Sifilografía

WRITING THE EARLY AMERICAS

Anna Brickhouse and Kirsten Silva Gruesz, Editors

❧ Sifilografía

A History of the Writerly Pox in the Eighteenth-Century Hispanic World

Juan Carlos González Espitia

University of Virginia Press
Charlottesville and London

University of Virginia Press
© 2019 by the Rector and Visitors of the University of Virginia
All rights reserved
Printed in the United States of America on acid-free paper

First published 2019

9 8 7 6 5 4 3 2 1

Library of Congress Cataloging-in-Publication Data

Names: González Espitia, Juan Carlos, author.
Title: Sifilografía : a history of the writerly pox in the eighteenth-century Hispanic
    world / Juan Carlos González Espitia.
Description: Charlottesville : University of Virginia Press, 2019. | Series: Writing
    the early Americas | Includes bibliographical references and index.
Identifiers: LCCN 2019015590 (print) | LCCN 2019019194 (ebook) | ISBN
    9780813943169 (ebook) | ISBN 9780813943152 (cloth : alk. paper) | ISBN
    9780813943732 (pbk. : alk. paper)
Subjects: LCSH: Syphilis—Spain—History—18th century.
Classification: LCC RC201.47 (ebook) | LCC RC201.47 .G66 2019 (print) |
    DDC 614.5/4720946—dc23
LC record available at https://lccn.loc.gov/2019015590

Cover art: *Touch of Evil,* Miguel Rio Branco, 1994. (© Miguel Rio Branco/Magnum
Photos; Metropolitan Museum of Art, purchase, The Horace W. Goldsmith
Foundation Gift, through Joyce and Robert Menschel, 2000)

Para Birgitte Bønning Espitia, siempre
Para Maya Espitia-Bønning, desde el principio
Para Alba Espitia-Bønning, hasta el final
Para mi madre, Doris Amanda Espitia. Para mis hermanas,
    Pilar y Juana
A la memoria de mi padre, Bernardo González Martínez
A la querida memoria de Herlinda Chitiva

Contents

Illustrations

ACKNOWLEDGMENTS

I can see it in some of the faces in the audience when I have presented about syphilis and culture in the Hispanic world. From their inquisitive faces—and half a smile—I know that they're wondering, "Is he interested in this disease because of some *personal* reason?"

Fortunately, all my reasons have been of the bookish type. I also feel fortunate that in the long process of writing *Sifilografía* I have encountered many willing partners who have shared with me this bookish contagion. Here I consign their names in salutary form, but my gratitude to them is infectious, viral, incurable.

At the University of Virginia Press my wonderful editor, Eric Brandt, believed in the project from the very beginning, back then when it was just a conference paper. Ellen Satrom and Helen Chandler patiently guided me through editorial meanders. Many people helped me to finally have something resembling a book manuscript. Peg Duthie skillfully edited the first, clunky version, and Ruth Melville expertly edited the still unwieldy second version. At the University of North Carolina at Chapel Hill, Rhi Johnson and Colleen McCallister helped me craft several of the sidebars. Rhi Johnson (again), Elena Casey, and Sarah Booker translated difficult quotations written in eighteenth-century medical and literary Spanish. Elizabeth Jones was key in securing image permissions. I am also deeply thankful to my friends Maricarmen Caña Jiménez, Oswaldo Estrada, Sam Amago, Vinodh Venkatesh, Federico Luisetti, and María Salgado for their constant encouragement. Logan Brackett and Nefi López-Chen have been solid support in the Department of Romance Studies. The UNC University Research Council provided much-needed funding for revising the first version of the manuscript; Beverly Gail Cummings-Whitfield's kind treatment at the council made me feel truly valued.

Sifilografía benefited from the careful reading and insightful suggestions of my friends and colleagues Irene Gómez Castellano, Nancy LaGreca, and Ellen Welch. The manuscript was greatly improved by the judicious comments and learned assessment of the anonymous readers. Their opinions were fundamental in framing the book as a whole and in honing several sections that needed elaboration.

I have left their names for the end. For them this is not a surprise: they know very well that I am *un ingrato.* But they also know that I am, beyond a fan of the oxymoron, un *ingrato agradecido.* Year after year, for many years, they have been there, steady. María Antonia Garcés, Christopher Conway, John Chasteen, Debra A. Castillo, Lee Skinner, Hernán Villamarín Abril. My friend with no equal, William Acree. Mi compadre y mi hermano, Stuart A. Day.

Sifilografía

In the Beginning, It Was Not Syphilis

In the beginning, it was not syphilis. The epidemic nature of the first recorded occurrence of the Great Pox in 1495 linked it with war, darkness, and despair, but there was no clear explanation of its nature or its etiology. The disease was so new to the world that it had, not one, but many names, almost always aimed at labeling the enemy, uttered to designate the Other. While there continued to be a great variety of localized terms, the main name for this venereal malady in Spain and its colonies in the 1700s was *gálico:* the French disease. The term "syphilis" derives from Girolamo Fracastoro's *Syphilis, sive morbus gallicus* (Syphilis, or the French disease), published in 1530, but it only became a common noun in the nineteenth century. Especially if we take into account the discovery of penicillin in 1928 by Alexander Fleming, which turned the disease from deadly to treatable, the understanding of syphilis in the Hispanic world during the eighteenth century is essentially different from our present view.[1] Nevertheless, as will become apparent throughout this study, today we still share with our unenlightened predecessors some beliefs, conceptions, preconceptions, and misconceptions surrounding the disease. To have a point of reference for discerning the dynamic of *gálico* in the eighteenth century, it is necessary to have a basic account of our own present conception of syphilis and to review its history immediately before the eighteenth century.

Venereal syphilis is acquired from infected exudations on the skin or in the mucus membranes or from organic fluids such as blood, saliva, semen, or vaginal secretions through direct sexual contact, including oral and anal sex. The infection is caused by the bacterium *Treponema pallidum* and develops through four distinct stages. The first stage is manifested between ten and ninety days after contact with the treponema in the form of syphilitic chancres on the genitals, lips, tongue, and tonsils. Patchy hair loss and the presence of cutaneous eruptions such as roseola, visible papules, and ulcerations of pustular origin characterize the second stage. After a latent stage, when all visible symptoms disappear, an ulterior stage, the third stage, brings consequences such as neurosyphilis, syphilis in the heart and blood vessels, and gummatous syphilis. Neurosyphilis causes a progressive general paralysis that hinders the

Naming the Enemy

After the epidemic outbreak in 1495, when the soldiers of Charles VIII of France invaded Naples, a veritable war of name-calling ensued. The French side named the malady the "Neapolitan disease," while the Naples side named it *morbus gallicus,* or the "French disease." Many later battles of vituperation likewise branded the enemy as the source of *gálico.* Persians called it the "Turkish disease," Turks called it the "Christian disease," Russians called it the "Polish disease," and Spain's enemies, of course, called it the "Spanish disease." In India it was known as the "Portuguese disease," in Tahiti and in France as the "British disease," and in Japan as "Chinese pox." As I will discuss later, *gálico* was also known as the "disease of the Indies" because of its supposed American origin.

Other names for the disease in Spanish include *avariosis, azul subido, bubas, doma potros, galan cortés, grande verole, grano, greñimón, grillimón, grillo, grimanas, griñimón, grosse verole, lúe, lúes, lüe venérea, malacatufas, mal francés, mal venéreo, morbo gálico, pudendagra, sarampión indiano, tenquedo, vicio venéreo, zurriache,* and *zurrión.*

It was 1832 before Philippe Ricord (1800–1889) differentiated syphilis from gonorrhea. In 1879 Albert Ludwig Neisser (1855–1916) described the gonococcus, the bacterium that produces gonorrhea. Fritz Schaudinn (1871–1906) and Erich Hoffmann (1868–1959) codiscovered the spirochete that causes syphilis in 1905. This *Spirochaeta pallida* is also known as *Treponema pallidum.*

---

coordination of muscle movement and can result in blindness and dementia. Cardiovascular syphilis generates problems in the heart and the aorta. Gummatous or late syphilis presents chronic inflammation in the form of soft balls, or gummas, manifested in the liver, the skin, and the bones, especially in the head. Bony matter in the nasal septum may be destroyed, and bone lesions can also appear in the clavicle, femur, fibula, humerus, radius, shinbone, sternum, ulna, and vertebrae. Syphilis may be transmitted from the mother to the fetus in the womb or at birth. A child with congenital syphilis may present a saddle nose or lack the nasal septum. Later in life, congenitally syphilitic children may suffer Hutchinson's teeth (a type of dental abnormality), blindness, deafness, and malformation of the shinbones. The main treatment for syphilis today is an intramuscular injection of benzathine benzylpenicillin, but the consequences of the disease, such as deformations in the bones, are not reversed after the destruction of the bacterium. Despite the availability of effective treatment with penicillin and the ability to prevent infection through the use of condoms, the spread of syphilis is increasing, most noticeably in the developing world, but insidiously in the developed world as well. According to a study by Molly E. Kent and Frank Romanelli, "Coinfection with both syphilis and HIV occurs frequently due to common risk factors. These 2 diseases interact with each other, making both diagnosis and treatment more complicated" (226). As it was three hundred years ago, syphilis continues to be an ominous presence that unfolds and inscribes its meanings in the body and in the writerly production of the times.

Later in this volume I will develop in detail the way physicians conceived *gálico* in the eighteenth century. It is beyond the focus of this book to offer an exhaustive history of the representations of syphilis from its first appearance in the late years of the fifteenth century until 1700.[2] However, at this point it is useful to have a brief overview of the situation of medicine and the treatment of *gálico* in peninsular Spain and the Spanish colonies under Habsburg rule, right before the end of the seventeenth century.[3]

Religion and the Crusades are the probable start of the Great Pox in 1495. King Charles VIII of France (1470–98) set his conquering ambitions at the Kingdom of Naples. He aimed at reclaiming power over Naples from Alphonso II, of the royal family of Aragon. He also wanted to use Naples as strategic headquarters for launching a military campaign against the Ottoman Turks in Constantinople. With a large and powerful army, Charles plowed through the north of Italy and entered the city in the spring of that year. A large conquering army of men eager to celebrate their victory with plunder, alcohol, and sex, in conjunction with the presence of a smaller number of forced or available women who became unwilling vectors of this highly communicable illness, staged the optimal conditions for syphilis to explode.[4] The pox became epidemic when the invading armies, fearful of being locked on the peninsula by a coalition of surrounding states, were pushed to abandon Naples. Charles VIII's soldiers came from different parts of Europe, and the retreat and disbandment of the armies meant a quick spread of the disease. Two years later, the pox was already present in England, France, Germany, and Switzerland. Five years later it had reached Greece, Hungary, Poland, and Russia. By the first quarter of the sixteenth century the Great Pox had attained virtually global proportions.[5]

Beginning in the 1970s, growing research on the history of medicine in Spain has proved that in the sixteenth and seventeenth centuries the peninsula was not a completely insular, detached, and benighted region, as sweeping assumptions had previously presented it.[6] It is true, as I will discuss further, that the incorporation of new knowledge had stagnated and that foreign ideas were doggedly rejected, but the practice of medicine was basically not that different than in many other places on the continent in relation to ideas, discoveries, and discussions. These recent studies have greatly advanced the task of presenting a more nuanced history, in which particular dynamics reveal the complexity of Spanish society and government. Nevertheless, it is apparent that science, and particularly medicine, were sluggish in comparison with the truly exceptional artistic developments in this period summarized under the name "Golden Age." Some of the most recognizable historical Spanish personalities belong to this time: in literature, Cervantes and Lope de Vega, Quevedo and Góngora, Calderón and Tirso de Molina, Mateo Alemán and Alonso de Ercilla, Santa Teresa de Jesús and Fray Luis de León; in the visual arts, Velázquez, El Greco, Zurbarán, Murillo, Machuca, and Berruguete; in music, Victoria, Morales, Guerrero, and Cabezón. This high level of production in the arts underlines the contrasting impervious attitude toward important scientific and medical developments happening elsewhere.

One of the explanations for the stagnation in medicine and science in Spain at the time is the success of the Counter-Reformation, which resulted in the strong role of the Inquisition in monitoring experimentation and the debate of topics suspected of going against dogma. Although there was no direct obstruction by the Santo Oficio (Holy Office) in disciplines such as math, botany, medicine, cosmography, or pharmacopoeia, one effect of the Inquisition was a generalized fear of new ideas or thoughts which stifled intellectual pursuit. Connected with this issue of religious dogma, another element that hindered the development of medical innovation in Spain was the expulsion and persecution of the Jewish and Moorish populations, which lasted until the beginning of the 1600s. The attack on these minorities meant the suppression of knowledge and practices that had until then enriched this area of expertise. One of the most salient forms of segregation of the Muslim and Jewish components of Spanish society was the requirement to show proof of *limpieza de sangre* (blood purity) to be able to study and exercise the profession of medicine.[7] There are several examples of physicians with Jewish or Muslim background accused by the Holy Office. Many died in prison or were executed, for example, the surgeons Tomé Quaresma and Francisco Maldonado de Silva, who died in the inquisitional fire in Lima, in 1639 (Granjel 3:68). The general fear was that non-Christians would kill their Christian patients, a recurrent topic represented in literary works such as Juan Ruiz de Alarcón's comedy *Quien mal anda, mal acaba* (Ruiz de Alarcón was born in the colony of New Spain of Spanish parents) or Tirso de Molina's *La prudencia en la mujer* (1634). Some Jewish doctors managed to continue practicing on the peninsula, but many others sought relative peace and quiet in places like Amsterdam and Hamburg, or tried a new beginning in the Spanish colonies. Some managed to surpass the vetting eye for their *limpieza de sangre* by securing forged documents.[8] The situation for nontraditional Morisco and Jewish healers and practitioners of popular medicine was perhaps even more ominous.[9]

Another reason for the suffocated state of development in the medical field was the powerful effect of Galenic doctrine, which rejected new discoveries or ideas that would contradict its prodigious but rigid system of organization. Since the Middle Ages, Galenism had been the most prevalent corpus of medical knowledge. Between the eight and eleventh centuries, Arab scholars revitalized Hippocrates's and Galen's classic teachings. The doctrine acquired a dominant position with the progressive inclusion of new commentaries and the refining of its internal logic, initially by the influential Al-Kindi, Averroës, and Avicenna, and later by other authors offering corroborations of its structure as late as the eighteenth century. Initially proposed by Hippocrates, the most important tenet of Galenism is the theory of humors, which understands health as a balance of four basic substances in the body: blood, phlegm, black bile, and yellow bile.[10] The role of the physician was to help in the balancing of humors through the implementation of procedures such as diets, purges, leeches, and bloodletting to attain *eucrasia,* or good equilibrium, and to avoid *discrasia,* or imbalance. The four-pronged structure of the humors is duplicated in the organization of life in a correspondence of macrocosmic and microcosmic interactions whereby the world is constituted by the four elements (fire, water, wind, and earth); the body is composed of the four principal organs (spleen, heart, gallbladder, and lung); and the four physical qualities (humidity, dryness, heat, cold) combine in different ways and in turn influence one another. Centuries of devotion to this doctrine, so well cemented in a closed logic and strengthened by the powerful tradition of irrefutable authoritative figures, made it very difficult to produce change or to defend conflicting new knowledge.

Although King Philip II's (1527–98) great interest in scientific matters has been proved, especially in regards to alchemy,[11] several of the political and administrative decisions implemented by him and his heir, Philip III (1578–1621), complicated the advancement of research, teaching, and debate from a practical perspective. The highly bureaucratic nature of measures such as the unification of hospitals or the imposition of the *Protomedicato* are two examples of the practical negative consequences of managing the large administrative machine of the empire. Even though he has frequently been depicted as an isolationist ruler, or as the stifling herald of Counter-Reformation, Philip II's scientific inclinations reveal that his persona and this period are more complex and nuanced than traditional interpretations of history lead us to expect.

The importance and power of the *Protomedicato* in Spain and the Spanish colonies merits a brief assessment of its history and bureaucratic mechanics. The Royal Tribunal of the Protomedicato was a board created in 1477 by the Catholic king to regulate the work of those providing healing services, including both the lower strata of spice sellers, midwives, and apothecaries and the more professionally trained physicians and surgeons. Being a tribunal, it had

the power to sanction those who did not yield to its verdicts. The Protomedicato ruled medical matters for over three centuries and exercised its power
over medicine and pharmacy on both sides of the Atlantic. According to John
Tate Lanning, before 1477 an administrative body existed with these duties,
but Ferdinand and Isabella officially gave it practical control by vesting *alcaldes
examinadores* (examining deputies) with the power to apply the law and to
impose monetary penalties (17).[12]

The Protomedicato was in constant adjustment as a result of changing
health and administrative needs in the kingdom. Initially, it administered the
licensing of those who practiced based on experience and not formal training, such as bonesetters (*algebristas*), tooth pullers (*sacamuelas*), those healing
external ailments (*ensalmadores*), oculists or cataract healers (*batidores de la
catarata*), those taking care of bladder stones (*sacadores de la piedra*), experts
in helping with hernias (*hernistas*), or the bleeders (*barberos*), who also functioned as barbers. After 1523, midwives (*parteras*), spice sellers (*especieros*),
and *ensalmadores* were taken out of its jurisdiction, and it monitored only
physicians, surgeons, apothecaries, and phlebotomists (Campos Díez 48n13).
But after 1537, under the rule of Philip V, the tribunal gained more and more
power, arbitrating all practices involving healing or the prescribing of major medications (*remedios mayores*) (Campos Díez 49). The Protomedicato
reached its apex of influence, complexity, and control between the reigns of
Philip II and Charles IV. The administrative apparatus grew over time, and
by the 1700s it included a wide range of licensing and auditing officials that
managed the examination of those receiving medical degrees, ensured the pay-
ment of fees, and monitored proper sanitary conditions. Because of the extent
of its administrative reach, the Protomedicato also involved other officers to
help with examinations and inspections such as surgeons, apothecaries, writing clerks, caretakers, bailiffs, and barristers (Campos Díez 46). In 1750 Ferdinand VI placed the practice of midwifery back under the rule of the Protomedicato, and by 1780 the institution was so large and complex that it was
divided into different branches—medicine, surgery, pharmacy (Campos Díez
49). The institution stopped functioning in 1799, and despite attempts to reinstate its functions in 1811 and 1820, its presence in Spain dwindled from then
on. Conversely, the particularities of the Protomedicato's implementation in
the American colonies, and its at times implicit autonomy, determined its un-
interrupted presence and its endurance, even after the emancipation, lasting
as far as 1879 in Chile (Gardeta Sabater 249n30).

The Protomedicato's territorial influence was not constant or homogeneous. At different times, some regions on the peninsula pushed for localized
control over the health professions and were not affected by its administrative
powers. At other times, especially during the peak of its power in the mid-

1700s, its control reached farther. In the colonies of the New World, the Protomedicato was officially established in Mexico City and Lima in 1646. There had been officials long before, for example, Dr. Hernando de Sepúlveda in Lima in 1537, who had a royal commission and the title of *protomédico* (Lanning 29). Nevertheless, there is a difference between individuals invested with a level of authority, such as Sepúlveda, and the regulatory institution of the Royal Protomedicato, which exercised a much stronger auditing power. The first person designated by Philip II for the post of General Protomedic of the Indies (Protomédico General de Indias) in 1570 was Dr. Francisco Hernández (Gardeta Sabater 239).

From the beginning of the office in the New Continent, one of the fundamental roles of the Protomedicato was to learn of plants, herbs, trees, or seeds with medicinal virtue, to compose well-organized reports on the use and properties of these medicinal products, and to send samples of these goods back to the peninsula (Gardeta Sabater 240). In the American colonies, the Protomedicato had more centralized professional control; for example, the chair of professor of medicine at the university was also the first *protomédico* exercising regulatory duties. However, from early on, the office lost its punitive power, since sanctions had to be implemented by policing authorities such as an *oidor de la audiencia* (court judge) or a governor. In addition, in terms of bureaucratic processes and structures, the vast extension of the territories and the idiosyncratic nature of each viceroyalty generated different practices compared to those of the peninsula (Gardeta Sabater 238, 244). The remoteness from the center of power, together with the constant desire for profit during the process of colonization, produced actions that were against the rules set forth for the office from the metropolis, such as charging fees to practice expressly prohibited activities like *curanderismo* (nontraditional healing) or stripping officers of their posts in order to transfer them to someone else for gain (Gardeta Sabater 245n17, 18).

Also different from the metropolis was the slow but growing presence in the colonies of persons practicing medicine who would not have passed the restrictions of *limpieza de sangre* on the peninsula. This situation was the natural outcome of, on the one hand, a steady and unstoppable intermixing of people from different provenances (indigenous, African, and Spaniards) and, on the other hand, the lack of trained doctors, which pushed authorities to be more lenient in the implementation of the segregationist practices that were more strictly enforced in the metropolis.

According to José María López Piñero in his *Medicina moderna y sociedad española: Siglos XVI–XIX,* at the beginning of the seventeenth century, under the rule of Philip III, any further movement of medical developments in Spain was merely the result of inertia. The initial push behind that inertial force had been the scientific humanism as manifested in the dynamic edition and commentary of classical medical texts and the positive reception of Italian humanism (18). Until that point, Spanish scholars and universities had engaged in vigorous discussion and incorporation of revolutionary forms of knowledge, such as Vesalius's approach to anatomy or Copernicus's heliocentric doctrine. But this process of advancement regressed after its condemnation in 1616 by the Sagrada Congregación del Índice (Sacred Congregation of the Index) (López Piñero, *Medicina moderna* 29). The previous unguarded attitude toward innovation was also visible in the interest in understanding and incorporating practical uses of the incalculable natural wealth found in Spanish possessions on the other side of the Atlantic, as well as the traditions of healing among the indigenous population in the conquered and colonized territories.

But friction with ideas that considered innovation a menace to the comfortable lethargy of tradition brought this inertial motion to a virtual standstill. However, this parochial climate could not negate or completely stop the influence and changes coming from science in the rest of Europe. By the middle of the 1600s there was a struggle between two factions of Galenic traditionalists: the *intransigentes* (obstinate ones), who rejected any innovation, even if obviously correct, affecting the coherence of traditional teachings, and the *moderados* (moderate ones), those opting to accept the indisputable innovations and changes as amendments to the prevalent doctrine (López Piñero 53). The quarrel between obstinate and moderate factions became radicalized in the last two decades of the century. A group of Spanish scientists who broke off from classic medical doctrine, dismissively referred to as the *novatores*— loosely translated as "the trendy ones" but more positively known today as the "pre-enlightened"—engaged in a strong defense of the incorporation of the new developments in science and medicine from the rest of the continent. This point of tension, which was in fact a crevice through which modern ideas in medicine entered and informed discussions and practices, sets the tone for what would happen in the treatment of *gálico* in the eighteenth century: a hesitation between tradition and innovation resulting in the phasing out of Galenic ideas by the second half of the 1700s. The most important representative of that interest in dispelling obscurantist beliefs and the modernization of attitudes toward science and medicine in the eighteenth century was Benito Jerónimo Feijoo, who systematically incorporated new knowledge from all over Europe in his pivotal *Teatro crítico universal* (1726–39).[13]

Crucial for the influential schismatic discussions of the *novatores* was the great breakthrough of William Harvey's (1578–1657) description of the systemic circulation of blood in his *De Motu Cordis* (1628).[14] According to Galenic theory, the heart was a producer of heat in relation to the blood, the lungs' function was to cool the heart, the liver was the producer of blood, and blood flowed in an open-ended bodily arrangement. Harvey's observations showed that if blood flow was indeed a one-way, oscillatory movement, the liver would be incapable of producing such large quantities of fluid—an amount larger than the weight of the human body itself—leading to his discovery that blood moved in a systemic, circulatory fashion. Relatedly, the *novatores* also criticized the extended and unnecessary use of bloodletting because it meant the loss of fluid from this circular system, and defended the use of chemical substances in the crafting of remedies to aid in balancing the composition of specific corporal fluids. Harvey's ideas on the circulation of blood became accepted in the Hispanic context by the eighteenth century.

According to López Piñero, one of the most representative texts of the *novatores'* departure from traditional doctrines and the quest for engagement with the new approaches to medicine is Juan de Cabriada's *Carta filosófica, medico-chymica* (1687).[15] The publication in 1697 and 1698 of at least two books defending the use of quinine (*quina*), a point of bitter contention for Galenic traditionalists, shows that a new direction in medical practice and inquiry was on its way (López Piñero 145).[16] Galenists thought of fever as a disease caused by a bile imbalance—for example, quartan fever caused by a black bile imbalance, tertian fever caused by yellow bile imbalance—but quinine, produced from the bark of the cinchona tree found in the Viceroyalty of Peru's high mountains, proved to cure fever without resort to purges or bloodletting, thereby shaking this long-held belief. Moderate Galenists, who could not challenge the practical evidence of remedies like quinine, opted for accepting them as products with exceptional curative qualities, and used the term *específicos* (specifics) to name them.[17] As I will show later, the "rediscovery" of American plants with intrinsic defined properties such as quinine, agave, or guaiacum became part of the search for components with specific iatrochemical properties to cure pervasive maladies like *gálico*. Promoted by Paracelsus (1493/4–1541), iatrochemistry combined chemistry and medicine. Its main goal was to explain physiological and pathological processes through chemistry. It also aimed at offering medical treatment through the use of chemicals to balance bodily fluids.

The foundation of the Regia Sociedad de Medicina de Sevilla (Royal Society of Medicine of Seville) in 1697 by a group in agreement with the ideas of the *novatores* can be interpreted as confirmation and tacit institutionalization of the new ideas that had been suppressed for the most part of the 1600s. The approval of the bylaws of this Royal Society in 1700 tellingly coincides with the death of the last Habsburg king.

As I will show in this volume, the strong tension between innovation and tradition in the field of medicine and the treatment of *gálico* that we see in the seventeenth century will continue without radical changes throughout much of the eighteenth century as well. But it would be a mistake to believe that this sluggishness in the reception and production of medical knowledge renders the period irrelevant for the study of the social implications of the disease. Here we find a vast wealth of significant developments in public policy and administration, the setting of benchmarks for the exercise of the profession and the implementation of future trends in research and experimentation in the sciences. Similarly, the multilayered study of this particular disease allows for a better and more nuanced understanding of Hispanic societies on both sides of the Atlantic. More than forty years ago, in his prologue to *Medicina moderna y sociedad española* (1976), López Piñero was already promoting the need to engage in a multifaceted and integrated study of societal activities. Beyond an accumulative synthesis of historiographic data, in which discrete knowledge from different disciplines is kept artificially isolated, he advocated for the organic imbrication of knowledge to shape an encompassing historical reality (12). The emphasis was to be placed on the reconstruction of complex webs of relationships, categorizations, and idiosyncrasies. This method has already rendered sizable investigative yield.[18] For the particular case of the seventeenth century in relation to the social manifestations of *gálico* in the Hispanic setting, the work of Cristian Berco, especially his *From Body to Community: Venereal Disease and Society in Baroque Spain* (2016), is an excellent model of this approach, and one to which my own work is kin.

Berco's study offers deep insight into social microconnections, providing valuable information about the quotidian web of economic and private life. My work is in line with his opinion that although we have a clear historical grasp on how syphilis was conceptualized and treated, there is a lack of studies on the wider social implications of the patients beyond the realm of the hospital; and it engages in the same type of interests that he signals by writing that "we need go no further than poverty, the presumed culpability of loose women as contagious, or the libertine attitudes attributed to men to encounter a maze of ingrained cultural assumptions that shaped responses to the pox" (5). While Berco sheds light on that void by skillfully tracing the ins and outs of several patients from different social strata through their recorded lives in the rich documentation of Spanish bureaucracy in the last century of the Habsburgs, I study the same crux through a multilayered discourse analysis in the eighteenth century. The organization of social experiences rendered by Berco's work necessarily follows the order, delimited structure, and logic of those managerial documents: the lists and descriptions of patients committed to treatment in a specialized hospital ward, the socioeconomic implications of their clothing, the changes in their fate and fortune, the record of legal procedures, or the details of inheritance proceedings. For *Sifilografía,* the ordering is equally dependent on the sources used to craft a cultural history of this sort in the 1700s, paintings and engravings, medical treatises, public policy discourses, obscene and humorous poems, pro-independence and invective essays, political satire, and periodical publications—thus the porous, interlinked, seemingly disconnected and parallel structure developed here that I explain in the next chapter by using the image of a tapestry. This method yields repositioned answers to questions regarding the locally framed reception and implementation of medical and scientific ideas in Spain and its colonies, the reinterpretation of artistic renderings of society such as those of Francisco de Goya, the strategic use of the image of syphilis to name friends and foes, the use of invective and obscenity to deal with taboo topics of sexual or socioeconomic nature, the reinterpretation of autochthonous products as valuable remedies and sources for self-identity for the regions outside the peninsula, the more nuanced understanding of the ideas of the Enlightenment, or the implications for insight into transatlantic dynamics.

So far in this introductory section I have explained our present understanding of the pathology of syphilis, which I will later contrast with the perception of the disease at the beginning of the eighteenth century. I have offered a review of the state of science and medicine during the last years of the Habsburg rule in Spain through the examination of historical and critical work developed by academics since the 1970s for the Hispanic case, positioning the present study among other works of the Hispanic early modern period. In the following chapter, "This Book Is (the Back of) a Tapestry," I introduce the methodological framework of the study. Through the image of the tapestry and its back side, I explain the structure and method I follow. The goal is to show how an apparently smooth surface (beautiful texts, organized medical discourses, picturesque representations) is tightly linked to practices, images, and facts that touch less visible realities in any given society. It presents the opposing yet mutually constitutive images of the homogeneous, "refined" front and the muddled, knotty underside of the tapestries used to decorate the palaces of the Hispanic nobility. Tapestries illustrate how overt "serious" discourses, such as aestheticized and didactic poetry, are counterpointed and supplemented by hidden discourses or realities where sexuality, unrestrained sensuality, and venereal disease—hushed, overlooked, or downplayed by critics—are rampant. The image of the tapestry also portrays in many ways the relations and tensions between peninsular Spain as part of a European milieu and the Spanish colonies in the American continent as complex, co-constitutive spaces of belonging and difference in relation to the Spanish metropolis.

In "A Mysterious Disease Changes the Political Map of the World" I investigate the medical perception of syphilis at the beginning of the eighteenth century. I use medical treatises and literary works to illustrate the logic of the disease, its symptoms and its cure. Through the particular case of the death in 1700 of Charles II, the last Habsburg king of Spain, known as "The Bewitched," I explore the clash between a Scholastic, Galenic medical discourse and a changing approach to medicine based on experimentation. The king's cause of death—perhaps syphilis—was described as resulting from a spell at a time when there was already a new way of explaining diseases in tune with the experimental method. European geopolitics changed radically after his death, which marked the beginning of the decline of Spanish power in the world.

The main treatment for *gálico* involved mercury and *Guaiacum,* a tree native to the so-called New World (in fact, *guaiacum* was the first word from the Americas to appear in print in the English language). Taking into account medical and literary texts, I discuss various meanings that resulted from the image of mercury (an arcane substance, a god of classic mythology, a medicine that caused terrible physical reactions), and the homeopathic logic of using American products to fight a disease that was thought to have originated on the American continent as result of sexual exchanges between Spanish sailors and indigenous women. I reveal how treatment for the disease varied according to the social and economic condition of the patient. The discussion covers the names, descriptions, and meanings of the physical symptoms of syphilis. Chancres, buboes, falling-out teeth or hair, and destroyed nasal septa became signs of fatalist revelation, conduits to ways of explaining ideas about the body's function—with the humoral theory, for example—and sources of harsh humor against those affected by the disease.

In "Judging Books by Their Covers" I show the wealth of information the cultural critic can gather from the often-overlooked preliminary pages of a book (dedications, legal declarations, epigraphs, prefatory material), considered by many as formulaic, unrelated or unimportant to the factual material a book may contain. I show how these paratextual instances offer key information about the linkage of *gálico* to the dynamics of power and influence that were behind the communication of knowledge and the crafting of public policies to control its incidence in society. The fact that medical books were items of extreme luxury (one book could cost as much as the daily bread for eight families) allows for an understanding of the stringent social conditions for the transference of knowledge, and the difficulty of creating an intellectual environment where ideas related to science could grow.

In the section "The Awakening of Reason Produces Befuddlement" I discuss the flow of knowledge between countries such as England or France and Spain and its American colonies. Drawing on an iconic figure of the Spanish Enlightenment, Benito Jerónimo Feijoo (1676–1764), and his *Teatro crítico universal,* I show the gradual incorporation of new ideas that challenged traditional medical theories. For example, the systematic use of the microscope, as noted by Feijoo, opened the door to a new understanding of maladies as transmitted by "animalcules," the origin of what we know as "germ theory," replacing the miasmatic theory or the theory of the imbalance of humors. Spain opened its doors to new notions from foreign countries, and these ideas served as new paradigms of self-understanding for the people of the colonies on the other side of the Atlantic. Observation, experimentation, and new technologies found rich soil for growth, not only in the geography of America but also in the minds of its inhabitants. Along with efforts at the reorganization of knowledge, there was at the time a strong impetus to deal with the negative social outcomes of the disease. Discourses geared to prevent the spread of *gálico* through unchecked sexuality usually showed up in literature, such as that of the famous writer Diego Torres Villarroel, who, as I show, used horrifying descriptions of patients receiving treatment in hospitals as a way to dissuade the reading public, in particular the youth, from recurring to "improper desires" and prostitution.

"All for the people, but without the people" was the classic statement of enlightened despotism's political doctrine. One of its instances was the creation or reorganization of institutions that dealt with syphilis and its associated outcomes. In the section "Inhospitable Hospitals" I investigate several of these establishments as veritable centers of meaning in the Hispanic eighteenth century. For example, when someone was jeered at as being an "Antón Martín," the implicit accusation was that he or she was the personification of the hospital of that name, an institution in Madrid exclusively dedicated to the treatment of syphilis. Therefore, institutions incarnated radiating connotations of power, geography, control, shame, and unavoidable reality. I show how the hospitals for syphilitic patients, the reformatory institutions for women in the trade of prostitution, or the jails for repeat offenders (i.e., prostitutes suffering a relapse of the disease) served as spaces to exercise control or to portray the idea of progress and equality, but for the common people they were also the embodiment of the proximity of the disease and a tangible reminder of the flaws in their society. Through the study of the Spanish author and bureaucrat Juan Meléndez Valdés's reports as executor of the unification of the hospitals in Ávila, and the *Historical Account of the Journey Accomplished by the Order of His Majesty to the Southern America* (1748), a report by Antonio de Ulloa and Jorge Juan, two Spanish scientific envoys to the colonies in South America, I show how hospitals functioned as double spaces of help and control on both sides of the Atlantic.

After dealing with the hospital space, in "The Transformation of the Medical Understanding of *Gálico*" I discuss the changing views on the pathology of syphilis and the ensuing dispute between different medical factions that defended either traditional Galenism or the new ideas about chemistry, the circulation of the blood, and the evolving germ theory. I show how changes in perspective were not a sudden revolution but a gradual process of modification traceable through the many medical texts of the time I analyze, including the widely circulated work of the Portuguese doctor João Curvo Semedo, whose remedies, imbued with an interest in iatrochemistry, may be read today as veritable conjuring potions.

A pervasive unmanageable scourge like syphilis was controlled, if only symbolically, by labeling it. In addition to several places where I discuss the different appellations for syphilis, in "Naming the Disease: The French Malady" I develop close readings of relevant Hispanic figures such as Gonzalo Fernández de Oviedo, José Francisco de Isla, Tomás de Iriarte, Eugenio de Santa Cruz y Espejo, Juan Pablo Forner, and Francisco Miranda to offer a strong argument on the resignification of syphilis's most common name in Spanish until the end of the nineteenth century: *gálico* or *mal francés* (French disease). As I have mentioned, the term "syphilis" was not widely used until the twentieth century, and *mal francés* evolved to name other forms of perceived menace to the body politic of Spain. Modes of thinking and aesthetic representations from France were rebranded with the same name as the malady, with the connotation that they were a disease in the minds of those who disdained their own identity, their own language, and their own allegiances. The use of this nexus to the disease was further exacerbated with the Napoleonic invasion in 1808, when images of expulsion, extirpation, and eradication previously used in connection with syphilis were repurposed to attack the French invaders as well as the Spaniards who were open to their ideas and presence. On the other hand, ideas derived from the French Revolution found fertile ground and affinity among the creole elites in the Spanish colonies: the military *mal francés* on the peninsula and the *mal francés* as a set of ideals of liberty and equality became catalysts of the revolutions that brought independence to this region.

In the chapters "Naming the Disease: *Mal americano*" and "The Rejection of the Origin of *Gálico* as a Nucleus of Self-Identity in the Spanish Colonies" I show that at the same time that the disease was rebranded to name a perceived invasion of ideas and a real military French invasion, syphilis was also named *el mal de las Indias,* meaning that the disease had originated in the New World and that the encounter with the indigenous population had resulted in illness for Europe. The term was appropriate for stressing the difference between colonies and metropolis, where the colonies represented a productive yet difficult appendage. Canonical American authors such as Francisco Javier Clavijero, Servando Teresa de Mier, and Andrés Bello worked not only to dispute the American origin of *gálico* but also to demonstrate that in fact the remedy for this universal blight was to be found there in the form of plants and animals with specific curing qualities that could be used to treat previously incurable diseases like syphilis. The intense rhetorical discussion of these two connected elements became the embryonic center of an argument for self-worth and self-determination in the Spanish colonies. I follow the course of this discussion in order to help dispel the long-held idea that this fight for self-definition began spontaneously around 1810. On the contrary, I show how eighteenth-century discourses on botany, American remedies, and American endemic plants or products opened an early space for thinking about autonomy and liberation. In connection with this push for meaning and self-worth, I study Manuel José Quintana's ode to Francisco Balmis's campaign to inoculate the crown's subjects in the American colonies against smallpox, the largest campaign of vaccination in history.

I study this association between *gálico* and the social implications of the colonial condition in "José Joaquín Fernández de Lizardi's Diseased Characters." Through close reading of several passages of Lizardi's *The Mangy Parrot, Sad Nights and Happy Day,* and *The Quijotita and Her Cousin* I trace the problems of administration derived from New Spain's ancillary situation. The lack of control over the medical profession in the colony resulted in characters like Lizardi's Perico, who at one point goes from town to town as a quack doctor, using stilted medical terminology and carrying a fake diploma. In criticizing this practice, the author also reveals the absence of professionals in the region and illuminates the state of medical knowledge at the time. Other characters, like the notary Chanfaina, who is described as lacking teeth, missing his uvula, and with a twangy, dribbling voice—all marks of a body touched by venereal disease—are used by Fernández de Lizardi to create an image of the rot within the colonial administrative apparatus. In his view, Chanfaina's dribbling on the common people who seek help from the bureaucracy of the New Spain's viceroyalty makes them unwilling or unwary vehicles of contamination within the rampant disarray of governmental affairs. A character like the spoiled brat Pomposita embodies what Lizardi criticizes as the negative upbringing of young women in Mexico. In this moralistic tale, the only viable outcomes are her well-behaved cousin Pudenciana's happy marriage and Pomposita's own doomed end as a prostitute ravaged by syphilis.

In the chapter titled "Sick Humor" I study the power of allusion and metaphoric portrayal in texts that make fun of individuals touched by the disease. I show how irony, double entendre, satire, obscenity, debased language, and dark and epigrammatic humor function as tools to make sense of the horrible consequences of a disease that started with just a brief moment of unsanctioned sexual exchange. Here I read works by writers such as Juan del Valle y Caviedes, José Iglesias de la Casa, Juan Bautista Aguirre, Diego de Torres

Villarroel, and José Francisco de Isla. The humorous description of the treatment with leeches in the anus, the account of the inevitable drooling that resulted from anointment with mercury, the covert mockery of Catholic dogma, and the scornful depiction of painful gummas on the head of the diseased underscore a moral denunciation of the consequences of improper behavior, but it is also a kind of sobering humor that points to the here and now, to the tangible, disturbing reality as summarized by the *gálico* experience, and signals that perhaps life should be weighed in a different scale: by living it intensely, one may reach transcendence and meaning, an understanding clearly akin to the budding Romantic mood.

Related to this discussion of humorous writing are the three following chapters, "Moratín's *Arte de las putas,* or the Distorted Art of Avoiding *Gálico,*" "An Epic Chant to the Syphilitic Bubo," and "Samaniego's Sticky Fable," in which I examine various representations of female prostitutes as vectors of syphilis. In contrast to the understanding of prostitution in the nineteenth and twentieth centuries, during the eighteenth century there was a tacit approval of sexual commerce as a way to satisfy what was considered the natural sexual drive of men, but fear of contagion drove the discussion toward regimentation and control of the practice. The consequences of this logic are multilayered. For some, like the author Diego Torres Villarroel, the solution was to hike up the prices of sexual encounters to sift out prostitutes with *gálico* or, more disturbingly, to allow sexual commerce with very young women who had not been exposed to the disease. Two possible ways to prevent *gálico* follow from this idea. One is abstinence, and the other is highly expensive prostitution. For other authors, like Nicolás Fernández de Moratín in his clandestine poem *Arte de las putas*—a text that I radically reinterpret in the light of syphilis control, and not just as a geography of prostitution as it has previously been read by many critics—prostitution should be self-regulated by guilds to control price and the health of the women, men should find very young women from the countryside, and clients should be offered condoms made out of sheepskin. In the same vein as my study of Moratín's *Arte,* in my reading of "The *incordio:* An Epic-Gallic Poem in One Canto," a lesser-studied work by the canonical author José María Blanco White, I investigate how in this humorous dream the traditional Cupid-like representation of love is debunked by a new fleshly and erotic god of sexual freedom who is empowered by a new medicine that can cure syphilis. The result of this absolute revolution is the possibility of imagining a society where all of those deriving power and money from the diseased—judges, physicians, priests, gravediggers—can no longer control society. I bring into my discussion works in the American context, such as Alonso Carrió de Lavandera's *El lazarillo de ciegos caminantes,* or the highly racialized poems by Fray Francisco del Castillo Andraca y Tamayo. Both of these authors offer subtle clues to the unsanctioned sexual exchanges—*gálico* and buboes included, of course—between members of colonial society's different strata that were not supposed to intermingle. Through this strategy of allusively uncovering scandal, both writers manage to acutely criticize the waning Bourbonic rule and its representatives on the other side of the Atlantic. This allusive uncovering is present in a different way in "Las moscas," a popular fable by the renowned Spanish author Félix María de Samaniego, which I reinterpret as a veiled reference to unchecked sexuality and prostitution leading to venereal disease.

The pervasive nature of *gálico* produced a mounting preoccupation with how to resolve the quandary of the perceived need to exercise one's sexuality given that sexuality was inextricably linked with prostitution. Those in the positions of administration and control were not necessarily against men attending to what they considered a natural sexual desire, even if this was accomplished through the unsanctioned frequenting of prostitutes. The problem was that they were at the same time frequenting ladies of society—as was the case with Leandro Fernández de Moratín. How to avoid the ever-present menace of *gálico?* In "*Gálico,* Prostitution, and Public Policy" I investigate how Francisco de Cabarrús, a high administrator close to the ear of some of the most influential people of his time, imagined a way of organizing prostitution by creating tightly supervised brothels to be concentrated in certain areas of the city where prostitutes could be monitored by doctors. In this way, sexuality could be exercised while *gálico* was kept at bay. After Cabarrús, other authors that I discuss, such as Valentín Foronda and Antonio Cibat, developed similar public policy ideas to curb the pernicious spread of the disease by controlling the providers of sexual services, but they rarely included the need to equally target their many clients. These viewpoints related to public policy are extensively connected with artistic and literary production, a conjunction I approach by studying Francisco de Goya's *Caprichos* as a document that portrays the situation of prostitutes in Madrid and the dynamic of *gálico.*

In the concluding section, "The Future in Jeopardy," I investigate the rising concern with the reduction in population at the end of the century, in part caused by the widespread presence of syphilis in Spain. The problem was not only about prostitution but about the fact that mothers were also being infected by their partners, therefore transmitting the venereal disease to their children. This mounting preoccupation with a decline in population was jumpstarted by the 1782 publication in France of an article by Nicolas Masson de Morvilliers in the *Encyclopédie méthodique* in which he insistently represented Spain as a lethargic nation. He characterized such indolence as a disease, and the country as a patient who rejected the treatment that could lead to health. The future of the nation and of its population was at stake; the aftermath of the Napoleonic invasion, the initial uprisings in the colonies, and political and administrative chaos would characterize the beginning of the nineteenth century: a period also marked by syphilis.

1 ❦

This Book Is (the Back of) a Tapestry

Let me use the image of a tapestry to explain the objectives and structure of this book. Francisco de Goya, the most iconic artist of eighteenth-century Spain, painted between 1775 and 1792 a group of about sixty *cartones* for the Real Fábrica de Tapices de Santa Bárbara (Royal Tapestry Factory of Santa Bárbara) in Madrid (Arnáiz 15). The *cartón,* or cartoon, was an oil painting made on canvas that served as a model for woven tapestries. Tapestries were both beautiful adornments and useful objects: they covered dull walls, created dignified spaces for the itinerant court, and protected the king and his entourage from the cold weather. Flanders had been the main provider of tapestries for the king until 1714, but after the War of the Spanish Succession and the Peace of Utrecht the monarch lost the Netherlands. As a solution, Philip V (1683–1746) installed the Real Fábrica in 1721 under the direction of Jacob Vandergoten, a tapestry master from Antwerp. The tapestries made from the *cartones* painted by Goya were used to furnish royal chambers and salons in the palaces of the Escorial and the Pardo.

The most important technical change in the production of Spanish tapestries during the eighteenth century was the introduction in 1727 of high-warp weaving from the French factories, especially that of the Gobelins, which allowed for better copying of the cartoon model and the crafting of bigger pieces (Tomlinson 8). Artistically, the most important change of the time was the incorporation of everyday elements in the paintings and tapestries by Francisco Bayeu y Subías (1734–95)—Goya's brother-in-law—and Goya himself. Even if the images developed by Goya for the Real Fábrica were based on daily life, they are highly aestheticized and do not reflect the crude or grim themes evident in his *Los caprichos* (*The caprices,* 1799)—which I will study later—or *Los desastres de la guerra* (*The Disasters of War*) (1810–15).

Although many of the cartoons present a detached reality that mirrors the activities of the few people in the higher echelons of Spanish society—hunting, picnicking, strolling around, playing childish games—others, like *El ciego de la guitarra* (*The Blind Guitar Player*), reveal moments of interaction among Spain's multiple social levels (see fig. 1). The blind musician and his young guide share the space with well-dressed women and a foreigner; the cloaked men see and hear the same things as the black water seller or the horse

Figure 1. *El ciego de la guitarra,* Francisco de Goya, 1778. Oil on canvas. (© Photographic Archive Museo Nacional del Prado)

rider who returns the viewer's gaze. I like to imagine that one of the figures in this painting—perhaps the individual in the background buying the watermelon—is that of an *indiano,* a well-off man born on the New Continent, or a Spaniard who has brought riches and new visions from the other side of the Atlantic.

Combined into a tapestry in the chambers of the Prince and Princess Royal, the many threads used to replicate a Goya image in the Real Fábrica present a homogeneous surface, with no gaps or bumps between characters, colors, or textures. But if one were to flip the tapestry, one would see its underside, where uniformity becomes inconsistency, transitions turn into abrupt chasms, and the smooth fabric disappears beneath loose ends and free-floating strands (see fig. 2). Cervantes had used this image to criticize the way translations, in the same way as the back of a tapestry, were like obscuring strands, imperfectly rendering the smooth beauty of the original work (*Don Quijote* II, 62:1143–44).

Cervantes uses the image to illustrate a process of artistic production in which the goal of recasting the original work is always in peril of failure, therefore showing an unfinished, unpleasant face. My own approach reads the image in the opposite direction. My goal is to *reveal* the imperfections that are part and parcel of representations that only *appear* to be smooth on the surface. *Sifilografía* is a study of Hispanic society's underside during the eighteenth century and the beginning of the nineteenth, from the 1700 death of Charles II—the last Habsburg monarch of the Spanish Empire—to the 1810 independence of Spanish colonies on the American continent. My proposal to supplement a reading of the smooth surface of sanctioned themes and images—the kind of texts imbued with reason and reasoning that since the nineteenth century and until recently had been considered as lesser and less meaningful, as irrelevant and minor in comparison with the previous Golden Age—with the assessment of less Panglossian texts, palpitating with passion and kindled with vital pulse or vital mortality, follows the same route as that announced by Guillermo Carnero in his Juan March Foundation conferences, published in 1983 under the title *La cara oscura del Siglo de las Luces* (The dark face of the age of Enlightenment) (25–29). This is the same methodological interest that accompanies David Gies's work, as attested in the trajectory of his writings published in *Eros y amistad* (Eros and friendship), or in Irene Gómez Castellano's *La cultura de las máscaras* (The masked culture).

From a political standpoint, the beginning of the conformation of ideas of self-rule in the Spanish colonies on the American continent has usually been considered a thing of the nineteenth century, not a consequence of radical reassessment in regard to identity deeply rooted in the eighteenth century. Through the study of the seemingly unlikely catalyst of venereal disease, *Sifilografía*'s approach offers a perspective on the consequential changes in this period. This study aims to connect the smooth and sometimes seemingly irrelevant surface of social behavior with the unwoven threads of meaning behind it, deemed by some as unsightly, lesser, morally dubious, or crude and usually kept out of sight. Nonetheless, and more importantly, the threads on the front and the back of the arras are one and the same. What appears only as a hint of color on one side may show all of its intensity on the other; when we see how tightly woven, very well placed threads on the front become less refined, freer threads on the underside, it challenges our perceptions of both reasoned discourse and decorative excess and forces us to reformulate our interpretations of the Hispanic eighteenth century. For example, as I will later show, Nicolás Fernández de Moratín urged his muse Dorisa to spend her time crafting poetry in poised and prim admonitions that would seem to be the opposite of the libertine and even obscene treatise on sexual satisfaction he composed as his *Arte de las putas* (The art of whoring), but the discursive material with which both the admonitions and treatise are made and the didactic aim that imbues them are exactly the same.

The tapestries woven in the Real Fábrica were not made with just one

Figure 2 *Abraham Entertaining the Angels,* from the *Story of Abraham.* Front and underside of tapestry, ca. 1600. Wool, silk, silver-gilt thread. (Metropolitan Museum of Art; gift of George Blumenthal, 1941)

type of thread or just one single color. Each image on the front or back is the combination of threads of different provenance. Although they may appear dissimilar if studied in isolation, they make sense as a whole. In the same way, this study weaves together threads related to literature, medicine, public policy, and the plastic arts to render an encompassing portrayal of social life in the Hispanic world. At the same time, I single out powerful threads of signification in the sidebars on these pages. Seen in these ways, the authors we usually study as paragons of aesthetic accomplishment, and the names we are used to reading as signposts of science, medicine, or public policy, become connectors of meaning that are as central or as ancillary—"importance" and "preeminence" are paradoxical and ambivalent categories when viewing a

tapestry or confronting a terrible disease—as the history behind a word or the origin of the medical use of a plant: all are threads that define an image only when entwined in a certain way. The singled-out threads in the margins of this book may seem to be included simply as colorful instances, but they in fact underline the pervasive nature of language and the shaping of history through occurrences that look merely anecdotal at first sight. The aim of my work has been to weave together these discrete significations to form a tapestry about the writerly manifestations of syphilis: a syphilography. Beyond this overarching theme of imbricated discourses related to the disease, I have avoided interpreting the presence of the malady or its writerly manifestations with my own metaphors or metonyms. Instead, I have focused on describing the threads, the tapestry, and the images on it in a clear, direct, and nuanced way. With this simple, even humble, exercise of judicious description alone,

I have been able to uncover several veiled features of the meanings of *gálico* during this period. In this sense, I have followed an exegetical method—the text and its context—and shied away when possible from the many temptations of developing an approach where my own subjective set of tropes could skew contextual interpretation. My goal is to offer readers from multiple disciplines a base they can use to develop perspectives related to their own specific fields of study and to initiate new exercises in discourse interweaving, with their own threads, images, and interpretations. This effort to follow and connect threads while avoiding reading into them my own ideas is not to be understood as rendering a simple sequence of anecdotes. The ordering of the threads to form the images on the tapestry produces its own meaning, renewed again and again by each reader and each reading.

To extend the metaphor I have allowed myself, the warp and weft of this study are, of course, *gálico*. *Gálico* was a disease that touched all levels of society, and it was the ailment that broached virtually every single discourse of the time and linked, in the same pervasive way as commerce or imperial administration, the territories in the New Continent with the peninsula. Another goal of *Sifilografía* is to show the deep and undeniable connections between both sides of the Atlantic, such as those suggested by the *indiano* in Goya's depiction. In many ways, disease levels the playing field. In order to better understand that the reality of sickness escapes traditional approaches—those that differentiate colony and metropolis—a study that encompasses the experience and meanings of the disease on both sides of the Atlantic is required. The eighteenth century is the peak of the Spanish Empire's cycle of rule in the American colonies, and a study that spells out the experience of the disease and its social consequences in a singular context may seem cogent and clear, but it risks being one-dimensional. *Sifilografía,* like the threads of the back of the tapestry, risks an apparent unevenness but gains in depth and perspective because it shows connections and correspondences that would otherwise be lost or downplayed.

Gálico is a disease that binds together seemingly disparate territories or social constructs. At its core, this is a border-crossing disease that breaks walls and reveals what is behind them. The distinction between public and private can be strongly demolished by its presence. *Gálico,* along with its derivative discourses, is so transgressive, yet so unifying, that every region has fought to avoid being named as its point of origin. No stratum of society can deny its rampant incidence, as its victims ranged from the lowly soldier to the rich noblewoman, from the self-assured *criollo* (creole) in a Spanish colony to the indigenous woman or the working slave, from the gambler who curses in the tavern to the pope who counts his beads in the cathedral, and from the artisan and the farmhand to the maid and the learned poet who pensively holds his quill: by the end of the eighteenth century, *gálico* was in fact as democratic and egalitarian as the American, French, and Latin American revolutions dreamed of being.[1]

In 1782, when Goya was painting his cartoons and slowly becoming favored by the court elite, Dr. Joseph Flores published his *Específico nuevamente descubierto en el reyno de Goatemala para la curacion radical del horrible mal del cancro, y otros mas frecuentes* (Newly rediscovered specific treatment for the radical cure of the chancre). Flores's treatise, one of many texts written about the treatment of syphilis at the time, might have been unexceptional were it not for three distinguishing details: (1) the author was from Guatemala, one of the remote colonies of the Spanish Empire; (2) the book was published in Mexico instead of in the Spanish metropolis; and (3) the proposed cure was not the inveterate use of mercury ointments, but the methodical ingestion of the raw, warm, essentially throbbing flesh of a large lizard found in the remote village of San Juan de Amatitán. While Flores bolstered his endorsement of the reptilian treatment with the arguments of eminent European authors entrenched in Enlightenment circles (Le Gendre, De Sault, Boerhaave), he also turned Western rationalism on its head by underscoring the importance of traditional Native American knowledge, asserting that "if we were not condescending of learning from this simple people, and tried to treat them with familiarity, we would be able to discover specific remedies more important than the most eloquent dissertations or the most curious discoveries in anatomy" (1).[2]

With its emphasis on empirical knowledge and its revision of medical dogma, Flores's defense of the lizard cure for *gálico* illustrates the reappropriation and relocation of the Enlightenment in Latin America. His gesture becomes even more complex if one considers that Flores's book was rapidly translated and republished in Madrid, Cadiz, Turin, Rome, Lausanne, Warsaw, and Halle. The circulation of Flores's text indicates the extent to which the Age of Reason incorporated inquiries beyond European modes of thinking, and shows that the Americas in fact played a crucial role in a global Enlightenment movement. Discourses on disease—syphilis in particular—became sites of scholarly contention that reveal alternative incarnations of "Enlightenment" beyond the North Atlantic. Through these discourses, one can perceive the way in which the relationships between empires and their colonies animated intellectual exchange. This is especially true in the case of Spain, a power that wielded the largest colonial administrative apparatus in the eighteenth century.

In this sense, *Sifilografía* is a cultural history of discourses about syphilis in the Spanish-speaking world on both sides of the Atlantic. By studying overlapping discourses of medicine, literature, and public policy, the book explores how fears of the disease and the search for its cure mobilized a transoceanic dialogue that remains on the underside of Enlightenment narratives of progress. With its protean identity—it was constantly rebranded as the French, Spanish, Indies, or Neapolitan disease—syphilis serves as a vehicle for following the transformation and retooling of ideas related to bodily contagion, which mirrored equally fluid exchanges in politics and philosophy. Concerns about syphilis's impact on everyday life—such as when distinguished members of society were driven mad by the disease, or when hospitals could not handle the increasing number of syphilitics—prompted writers and policymakers to transgress the boundary between public and private matters, thus creating an avenue for the strategic discussion of until then unmentionable topics. By calling our attention to the neglected cultural production of eighteenth- and very early nineteenth-century Spain and the Americas, this study demonstrates the Spanish-speaking world's crucial relevance to a global understanding of the period and engages with the current reassessment of Enlightenment thought in English and French area studies (see, e.g., works by Edelstein, Fleming, Lloyd, Monod, Roberts, Sala-Molins).

In addition to its attention to the relationship between syphilitic discourses and the global Enlightenment, this book is interested in syphilis's political significance in the countries and regions from which these discourses emerged. Throughout this period, the peripheral involvement of Spain and the Spanish colonies in scientific discourse, including its approach to syphilis, served as a platform for discussing the ideas of self-representation and autonomy that informed Spain's struggle for independence from the French, the colonies' struggle for independence from the Spanish metropolis, and their respective projects for creating viable economic models. The critical approach developed here understands syphilis in Latin America and Spain as an organic construction that goes beyond traditional classifications in terms of movements or historical progress. As such, the book is interested in the way that writings about syphilis crossed not only geographical borders but also boundaries between disciplines and genres. In contrast to the approach of traditional studies that deal with single layers of discourse related to a particular discipline, the aim here is to gain perspective through the extensive corpus of medical treatises, literary essays, poems, novels, music, art, and governmental documents. The authors and texts broached here subvert the idea of a homogeneous interpretation of syphilis and contribute to recomprehending the wide-ranging historical, cultural, and philosophical impact of this disease in the Spanish-speaking world. *Sifilografía*'s goals are to rediscover the significance of syphilis, to reassess the global understanding of the Enlightenment, and to engage in dialogue with other area studies about the disparate meanings of science.

2

A Mysterious Disease Changes the Political Map of the World

November 1, 1700. The first year of the century. The Habsburg dynasty in Spain comes to an end. Charles II has died without succession. When Charles was born in Madrid in November 1661, Jacques Sanguin, emissary of the French king Louis XIV, described in a letter the hopeless features of the heir of what was then the biggest kingdom on earth: "The prince seems extremely weak, both cheeks have a herpes-type rash, the head is covered with scabs, and below the right ear a type of suppurating duct or drainage has formed" (qtd. in García-Escudero López et al. 180). Charles II's life and diseases are veiled by secrecy, the dust of time, and diverging opinions. All we know is that he lived through almost four decades of bodily and mental weakness. At the time, the causes of his disease were to be found in the metaphysical world of potions and curses, and he is known as *El hechizado* (The Bewitched) in history books; the Holy Inquisition and his own confessor secured an exorcist, who after a heated discussion with the devil was able to report that "the spell had been cast in a cup of chocolate on 3 April 1675," with the beverage "containing the dissolved brain of an executed criminal to take away his reason, intestines to take away his health and kidneys to corrupt his semen and prevent him from engendering offspring and that the cause was the widow queen Mariana so that she could stay in power" (García-Escudero López 182). More recently, his condition has been interpreted as the outcome of extreme inbreeding within his family. There are theories that diagnose him with medical conditions ranging from Klinefelter's syndrome to hermaphroditism (179). According to others, his unfit constitution was the result not only of a long lineage of endogamy but also of congenital syphilis inherited from his father, Philip IV (1605–65), the "Planet King" (*Rey Planeta*).[1] Although we do not know if *El hechizado* was treated specifically for the French disease, and even if we do not have reliable information on whether he was diagnosed and treated for it by any of the royal doctors, the fact that his life has been interpreted under the lens of syphilis signals the high metaphorical power held by this disease.

Regardless of the theories concerning Charles II's malady, his life and his death at the onset of the new century reflect the medicine, politics, and culture of the time. Medicine was a kind of knowledge that mixed the judicious study of well-followed cases with inveterate belief based on Galen's (129–210 CE) theory of humors, or the theory of miasma favored by Avicenna (980–1037 CE), accompanied by a good amount of speculative reasoning—as seen in the above story about Charles II's laced chocolate—or astrological observations that interpreted diseases as the result of the alignment of the stars. Edicts and urban laws, specialized hospitals, and increasingly systematic medical training had begun to contain the spread of disease, but there was no concerted, effective effort to deal with problems that affected all strata of society. The fact that the outcome of disease was still a matter of fate left the sick and those close to them reacting with grief, terror, and scornful laughter, as expressed in poems, theater pieces, and written comments.

The general understanding of syphilis at the time is summarized in the definition crafted by the Venetian anatomist and doctor Niccolò Massa (1489–1569), one of the most commonly cited authors in Spanish books. Massa stated: "The French Disease is the bad disposition of the liver to the cold; some time after turning dry, it goes by hidden qualities through the veins and porosities and communicates with the whole body, and it is contagious, which occurs most often with bad blisters on the whole body, or in some of its members, and often appears first in the head, and in the forehead close to the root of the hair, and in the penis, and the vulva, and in those who are tainted through coitus" (5).[2]

Three years after the death of Charles II, when the War of the Spanish Succession (1701–14) was in its initial stages, a new edition of a popular treatise on surgery by Dr. Juan Calvo (1535?–99) was published in Valencia. This *Primera y Segunda Parte de la Cirugia Universal* (First and second part of the universal surgery) included a treatise on *morbo gálico,* one of the many names by which syphilis was then known. The ideas expressed by Calvo in his book not only illustrate how people like the ill-fated Charles II may have been treated for their health problems at the onset of the eighteenth century but also serve as a point of departure for examining medical views of the disease and its consequences in society. Like the disease itself, all these ideas will unfold and spread for the next three hundred years in a veiled, continuous, and pervasive way.

The term *morbo gálico,* which was frequently used by medical professionals in Spain, was the translation of *morbus gallicus,* "the French disease," a name that had been popularized in previous centuries. The use of the word *gálico* was so extensive and common that it was employed not only as the name of the disease but also as a term for those who suffered it. Other derivations of the name include *galiquiento, engalicado,* and *galicoso.* Today's term for the disease, "syphilis," did not become common until much later, but the word was already familiar to Calvo, who had read it in a three-volume poem by

Girolamo Fracastoro (1478–1553). Fracastoro had coined the word for his *Syphilis, sive morbus gallicus* (Syphilis, or the French disease) (1530), in which Syphilus, a shepherd, is punished with the disease by a solar god from Haiti, in the New World. In *La Cirugia Universal*, Calvo gives a moral interpretation to the name that is very telling of his interest in reducing the sexual encounters he blamed for spreading the disease: "Others like Geronimus Fracastoreo [*sic*] call it *sifila*, which means, ailment born out of too much love and accord that happens between women and men, although it would be better if it would please God there was not that much of it here" (540).[3] As I discuss the historical development of the concept and the names of the disease, I will avoid the word syphilis and instead employ terms common during this time, such as *gálico* and *bubas* (buboes).

First published in 1580, Calvo's book was widely studied and reedited on multiple occasions.[4] The eighteenth-century use of dated medical literature was common, given that advances in treatment were generally slow, burdened by continuous disputes between Galen's or Avicenna's partisans, and hindered by a dynamic in which tradition and previously received knowledge were favored over experimentation and testing of divergent opinions.[5] The explanations in Calvo's treatise are written in a clear literary style, but from a scientific standpoint they are reformulations of Galen's ideas, which by then were fifteen hundred years old. The main goal of traditional, didactic treatises like Calvo's was to summarize and organize previous knowledge, not to present novel interpretations or untested medicines that would not be easy to incorporate into established practice. In spite of its problematic perspective, this treatise was successful because it was practical, its focus already clear in its long subtitle, which stated that it would teach the French disease's "origin, causes, and cure," as well as "the method to make Holy Wine, apply anointments, and correct its accidents."[6] Along the same lines, to reach a wider reading public, Calvo's book was written in Castilian rather than the traditional medical language of Latin.

Calvo explains that the clearest manifestation of *gálico* was *bubas*, pustules that could be either open suppurating ulcers—in contemporary medical terms, the chancres of first-stage syphilis—or enclosed soft tumors. The "pustulas gálicas" are formed "from acrid corrosive and malignant humors, or from a corrupted blood mass, which at times becomes bilious, at others melancholic, and even at other times black bile" (538).[7] These putrid vapors would travel to the heart, ignite its "natural warmth" and produce fever, and then spread to different parts of the body. If the pustules appeared, they were a "sign that the person has confirmed *bubas*,"[8] and that the humors were malignant (544). If the pustules disappeared suddenly, that too was a bad sign, because it meant that "the humor has turned from the outside parts to the inside parts."[9] It was even worse if the patient fainted, because it meant that the humor was "back to the heart, and will suffocate its natural warmth, and the sick will die without a doubt" (546).[10] The inguinal pustules were called "*incordios* by the common people, and with good reason, because those who have them cannot walk freely but limp, and with great pain" (562).[11] As I will show later when discussing José María Blanco White's "El incordio: Poema épico-gálico en un canto" (The *incordio:* A epic-gallic poem in one canto) this symptom of the disease was featured in numerous poems and essays.

In documenting the progression of the disease, from simple fever to *bubas,* and from outside pustules to humors getting back inside, Calvo shows that there was already an understanding of its stages previous to the modern description, but he organizes all his conclusions around the idea of humors in flux. This rationalization of the disease was further codified in Juan de la Torre y Balcarçel's *Espejo de la philosophia* (The mirror of philosophy) (1705), a book that, like Calvo's, had first appeared in an earlier edition, in 1668: "This ailment has three kinds; in the first, and for those that suffer it, there are no pains, and it is difficult to recognize it. It can be traced by seeing that there are disorders and obstructions in the liver, and weakness in the stomach. In the *gálicos* of the second kind there are usually gonorrheas and general pain, as if they were arthritic. In the third kind there are gummas and tumors over the bones; and in all of them, finally, the symptoms of the first kind are found" (229).[12]

Other consequences of *gálico* discussed by Calvo were damage to the nasal bridge (545), hoarsening of the voice, and loss of hair. All these physical outcomes can be found in written representations from the previous century, such as *El buscón* (The swindler) (1626), where Francisco de Quevedo describes a *licenciado* (lawyer), Cabra, as having a nose that is "half Roman, half French, because it had been eaten by the pustules from a cold, and not from any vice, because those cost money (35).[13] Here, Quevedo plays with words by mingling geography and disease: the city of Rome is a way of saying "snub-nosed" (*romo*) in Spanish, and the country of France alludes to the appellative *gálico,* or Gallic—French—disease. In addition, Quevedo accuses Cabra of being a miser because his disease did not come from paying prostitutes for sex, but from a prosaic common cold.

Calvo also pays special attention to the issue of baldness. People made fun of the bald because hair was a sign of beauty and manliness, so "the ones that lack hair are seen as effeminate persons, and because the *morbo gálico* is many times the cause for it to fall out" (570).[14] Torre explains that the *bubas* provoke the loss of hair over the whole body "because the vicious humor that has settled in the liver, comes out not only in the mouth, but in the whole body" (17).[15] Believing in the theory of humors and of the body constantly seeking balance, he adds, "Some doctors claim that baldness usually helps to get rid of other, more dangerous ailments when the vicious and malignant hu-

Losing More than Just Hair

In his poem "Cubriendo con cuatro cuernos," Francisco de Quevedo mockingly describes the tokens of love that Benita—a dissipated and unfaithful woman—gives to
a church sexton. One such proof of love is a lock of hair that the enamored man con-
templates: "She took out then some hairs / between oak and chestnut, / Which, at the
intercession of some buboes / had fallen from her some time past" ("Sacó luego unos
cabellos / Entre robles y castaños, / Que á intercession de unas bubas / Se le cayeron an-
taño") (*Obras* 188). The fading color of the hair—a shade between brown and yellow—
refers either to the theory of humors or to treatment with mercury.

mor exits the body through the skin" (17),[16] and that the doctor should apply
different treatments according to the color of the patient's hair roots. White
roots meant that the phlegmatic (passive or calm) type of humors had to be
expulsed. If the roots were yellowish, the excess was of the choleric type, and if
black, the excess of melancholy needed to be purged (17).[17]

Following Galen, Calvo catalogs the disease as epidemic, but transmitted
not in the "proper" fashion of the bubonic plague in the late Middle Ages—
through the "infected and putrefacted air"—but in an "improper" fashion,
"by contact with bubous persons" (536).[18] Calvo's method of description
shows that knowledge was still measured scholastically, by organizing observations, and not necessarily obtained through trial and error—that is, experimentation—which was the approach of barbers and bloodletters, the kind of
empirical practitioners that doctors like Calvo considered of a lower strata.
When authors like Calvo discarded the old belief that the French disease was
"properly" epidemic, those who until then had attributed their symptoms
to bad air rather than physical contact started to have problems accounting
for how they had become infected. One can just imagine how many supposedly celibate priests, cloistered nuns, devoted husbands and wives, and self-
important nobles who until the early seventeenth century had blamed innocent causes—such as breathing the same air as a diseased person—were
now forced to explain to doctors, superiors, and spouses the all-too-corporeal
origin of their throbbing pustules. But the sources of contagion were still multiple, and excuses could be given without much twisting of reality, especially
since the disease was seen with a certain degree of leniency because it remained
within the domestic realm: it was discussed with the doctor or the barber,
but not yet regarded as a clear danger to society. Calvo believed that mainly
women disseminated the disease (Berco, "Syphilis and the Silencing" 101), but
Torre thought that *gálico* could be spread by men and women alike, and in no

particular order (229). The tangible ways of contagion described by Calvo are sleeping in the same bed as someone with the disease, using the same shirts, getting close to their breath, drinking from the same cup, and most especially through having coitus (537).

Pedro López Pinna (1667–?), who practiced in the Hospital de Gálicos de San Miguel de Zafra, wrote *Tratado de morbo gallico* (Treatise on the French disease), which was published in 1696 and reprinted in 1719. The author begins his treatise by citing medical authorities to stress that "unnecessary coitus destroys and universally disarrays the entire machine of the human body" so that "it sways, crumbles, and trembles." He adds, "The venereal acts destroy, wither, deflower, and make ugly all the beauty, grace, and spirit of the man, leaving him dry, and withered" (1).[19]

As a consequence of their "immoderate appetite," humans are subject to all kinds of sicknesses, which López Pinna meticulously lists: "Stomach ailments, sweating of the limbs, weakness, dullness of the senses, memory loss, palsy, gout, sickness of the kidneys, and urinary pain, colic, bad breath, toothache, inflammation of the tonsils, phthisis, dropsy, [...] aches of the head, neck, back, arms, haunches, knees, feet, and of the whole body. Gummas of the head, arms, and legs, corrosive ulcers on the whole body, throat, uvula, and palate emerge; patches of hardened skin, pustules, eczema, warts, genital ulcers, *gálico* gonorrheas, buboes, hair loss, scrofula, moles, abscesses in the head, bone lesions" (3).[20]

The afflictions range from loss of memory to colic and include 234 simple and complex species of *bubas* (4). It is not a stretch to conclude that López Pinna thought badly of sexual relations. Like his contemporaries, he does not use the now common term of "infection" or "contagion" to name the way the disease was spread, but instead the word *inficionar*, which is closer to the Latin *inficio* and means "to taint" or "to corrupt." He also uses the word *comunicar*, in the sense of communicating or transferring something (6).

For Calvo, following the teachings of Gabriel Fallopius (1523–62), the longer coitus lasted the more exacerbated the disease would be: "The more they keep on, the more open are the porosities, the more heated humors become, and the more apt and ready they are to receive such disease. Hence we gather that those who feel more pleasure in the venereal act will become infected more quickly; and for this reason young people will become infected more quickly than the old, and the sanguine more than the melancholic, and women more than men, because they feel twice as much desire as men" (542).[21]

But, whether lust was felt twofold or by halves, coitus happened, and the exchange of humors happened, even if Calvo and his peers thought that women were more prone to sexual desire. The inevitability of contact led to a burgeoning interest in preventing the disease: for example, the use of condoms would become more common in the second half of the 1700s.[22] There were also calls for early intervention, as explained by Torre in an entire chapter of his treatise, conveniently titled "How is one to defend oneself of this disease after the coitus," which he starts by saying that "the one who stops and averts a person from falling does more than the one who helps him get up after having fallen" (7).[23] The author advises that if there is suspicion of contagion, the sexual organs of the patient must be washed with hot water for at least "half a quarter of an hour" ("medio quarto de hora"), a provision that should equally be applied to the breasts of wet nurses, breastfeeding mothers, and the mouths of children. This preventive cleaning could get rather radical; Torre mentions that if there was a lack of hot water, the patient was to use his own hot urine to wash properly (8). Still, once infected, patients were to refrain from having sex; in Calvo's words, this was "so they do not get debilitated in a way that the cure may be hindered, and also because with all that agitation the humors become inflamed and many accidents may happen" (548).[24]

For Calvo, the theory of humors, which would not be debunked until well into the nineteenth century, serves to explain the mechanics of the disease's transmission and treatment. The logic of this theory is based on a balance of contrasting qualities; as a result, the physician had to observe the patient and prescribe a treatment to maintain an even performance of the diseased body (see fig. 3). But the consequences of this viewpoint were more than simply physical. Calvo's interpretation of humors reflects the way people—old and young, men and women—were cataloged. From this perspective, women, being twice as inclined to sex as men—that is, being more hot and more humid—were more likely to produce symptoms of the disease. Descriptions of the dissimilarities between men and women reveal a recurrent logic that gave further space for a logic of differentiation in treating and understanding gálico. For example, Torre claims that gálico appears less frequently in women than in men because of their "monthly evacuations" ("purgaciones de cada mes"), while the disease is more present in men, children, and pregnant women because they cannot menstruate and the "venom" thus remains inside, without a natural form of elimination. This logic also explains for him why people exercising continuously, and those working in ovens and kitchens, tended to get rid of the "bad humors" ("malos humores") more easily (5). The resulting prescription from this logic was to concentrate on avoiding sexual contact with women in general, and more specifically with the kind of women who catered to men for a price.

From Calvo's perspective, the course of action was clearly defined. The life of the patient was to be organized through a regimented diet. The patient was restricted to bread of good quality, mutton, veal, young goat, chicken, young pigeon, partridge, and mountain birds, all preferably grilled because that

Humoral Equilibrium

The doctrine of humors was initially developed by Greek polymaths Hippocrates (c. 460–370 BCE) and Galen. According to their teachings, the health of an individual depended on the proper balance of four bodily fluids: yellow bile, black bile, phlegm, and blood. The grouping of these four elements resonated with previous theories about matter (air, fire, water, earth), their corresponding qualities (cold, hot, moist, dry), and even the four seasons. The instability of bodily fluids resulted in disease. The treatment to restore balance included the consumption of a particular diet or a variation in daily routines, and more invasive practices such as purges, enemas, and bloodletting.

The tight logic of correspondence and balance was the main factor behind the prevalence of the humoral theory until the eighteenth century, and it is still palpable in our everyday life. For example, when we describe someone as "sanguine," we are using humoral ideas that believe that an excess of blood causes an active, optimistic temperament. The chart in fig. 3 of correspondences between physical and nonphysical qualities explains the broad system of meaning derived from humoral theory.

---

would help dry out the humors of *gálico*. Fish, water birds, bacon, and salted meat were proscribed because they tended to produce thick, melancholic, and *adusto* (burning) humors that affected the liver and intensified the sadness of the diseased (547). *Gálico* was a disease closely linked to melancholy, in the same way that plague or leprosy had been many years before. The treatment was geared toward addressing the physical effects of the disease, but ultimately the goal was to balance the humors. Torre adjusts the patient's regimen to counter the negative consequences of unbalanced emotions: "Other procedures will help them, like doing physical exercise, more than they are used to; to be well wrapped up, to avoid the cold of the night; to wash the hands and face regularly; to cut the nails of hands and toes; to not have access to women, even if they are married, but as little as they can; to not get angry, or sad, or melancholic, but instead to try to sidestep any sorrow" (230).[25]

According to Calvo, wine was to be avoided because it was vaporous (*vaporoso*) and diluted the excess humor, which should be extracted in a condensed way: "What [the patient] must drink is boiled water with the *palo santo*, or sarsaparilla, in a very simple preparation. How it is to be prepared, we will say later" (547).[26] Leafy and garden vegetables, as well as olives and raw salads, were to be avoided because they also produced thick humors, but the broth of chickpeas and parsley was allowed (548). It was thought that extreme cold or heat would produce adverse humors that would work against the patient, so the dwelling was to be kept temperate by using artificial heating or cooling.

Figure 3. The four humors and their qualities

Humor	Organ	Characteristics	Physical type	Temperament	Element
Blood	Liver	Hot and moist	Chubby, ruddy	Sanguine (optimistic, carefree, generous, happy, amorous)	Air
Phlegm	Lungs	Cold and moist	Overweight	Phlegmatic (cowardly, lethargic, lazy)	Water
Black bile	Gall bladder	Cold and dry	Thin, pale	Melancholic (apathetic, introspective, sentimental)	Earth
Yellow bile	Spleen	Hot and dry	Muscular, wiry	Choleric (ambitious, vindictive, volatile)	Fire

Moderate exercise was accepted, but sleeping during the day was prohibited because it would produce burning humors and unwelcome flatulence.

After organizing the routine of the patient, the next step was to "evacuate the precedent matter" ("evacuar la materia antecedente") by using radical treatments such as bloodletting, purgatives, and leeches. More moderate actions, such as suction with cupping glasses, medicated baths, and massages, were considered too weak and therefore useless. These measures were followed by the "elimination of the conjoined matter" ("quitar la materia conjunta," 552), which was the poisonous humor that remained in veins and joints after the aggressive procedures of evacuation. The elimination of these remnants was pursued through the use of medicines that had their own array of meanings based on their use, origin, and shape. The main components to attack *gálico* were China root (*Smilax china*), *palo santo, zarzaparrilla,* and mercury: "these four things with all their substance, and with properties unknown to us, admirably cure all types of *bubas*" (552).[27]

At this point there was an important crux in the way *gálico* was understood. The line of Scholastic reasoning that dealt with discursive organization and a desire for formal balance—that is, the kind of knowledge that could be acquired only in establishments of higher education—had to bow to the cryptic properties attached to specific plants or minerals whose effectiveness could not be unveiled through reasoning but whose use had been established by practitioners who had no formal training (e.g., barbers and bloodletters), and by people who were not considered part of the civilized sphere because their knowledge was supposedly unorganized (e.g., indigenous doctors, shamans, and healers). Doctors like Calvo solved this tension between *doxa* and *episteme* by trying to impose order on the measurements, processes, and times of preparation and administration of the remedies. Such is the case of *palo santo* (guaiacum, *guayacán, palo de Indias,* or more tellingly *lignum vitae,* which can be translated as "wood of life"). Calvo explains that "the remedies that cure this disease were found by experience. This experience came to us from the Indians, who by drinking the water in which this twig was cooked, or *palo santo,* and sweating with it, and keeping a good regimen, can cure the *bubas* perfectly. [. . .] This is the *palo santo* brought to us from the Indies. It is indeed a great gift from God that the medicine comes from where the disease came" (552).[28] According to the Spanish doctor Nicolás Monardes in his *Historia medicinal de las cosas que se traen de nuestras Indias occidentales, que siruen en medicina* (Medical history of the things brought from our West Indies, that can be used in medicine), the first time Spaniards—and Europeans, for that matter—learned about the medicinal properties of guaiacum was on the island of Santo Domingo or Hispaniola. The knowledge of its supposed curative power passed from the indigenous pharmacopeia to the European medical system: "An Indian gave notice of it to his master in this way. Seeing that a Spaniard was suffering great pains from the buboes that a Indian woman has stuck to him, the Indian who was one of the Physicians of that land gave him the water of Guayacan, by which not only was he rid of the pains that he was suffering, but the illness healed very well; with such results many other Spaniards, who were infected with the said illness, were made well; which was later communicated by those who came here from Seville, and from here it is made public across the world" (10).[29] The idea that the New World was the source of both *gálico* and the medicine that purportedly cured the disease made a lot of sense within a medical perspective that believed in the homeopathic interconnection between cause, effect, and cure. This logic also meant that wood of a certain origin—guaiacum from Honduras was thought to be the most effective—was considered of better quality than others, and therefore acquired higher prices: today's tension between generic and brand-name remedies has indeed a long history. Also, as is the case today with other remedies, many fake wood slivers and branches were sold as real American guaiacum.

Spain was the biggest empire on earth, but its possessions beyond the sea were a different world, a place understood from the metropolis's perspective as the source of incalculable riches that had financed the magnificence of their harbors and the court. But this world was also a place not easily connected to

Guaiacum, First Word of the Americas in the English Language

Ulrich von Hutten (1488–1523) was a German scholar known for his satirical writings and his strong defense of the Lutheran Reformation. He is also known for dying of syphilis. He wrote an early work on the disease titled *De guaici medicina et morbo Gallico liber unus,* published in 1519. The text's main feature is a discussion on the treatment of *gálico* with guaiacum. The book was translated into English by Thomas Paynell and published in London in 1533 as *De morbo gallico.* In this translation, the word *guaiacum,* an indigenous Taíno name from the Antilles, is printed for the first time in the English language. The title page of the 1536 edition states the word directly: *Of the vvood called gvuaiacum, that healeth the Frenche pockes.* One of the earlier depictions of guaiacum in the treatment of *gálico* is *Hyacvm, et lves venerea* (Guaiacum and the venereal plague) (ca. 1591), painted by the Flemish artist Jan van der Straet (1523–1605; also known as Stradanus) and engraved by the Dutch publisher Philip Galle (1537–1612). Other names for guaiacum, such as *palo santo* (holy wood) attest to its medical good standing. *Guayaco* or *guayacán* is also highly prized for its hardness and density. A very valuable and scarce wood, it has been cataloged as an endangered species by the International Union for Conservation of Nature and Natural Resources.

---

the identity of the kingdom. For Europeans of the time, it made sense that the remedy for a disease from the Indies was to be found in the Indies. That logic followed Paracelsus's (1493–1541) principle of *similia similibus curantur* (like things are cured by like things), which was further developed during the second half of the seventeenth century in relation to homeopathy. This principle is related to the logic behind today's production of vaccines. As I will discuss later, by the end of this century several educated men in the New World were laboring to change the interpretation of this belief's components by rejecting the Indies as the source of the disease and reinforcing their role as the provider of a cure.

A similar set of meanings was attached to sarsaparilla, a plant "that cures the *morbo gálico,* or *bubas,* with all of its substance, and not through manifested quality." It "was brought for the first time from New Spain, and later from Honduras, which is the best, and the one that produces the best effects" (Calvo 553).[30] A kind of sarsaparilla could be found in Spain, but according to Calvo it was not as effective as the one from the Indies, reinforcing the idea that doctors could not understand the hidden qualities of the plant, and that the foreign origin of their properties was somehow related to their effectiveness. Calvo also mentions China root as an effective remedy, but he cannot give any specific morphology, saying only that it too comes from afar, somewhere close to Scythia (in Central Eurasia) (551). Guaiacum, sarsaparilla, and China root all were used almost exclusively as electuaries or in concoctions such as *agua de palo* (wood water) or *agua de zarza* (sarsaparilla water), which were mixed with other fitting ingredients, using very formalized methods of preparation.

In addition to brews, there were other ways of administering remedies. Electuaries are conserves or pastes made with syrup or honey into which medicinal components have been folded. The sweet flavor of the base facilitates the medicine's administration, since it can be given with a spoon or rubbed onto the gums of the patient. Since *gálico* was usually treated with mercury, or a combination of mercury and guaiacum or sarsaparilla, these ingredients were typically mixed with lard to make ointments (*unciones*) that were applied directly to the buboes and the joints of the patient or spread on a cloth and applied to specific areas as a patch (*parche*). Fumigations—the burning of mercury in the form of cinnabar grains, the use of its smoke on the body, and the breathing in of its vapors—lost prevalence by the seventeenth century, when guaiacum became the medicine of choice. A logical consequence of *gálico*'s pervasiveness and this homeopathic logic was the constant search for new medicines from the Indies. There was the milk extracted from *mechoacán* or *tacuache* root (*Convolvulus mechoacan*) (see fig. 4) (Suárez de Ribera, *Arcanismo* 156), a plant from Mexico and Peru known for its purgative properties, expelling "especially flegme, and then waterish humors" (Gerard 723–24). Another example was *calaguala* (*Polypodium angustifolium*), a type of fern found in Central and South America, which according to the Spanish doctor Pérez Bravo had been brought from Peru and was believed to cure all symptoms of *gálico* (13). Another kind of medicinal wood used for *bubas* was sassafras (*Sassafras albidum*) (see fig. 5), which according to Jean Astruc (1684–1766) had been brought especially from Florida and was called *pabamwe* by the natives (*Traité,* 90). Astruc also mentions the use of tortoise meat found off the coasts of America, a remedy commonly employed by buccaneers: "They say effectively, that if a person sick with the venereal disease does not have any other food, at first many pustules break out all over the body, which rising to a point, fester very much, and in this way they believe that in a month all the virus hidden in the body is cast out [...] the pirates commonly called buccaneers, that infest the seas of America, do not cure themselves by any other means" (102).[31] In a similar vein, Dr. José Flores, an important author I will study in more depth later, and who was born in "The Kingdom of Guatemala" (*El reyno de Goatemala*), informs us of native species of lizard whose fresh meat was a proven cure of *gálico* (6).

Another powerful and radical remedy against *bubas* was *azogue,* or mercury. Like the plants and animals mentioned above, it had hidden properties

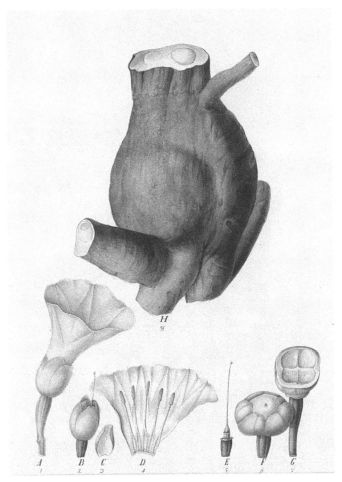

Figure 4. Mechoacán (*Convolvulus mechoacan Arruda*), Javier Cortés y Alcocer. Drawing of the Royal Botanical Expedition to the Viceroyalty of Peru, by Hipólito Ruiz and José Pavón, 1777–1816. (Real Jardín Botánico, CSIC, Madrid; © RJB-CSIC; image ARJB, DIV. IV, D-1811)

that expelled the disease from the body, in this case through copious sweating and profuse salivation, which evacuated the "predominant humor" ("humor pecante") (Calvo, 555). Following the teachings of Niccolò Massa, Torre explains that the benefits of mercury in the treatment of the disease were myriad: dissolving and tempering humors dispersed through the body, relieving pain, healing pustules, maturing abscesses, cleaning and dissolving ulcers, cleaning the infected blood through elimination and urination, and vaporizing any remnants of excrement through sweat (36). The belief in mercury's supposed efficacy could be attributed in part to its cryptic properties: it was a liquid mineral, deemed by many as a curing substance and by others as a venom, and

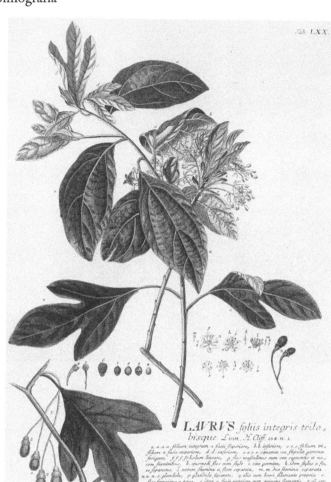

Figure 5. Sassafras (*Sassafras albidum*), G. D. Ehret, C. J. Trew, and B. C. Vogel, 1765. *Plantae selectae*, vol. 7, plate 70. Norimbergae: Nonas Martii. (Peter H. Raven Library/Missouri Botanical Garden)

described as cold or hot, depending on which side the author or doctor felt more inclined to defend. Treatment was administered through tinctures, infusions, and fumigations. Following the teachings of the Italian anatomist and doctor Gabriel Fallopius, Calvo and other doctors of the time favored *unciones* (ointments) and concoctions taken orally (557). The *unciones*—mixtures of mercury, saliva, laurel oil, and pork fat—were smeared on arms and legs, but never near the heart or liver (558). Treatment was administered for several days, with the patient on a strict diet, and the goal was to provoke the expulsion of the excessive humor through profuse salivation and sweating, and even *cámaras* (diarrhea), although this was not desirable because it was difficult to cure the internal wounds that resulted from such a radical evacuation. Sweating was good, but it got rid of only the "subtle" component and not the bulk of the excessive humor (558). The patient's room was to be kept lukewarm because hot or cold temperatures would hinder the cure of *gálico;* for this reason, Calvo was against using *unciones* during the winter or on hot days, and preferred the "dos Primaveras" (the two Springs)—fall and spring proper— as more appropriate times for intervention (558). After this strong treatment, patients experienced loss of hair and teeth, severe digestive problems, and, on more than one occasion, death.

It would be a mistake to infer from Calvo's organized description of treatment with mercury that every patient had an equally organized and complete means of cure. Torre's comments remind us that not all patients had the same treatment; the administration of mercury varied according to the patient's constitution and in relation to social position or physical constitution, "because rich and noble men, who are to be cured with this remedy, wish their ointments to be more delicate and fragrant, while the poor are happy with what suffices to cure them. The young and frail men, and others who sweat easily, and progress, are to be treated more delicately and softly" (27).[32] But the difference in treatment because of social position is shown even more tellingly in a section titled "Como se han de aver los pobres con las unciones" (How the poor are to have the *unciones*), which deals with the need of poor people to keep working in spite of their ailment. Torre's discussion leaves the discourse of medicine and enters the realm of public policy: "The poor, or the beggars, or serfs, who do not have a place to get cured, or money to pay, after having been bled and purged can gently apply the ointment with their own hands to all the joints, or the places that are more convenient in each case, using one of the light ointments already described, and then will get dressed, and will go to their business, and when they see some of the signs we mentioned will stop the application" (30).[33]

For the rich or for the poor, *gálico* ultimately meant death. In contrast to this close-ended imminence, *gálico's* immanence rested in its power of representation—that is, its far-reaching and open-ended meanings—which is epitomized by mercury. The extensive use of this component in treating the disease provided a fertile ground for cultivating the meanings that became material for poets and playwrights. The contexts of Greek and Roman mythology produced oblique meanings, masked criticisms, and humorous double entendres when mercury was mentioned in relation to *gálico*. The same thing happened among alchemists, who thought that mercury could be transformed into silver, and its unstable qualities helped writers characterize love and sex as ever changing, treacherous, and dangerous. The use of mercury was so generic, and the number of patients suffering *gálico* so large, that the poet and courtier Francisco Benegasi y Luján (1659–1743), an author who will be discussed later, commented on the shortage of the remedy in a somewhat cryptic stanza: "The mercury of the apothecaries, / Is not enough to reach all the bubous persons, / And so I named God Mercury, / Because in the end: God [reigns] over all" (50).[34]

For Benegasi there are so many people affected by *gálico* that there is not sufficient mercury in the apothecaries to treat them all. Having no access to material mercury, these people must hope for help from the more ethereal but readily available god Mercury. Benegasi takes the connection a step further by conjoining the Christian god's qualities of ubiquity and omnipotent power with the defunct and failing qualities of the god belonging to the Greek pantheon. Benegasi's poem is not easy to understand because it is a response to a specific context for which we have no reference, but it certainly shows the overlapping meanings among mercury the mineral, Mercury the god, and mercury the medicine.

In the same manner, the culteranist poet Francisco de Trillo y Figueroa (1618–80) functions as a bridge between the literary production of the seventeenth and eighteenth centuries. His poem "Al sepulcro de un medico astrólogo" (For the tomb of a medical astrologer) (Castro 94–95) plays with the connotations of the signs of the zodiac. The satirical text makes fun of an astrologist and describes his meteoric career. Trillo explains that the character "de Virgo hizo figuras treinta veces"—drafted charts for many people born under the zodiac sign of Virgo, the virgin—but at the same time Trillo implies that the astrologer deflowered thirty women, thus "repairing" thirty virginities. The poet also says that many fish swam in the astrologer's aquarium ("Acuario nadaron muchos peces"), an image that plays with the double meaning of *acuario* as both "aquarium" and "Aquarius," implying that this man was prone to having sex with many people, an idea that Trillo reinforces by stating that the astrologer was "de Géminis retrato"—that is, a person with a double life, who was perhaps having sex with both men and women, given that the sign of Gemini is represented by twins. Trillo further develops the sexual voracity of the charlatan astrologer in the following lines: "Without becoming gold rain, ten husbands, / He converted into Aries, Capricorn and Taurus" (vv. 12–13).[35]

Trillo is playing with the fact that these three zodiac signs are represented by animals with big horns—the ram, the goat, and the bull, respectively— which in turn alludes to the horns of cuckolded men; that is, the husbands of the astrologer's conquests. To seduce these ten wives, the man did not have to become gold rain, as Zeus did to possess Danae. This observation can also be interpreted to mean that the man had sex with the women without spending money. Making other allusions to the zodiac, Trillo states that the soothsayer was not a decent person and attacked people like a lion (Leo), spread his killing venom like a scorpion (Scorpio), and swindled others with his archer-like ability (Sagittarius). But in the end, "in the best of these tricks / *Gálico* Cancer ate away his years":[36] this cancer in Trillo's poem is not really that of the zodiac sign of the crab, but the creeping disease of the *bubas—gálico*—that gnaws up the astrologer's life in a sort of poetic justice that punishes him for his excess and treachery.

The renowned Spanish author José Cadalso (1741–82) also alludes to the intersection of planets, gods, mercury, and *gálico*. Cadalso is the author of the classic *Cartas marruecas* (Moroccan letters) (1789) and *Noches lúgubres* (Lugubrious nights) (1789), both published posthumously in installments by *El Correo de Madrid*. The second of these works served as inspiration for the novel *Noches tristes y día alegre* (Sad nights and happy day) (1818), by the Mexican author Fernández de Lizardi (1776–1827), a text I will study later in the context of social dynamics in colonial Spanish America, specifically in Mexico. In one of Cadalso's poems, titled "Anacreóntica," he comments on life during winter, when some people are inside reading serious books and others are counting their ill-gotten coins while the poet and his friends are in the countryside sharing good food and good wine by the fireplace. Anacreontic compositions derive their name from the Greek poet Anacreon. They came to be popular in Spain especially in the eighteenth century, with poets such as Juan Meléndez Valdés and Cadalso. *Anacreónticas* deal with themes of love, and with the celebration of pleasures such as food and drink. These poems provided an outlet through which poets could explore excess and indulgence, as opposed to the highly regulated, organized style and practical themes that neoclassical poetry demanded. Both types of poetic composition in eighteenth-century Spain looked to ancient Greece as their origin, but they diverged in their approach and conceptualization of poetry. Irene Gómez Castellano has shown in *La cultura de las máscaras* that the use of symbolism and metaphor in *anacreónticas* allowed poets to test and question their sexual desires, which they would not have been able to do openly.

Exhibiting these ambivalent anacreontic features, Cadalso's poetic character thinks of what may be happening outside the balcony of his beloved Cloris, while depicting plowmen walking under rain, snow, and ice, as well as "Others [standing] with pikes on their shoulders, / Positioned atop ramparts, / Hungry and naked / But full of glory" (*Poesías* 114).[37] The poet ambiguously describes one more group that goes to the "open fields" ("campo raso") to measure the distances "That lie between Venus and Mars, / That lie between Mercury and Venus" (115).[38] The verses are a variation of an infamous phrase, "una noche con Venus y una vida con Mercurio" (a night with Venus and a life with Mercury), which refers to the prolonged and painful treatment with *unciones* that persons touched by *gálico* must undergo, even if they had sex only once with a carrier of the disease. In this case the terse verses seem to hide the idea of men going to the "open fields," which may be a euphemism for men seeking sexual gratification with prostitutes, thus engaging in love battles with a Venus, and consequently traveling the short distance between venereal love and venereal treatment. Cadalso makes another oblique reference to the use of mercury in letter 78 of his *Cartas marruecas.* The character Gazel describes to his preceptor, Ben-Beley, the features of a Spanish "scholastic man of wisdom" ("sabio escolástico," 255). He describes such a man as scrawny, tall, smelling of tobacco, and wearing heavy glasses, with affected speech and a reactionary mind. Gazel's scholastic man despises poetry as a waste of time, physics as puppetry, and the study of electricity, movement, or light as heresy, and he views mathematics not as a useful discipline for advancing the economic situation of the country but as a field equivalent to astrology. According to Gazel, this kind of backward character does not acknowledge the advances of medicine and thinks that patients can be cured with the precepts of Galen or Hippocrates or with syllogisms and aphorisms: "If you tell him, that without discounting the merit of those two great men, modern physicians have made advancements in this field through a greater knowledge of anatomy and botany than that which the ancients possessed; in addition to many medicines, like quinine and mercury, that were not used until a short while ago, he will also make fun of you" (257–58).[39]

From Cadalso's point of view, physicians of the end of the eighteenth century are fortunately distant from the earlier medical discourse of Calvo and Francisco Suárez de Ribera, and closer to the rising scientific ideas that were being disseminated from England or France. For Cadalso, speaking through his supposedly objective and detached Moroccan character Gazel, the *sabio escolástico* represents an old view of knowledge; he is the enemy of enlightened progressive ideas. Nuño, the third character of this epistolary novel, thinks that the best course of action is to let this kind of scholar continue screaming his syllogistic nonsense until he dies. Meanwhile, the younger generation must keep working on the "positive sciences, so that foreigners don't call us barbarians; let our youth make whatever progress it can: let it seek to give works to the public about useful subjects. [. . .] Within the next two years the scientific system of Spain must change imperceptibly and without fuss" (258).[40] Nuño describes the backward state of medical discourse during the first half of the seventeenth century and drafts a programmatic idea to advance the state of knowledge, as summarized in the closing statement of his letter: "Well, let the

José Cadalso y Vázquez de Andrade

Cadalso was a man of letters and arms. His life as writer, essayist, and poet ended in 1782, when he was killed during the Great Siege of Gibraltar. An English and Dutch force had occupied this territory in 1704—after the death of *El hechizado*—and Cadalso was active as a colonel of the Royal Spanish Army in the failed effort of the Spanish and French armies to recover it.

His most relevant work is the *Cartas marruecas* (1789), a novel written as a series of letters between two Moroccans and a Spaniard. They discuss different perspectives on the customs in Spanish society. The overt criticism of several Spanish cultural and administrative habits represents a peak of enlightened thought in the peninsula. By contrast, his novel *Noches lúgubres* (1789) is usually considered a precursor of Spanish Romanticism. The story of the novel (which was never finished) relates the three-night effort of the protagonist, Tediato, to disinter the body of his beloved with the help of the gravedigger Lorenzo because he wants to commit suicide by the side of the corpse. Critics have argued that the story originates in Cadalso's wish to unearth the body of his lover, the actress María Ignacia Ibáñez (1745–71). David Gies suggests that Ibáñez, known by the poetic name of "Filis," died as a result of syphilis ("El cantor" 320).

---

past count for nothing, and let us mark the date from today, supposing that the peninsula sank halfway through the seventeenth century, and has again risen from the sea at the end of the eighteenth" (259).[41] For Cadalso, mercury and quinine represent modern medicine, even though the treatment for *gálico* has not changed during the previous two hundred years. What is modern are not the remedies, or the rudiments of math and physics, but an openness to new perspectives from outside Spain—an attitude that was natural to Cadalso himself, as he had resided in England and France and traveled to Italy, Holland, and Germany. According to Nuño—speaking for Cadalso—the regressive stance of traditional scholars could be countered only by secretly studying foreign sources, a course of action followed by other authors of his time, who later were forced into exile.

Years after Cadalso's death in Gibraltar, Juan Nicasio Gallego (1777–1853)—an Enlightenment poet, a friend of Juan Meléndez Valdés, and a transitional figure in the move toward literary Romanticism *in* Spain—laments what he sees as the decline of Spanish theater in a satirical sonnet titled "For Contemporary Literature: A Sonnet Improvised in Jest and in the Obligatory Verse Form" (191).[42] According to Gallego, the Spanish public is no longer able to see dramatic works with grand characters like Shakespeare's Mark Antony or Julius Caesar. Gallego grouses that when characters vanish from the stage,

Juan Nicasio Gallego

Nicasio Gallego (1777–1853) was born in Zamora, studied in Salamanca, and upon entering holy orders, went to Madrid, where he was given a position at court. There, his
patriotism and literary spirit led to his inclusion in the circle of Manuel José Quintana,
who was both a close friend and a literary inspiration for Gallego. His imitations of
Quintana's style place him among the most important poets of the turn of the nineteenth century, though his oeuvre consists of only seven poems. The most famous of
these is the elegy "El Dos de Mayo," which commemorates the 1808 uprising against
the French headed by three Spanish soldiers. His liberal tendencies led Gallego to be
elected as a delegate to the 1808 Cortes de Cádiz. There, he was one of the strongest
voices in support of the decree of November 10, 1810, which recognized the freedom of
the press for the first time in Spain's history. Gallego consistently demonstrated his opposition to the French invasion, in both discourse and verse, yet, restored to the throne,
Ferdinand VII imprisoned him in 1814 for his political liberalism. Nicasio Gallego
spent much of his imprisonment in the monastery of Loreto, where he was relocated for
his health. He was freed after the revolution of 1820, and briefly served as archdeacon
of Valencia. The Royal Spanish Academy took him into its membership, and made him
its perpetual secretary, in which position he was very involved in the administration of
texts for education.

---

they succumb to the undignified use of opium, arsenic, or antimony, instead
of tragedy-intensifying weapons like daggers or swords. In the third stanza, he
criticizes current standards: "Delirium, fury they call *genius;* / Diana is no longer anything more than a *full moon;* / *Cyllenian* is only used for *gálico*" (191).[43]

Gallego criticizes the Romantic propensity to understand unconventional-
ity, in this case plain craziness and mad asocial behavior, as an individual expression akin to genius. Mythology had been employed by authors in previous
literary movements to make their works more complex, given that a god was
a representation with many different meanings. This practice has given way to
prosaic analogies, such as using the multifaceted Roman goddess Diana as a
mere synonym for the moon.

The reference to *gálico* in this stanza is more complicated. Gallego mentions
the name "Cyllenian" (Cilenio), the gentilic for someone born on the Greek
mountain of Cyllene (Kyllini). According to Greek mythology, the Pleiad
Maia gave birth to the god Hermes on this mountain, and therefore the god
was also known as "The Cyllenian," an appellation going back to Homer's
Odyssey and Virgil's *Aeneid.* The Romans integrated the qualities of Hermes
with those of the god they called Mercury, hence the connection between the

geographical place, the Greek divinity, and the Roman god of eloquence and commerce. Going one step further, we know that the name of the god has been transferred to mercury, the element used extensively to treat *gálico*. Thus, Gallego is ultimately bemoaning how "the Cyllenian" appears only in a pedestrian form, when naming the ingredient of an ointment to cure *bubas*.

This brief review of mercury's literary appearances shows the wide and profound penetration of the disease's meanings and its treatment throughout the century. I will return to mercury later in this study; for the present, I continue reviewing the medical understanding of *gálico* and its societal expressions.

Early in the eighteenth century, physicians like Juan Calvo combined the received knowledge of centuries-old theories with new facts that were slowly incorporated into the general structure of medical discourse. For example, after repeated observation, Calvo is able to affirm that the disease is transmitted to infants through lactation, and tells parents to be careful about the women to whom they entrust their children's breastfeeding (542). More important, at the social and public policy level, Calvo concludes that a fetus in the womb can inherit the disease, which hypothetically could have happened with Charles II of Spain: "There are many that get it from their mother's womb, these are the ones engendered by parents who have the same disease. Given that semen is the efficient cause of generation [...] when husband and wife are infected, it is certain that the menstrual blood as well as the semen (from which the creature and its parts will be formed) will also be vicious and corrupt, and even if they mix in the uterus, given that they are bad, there will not be generation, or it will be a sickly being: because from bad principles in the natural things, good end is never derived, unless God provides a remedy" (536–37).[44]

This description, found in a well-known medical text, helps explain why the disease started to fade from the public arena. It had been openly mentioned in poems and novels by popular literary authors like Cervantes, Quevedo, or López de Úbeda in the previous century, but it became confined to a more veiled context, with authors fearing that they would be seen as bad, vicious, corrupt, or a negative influence on the next generation.[45] Calvo's stance on "bad principles" suggests why Spanish courtiers chose to blame the feebleness of the Spanish heir on a mysterious concoction rather than on the union of corrupted origins inside Queen Mariana of Austria's womb. Calvo's observation would produce a radical reinterpretation of the disease, but a radical change of attitude in society at large would not be seen until almost two hundred years later, with the onset of a new eugenics movement.

In the eighteenth century, the tangible consequences are more important, and Calvo laments that in Valencia, the city where he practices, he has seen people who had been cured of *bubas* relapsing because they act "(like the dog going back to the vomit) and again have excess with tainted women, which will infect them again one and many times."[46] Calvo is alluding here to the biblical verse Proverbs 26:11, on the repetition of wrong behavior: "Sicut canis qui revertitur ad vomitum suum sic imprudens qui iterat stultitiam suam," meaning, "As a dog returneth to his vomit, so a fool returneth to his folly." The tainted women are prostitutes, and the frequency of men going to brothels or the streets to find women, like dogs going back to eat their own vomit, was all too frequent and real. As a result, prostitutes were at the core of the debates that took place when administrators were asked to help prevent transmission of the French disease. Prostitutes also commanded the attention of poets and writers, who sang to them as sources of pleasure, malady, and fear. Calvo reflects this dynamic of terror, containment, and abhorrence when he claims that women possess the same slowly corroding effect as that of the *gálico*-causing humor, and that men should avoid them like the plague (545).[47] Prostitutes in particular and women in general had become scapegoats for the disease, and this narrow view kept its containment to short-term, short-sighted solutions; concerted efforts to eradicate *gálico* as a multifaceted problem would not be implemented until much later.

Calvo defends the idea that *gálico* is a disease unto itself and criticizes those who see it as an old disease such as "the elephantiasis of the Arabs" ("elefantiasis de los Arabes"), cancer, "inguinal eczema of the Arabs" ("lichinas de los Arabes"), or "the afflictions of the Greeks" ("las acoras de los Griegos") (537–38). Instead, he asserts that it has been "known for less than a hundred years, at least in our land, because in the Indies it is older" (539).[48] Although for Torre, in the "Tratado de morbo galico" section of his *Espejo,* the dispute about the antiquity of *gálico* is "more a curious than a beneficial matter" (2),[49] he argues that the disease was ancient and already mentioned, at least its symptoms, by Pliny, Hippocrates, and Avicenna. Still, he infers that the disease may have been forgotten, reappearing as a new malady after Columbus's travel to the Indies and his return with native men and women from Santo Domingo. Subsequently, according to Torre, the disease was brought to the war in Naples by Spanish soldiers that had previously been "conversing with the Indian women who were touched by the disease" (2)[50]—indeed, engaging in more than conversation. From there, the French army spread the contagion, also present in Naples, leading to *gálico*'s christening as "the French disease." López Pinna explains that the disease was so horrible and dreaded that no one wanted to be blamed as its source: "Its name alone produces disgust and fear; and it is so detestable that none of the nations suspected of catching it for the first time wishes to give it their name, seeing it as an affront that such pestilent evil may have been theirs in origin, and that it may bear the name of their fatherland, and then choose to ascribe it to another" (4).[51]

Torres's and Calvo's opposing postulates reflect a narrativization of the origin of the disease that led to long and complex consequences in the Hispanic world. Establishing the origin of the disease was not as inconsequential as Torre claimed. Its connections with the logic of treatment included the way it shaped attitudes toward those who were considered the cause of transmission: the prostitute at home, or the people of the Indies outside of Spain. In this regard, when Calvo writes about the origin of the disease, he adds several features that mirror a dynamic of rejection and signal what is considered inferior, debased, dangerous, and removed but at the same time unavoidably present, ubiquitous, and near: "In our parts this disease originated from the said Indians, and they were the ones who passed it to the French, the Italian, the Spanish, and other nations, who during that time were found in Naples, because in the Indies it is very common and familiar, being as they were, very lecherous, carnal, and so voracious that they ate not only the meat of animals, but even of men" (541).[52]

The link between *gálico* itself, its origin, its possible cure, and the view of the people from the American continent as intellectually or physically unfit is at the core of a discussion about the identity of those outside the Spanish metropolis. As I will show later, some Spaniards, like the writer Pedro Estala (1757–1815), saw the disease ravaging the bodies of the indigenous people of California as a just, divine punishment for not being Christian, whereas Francisco Javier Clavijero (1731–87) and Andrés Bello (1781–1865) not only disputed the American origin of the disease but also claimed that the cure for this universal ailment would come from the New Continent. The tension between these two views would later be expressed among intellectuals in the colonies as a discourse of dignity and pride, as a contemplation of autonomy, as a possible path to coveted equality with the Spanish parent state, and ultimately as a form of armed uprising and independence.

☙ 3

Judging Books by Their Covers

When reading antique medical texts with the goal of obtaining information about the disease, it is easy to leaf quickly through the preliminary pages, seeing them as formulaic, unrelated, or unimportant to the relevant factual material that the book may contain. But our understanding of *gálico* would be incomplete without taking into account the dynamics of power and influence that were behind the communication of knowledge and the crafting of public policies to control its incidence in society as presented in these paratextual instances. More importantly, these documents reveal the connections between medical and literary discourses, especially because all texts, be they treatises or poems, had to conform to the same set of regulations imposed by church and king. The contents of these books would not have seen the light of day without clearing multiple requirements under royal and ecclesiastical oversight. The front matter usually consisted of a dedication, brief notes approving the contents of the book, a permit for publication, a document stating the approved official price of sale, and a prologue by the author or the person in charge of the new edition or printing. The book was usually dedicated to a member of the nobility or the church, and written in a clearly literary style with the aim of gaining protection for the book and its author; it is apparent that this support also meant the possibility of obtaining promotions, annuities, or links with other influential individuals. Some authors, like Matheo Giorro y Portillo in his *Discurso sobre la naturaleza del cancro* (Discourse about the nature of the malignant tumor) (1738), played it safe and went directly to the source: instead of dedicating his book to a simple count or bishop, Giorro offered it to the "Most holy Mary, mother of the Word made human; mother of the beautiful love, fear, and wisdom; munificent ocean, celestial star, and trusted patroness of all mortals" (López de Araujo et al. iii).[1]

The books had to be read by medical and religious censors, people usually entrusted with vetting these publications by someone higher on the scale of power. They had to verify that each book did "not contain anything against our Holy Catholic Faith, or our Christian customs" (Suárez de Ribera, *Arcanismo* 4),[2] and that it followed the norms of the medical profession as regulated by universities and physicians in high positions in the court. This medical censorship was geared to attest that the book was not harmful to the royal rules or the good customs of the land, and that its contents were backed by many practical observations of the outcome of remedies and treatments. The documents of approval range from succinct letters that go to the point and assure that the contents are not offensive, to true disquisitions and laudatory discourses praising the prodigious wisdom of the doctors who are giving humanity a ray of hope to cure this terrible malady.

The other document of approval was an authorization from the church, usually from the bishop's quarters or a clerical judge, titled "licencia de ordinario" (ordinary license). It functioned as a printing permit that was given after appropriate assessment of the book. The revenue authorities also weighed in through a document known as a "suma de la tassa" (amount of the rate), which reported the approved price of the book based on its number of broadside sheets. Each sheet cost 6 maravedís, and an average book had about thirty-two broadsides, making the average price 192 maravedís. At the time, a twenty-two-ounce hunk of bread in the Murcian town of Lorca cost between 16 and 20 maravedís (Hernández Franco 85). One medical book might therefore cost more than the daily bread for at least nine families. It is clear that the understanding of the disease and its cure was restricted to a few dedicated and well-heeled medicine students, a few practicing doctors, and even fewer lettered men interested in medicine. Information for regular folk was restricted and fragmentary, limited to received knowledge and myths surrounding the disease, and concerned mainly with its visible consequences (*bubas,* loss of hair, roughness of the voice) and its treatment (bloodletting, or the profuse salivation caused by mercury). Given its liminal condition between lettered discourse and popular beliefs, literature is the medium through which *gálico* is more clearly presented. That both types of writing, the medical and the literary, were valued at the same rate of 6 maravedís a broadside, evinces the need to pay equal attention to both types to gain a nuanced understanding of *gálico* during this period.

After the death of Charles II and during the War of Spanish Succession between 1701 and 1714, Philip V of the House of Bourbon reigned in Spain. By 1718, when he was well established in power, books started to include one more document, which was called a "suma del privilegio" (summary of the right to print). In each "suma," the king himself granted the book's printer exclusive rights to print the work in question, usually for a term of ten years. As with the permits that had been institutionalized during the previous centuries, the license implemented by the new monarch not only raised money for his treasure chest but also served as an effective way of monitoring and controlling the dissemination of information and opinion among the lettered elites. The amount and repetition of the structures of approval reveal that the system of administration in Spain was large and complex; to publish their work, authors and printers had to ease the bureaucratic process and win the favor of those in power, which required them to develop rhetorical abilities as well as resorting to the ever-present pedestrian use of money. Printing was expensive, and a review of dedicatory notes suggests that in addition to obtaining the protection of powerful individuals, authors were seeking monetary help for their projects.

The extremely slow distribution of knowledge and opinion benefited those in positions of power, giving them time to accommodate to new ideas without having to fear sudden eruptions of dissent. Religious institutions, for example, needed time to adjust elements of dogma to changes resulting from new scientific discoveries. This refractory characteristic, which had been beneficial to high clerics and noblemen, was operational for many years, but after the Bourbon dynasty came into power, with its direct connections with the French, the developments in science and thought on the other side of the Pyrenees slowly sifted into the Spanish society. The French influence—the *mal gálico*—made itself known not only in the name of the venereal disease but also in the progressive incidence of French culture on the Iberian Peninsula.

These preliminary texts also reveal the entrenched system of monitoring and vetting the production of knowledge with the aim of preserving the status quo. Both in medicine and in the literary realm, dissent was expressed primarily through the strategic crafting of texts in which images, doublings, similes, metaphors, and parallel meanings were used to reach the reading public. The other way of presenting diverging or unsanctioned viewpoints was through the publication of texts by pseudonymous or anonymous authors, as in the case of "Bachiller Philaletes," whose treatise against the use of mercury to cure *bubas* was at the same time a personal attack against Dr. Francisco Suárez de Ribera (1686–1738), a prominent graduate of the University of Salamanca and author of *Manifiestas demostraciones* (Clear demonstrations), which I analyze later. In the literary realm, we find the indecorous *El arte de las putas* (The art of whoring) (written ca. 1776, published in 1898), a long poem that circulated widely in manuscript form without the name of the author, penned by Nicolás Fernández de Moratín, the well-known author of *La petimetra* (loosely translated, The fashionista) (1762). I will later discuss Moratín's poem as a proposal to contain *gálico* and as a manual for avoiding the disease. The masking of authorship is one of the ways in which literature and medical discourse were tightly connected during this period, and writing style is another: The writers of medical treatises compensated for their lack of experimental innovation in the treatment of *gálico* with a steady flow of rhetorical flourishes and, on many occasions, brilliant argumentation, generally the province of literary authors. Like their literary counterparts, the authors of medical treatises had to confront not only censorship from on high but also the stern criticism of their peers. Diego Pérez Bravo explains in the prologue to his *Dissertacion botanico-pharmaceutica sobre la Calaguala* (Botanical and pharmaceutical dissertation about the calaguala) (1754) that such feedback was not intended to advance science but to make personal attacks, and that the results were harmful to the profession in Spain:

> Who will not lose enthusiasm for the task of writing when noting that great heroes, like the acclaimed (more by foreigners than by our own Spaniards) polymaths Feijóo, Rodríguez, Martínez, and others, whose every mark from their quills should be engraved in gold—that, not long after they make public their precious letters, their emulators, almost immediately, with daring impudence, want to attack them; but the impertinent contestations they [the emulators] want to fight with are not the worst thing they [the heroes] must be on guard against, but also that, stepping over the bounds of propriety, they [the emulators] are used to tarnishing those who are respectable, perhaps with untidy satirical invective. (xv–xvi)[3]

These treatises are heavily narrated accounts in which the disease—or the author or doctor—is the main character. Several of these texts are written in the form of case studies, with a plot that describes the patient; the details of her or his situation; the proximity of death, which provides climactic tension; the effectiveness of the cure; the dénouement, in which there is usually victory over the disease; and a moral, condemning fornication. In the background there is the presence of a streamlined scientific language; more specifically, the discourse follows syllogistic rubrics. The *Arcanismo anti-galico, o Margarita mercurial* (Anti-*gálico* arcanum, or the jewel of mercury), which was published in 1721 and printed again in 1731, was authored by Suárez de Ribera and displays the imbrication of literary and epistemic discourses:

> When I was the main doctor of the town of Gargantalaolla, I was called from Aldea Nueva to visit a certain young woman who suffered from an immoderate and periodical menstrual discharge [resulting from *gálico*]. [...] Then, with generosity of spirit, I tried to use my anti-hemorrhagic medicine. [...] I tried to destroy the *gálico*'s ferment, which is the palpable matter of that shadow, by using mercury, which I trust from experience to be the fire that consumes the venereal acids, the jail that imprisons them, and the monarch that tames them, because it is the most noble solidifying, absorbent, and corrective element discovered up to our time. (li–liii)[4]

In this book the overlapping of different modes of understanding of the world is evident, and even more striking when one reads a group of paratexts that precede the medical treatise. The texts are sonnets and *décimas* (stanzas composed of ten octosyllabic lines) written by disciples of Suárez de Ribera to honor their teacher. A poem crafted by his former student, a *bachiller* (graduate) by the remarkable name of don Antonio Ramos de Vergas, shows the connections between medicine, chemistry, and alchemy, represented by chemical components and their veiled relation to planets and stars:

> All seven planets
> You include in your first volume,
> And in this way you are ahead
> Of all other influences;
> Because of the sciences a Minerva
> You are the one that can see how metals,
> Present in sweet minerals,
> Copper, lead, mercury, tin,
> Are able to confront so much evil,
> More than streams of Mars, Sun, or Moon. (lxxxi)[5]

This poem of praise evinces how, at the onset of the eighteenth century, the inscription of *gálico* negotiates the early and ongoing conformation of disciplines. Between the measurable methods of chemistry and the idiosyncratic interpretations of alchemy or astrology, physicians and authors of medical treatises are trying to establish a balanced discourse that can give them the tools to make sense of the disease and its treatment. The discourse appears cohesive because it still uses the convincing power of rhetoric, but deep down there is confusion.

4 ࢭ

The Awakening of Reason
Produces Befuddlement

A clearer differentiation of disciplines is seen in Bernardo López de Araujo y Ascárraga's *Impugnacion de los triunfos partidos entre el cancro obstinado y el cirujano advertido* (Contestation of the victories divided between the obstinate malignant tumor and the wise surgeon) (1738), in which he deviates from rhetorical modes and literary language. He studies multiple real cases, explains particular treatments, and reflects on their outcomes, emphasizing that knowledge comes from experimentation and not only from argumentation. He shows that the different circumstances of the patient must lead to equally different courses of treatment, a point he bolsters by recording the name, age, and address of each patient he uses as a case study. This organization of knowledge illustrates the rising influence of the modern scientific method, which had been cultivated since the late fifteenth century by physicians such as Niccolò Leoniceno (1428–1524) and Francisco Sánchez (1550–1623), and by Galileo Galilei (1564–1642), who had combined mathematics and direct experimentation in his studies of astronomy and motion. The method had found its apogee in the seventeenth century, with William Harvey (1578–1657), who after direct observation had explained the circulation of blood in the human body; René Descartes (1596–1650), with his *Discourse on Method* (1637); and Robert Hooke (1635–1703), with *Micrographia* (1665), where he published observations obtained by using a microscope and coined the word *cell,* which we still use today. This form of acquiring knowledge would bear fruit in the eighteenth century after the dissemination of Isaac Newton's (1642–1727) *Principia Mathematica* (1687), where he stated the three universal laws of motion he had inferred from direct observation and experimentation, and Gottfried Wilhelm Leibniz's (1646–1716) developments in calculus and mathematics. In the medical treatises I discuss here, it is possible to see the budding influence of the scientific method and its characteristic stages: formulation of a question, construction of a conjecture or hypothesis, verification through experimentation, and assessment of the experiment's results. But even more important, the initial approach to these treatises demonstrates that the disease was cured not only with mercury and guaiacum but also with a complex textuality that explained it, organized it, and tamed it as a discourse.

The deep urge to record and capture life experiences and knowledge through organized language was manifested in ways beyond medical treatises. The Real Academia Española was dedicated to regulating and documenting the Castilian language as a unifying medium of communication. The Academia was officially founded in 1714 under the protection of Philip V, almost immediately after the main documents of the Peace of Utrecht were signed. This group of treaties closed out the war that had resulted from the death of *El hechizado* without an heir. The cover of the first edition of the Academia's bylaws, published in 1715, already bears the motto "Limpia, fija y da esplendor" (Purifies, fixes, and gives glory), illustrating the need to create a common discourse that would be free of warring viewpoints or interpretations and clearly concerned with things that were seen as pleasant or appropriate. The *Diccionario de autoridades* was the first dictionary published by the Academia, and its first volume (1726), containing words beginning with the letters A and B, offers this glorified, fixed, and purified entry for "buba":

> Usually used in the plural. Well-known and contagious disease, also called French disease, and *gálico,* because (according to some) the French got it when they went into Italy with King Charles VIII, through the illicit relationships they had with women from that country, but others affirm that the Spanish suffered it during their discovery of the Indies, also as a result of the improper contact they repeatedly had with the women of those new regions. What is certain is that it is an extremely old disease, known to some provinces before others, and because of its indecency no one wants to confess to having been the first to have it and transmit it.[1]

This characterization of the word is instantiated in the *Diccionario* with passages from Francisco López de Gómara, who narrates the sufferings of the Spanish soldiers in their conquest of the New World; Luis de Mármol's description of maladies in Egypt; and Quevedo's *Musas castellanas,* in which a street tough laments the closing of a brothel where sex, and *gálico* with it, could be bought for a low price: "*Bubas* were cheaper, / than a pound of cucumbers" (*Obras* 308).[2] This explanation of the word—it is evident that this is not a proper factual definition—imparts a reading of the disease that casts it as removed from the present, as foreign in origin, as moving stealthily from one region to the other, as a consequence of improper contact with foreign women (or with women who are foreign to the norm), and as a source of shame for those who do not wish to be seen as connected with it. The wide range of works and authors employed to exemplify the use of the word shows the pervasive nature of the disease, and how it was a hidden yet a well-known occurrence, familiar to epic historians, taunting writers, doughty soldiers, and street ruffians, and to the French, Spaniards, and Italians alike.

The disease touched men and women from all walks of life, but according to Suárez de Ribera, *gálico* manifested itself differently depending on the occupation or profession of the patient. Following the claims of the Italian physician Giorgio Baglivi (1668–1707), Suárez states that *gálico* becomes especially active in muscles, nerves, and joints when the person is a plowman or a peasant; musicians are affected in the lungs, because the constant action of this part of the body causes their "fibers" to deteriorate into phthisis, bloody phlegm, or asthma; while women and inactive people experience problems in the area of the stomach (*Arcanismo,* 58). The evacuation of the bad humor of the disease was also seen as connected to the livelihood of each individual, and Suárez explains that it is easier to cure the *bubas* of a plebeian than those of a nobleman, reasoning that commoners usually move around briskly, which cleans obstructions out of the glands and opens the pores, diminishing the "fermento galicano" (Gallic ferment) via transpiration and sweat. Nobles are intrinsically idle, and therefore more difficult to cure (66). Along the same line of logic, Suárez states that "in businessmen (such as those dealing with written papers and those given to literary endeavors) the *gálico* ferment settles especially in the head and in the stomach. [. . .] Their head weakens greatly as a result of the continued study [. . .] and for that reason so many head ailments [lit. "accidents"] appear, such as migraines, deafness, etc." (57).[3] According to the author, those given to literary work are "are no less disproportionally given to venereal acts" (xxiii).[4] In sum, people like writers were more difficult to cure because they did not sweat enough, did not work enough with their bodies, and mainly because they liked the strenuous activities that were the chief cause of *gálico.* Their constant reading debilitated them, and their inclination to have sex did not help. As a result, the disease attacked mainly their heads and stomachs.

Although it is not directly related to *gálico,* a relevant eighteenth-century text is a sonnet about a not very amorous situation titled "Dialogue between a sick man and his guts when he was about to drink broth, because his doctor commanded him not to have any other food until he threw up, which he could not" (Benegasi 20).[5] This literary text narrates the experience of following a medical remedy such as the one Suárez would have prescribed. The sonnet was written by Francisco Benegasi y Luján (1656–1742), who was a well-known figure in the court of Philip V for the literary gatherings he hosted, and because he worked as an administrator for the king in different posts. Besides poetry, Benegasi y Luján also wrote light theater pieces that were presented with success in Madrid.

Francisco Benegasi y Luján

Francisco Benegasi y Luján (1656–1742), born in Arenas de San Pedro, was the lord of Terreros, Val de los Hielos, and of the mayoralty of Luján. During his education in Madrid, he was recognized as a prodigy of the harp, and studied under the harpist of the royal chamber, Juan Hidalgo de Polanco. At seventeen, he was named a member of the order of Calatrava, and served Philip V as governor of several priories. At court, he lived large and formed friendships with many of the brightest stars of the age. He married doña Ana de Peralta Irigoyti, a Madrid native, and with her had a son in 1707, José Joaquín Benegasi y Luján. He died outside Spain, probably in Milan, where his writing attests that he spent some time. Don Francisco wrote much poetry, most of it festive, and his *entremeses* and dances were enormously popular. His work ridicules vice and abounds in comic revelry, but does not cross the line into giving moral offense. In 1744, his son published don Fernando's work posthumously, though José Joaquín included more of his own work than his father's.

Benegasi is using a witty discourse, but he exposes the precariousness of medical treatments of the time. His literary rendition offers us a complex and rich view of disease and cure, revealing that medical treatments were not as sanitary or organized as described in treatises. Illustrating Suárez's claim that writers tend to have head and stomach problems, Benegasi quarrels with his innards—which are threatening to prolapse—because they are failing to let him eliminate his sickness through vomiting or diarrhea:

SONNET

Sick (patient): There goes water, my dear guts, there goes water.
Guts: No, for the love of God, please stop,
   Let us get out, and give us mercy.
Sick: What do you mean by getting out? Stop right there.

Guts: So let the assassin return. **Sick:** It will return.
Guts: Careful, or we will die. **Sick:** Are you thirsty?
Guts: We are in need. **Sick:** Then have
   That substantive broth. **Guts:** Good enough.

Sick: You had already a hundred broths. Great endurance.
Guts: Take into account that we carry the greatest risk.
Sick: Then swim, without trying to get out.

Guts: Saint Blas! Saint Blas! **Sick:** Wait for the doctor,
   Stop your uproar; he will come,
   And there is no reason for noise if he is not here. (20)[6]

Benegasi is describing the common procedure of expelling bad humors through purging, a method that was also used in the initial steps of treating *gálico*. In order to secure an effective treatment, the physician had to help the body get rid of any noxious matter (*materia antecedente*) by purging or blood-letting. The scatological aspect of Bengasi's verse can also be seen in works by his predecessors during the Spanish Golden Age, such as Francisco de Quevedo's poems on flatulence and Luis de Góngora's (1561–1627) "¿Qué lleva el Señor Esgueva? Yo os diré lo que lleva" (What is Mr. Esgueva carrying? I will let you know what he is carrying). Like his predecessors, Benegasi approaches the crude reality of the body by using oblique references and retooling the qualities of poetic allusion. The result is humorous but at the same time sobering, because it contrasts the limits of the human body with man's longing for idealization.

In a sequence of *quintillas*—stanzas similar to limericks—titled "The day they put leeches on him, he made this *Quintillas*" ("En el dia que le echaron unas Sanguijuelas, hizo estas Quintillas"), Benegasi uses a mocking tone to describe the medical procedure of applying leeches to the anus:

> The first leech
> attacked me with great fury,
> and when I saw it was so fierce,
> to make it even angrier,
> I winked my eye at her (130, vv. 16–20).[7]

The author makes fun of the experience of bloodletting, but he is also intent on connecting the procedure to the public sphere. For a moment, he stops the scatological double entendres (e.g., winking an eye that is not an eye) to point out that by sucking the blood that is not their own, the leeches

> reveal to me the many ruses
> employed by the commoners of this town:
> Ah, poor little Madrid,
> full of leeches! (130, vv. 52–55).[8]

Benegasi uses disease as a medium to obliquely share his opinions and to position private and public reality in coordinates of place and time. He similarly connects the realm of public imaginary with a perception of the geography

of the city. In his "A Dialogue in *seguidillas*" ("Dialogo en seguidillas")—
seguidilla is a string of verses—he gives new order to an abstract layout of the
urban space by naming streets with the personal qualities and desires of particular inhabitants:

> Here is a gentleman,
> who is very gallant:
> 2. He must have his lodgings
> on the Street of the Franks.
> 1. Where is he going, the one who has
> the ailments of France?
> 2. To the Street, they call,
> of the Zarza. (119, vv. 111–16)[9]

By itself, Calle de la Zarza would be an innocent street name, with *zarza*
simply meaning "blackberry bush"—one would call it Blackberry Street, and
it would be as unremarkable as an Oak Street or a Magnolia Avenue. Within
Benegasi's reverse parallel, however, "Zarza" becomes shorthand for the plant
brought from the Indies (*zarzaparrilla*) to help cure "the ailments of France."
The city, which in general was the stage on which *gálico* showed its representative abilities, is reorganized in terms of such representation, and the mark of
the disease is consequently inscribed in its streets, and in popular poetry like
that of Benegasi: an eye is not only an eye, a blackberry bush is a medicinal
plant from the New World as well as a street, and a sore on the body is also a
sore in the urban geography.

Straddling the seventeenth and eighteenth centuries, Benegasi is also the
first author to narrate the presence of *gálico* in connection to a literary figure.
He wrote a *romance,* a series of octosyllabic verses, titled "Giving Thanks to
Señor Don Gaspar de Mendoza, Son of the Most Excellent Señores Marquises
de Mondejar, for Having Sent Him the Works of Pantaleon."[10] Anastasio Pantaleón de Ribera (1600–1629), a poet who wrote in the style of Góngora, had
been a well-known satirist, the private secretary of noblemen, and an individual protected by King Philip IV himself. This superior status was not enough
to defend him from *gálico,* a disease that apparently ended his life at a very
early age. When Benegasi received his copy of Ribera's works—perhaps the
edition published in 1670—he wrote a poem that incorporates many elements
characteristic of literary portrayals of *gálico,* in particular the use of raw humor
(which I examine at length in the chapter below titled "Sick Humor"), the
masking of the disease through mythological or alchemic references, and the
description of the consequences of treatment with specific medicines such as
sarsaparilla and mercury.[11] The common topos of praising the poverty of poets

Anastasio Pantaleón de Ribera

Of unknown parentage, Anastasio Pantaleón de Ribera (1600–1629) was born in Madrid and studied law at the universities of Alcalá de Henares and Salamanca, but paid much more attention to the arts than to his degrees. Lauded and famous for his poetry from a very young age, Pantaleón de Ribera quickly made a place for himself among the literary elite of the court, under the patronage of the Duque of Cea (later also of Lerma). His poetry falls into the mode of *culteranismo,* and he defined himself as a Gongorist. He wrote serious poetry, as well as comic verse and satires of the literary elite of his day. A rising star of the literary world, Pantaleón de Ribera died in February 1629 and was buried by his patron. His good friend and autobiographer, José Pellicer, was granted permission to publish his works in 1631, though they did not see print until 1634.

---

is countered with a mix of mockery and double entendres: Benegasi indicates that Ribera died with little money, for which he uses the colloquial "poca lana" (lit. "little wool"), which he extends into an image of sheep's hair tangled in bramble (*zarza*), which in turn refers to sarsaparilla, and ultimately to how Ribera used what little money he had for remedies against *gálico*. Benegasi also employs allusions and postponement of meaning in his use of mythology, which attributes Ribera's force of creativity to the god Apollo; his will to Venus, the goddess of sexuality; and his energetic wit to Mercury, the mutable god whose name invokes the treatment of *gálico* with quicksilver. In Benegasi's buoyant satirical work, high classical culture overlaps with his morbid recounting of Ribera's ailments.

Benegasi uses a type of humor in which reality is turned upside down, and he plays with Inquisitional fire. He uses the image of the last rites received by terminally ill patients, what Catholics call the sacrament of extreme unction, to mask the gruesome treatment of *gálico* with *unciones*—the smearing of a remedy on the body. In the Catholic rite, a priest—a representative of Jesus on earth—anoints the dying person with holy oil (blessed every year on Holy Thursday by the pope or the bishop) to strengthen his soul and his faith and to prepare him for death. Benegasi replaces the priest with an uninspired neighborhood barber (not even a physician), and replaces the holy oil with a mix of mercury, pork fat, and spit, which was smeared onto the joints and flanks of the *galicado.* The sacrament of the last rites was aimed at creating an atmosphere of peace, but the anointment with mercury only brought distress, as it caused nausea, fever, diarrhea, and uncontrolled salivation.

Beauty can produce astonishment or ecstasy in a sensitive soul, and therefore evokes individuals in a state of awe, but Benegasi prefers to invert such images, showing a poet who unwillingly presents himself in public, disagreeably drooling (*caer la baba*), not because he is dazzled by the world, but because mercury has overtaken him. Benegasi's goal in this romance is not to present himself or Ribera as sensitive or refined creatures, but instead as individuals who reject idealization. He is an artist who uncovers, at least temporarily, an apparently fissure-free reality. The result is not necessarily pessimist or nihilistic; rather, it confirms the victory of artistic pursuits over the ugly yet worthwhile condition of being human. For Benegasi, it does not matter if Ribera's life was consumed by disease; what matters is that his achievements surpassed the limits of his body.

Very much in the vein of literary predecessors like Francisco de Quevedo, who used satire as an important but somewhat hidden literary tool, Benegasi transmutes the horror of the pustules and the mercury into crude humor. He literarily documents the pain of the buboes, the horrible outcomes of the cure, and the disfiguring consequences of the disease, but does so through the waggish revelation of reality, making the dreadfulness more human and more present. Even as he follows the path of writers before him, he reframes and perhaps intensifies their precepts, because he is not narrating episodes of harmless or inconsequential conditions like flatulence, but speaking about a death that appeared as a gift of Venus. This change of perspective goes beyond his predecessors' portrayals of how the senses deceive us, or their disenchantment with the state of the empire, or their recognition that material things are ephemeral and that life is fleeting. Instead, Benegasi's sobering humor points to the here and now—to the tangible, disturbing reality of the *gálico* experience—and signals that perhaps by becoming *apantaleonado* (that is, like the poet who had the disease and died, but who also lived a full life by living it intensely) one may reach transcendence and meaning. This kind of humor, which tests the boundaries of the acceptable, is also a kind of soothing medicine—a purgative of sorts—palatable only because its acrid flavor is masked by a type of wordplay that reveals by hiding, hides by revealing, and uncovers through allusion.

As evidenced by the purgatives, leeches, and ointments in Benegasi's narratives, medical treatments had remained the same for many years. Scientific inquiry was bogged down, since, as I mentioned before, the books used to teach and explain *gálico* were three or four generations old. Halfway through the century, Benito Jerónimo Feijoo (1676–1764) criticized the stagnation of medicine. Feijoo, one of the finest Spanish minds of his time, applied himself to attacking irrational beliefs and advocating for a factual, experimental approach in line with the scientific method. In one of his most important works, the five-volume *Cartas eruditas y curiosas* (Erudite and curious letters) (published between 1742 and 1760), Feijoo summarizes the state of medicine at the time:

Benito Jerónimo Feijoo

Fray Benito Jerónimo Feijoo y Montenegro (1676–1764), considered the father of the Spanish Enlightenment, was born in Orense in Galicia. At fourteen, he entered the Benedictine order at the monastery of Samos, near Lugo. He later studied and taught at the universities of Galicia, Salamanca, and León. At thirty-three, he went to teach in the Benedictine convent of San Vicente, in Oviedo, where he obtained degrees in art and theology, and where he lived until his death. Though he did not begin to publish until he was fifty, the nucleus of Feijoo's work, the *Teatro crítico universal* (1726–39) and *Cartas eruditas y curiosas* (1742–60), is 7,000 pages covering over 500 different topics. According to Vicente de la Fuente in his introduction to Feijoo's *Obras escogidas,* there were at least 420,000 copies of Feijoo's work in print in the eighteenth century (xliv). The organization of his work, in conversational letters rather than discourses, and in Castilian rather than Latin, demonstrates his opposition to systematizing philosophies as the replacement of Aristotle led Enlightenment thinkers away from the grounding of science and empiricism (Martínez Lois 87). Feijoo's attempts to bring popular ideas into the Enlightenment, where they conflicted with church doctrine, brought him much criticism, but King Philip V issued an edict making attacks against the friar punishable by law. Feijoo's intended audience was the literate public, not the academic elite; he pushed people toward questioning everything and trusting their own reason. Feijoo thought that the role of the philosopher was to base himself in reality and render service unto society. Therefore his essays are utilitarian and practical in nature and content; his goal was to eradicate unfounded superstition and introduce the scientific method into social and educational reform.

Among the modern [medical minds of today], some blame acids for fevers, and want them to be cured with alkalies; others blame alkalies, and want them to be cured with acids; and others meanwhile make fun of how much is said of acids, and alkalies. Did God instill three such contrary opinions in Adam and Solomon? But in as many parts of my Works I hold it to be shown, that there is nothing well established among doctors, with the exception of curing intermittent fevers with *quina, gálico* with mercury, dysentery with ipecacuanha, and scabies with sulfur (and even in these remedies, with respect to when, how much, and how there are battles at every step), so it is unnecessary for me to dwell any more on something so obvious. (67)[12]

According to the Galician polymath, science and medicine were at a standstill because the debates about which treatments to pursue were being conducted in Scholastic terms, producing a kind of knowledge that had no bearing on actually curing diseases. A patient could not be cured with syllogisms, inferences, or quotations from the forefathers of medicine. The skeptical doctors who mocked the outcomes of these verbal disputes were themselves not helping to advance the state of medicine, because they too were constrained by words. To fight disease, doctors had only a few tangible tools—unreliable medications, with arguments about dosages and regimens that did not get them any closer to a reliable cure.

The exasperation with the state of medicine exemplified by Feijoo is all the more understandable in light of real advancements that were signaling the possibility of shifting from discourse to experimentation. Feijoo knew that observation had already yielded fruit that could change the view of disease. In his earlier and widely known *Teatro crítico universal* (Universal critical theater) (1726–39), he had discussed alternative explanations of *gálico* that departed from the theory of unbalanced humors. In a discourse titled "Lo máximo en lo mínimo" (The greatest in the smallest), published in 1736, Feijoo describes the work of the English doctor Richard Mead (1673–1754), who had stated that scabies "consists only of some small worms, or small insects, whose figure is very similar to that of the turtle. These worms live two or three days outside the body, for which reason it is easy to contract scabies through contact with the clothing or gloves of the person who suffers from this infection" (*Teatro* 7:16).[13] Mead's observations stemmed from the use of the microscope, the great seventeenth-century invention that had been perfected by Galileo Galilei and employed methodically by the Dutch scientist Antonie van Leeuwenhoek (1632–1723) to study blood, sperm, and bacteria. Rather than going back to the observations of physicians of previous centuries, Feijoo relied instead on the new knowledge he gathered from periodicals dealing with current advancements, such as the French *Nouvelles de la république des lettres* (News from the republic of letters) and London's *Philosophical Transactions of the Royal Society*. The greatest impact on scientific thought for Feijoo and his peers was thus being made not by Italy but by England and especially France, the country that was to exercise increasing influence on cultural discussions on the Iberian Peninsula. A few lines after his comment on Mead's discovery, Feijoo adds that Antoine Deidier (1697–1732), a professor of chemistry at Montpellier, has inferred that *gálico* should be attributed "à unos gusanos de especie particular" (to certain worms of a particular species), and even if there has been no direct observation, one can extrapolate the unknown from the known by applying the scientific method: "It is true that this opinion is not founded upon visual inspection, but upon mere conjecture, taken from the fact that mercury, which is the great antidote to the worms, is the specific remedy for this disease" (*Teatro* 7:16).[14] This meant that the solution was not to be found in seeking to balance humors, but instead by eradicating the cause,

Hipecuana

Hipecuana, also commonly known as ipecacuanha and ipecac (*Carapichea ipecacuanha*, also *Cephaelis ipecacuanha*), of the family Rubiaceae, was a widely popular emetic and treatment for dysentery from the late sixteenth through the nineteenth century in Europe. The name derives from the Tupí word for the plant, *ipekaaguéne,* which translates literally as "low creeping plant causing vomit." The plant, found primarily in Colombia and Brazil, is a low perennial shrub, with oblong leaves and white flowers. Its active compounds (emetine and cephalin) are in the lining of the root, which looks like a tightly packed string of beads. The first reference to it by a European author was in 1648, but the first substantial shipment to Europe arrived in Paris 1672. It was used from that time to treat both dysentery and fever—sporadically at first owing to limited supplies and secrecy about its properties. In 1684 a merchant imported 150 pounds of the root, which led to increased usage, but the Dutch physician Jean-Adrien Helvetius is the key to its rise. He successfully treated both the French dauphin and the queen of Spain with ipecac, and was granted sole license for its sale by Louis XIV, though it proved so lucrative that the French government bought the rights back. Apart from its use in the treatment of dysentery, hipecuana was also popular as a general emetic; through the nineteenth century this is its primary listing in drug manuals.

which was now, at least hypothetically, to be seen under the microscope.[15] Feijoo signals that the cause and cure of the disease was not to be based on obscure, cryptic explanations, but on a new understanding of the world by using tools that facilitated the study of the big and the small, which until then had been invisible. By formulating hypotheses, and then trying to prove them, medical knowledge would become more flexible and daring.

The Spanish author also ventures to make public a type of approach that challenged traditional teachings in Spain: "Several physicians, with señor Paulini, cited in the Parisian Journal of the Sages in the year 1704, expand on this much more, asserting that all, or nearly all, the epidemic illnesses consist of some insects that pass from some bodies to others, in which, by means of propagation, they increase their number; for which reason it is not surprising that from one single body touched by the contagious illness the damage spreads through a whole realm" (*Teatro* 7:16).[16] This dynamic of hypothetical exploration is reiterated by Feijoo in one of his "Paradoxas médicas" (Medical paradoxes), which are part of the *Teatro crítico universal:* "It is probable that all contagious illnesses come from various species of insects that are conceived in the human body" (*Teatro* 8:327).[17] In this discourse, Feijoo seeks to demystify inveterate medical practices. His readings of foreign works, together with his own witnessing of doubtful traditional remedies, spur him to debunk ideas, such as the claim that by knowing a disease—that is, by being able to describe it—its cure is assured (8:263); that leeches applied to the anus, like those Benegasi had to suffer, were able to suction "thicker" blood than that drawn from the arm (8:271); or that the use of precious stones functions as a cure, to which he counters that "the princes, who possess precious stones of better quality, and in greater quantity, adorning themselves continually with them in rings and other furnishings, not only do not live any longer than the rest of men, but, proportionately, much more than those of lesser status, they suffer the malice of poisons" (8:267).[18] It can be seen that at the level of discourse there is also a change of perspective; knowledge becomes the result of constant exchange among those who are conducting experiments, in a conversation that slowly shifts from Latin to English and French.

But many years would have to pass before viewpoints like Feijoo's became incorporated into the understanding, teaching, and practice of medicine. There was a slow inclusion of experimentation and scientific method, but a structural change would not come until one hundred years later. One example of how new ways of viewing *gálico* were gradually added to frameworks entrenched by tradition is visible in Francisco Suárez de Ribera's *Manifiestas demostraciones de las mas seguras y suaves curaciones del morbo galico* (Clear demonstrations of the most safe and gentle cures for *gálico*) (1745). Suárez de Ribera starts his book by dedicating it to "the famous male and female doctors, who having died in a saintly fashion, are worshipped by our Holy Mother the Roman Catholic Church" (iii),[19] and stating, "Disillusioned, my saints, with the glories of the world, I sacrifice this first volume of my work" (viii).[20] Suárez de Ribera tries to negotiate a middle ground between the theory of humors and the outcomes of experiments with technological innovations such as the microscope, the thermometer, and the barometer. For example, mercury in a thermometer stays in the middle of the crystal cylinder during spring because the season is neither too hot nor too cold, so Suárez de Ribera concludes that it will act in the same balanced way when given to a patient at that time of the year, making spring the best time to treat *gálico* (152). He later considers that the mercury used in the treatment of *gálico* is expelled through saliva, sweat, and urine, and studies a sample with a microscope to verify whether elements with its shape will be found in those substances: "And since the eyes of the body cannot discern for themselves what has been said, it will be achieved by applying some sort of microscope to them; then yes, they will see mercury dissolved in the urine, forming different prickles, or saline points, like sharp knives; because the aforementioned venereal saline acid made Mercury lose its spherical shape, the most delicate and soft of all the shapes" (271).[21]

The growing presence of French medical authors and studies is visible

Calaguala

While several species of ferns are referred to by the common name of calaguala, the one we are concerned with here is the *Campyloneurum angustifolium* (also *Polypodium angustifolium*). The calaguala fern, in English the narrow strap-leaved fern, is an epiphytic fern (meaning it grows without soil, either on rocks or on the trunks of trees), with fronds up to seventy centimeters in length, which grow from a short, creeping rhizome (Huxley XX). The fern was used medicinally by the indigenous populations of southern Mexico to treat chest ailments and as a diaphoretic, and in Peru for fever, dropsy, and as an antirheumatic and anticoagulant (Uphof 291; Ruiz López, *Memoria* 4). The name of this plant was derived from the Quechua *Ccallahuala*. According to Hipólito Ruiz López, the Quecha word means "batidera de muchachos," since playing children would use the plant to imitate the beater (*batidera*) of a loom. According to Diego Pérez Bravo, calaguala was first discovered in the province called Caxamalca, and its use then spread to Cuzco, Huamanga, and farther afield.

---

in a text I mentioned earlier, Diego Pérez Bravo's *Dissertacion botanico-pharmaceutica sobre la calaguala* (1754). Pérez Bravo was a member of the Real Sociedad de Sevilla (Royal Society of Seville), an institution similar to the Académie Royale des Sciences in France and the Royal Society of London. *Calaguala* was a fern from America medicinally used by doctors in Spain. In Pérez Bravo's treatise, French scientists and French science are referred to as models, almost in hyperbolic fashion: "The most expert physician Count de la Garaye deliberates about hydraulic salts: this eminent man tells us about the proven value of the famous virtues and the efficacy of these salts," and later "The famous academic chemist Mr. Geofroy, of the Royal Academy of Sciences of Paris, presented a report at that wise conference, which was summarized afterward by the Journal of the Sages" (36).[22] But the practice of medicine was precisely that—a practice—which meant that many of the principles from the north were transformed or reapplied in the everyday work of Spanish doctors like Pérez Bravo, who illustrates this dynamic by studying a plant from the Spanish colonies to garner scientific knowledge based on chemical analysis, in hopes of improving the cure of Spanish patients. Although the connections with authors from abroad helped energize the profession in Spain, by 1758 Ramón Brunet de la Selva, a member of the Real Sociedad Médica de Madrid, complained in the prologue to his *Dissertaciones physico-medicas, sobre varios curiosos assumptos de Medicina* (Physical and medical dissertations about various curious assumptions of medicine) about the growing influence of French culture in Spain: "They see the light in a time so full of writings, that there are many more authors, without exaggeration, than people that should read them. I have said authors without them really being so, because I have hardly seen a time so lacking in this type of men. For ten years now, in Spain nothing is done, save translating many writings of other nations into our language, as if all ingenuity had died in her [Spain], foreign writers are sought, to pay them that honor, which should with great reason be awarded to our own" (xxi–xxii).[23] As I will discuss later, this complaint was connected to the name of the disease that affected every strata of the Spanish population. The *mal gálico* or *mal francés* became a double term that labeled at the same time the venereal disease and the feared effect of a foreign culture.

Although many, including Suárez de Ribera and Feijoo, deemed mercury the only certain cure for *gálico,* other doctors considered it ineffective and destructive. In a letter that reached a wide public among the court elite, Bachiller Philaletes claimed that mercury was not the antidote for *gálico*. In addition to criticizing *unciones,* and arguing that mercury was actually a venom, Philaletes openly jeered at Suárez de Ribera. Philaletes's opinion on mercury would reverberate for the rest of the eighteenth century and a good part of the nineteenth; similar objections to mercury would arise at the beginning of the twentieth century, with the discovery of Salvarsan as an effective medicine against the disease. With its constant flux of discussion, glossing of previous authorities, proof by examples, and use of syllogisms, the quarrel between Suárez and Philaletes exemplifies the unempirical kind of medical practice that Feijoo criticized. Suárez reacted to Philaletes by writing *Arcanismo anti-gálico,* seeking to overthrow an idea he considered dangerous to public health. With a telling lack of modesty, he presents himself in a long prologue as a champion of effective medicine and claims that his book is to serve as "master key, to open the doors to the true knowledge of mercury, the remedy, that in the form of ointments, overcomes fatigue, the daughter of *gálico*" (iv).[24] Although he continues to follow the precepts of the theory of humors, he refashions and modernizes his discourse by calling the cause of *gálico* a "ferment," some kind of substance that is able to multiply within and corrode the inner body.

In a document of approval for the book, Dr. Joseph Ximenez Curto also defends mercury as the sole medicine against the disease and rejects others as ineffective. For him, treatments such as "aguas antimoniales" (antimony waters) and the "caldos de Septalio" (Septalio's broth) do not contain enough alkaline power to absorb the "accido venereo" (venereal acid). Even if they are able to interact with the acid, the good they might do does not last (ix), but that problem is surmounted by mercury; a purgative injected into the vein of a soldier with *gálico* works because mercury's "volatile salt is able to touch the mass of the blood immediately, and without refraction" (x). Suárez fur-

The Curing Names of Mercury

In 1733 Francisco Suárez de Ribera published an augmented and illustrated edition of the book by the medical founding father Pedacio Dioscorides Anazarbeo, which had been previously annotated by Dr. Andrés Laguna. Suárez and other doctors wanted very much to vindicate the qualities of mercury, in part to guard their power as arbiters of the medical institution (Suárez himself was doctor to the Spanish king). One of his strategies is to trace the origin of the words used to name the substance. In book 5 he includes the names for the mineral recorded by Dioscorides: "Llamase en Griego *Hydragiros;* en Latin *Hidrargyrus,* y *Argentum vivum;* en Arabigo *Zaibar,* y *Zaibach;* en Castellano, y Portuguès *Azogue;* en Catalàn *Argent viu;* en Italiano *Argento vivo;* en Francès *Arjant vif;* en Tudesco *Quechksilven*" (65). He also lists mercury's many other names in the civilized world: "El Azogue se apellida por los Latinos *Mercurius,* y *Hydragirum,* por los Chymicos *Aqua argentea, Argenteum aqueum, Aqua non madefaciens,* y tambien *Servus fugitivus;* por los Castellanos *Mercurio;* por los Franceses *Vis argent,* y tambien *Mercure;* por los Barbaros *Quikzilber;* por los Ingleses *Quicke Silver,* por los Alemanes *Quecksilver,* y tambien *Levendis*" (68).

ther develops this chemical theory of *gálico* by claiming that the more volatile part of the venereal "false" acid is able to fasten to solid elements, such as the membranes in the body. The acid or ferment takes nourishment from its host, becomes part and substance of the body, and continues its dynamic of overtaking the diseased (29).

The terminology used by Suárez and his peers is part of their strategy to convince the medical establishment of the effectiveness of their approach. They defend the use of mercury by calling it *hydragiro* rather than *mercurio* because they are trying to present the remedy in a new light. The terminology derived from the rapidly developing discipline of chemistry allows for a discourse in which, for example, mercury extinguishes the galican "ferment," "acid" is countervailed by "alkaline" and "volatile" substances, and mercury does not suffer the consequences of "refraction." Nevertheless, these theorizations of *gálico* have the same gaps that any discussion based on opinion would have. The logic of an acid that fixes itself to a solid in the body is deeply problematized by other beliefs of the authors. For example, while acknowledging the active quality of the acid, Suárez intends to preserve the deep-rooted theory that diseases are inherent to humans; that is, the *seminio* (seed) of an ailment like *gálico* is already in the body, and it is "communicated" or made active by the venereal act or similar causes. For Suárez and many others following this doctrine, God punishes humankind for original sin through these seeds, which are

Septalio's Broth: A Mystery in the Name

The term "caldos de Septalio" may refer to a treatment devised by Ludovico Settala (1550–1663), also known by his Latin name of Ludovici Septalii. Settala was an eminent physician from Milan who helped treat victims of the plague outburst in that city between 1629 and 1631. In 1622 he published *De peste, & Pestiferis affectibus*, a book that dealt in part with the treatment of infectious fevers related to the plague and the source of several remedies to treat the symptoms of the disease. The term Septalio's broth may also be related to a purgative made by mixing ground Lemnian earth, oil, honey, and water. Lemnian earth, a kind of clay with medicinal properties, was used in antiquity and found on the Greek islands of Samos and Lemnos. Galen himself traveled to Lemnos and acquired this component to administer to his patients (Manetti 172). The clay was formed into tablets and sealed with a stamp by a priestess of Artemis in the city of Hephaistia on Lemnos (Macgregor 118). Besides being used as a purgative, Lemnian earth was considered to have astringent properties, to absorb toxins, to neutralize venom in the stomach when consumed mixed with wine, to treat wounds when mixed with vinegar, and even as a cure for the plague (Macgregor 120). Manfredo Settala (1600–1680), son of Ludovico, also known by his Latin name Manfredus Septalius, was a great collector from Milan who owned a famous *Wunderkammer* or cabinet of curiosities. Among his rare possessions was a vessel containing Lemnian earth. It is possible that the medicine named by Suárez is connected to Settala in this way. It is also possible that the name of Septalius associated with the medicine to treat *gálico* has to do with an observation Manfredus sent to the Royal Society of London explaining the finding of mercury in the roots of some plants in the valley of Lancy, in the mountains near Turin (Septalius 493).

potent but unlikely to develop into disease. But on particular occasions divine punishment emerges in the form of something such as *gálico*. In the same way, this theory of inherent disease is not tightly compatible with Suárez's claims several years later, in *Manifiestas demonstraciones* (1745), that *gálico* is communicated by exhalation—that is, through breathing the air where a diseased person has been—like phthisis, which can be acquired without direct physical contact. Suárez also indicates that *gálico* can be transmitted through direct contact, through *concubito* (lying down with someone), through inheriting it at birth, and through breastfeeding. None of these forms of communication seem to play well with the theory of inherent disease, because if God indeed sows disease in advance, one could argue that an ascetic, solitary monk in a desert would be equally at risk for *gálico* as someone regularly exposed to people who have it.

Nevertheless, the use of the old-fashioned word *seminio* and the novel, scientifically derived "refraction" by the same author illustrates the moment of vacillation between discourses that fought to maintain the relevance of God and church in everyday life and discourses that aimed to explain nature through factual observation. This tension was not confined to the realm of medicine; it was present in other forms of discourse, like literature, where mercury flourished with multiple meanings. The words, definitions, and theoretical explanations found in medical treatises of the time seem to describe a well-organized, clean, effective, and convenient system of curing *gálico*. There are exact measurements and schedules, logical methods, and sensible advice. Yet the treatises fail to document the tangible effect of mercury on a person, and only literature, by authors like Benegasi (whose humorous commentary on the experience of leeches and purging broths I discussed above), can begin to give us a glimpse of what is beyond the medical texts. Although humor is the main vehicle for descriptions of *gálico* in the eighteenth century, not all texts are written exclusively in that key.

Diego de Torres y Villarroel (1693–1770), another great author of the century, wrote poetry, autobiography, essays on a wide range of subjects, and even prophecies and weather forecasts based on astrological observations. He offers a more poised yet extremely entertaining view. Torres Villarroel is especially known for publishing the story of his life, ranging from his unruly youth to his appointment as a professor of math in Salamanca and his later days as a protégé of the Duquesa de Alba. His *Vida,* which he divided into six *trozos* (parts), was later republished in multiple editions and in many Spanish cities. In Part 5 (*Quinto trozo;* 1750), Torres Villarroel comments about a difficult period he experienced as a result of a bureaucratic muddle and the death of his friend, the statesman José Carvajal y Lancaster (1698–1754). Torres Villarroel began to have stomach problems and to feel low in spirit, which he describes as "a melancholy so deep, and so desperate, that no shape was seen by my eyes, nor any idea in my soul" (20).[25] Doctors treated him with "the fury of their prescriptions, and their mistakes [. . .] and without knowing the first name, the last name, the class, nor the temperament of the sicknesses they were curing, and pursuing them at the cost of my own skin with all the nonsense, and trifles, that are sold in the apothecaries" (22).[26] Believing that the classification and naming of a disease was the beginning of curing it, each doctor brought a new label to Torres Villarroel's ailment: "Many times I heard it called hypochondria, others a blood clot, buboes, jaundice, a passion of the soul, the disease of melancholy, obstructions, witchcraft, spells, love, and demons" (22).[27] He suffered almost all the treatments that logically followed each new christening of his disease. Among his doctors, there was a foolish one who said that "all the ailments that are resistant, that trouble the bodies, and that jeer at other

Diego Torres y Villarroel (1693–1770)

Torres Villarroel was born in Salamanca to a family of booksellers: his father and maternal uncle became his primary publishers. However, in 1703 his father left the bookshop to serve Philip V, worsening the family's precarious finances. It was serendipitous, therefore, that Diego received a scholarship to the Colegio Trilingüe of Salamanca in 1708, where he stayed for five years. Many of the picaresque stories of his *Vida* are set during this time. In the spring of 1715, after one scandal too many, he left for Portugal, only to return in the fall, ready to mend his ways, and was ordained a subdeacon. He threw himself into study not only of the arts but of many disciplines, including mathematics, philosophy, medicine, and alchemy. At thirty, he obtained a professorship in mathematics at the University of Salamanca. In 1745, the year he suffered the illness detailed in part 5 of his *Vida*, Torres Villarroel was ordained a priest, and in 1751 the Real Consejo allowed his early retirement. His work continued to be popular, as is apparent in the subscriptions to his later writings, a list headed by Ferdinand VI himself; the only library to not subscribe was that of his own university, though he later gifted a set of his works to the Colegio Trilingüe. His renown during his life was largely due to his almanacs and imitations of Quevedo, though he also wrote, apart from his *Vida*, one-act farces (*sainetes*), lyrical verses, and texts in science, religion, and criticism.

---

medical treatments, should be known as buboes, and cured with ointments" (23),[28] and decided that mercury ointments were in order. This was the only treatment Torres Villarroel refused, because "even though like them I did not know the class of my condition, I knew well that it was not buboes, because I was certain, that not by inheritance, nor by theft, nor in exchange for anything, nor by loan had I received any such furnishings; nor ever in my life did I house in my humors such tenants" (22–23).[29] Even though his illness baffled the doctors, he knew that there was no reason for him to be diagnosed with *gálico*. He calls the treatment with mercury a sentence or punishment, and explains that rejecting the treatment saved his life, or at least enabled him to free himself "from the multitude of afflictions, and pains, that this most useful medication carries with it" (23).[30]

Scornfully, he calls *unciones* "most useful" because he had learned about the horrifying effects of the treatment. In 1736 he had published *Los desauciados del mundo, y de la Gloria* (The terminally ill of the world, and of the Glory), a book that describes the deaths of people with terminal diseases. A *desauciado* (terminally ill) is a person who has no hope of getting better, a person deemed incurable by the doctors. The title of each chapter corresponds to a different illness, and the book is a veritable record of ailments thought to be connected to the spiritual weakness of the patients who suffered them: the phthisic, the apoplectic, the *gálico,* people behaving frantically, and people with chronic renal disease, cholera, dysentery, colics, fevers, or kidney failure. Among women, he describes the hysteric, the one wasting away, the one with an inflamed liver, the epileptic, and the one who just had an abortion. While taking a siesta by the Tormes River, which runs by Salamanca, the narrator dreams of an "Etyope" (Ethiopian) demon. Its skin color reveals the prejudice of Torres Villarroel and his contemporaries, and its depiction as a composite of animalistic parts is reminiscent of the excess in and monstrosity of portraits by the Italian painter Giuseppe Arcimboldo (1527–93), or the convoluted decorations of Baroque style. Its repugnant features clash with the light background of the placid Tormes River. The way this demon is described—as a guide and a revealer of hidden truth, but at the same time as related to the traditional idea of Satan—makes the demon a knowledgeable companion for the narrator as they explore the reign of the occult and evil. The demon passes judgment on the situation and the conduct of the different patients they visit, functioning in much the same fashion as Ovid in Dante's *Inferno* and *Purgatorio.* The goal of Torres's book is to instill good behavior in readers by revealing the causes and consequences of the ailments, which are usually connected to a lack of temperance and a proclivity for sensual pleasures.

The case that best embodies the author's criticism of a terminally ill patient is that of the fourth *desauciado.* The demon takes the narrator to the room of a *gálico* patient being treated with mercury ointments. The young man belongs to high society, or at least is a man with some economic means, because they find him in "a beautiful room, capable, and elegant with several crests, and cards" (57).[31] The room follows the specifications for patients of *gálico* as prescribed in medical treatises: the bed is covered by a canopy, and its curtains are made out of different types of cloth, which were supposed to maintain an even temperature within the enclosed space, as well as stopping air from getting in or out. The servants and family members in the house are fretting and whispering comments to one another. When narrator and demon open the curtains, the sight is ghastly; the narrator lists what they behold: "swamped in sticky and fetid sweat, caught up in afflictions, and swallowed by anguish, and hot flushes. [. . .] The head hairless, and covered in patches of scabs, warts, small pustules, tubercles, and other promontories, and bumps. The mouth covered in blisters, pooling with drool. [. . .] The lips black, hard, and curled back, like the edge of a wash tub; the nose full of large bites, and so scratched, and eaten away, that it showed the bones of the tear ducts, and the eye sockets through the openings: he barked instead of saying words" (57).[32] The patient had possessed youth, handsomeness, health, riches, and intelligence, but these very same assets had brought him misfortune. He had learned how to woo the ladies, and found it easy to conquer them—even those who had tried to reject his advances and keep their honor intact. His courtly ways, his smooth talk, and his proximity to distinguished women at dances and soirées, in collusion with the sweetness of the music at these gatherings, had helped him vanquish any feminine obstacle in his way. But, at some point, the women of high society were no longer as savory as he wished. He had then turned to "rooting around in other dirty, and rude vices" and had gotten sick (59).[33] Instead of learning from the early signs of the disease or heeding his doctor's advice, he had gone on with his lewdness, disregarding the symptoms that eventually ravaged his body. Although it is not clearly stated, the ill-bred vice to which Torres is referring is very possibly the habit of visiting the brothel. The young man's body "gave him a second warning with more raw and sensitive displays, strewing small spots like multicolored sequins over all his skin, and [they were] so agitated, that he could not calm them with his nails, blood-lettings, ointments, horchatas, mallow waters, and other absorbents, and sweetener" (59).[34] But like the aforementioned dog returning to its vomit ("como el perro al vómito")—Torres Villarroel, like Calvo before, uses the words from the Bible *verbatim et literatim*—he had revisited his clandestine lascivious steps, only to experience a renewed bout of "small pustules, tubercles, scabs in the forehead, ears, mouth, head, and other shameful parts of his body" (59).[35] The power of medicine was brought to his bedside in the form of various products: "the pills from the guaiacum wood, sassafras, sarsaparilla, China root, soapwort, and the most exquisite substances that countered the effects of venom, like antidotes, heart water, and palmar powders, the curative water of Rondeleto" (59).[36] But no medicine could stop the disease caused by his untamed desire, and his health continued to deteriorate.

The author knows the array of palliatives for *gálico* patients very well; in fact, the fourth *desauciado* functions as an excellent abridgment of medical treatises of the time. The character who has the wisdom worthy of physicians is the demon that accompanies the narrator. He can explain the "communication" of *bubas* as well as Calvo, and he describes the way the disease evolves in terms of the theory of humors more succinctly than Suárez de Ribera: "That part of the body that receives the venom, is that which is first damaged, then it is communicated, and runs through the veins, and from these to the liver, where it acquires a depraved disposition, with which it destroys the goodness of the blood, and of all the other liquids" (63).[37] In this regard, the clearest difference between Torres Villarroel's text and the medical treatises is that he is not a physician and therefore is not invested in assuring the reader that a particular regimen—be it mercury, guaiacum, or sarsaparilla—will lead to any improvement: the patient is hopeless—a *desauciado*. Torres Villarroel states that almost all of the stages of *gálico* and its manifestations are incur-

Malos hígados

"Malos hígados" (lit., "bad livers") is an expression still used to denote an ill-inclined person or someone of ill will or malevolent character. While having a "good heart" means being caring, benign, or altruistic, having a "bad liver" means completely the opposite. These idioms are derived from the humoral theory inherited from the Hippocratic system that informed medicine during the eighteenth century. Each of the four humors represents a corresponding cardinal fluid and a time of the year. Yellow bile corresponds to the summer season and to the organ of the liver, while black bile corresponds with autumn and the spleen, phlegm with winter and the brain, and blood with spring and the heart (see fig. 3). Given that each organ was supposed to be the seat of a particular strong feeling, metonymical qualities followed. Usually written in the plural in Spanish (*hígados*), the liver was connected to the idea of courage and bravery, or spirit, willpower, and grit—that is, "guts." Common expressions in this regard are *tener hígados* (to have a liver, or to have grit) or *echarle hígados* (put the liver, or effort, into it). The idiom *tener malos hígados* (to have a bad liver) refers to a cowardly person who springs into action only to do evil. For more on idioms related to body parts, see Cantera Ortiz de Urbina's "Refranes y locuciones."

---

able: "*Gálico* is regularly a slow and long-lasting illness, and those that suffer it go dragging on with life for many years" (66).[38] Torres Villarroel's depiction of the slow progress of the disease—"diuturno" means that it lasts for a very long time—shows that there was an understanding of the intermittent quality of *gálico,* in this case attributed to the patient's persistence in having sex, but not yet of the disease's stages. The author is able to explain that the first signs of the disease were not as harsh as later indicators, but general depictions of *gálico* patients at the time tended to illustrate only the secondary and tertiary stages, when the symptoms were much more extreme.

While a goal of Torres Villarroel's exemplum is to inform the reader about the characteristics of *gálico,* for him it is more important to instill in sane young men the ideas of sexual temperance and restraint, and to suggest that the disease could be abated if patients could stop following improper desires. In his eyes, the only feasible way to reduce the incidence of *bubas* is to prevent their transmission. His call for self-restraint is not necessarily to pursue a common good, or to protect society at large, but to provide individual, focused help. Yet, if a person could not control sexual desire and continued acting like a hog (I am using the author's image), rutting in dirty and ill-mannered vices, punishment would come, as it had in this particular case: "the brutality of his habits [. . .] corrupted the solid parts of his bones, tendons, membranes, and nerves, tearing, and eating away at all its texture, and symmetry. It covered him in ulcers, fistulas, cavities, cankers, and moles: it pulled out all the hair from his beard, and head: it ate away his nostrils, it swallowed his throat, it covered up his ears, and finally it led him to consumptive fever, which is the one that is most quickly absorbing his life-giving fluid" (59–60).[39]

Even the demon, with all of his horrible features and supposedly obscure provenance, is ashamed of the patient's deeds: "I don't want to speak to you anymore about the causes of the condemnation of this convicted man; for although I am a demon, I am ashamed that the tale of his ugly crimes passes through my black lips" (69–70).[40] Note that the demon uses the word "ajusticiado"—that is, a person punished by the law in order to restore balance after a proscribed action. The demon explains to the narrator that young men do not learn from the many examples they see because their vice "erases from their knowledge the dangers, the pains, and even all the horror of hell" (60).[41] As the demon imparts these moral reflections to the narrator, the pained wailing of the patient interrupts their conversation. They open the heavy bed curtains once again and see him "submerged in more abundant, and reeking sweat, all the harmony of his countenance broken down, furious in his gazes, and fighting with such extreme injuries, and pains, that I suspected that they were the ones giving the final end to his life" (61).[42] For Torres Villarroel, this is a form of purgatory. The narrator thinks that this must be the end of the patient's misery, but the demon states that death will take longer because the "strength of live quicksilver, and the rebelliousness of the humid humor produce such a furious battle" (61).[43] Mercury is thought to have a powerful quality that can prolong life, but the extension of life under the terrible effects of the medicine is in truth a prolongation of death and suffering. At this point the main impetus of the story is revealed: punishment for lecherous behavior is not necessarily experienced in purgatory or hell, but is true and real on earth thanks to *gálico*. Even as the demon tries to teach the causes and characteristics of the disease, the narrator remains astounded, struggling to make sense of the devastation of the patient. Torres Villarroel criticizes those who turn a blind eye to unregulated sex, or those who think that lasciviousness is a minor sin—a mere by-product of the fragility of good men. He defends the idea that sex without boundaries destroys lives; he considers all other diseases in which human will is not present worthy of pity, but "the illnesses that men ask for, by not displeasing their gluttony, and by lavishing upon their lust, do not deserve compassion, nor feigned ignorance" (68).[44] *Gálico* is a deserved death sentence.

There is a solution, though. For Torres Villarroel, this disease, fueled by untamed desire and punished with painful wounds, is not to be treated with "antigálicos" but prevented from ever taking hold. The nightmarish narration of the lustful causes and chastising consequences of the disease is the real cure for *gálico* because preventive words, in this case in the form of a moral anecdote, penetrate even more deeply than mercury. The reader is advised to carry around, not the portrait of his beloved, but a copy of this book instead, because it would be "without doubt the antivenom to all his troubles, and it would not allow for his thoughts to become infected, nor for the more penetrating and sharp thorns of lust" (62).[45] In this crusade, all literary tactics are accepted, as is the scornful tone that people use when referring to *gálico* or to those affected with *bubas,* which Torres Villarroel frames as one more compelling reason to avoid its transmission: "Even if this volunteer and revolting insult had no other enemies, nor afflictions, than anger, disgust, disdain, and coldness with which the patient is treated, men must flee a hundred leagues from his contagion" (62).[46] Although his purpose is to bolster the idea that taming sexual desire is the only real way of avoiding the disease, his comments on the sardonic humor aimed at sufferers of the disease offer a glance, a kind of opening of the curtain shrouding the *gálico* patient, that is more accurate than the formal medical discourse.

Torres Villarroel points to the connection between disease and disdain. For him, *gálico* does not merit sympathy or pity; instead, "all who see themselves free from its mark laugh, and mock he who suffers from it" (62).[47] Diseases like the plague may elicit empathy or sympathy because they are not the fault of the person who suffers them. These diseases are not the result of an activity that produces pleasure, and in general people run away from them because there is no happy return from being in their proximity. The defining characteristic of *gálico* was that its main source was pleasurable sex, and those who attached to sex a meaning beyond reproduction—those who sought in it pleasure by itself—were seen as willing to pay any price for their inclination, even in terms of their health. The self-indulgence of such people had been secretly viewed with antipathy, mixed with a certain level of envy; this became open mockery and disdain once their diseased state was revealed in the form of *bubas.* The structure of this logic becomes apparent in the colloquial expressions that Torres Villarroel has garnered related to *gálico,* which can be studied as genuine snapshots of the common understanding of the disease: "it serves him right, with this we'll see if he learns his lesson: if he were cozy at home, or spending his time with honorable people, this wouldn't happen to him: it is not necessary to take pity on one who seeks sicknesses for himself, and takes them by the hand; you've made your bed and now you must lie in it" (62).[48]

The element of mockery and disdain, which we also saw in Benegasi's poem on Anastasio Pantaleón de Ribera, is further illustrated in these sayings, but it is important to stress that these expressions come from those who were not affected by the disease. It is almost a rule in all written instances of *gálico:*

the perspective of the diseased is virtually absent, and what survives as textual evidence are the viewpoints of those who observed it from outside, and those who having had it saw it as something removed, as an incident in the past, or as a transitory situation that has been surmounted. Consequently, all these texts appear within a moral frame that at once reveals and hides the experience of the diseased. Their humor discloses the fact that *gálico* was seen as a retaliation, as a path to knowledge through pain, and as an enforcer of social conduct. Conversely, the perspective of the patient could have been that of either a victim or a morally recovered person retelling her or his experience as an act of contrition after escaping from death. A third way, that of the disease as a source of somewhat positive or productive literary work, would not clearly appear until the second half of the nineteenth century. For now, Torres Villarroel is mainly interested in the moral implications of the narrativization of *gálico* as encapsulated in the last image that the narrator kept in his mind of the *desauciado:* "I had hardly righted myself, when I saw the bedchamber blacken with rowdy, great dark cloud of the demons that were following us, which with furious din carried away the spirit of that revolting flesh to suffer greater punishments for eternity" (63).[49] After experiencing the pain of purgatory while the patient was alive, the spirit leaves the rotten flesh. But the suffering on earth was not enough, because now the soul will continue its punishment in hell. There would be no way out: for Torres Villarroel, *gálico* was a terrible malady indeed.

Torres Villarroel effectively uses humor-laced depictions of *gálico* as a punishment, as a source of knowledge, and as a disciplinary medium in several pieces in his wide range of published material. One of his most important publications was the "Pronosticos del gran Piscator de Salamanca" (Predictions of the great Diviner of Salamanca), a series of almanac-style booklets in which he delivered astrological predictions and cryptic *jácaras* (comic ballads of low life) and sonnets with acid commentary on the politics of the time. The "Piscator" appeared between 1725 and 1753 and is considered an early example of journalistic work on the peninsula. The author republished most of the issues in a single volume titled *Extracto de los pronosticos del gran piscator de Salamanca* (Abstract from the predictions of the great diviner of Salamanca) (1753). Torres Villarroel frames the predictions for 1741 in the environment of the Antón Martín Hospital, the main location for the treatment of *gálico* in Madrid. The introduction to the text is written as a compilation of humorous double entendres, and it connects directly with the theory of balance of humors in vogue at the time. The narrator, who is the "Piscator" (diviner) himself, comments that he was seeking cover from heavy rain when he slipped into the hospital "either because it was it was the closest and least occupied easy shelter, or because that place is the most opportune for shaking off the humid-

ity that sticks to those who wander at leisure through the court" (335).[50] The
"humedades" that idle men get in Madrid are of course the bad humors they
catch from their commerce with those tainted with *gálico*. The Piscator finds
it fitting to get rid of the wetness—that is, the humidity or humor—he got
from walking in the rain. The men at the hospital had acquired the humidity
or phlegm of *gálico* from their idleness in the same way that the Piscator got his
humidity from walking idly in the rain in the streets of Madrid. The narrator
is asked to come into the ward of *gálicos* by an olive merchant from Seville who
is being treated with mercury ointments. In his welcoming remarks, the man
uses parallel meanings that connect features of the *gálico* treatment with the
author's profession as diviner or forecaster: "Enter, Mr. Diviner, for this is the
very place for stargazers. Come here, for here you have the mercury you need,
and give up on pursuing that [mercury] of the heavens, for that one won't
absorb harmful humors. Go ahead, for here you will throw up the Catalinas
that have stuck to you in your affairs with the Pepas and the Antonias" (337).[51]
With his Andalusian accent compounded by the raspy and drooling intona-
tion caused by the mercury, the patient tells the astrologer that the Antón
Martín is a good place for "estrelleros" (stargazers), which alludes not only to
those interested in the stars in the sky, but also the star-shaped wounds of the
bubas that *gálico* patients had on their face and other parts of the body.[52] It is
suggested that the Piscator will read the future not only in the heavenly stars
but also in the terrifying starry marks on the face of the diseased. The man
from Seville believes that the narrator is seeking treatment for *bubas* at the
hospital, and advises him to stop trying to find a cure in the planet Mercury
in the sky, and instead attempt to find a cure with the mercury ointment he
will receive in the hospital. Everyone else in the place acts as a mocking chorus
to the olive merchant. The narrator is offended by the intimation that he has
the terrible disease that produces oozing stars and points disdainfully to the
drool of the irreverent patients: "May the babblers shut the hell up [...] for
buboes only snatch the idiots, the idle, and those bored with honorable conversations" (338).[53] Although the narrator has been practicing the same kind
of commerce as the Sevillian, he has been more careful, perhaps more fortunate (i.e., having a better star), and is suffering less than those in the hospital
(338). This assertion confirms that at the time there was no overt criticism
of prostitution—the narrator regards himself as morally correct—but prostitutes were feared as the source of the disease. An outcome of this viewpoint
was the idea that habitués tended to look for younger women who had had
less contact with men.

In addition to playing with double meanings, Torres Villarroel adds a kind
of humor that he inherited from his Quevedian model—a debt so deep that
one of his early books is titled *Visiones y visitas de Torres, con D. Francisco de*

Emetics

First discussed in writing in the Hippocratic canon and shaped and formalized by Galen, the humoral theory is one that is both holistic and based on the primacy of balance for good health. The four humors (blood, phlegm, black bile, and yellow bile) must be maintained in balance, through diet and daily regimen, to counteract the weather, season, and natural preponderance of one humor or another. While the humoral theory of medicine is, in practice, much more focused on diet and preventative care than direct intervention, it does have a system of internal medicine. This system grants primacy to bloodletting (phlebotomy or venesection) for both prophylactic and curative usage, but also makes use of other purgatives to flush excess humors from the body. Therefore, emetics, cathartics, diuretics, diaphoretics, expectorants, and so on were a highly valued element in the medical pharmacopeia through the nineteenth century, with more value placed on those drugs that achieved their desired results most efficiently. Emetics have the additional advantage of great efficacy in treating cases of poisoning, though many emetics are themselves toxic, and indeed poisonous, given a high enough dose.

Quevedo, por la Corte (Visions and visits of Torres, with D. Francisco de Quevedo, around the Court) (1727).[54] This stylistic legacy, which is akin to grotesque humor, is scatological in nature, and it presents the reader with exaggerations, underlines characteristics that make an impression on the senses, and intensifies reality to produce a discomfort that catalyzes the humorous effect. The awful smell that makes the narrator recoil when he enters the ward in the hospital is not just an awful smell but "a stench more intolerable than the belch of a vinegary stomach, more sticky than the phlegm of an old glutton woman, and so thick and dense that it could be sawed off" (335).[55] In spite of the offensive, repugnant odor, the narrator still wants to "examine the dung heap" (*examinar el estercolero*), just as the reader feels compelled to keep reading in spite of the disgusting description. The grotesque intensification Torres Villarroel had used as a comical device a few lines before is now retooled to condemn the habits of the other men at the hospital: "there were purging their scandalous delights, and their guilty nonsense, up to dozens of foolish delinquents, gallant-bats, lascivious mouths of the night, that go around covered in lust, lying in wait in dark doorways and hidden urinals, smitten simpletons, who buy crimes and condemnation at the cost of their own skins, and finally dirty sinners, and infatuated morons, who think that for a little money one can find a good woman and happy health" (336).[56]

Knowing that their behavior is not condoned by society, these men take cover in the shadows of the night, like bats, and like rats or flies they linger in the stench of urinals, which were some of the places where prostitutes looked for clients. According to Torres Villarroel, those affected by *gálico* are unwise precisely because they fail to comprehend the consequences of careless sexual exchange; they are thoughtless or inexperienced because they do not want to understand that safe sex comes with a higher price. Being stingy—that is, seeking sexual commerce with women who have sex with many men for just a few coins—translates into foolishness, because no money can pay for the return of one's health. The corollary of this logic is that it tacitly approves of sexual commerce, but only when the transaction is sufficiently expensive to sift out prostitutes with *gálico* or, more disturbingly, when it takes place with younger and younger women who have not been exposed to the disease. Following the ideas gathered by the author in this text, there are two possible ways to prevent *gálico:* one is abstinence, and the other is to limit one's use of prostitution to a chosen few.

The excesses of Torres Villarroel's writing style create an ambiguous dynamic of attraction and repulsion, but in the end their goal is to make more potent his criticism of those who have acquired the disease from what he considers dirty desires. The language is baroque in nature because it aims to saturate the sensibilities of the reader. In this case the intensification is not to promote a feeling of beauty but instead to corroborate the sense that regulation of personal and social behavior is necessary; that is, to reassure readers of the beauty of order and limits. The thick, fetid, copious slobbering and the broken, raspy, inarticulate speech that Torres underscores are the two most important physical markers that characterize *gálico* patients: "the prostrate libidinous [patients], began to unload upon me another downpour of insults rolled in large skeins of froth and strands of phlegm, because they were throwing the words from the trash heaps of their rotten mouths, smeared with grime, filled with rot, and so filled with the greasy dung of their drool, that what they [the words] could not be distinguished, nor in a million years could their meaning be known" (336–37).[57]

These diseased men can barely make meaning. They do have a voice, but one that is immediately qualified as vile, dirty, and rejectable. When they attempt to utter their feelings, or when they try to call for pity, the narrator describes them as tainted and foul and clearly regards their pain as their well-deserved punishment for past actions. Nevertheless, from a medical standpoint, the men in the ward are responding to the treatment with mercury by the book. Thick saliva and heavy sweating were good indicators of the bad humor leaving their bodies. Hoarseness, an expected result of the disease's progression, was also a side effect of mercury working its intrinsic powers.

The intensified language of Torres Villarroel brings new meaning and verve to the detached descriptions of *gálico* in medical texts of the time. The words coined or retooled to name the symptoms and manifestations of the disease, which in general would lose their semantic charge as a result of repetitive use or the passing of time, retain their power to offer meaning through literary language used by authors like Torres Villarroel. Such is the case of "Don Babilés," one of the *gálico* patients at Antón Martín. He is being treated with mercury and does not need a clairvoyant like the Piscator of Salamanca to know that he will die soon. Babilés has crafted several stanzas, supposedly in the course of interpreting some poetry. In truth, the activity is an excuse to make political commentary about the events of the year. He does not want his literary efforts to go to waste and thus asks the Piscator to include the composition in his "Pronosticos" after Babilés's certain death. "Babilés" is another play on words: *baba* (dribble) signifies that the patient is a personification of mercurial slobbering, and could also be interpreted as a term for unbridled slandering. What we know from the description for sure is that Torres Villarroel's character was in the last stages of the disease: "He scratched his lips with his large shirtsleeve, and rising up with painful slowness upon his elbows, he showed us his face; but, Jesus a thousand times! How deformed, and how abominable, for even hell itself cannot have a similar monstrosity. He had a stony ground of gummas, and abscesses the size of large sweet cherries, heaped upon his forehead and skull; in his throat an anthill of large warts; and on the arms a swarm of exostosis, bumps, ticks, and other raised and angry lumps. His mouth was wide-open, the lips curled back over the nostrils and chin, the cavities of his jaws so stuffed with filth, that it seemed to me a washbowl at the time of making sausages, full of fat, rotten blood, and whole onions. His teeth went scattered about the outskirts of the cavern of his mouth, and when he wanted to turn his tongue (which was more useless to him than a cowboy's cudgel) to utter some word, his set of teeth sounded like a sack of walnuts in the hands of young boys" (338–39).[58]

Babilés's head is cobbled with *gomas* or gummas, known in present-day medicine as syphilomas, the tumors of tertiary syphilis, which may spill a resinous liquid similar to the oozing gum produced by trees and other plants. *Talparias,* wounds that appear on the head and other parts of *gálico* patients, are named after the word *talpa* (mole) in Latin, because they look like the mounds made by moles when digging underground. In some medical treatises, these eruptions are directly called *topos,* the common name for a mole. Babilés has so many *talparias* that the narrator identifies them as *garrafales,* a kind of prolific sweet cherry, which by extension names something that is excessive. Like the fruit, *talparias* are dark red and grow in clusters. The warts on Babilés's neck look like massive anthills, and his arms are covered with swarms of *sobrehuesos* or exostosis, tumors that appear over the bones. As if all this were not enough,

Babilés must contend with other bumps and lumps (*burujones*). His mouth is compared to a washbowl filled with pork chitterlings, tripe, lard, rotten blood, and whole onions ready to be cooked. These grotesque images reinstantiate the spirit of Quevedo's *picaresca,* specifically in *El buscón,* where the disgusting contents of a pot test the strong stomach of the reader.[59]

Babilés bases his political commentary on some very popular verses written by Quevedo about a character named Marica: "A Marica la chupona" (To Marica the moocher) (4:497) and "Tomando estaba sudores" (Taking the sweats) (4:414). In one stanza of the last poem, Quevedo explains that "Marica was taking the sweats / in the hospital; / for taking was her custom, / and the remedy is to sweat" (vv. 1–4), and in the first poem, Quevedo begins stating that "The drippings in the bed / of Marica the moocher / took her health away / in the sarsaparilla stand" (vv. 1–4).[60] The first quatrain deals with the verb *tomar,* which means "to take" and refers not only to the act of absorbing or accepting something—in this case a treatment that produces sweat—but also to sexual intercourse: to "take" someone is to have sex with them, especially anally, while they are in a passive position. The other quatrain initially seems to denote the adornments (*goteras*) hanging over Marica's bed, but a second reading hints at drops or drippings—very likely of seminal fluid—that are connected to the transmission of *bubas* and consequently to buying sarsaparilla for brewing medical concoctions. The outcomes of *gálico* in Babilés's gloss feature women as well, although their names could be hiding those of male politicians: as a result of the disease, a woman of noble origin named Angelina has turned "turba"—that is, the color of coal; "la Cusculina" is paying the price of living the good life (*vita bona*); Constanza is balding (*está pelona*), a sign of the rampant disease; "la Perales" has lost her cassock; "la Roma" is soaking, likely in mercury ointments; "la Meneses" has retired to a convent; and "la Lema" is being singed (*emperdigada*). In this last example, Torres Villarroel uses a hunting term that typically describes the process of briefly roasting partridges over coals to prevent the meat from rotting, but in this case "emperdigada" is related to the heated rooms used to provoke sweat in *gálico* patients.[61] Of all the women in the verses intended for "Pronosticos," only "la Galarza" has avoided the disease, but even she is now using her own pot "in the brambles stand" (*en la venta de la zarza*)—that is, in the place where people drink water infused with sarsaparilla to cure *bubas* (344). The description of Babilés's face and body and the developments in the lives of the mentioned women bring to life the medical and popular language for naming the symptomatology of *gálico,* which makes Torre y Balcarçel's *Espejo de la philosophia* or López Pinna's *Tratado de morbo gallico* appear almost lacking when compared with Torres Villarroel's more intense account.

Torres Villarroel incorporates the voice of Quevedo in order to craft a discourse that connects popular tradition, as evidenced in the well-known verses of the Spanish Golden Age author, to the current political situation through veiled commentary that alludes to facts known to his intended public. The disease suffered by Babilés and the proximity of his death invest him with an aura of harsh sincerity: "through the mouth of the dying man: / with profound disillusionment / I will denounce your mistakes, [...] one who in Martín Antón / *was taking the sweats*" (341).[62] The gloss is written in a cryptic language, and its purpose is to prod readers to use their contextual knowledge to extract meaning and for comical effect. Although it can be difficult to interpret the text politically today, it does reveal important significations on literary or narrative levels because of Torres's purposeful use of the theme of *gálico*. We can confirm that mercury was deemed a venom by some physicians, as previously demonstrated by Bachiller Philaletes's attack on Suárez de Ribera for the latter's blind trust in *hydragiro* (mercury). Babilés writes about this more humorously in this *jácara*—a type of song describing low life—narrating that "Disguised as Galens [doctors] / go around Perico and Marica, / and both one and the other apply / venoms calling them theriacs" (341).[63] A theriac (*triaca*) was a mixture of several medicines, usually laced with opium and honey, which was considered a universal remedy. In this case Babilés claims that the characters of Marica and Perico prescribe as medicine what in truth is venom, a comparison that seems analogous to the ever-present issue of politicians who sell as the perfect solution what in truth is society's ruin. In the same vein, the commentator refers to the tendency among physicians to engage in rhetorical wars and badly written manuals, and their inability to produce effective medical treatments:

> the Anti-Medicato goes about
> voicing his aphorisms:
> he is letting loose solecisms
> that he will not be able to correct,
> and the cure must fail,
> because in this hypochondria
> blood-letting is prescribed,
> *and the remedy was sweating.*" (341–42; emphasis in original)[64]

In a continuation of his mocking of structures of power, Torres's "Anti-Medicato" is a play of words with "Protomedicato," the administrative machinery that regulated medical practice in the empire, as I discussed with more detail in the introduction.

Triaca, treacle, theriac, theriaca

A *triaca* was a mixture of several medicines that was considered a universal remedy or panacea. The term "theriac" was originally used to designate an antidote against poisoning that included the mashed flesh of venomous snakes and was usually laced with opium and honey. Since the concoction had so many components—the formula for *triaca magna* contains at least seventy-five ingredients—and a complex method of preparation, it was a scarce, expensive medicine. Until 1736, the Roman and Venetian *triacas* were considered the best, and held a kind of electuary monopoly. Around 1766, the Spanish king tried to protect sales of the concoction by granting pharmacists in Zaragoza, Valencia, and Barcelona the exclusive privilege of selling it. In the same way that Venice exported the medicine to the rest of Europe, Spain exported *triacas* made on the peninsula to the colonies overseas. In *La Triaca Magna* (2009), Francisco Javier Puerto Sarmiento quotes Hebbe Isabel Campero Carrasco, explaining that the inventory of an apothecary in the Real Audiencia de Charcas, now Bolivia, included "Triaca de Toledo" (88). Even though the formula for the *triaca* continued to appear in official pharmacy annals, by the end of the eighteenth century *triacas* were used no more.

All these manifestations of *gálico* function as a structure for moral teachings; the tone of the *jácara,* a form normally used for humorous depictions of low life and unbridled pleasure, both cloaks and reveals a nascent preoccupation with a disease that was corroding the social tissue while people continued seeking sensual gratification. Although the disease was usually kept in the realm of private life, by using the far-reaching medium of the almanac (acquired by many people because its cost was low and it claimed to predict the future), by writing in the public and festive style of the *jácara,* and by describing hospitals to the general public, Torres Villarroel brings the private to the public sphere and repositions the private consequences of public actions. These moves are even more clearly portrayed in a moral sonnet that appears in his book *Juguetes de Thalia* (Thalia's toys) (1738). Written in a jeering tone, the sonnet is titled "Difine unos grados de pompa en Salamanca" (Describing an ostentatious commencement in Salamanca) and criticizes the celebratory excesses of a group of recently graduated students:

> Upon venerable beasts rode
> all the school, which Mercury endorses,
> and each one on his head wears,
> signs of the science he studied:

"Long life!" and "drink!" were heard in the disorder,
in the colorful rasping shrieks of a new voice,
and in the whole graduating class, there is reproduced,
upon hearing "long life!" so much drool:

All the people, and the city becomes silly,
around the Plaza they arrive,
they run the bulls, they drink a cask;

They dine, and they get sick from the fondling,
and the party ends, as I said above,
in "drool!" "drink!" "long life" and "buboes!" (19)[65]

On the surface, Torres Villarroel is merely describing a group of school-fellows riding thoroughbred mounts. But the real story is that of young men getting joyrides with women of ill repute, here called "beasts." The patron god Mercury, the divine messenger who bridged the gap between mortals and deities, apparently endorses the college to which the students belong, but the true "approval" of their actions will come from mercury, the remedy for the *gálico* being communicated to the merry partygoers. Torres Villarroel mentions the custom of hanging emblems of academic achievement from hats, but these rowdy pupils will show the outcome of their raucous inquiry as blisters and gummas embellishing their foreheads. At the same time, amid the hustle and bustle of people cheering and toasting, someone wishes long life to the newly robed alumnus, shouting with the piercing or raspy voice of a person affected by *gálico*. Torres Villarroel claims that every newly graduated (*licenciado*) man at the university may reproduce the disease, so much that every toast and cheer seems to suggest more mercury-induced drooling.

For the author, the people of Salamanca are blind to the health problems that stem from the lack of continence among the young population of the college city. The inhabitants boisterously celebrate by drinking full barrels of wine, parading in the streets, and enjoying bullfighting, an iconic Spanish activity that became more organized and formalized during the eighteenth century. But behind the mask of merriment lies the truth of sickness. On first reading, the poem simply notes that once the performance (*función*) is over—once the feast has reached its end—all that is left is the hangover. But at a deeper level, the poem asserts that everything ends in slobber, drinking, cheering, foolishness, and *bubas*. Its last verse summarizes the dynamic of *gálico* in Salamanca. The final outbreak of the *bubas* to which the graduates will succumb will be the result of a gradual lack of vigilance; that is, the outcome of self-indulgence and the prospect of death are both blurred by the noise of

De tales romerías se sacan tales veneras

Venera is the name of the shell of the scallop, a mollusk in the Pectinidae family. This shell, specifically the species *Pecten maximus,* is the traditional emblem of Santiago (Saint James), Spain's patron saint. Brothers of the Order of Santiago would bear the shell as a medal in their cloaks. Pilgrims who completed the Camino de Santiago (Way of Saint James) to Santiago de Compostela in the region of Galicia also displayed shells on their clothing. In his *Tesoro de la lengua castellana o española* (1611), Sebastián de Covarrubias (1539–1613) includes a proverb with metonymic connections with *gálico:* "from such kinds of pilgrimage you get that type of scallop-shell medal" ("de tales romerías, se sacan tales veneras," 1338). Covarrubias explains that the saying refers to the *bubas* or sores afflicting those who journeyed to visit prostitutes: "when men get swollen from the buboes that result from their harlotry and conversation with despicable women" ("quãdo de las ramerias y conversaciones de ruines mugeres, se hinchē los hombres de bubas"). The medal-shells correspond to the *señales* or signs left on the face or body of those with *gálico.* Covarrubias engages in wordplay, contrasting *romerías* (pilgrimage) with *ramerías* (whoring). The moral of the proverb is connected to the negative outcome of following a wrong path in life. Although mentioned in earlier editions, by 1739 the connection of the shell with the proverb mentioned by Covarrubias does not appear in the dictionary of the Real Academia.

celebration. The moral of the sonnet is that the more younger people learn, the less they know, and their lack of knowledge will translate into their prompt demise.

From a literary perspective, it is significant that Torres is retooling what is perhaps the most-anthologized poem by Luis de Góngora, titled "Mientras por competir con tu cabello" (As it strives to compete with your hair). The graded, climactic asyndeton in Torres Villarroel's last verse mirrors Góngora's "en tierra, en humo, en polvo, en sombra, en nada" (in soil, in smoke, in dust, in shadow, in nothing), which stresses the inexorable advent of old age and death. Torres's sonnet differs from Góngora's poem by pointing out that *gálico* produces an early and monstrous death, which does not allow for the golden hair of youth to turn into venerable silver. The Gongorian ideal of seizing the day—that is, of enjoying youth—becomes a fear and condemnation of enjoyment, because instead of Góngora's somewhat comforting vision of final repose once the body becomes dust and nothingness, there is the specter of protracted pain, humiliation, and disfigurement.

In short, the foolish students of Salamanca can expect to end their days in a hospital like the one depicted in "Pronosticos del gran Piscator de Salamanca."

As discussed above, physicians like Calvo had identified the "two Springs" as the best time to administer sudorific treatments like sarsaparilla and mercury, and the hospitals that accepted this kind of patient arranged their calendars accordingly.[66] Some graduates would probably be among the *gálicos* who could not get the ointments at home and would thus receive them at the hospital. It was customary for people with money to sponsor patients to secure a place in the upcoming cohort in the *gálico* ward. By streamlining treatment, hospital administrators ensured correct dosage, reduced the price of medical components, and allowed for better organization of the treatment and more effective monitoring of patients.

5

Inhospitable Hospitals

The Antón Martín was the primary center of treatment of skin ailments, *gálico,* and other venereal diseases in Madrid. Its official name was Hospital de Nuestra Señora del Amor de Dios, but it was better known by the name of the cleric who founded it in 1552. After the death in Granada of the famous San Juan de Dios, founder of the hospitaller order that bears his name, Antón Martín continued his work and started the hospital on Calle de Atocha. By 1600 it was the main hospital of the city, and most of the Madrilenian doctors lived in its neighborhood in order to be closer to the patients they had to visit every morning. The plaza in front of the hospital, also named Antón Martín, had a market and was so central to the life of the city that the infamous "Motín [riot] de Esquilache" in 1766 started there. The name of the hospital became a metonym for *gálico,* and mentioning that someone was in the Antón Martín tacitly meant that the person had acquired *bubas.* Francisco Benegasi offers an early eighteenth-century reference to the hospital in a poem mocking the Marqués de Valparaíso, most likely Bartolomé González de Andía-Irarrázabal y Howard, in retribution for some satirical verses the nobleman had written. Benegasi plays with meanings, specifically in terms of sending mercurial verses—that is, satirical or scalding poetry that may cure the marquis of his poetical and physical venereal disease: "If Castro went to Anton Martin / with his funny romance, / that I sent him mercury, / should not surprise the learned man" (50).[1] But perhaps the most radical instantiation of Antón Martín as a metonym for the horrors of *gálico* is one crafted by Torres Villarroel in the introduction to Piscator's predictions for 1739: "There once was a drunkard and a rogue, with the airs of a conman, blond, one-eyed, mangy, with a scraggly beard, covered in mumps, devoured by scabies, crammed with buboes, and an everlasting slave of the universal misery with which señora lust pays the wicked inclinations of impatient, despicable, and cheap appetites. It was his grace the aforementioned Señor Don Misfortune, a living and revolting portrait of rot, a walking copy of disgrace, a map of the drunkenness, and an abbreviated Anton Martin" (*Extracto* 299).[2]

The scope of the insult is based on the multiple layers of meaning surrounding the hospital. Being a public, charitable institution, the Antón Martín was

Motín de Esquilache

Leopoldo de Gregorio, Marqués de Esquilache (1699–1785), was a Neapolitan politician and favorite minister of Charles III. He developed a program of modernization of Madrid that included the cleaning of streets and the installation of streetlights. Esquilache considered the traditional use of long capes and hats with wide brims a signal of backwardness in Spanish society. He believed that the concealment provided by these garments did not help in policing the streets of Madrid because men could hide weapons while covering their faces, making it difficult to find culprits after fights. Esquilache proposed to make obligatory the use of garments closer in style to those in vogue in France. Traditional Spaniards, unhappy about the changes implemented by a foreign minister, and rattled by the increasing cost of food—in part the result of Esquilache's idea of freeing the grain market—rebelled in March 1766. Donning the illegal outfit, protesters crossed the square in front of the Antón Martín hospital. The mob destroyed the lampposts placed by the well-intentioned urban reformers and threatened to take the royal palace if their demands were not met. The king acquiesced grudgingly. Esquilache was sent to Venice as ambassador; the price of staple food was lowered; the disliked guard of Walloon men from Belgium was dissolved; and, of course, the fashion of wide hats and capes was restored. Advisers to the king alleged that the Jesuits in their sermons had promoted the riot. As a result, the Jesuits were expelled from Spanish territory, including those in the American colonies. Some leaflets sold in the street claimed that El gran Piscator de Salamanca (Torres Villarroel) had predicted the riots. Torres was quick to disengage his predictive writing from the reality of the insurrection.

---

populated by those with scarce resources to treat their ailments. Many regular clients of the street prostitutes—incidentally, there was a lot of prostitution in the vicinity of the hospital as well—ended up, perhaps for the last time, in a ward similar to that previously described by Torres Villarroel. The author describes not only the repulsive physical traits of the man but also the way in which the marks of disease reflect his depravity and corruption. The feared wickedness of soul and body is summarized by Torres in the image of the Antón Martín hospital, its location, and its inhabitants, as a kind of people and type of space that mirror the supposed depravity of individuals and society. What is more relevant is that Torres tacitly fears a disease of the soul that does not become apparent in the body. For now, for him, the only possible front of attack is to point the finger at what is evident and immediate—that is, the metonymic abbreviation of what the Antón Martín stands for. When the hospital was demolished in 1899 to give way to another urban restructuring in Madrid, there was still no reliable cure for the disease its name once represented; today "Antón Martín" names only a small plaza squeezed between buildings and a stop on the Madrid metro system.

Like the Antón Martín, there were hospitals for the cure of *bubas* in other parts of Spain.[3] José Iglesias de la Casa (1748–91)—an important poet associated with the Escuela Literaria Salmantina (Literary School of Salamanca), a circle in which he was known by the nickname of "Arcadio"—refers to the hospital of Santa María la Blanca in Salamanca in a poem:

> The young man, who without knowing
> What a thing lust was,
> After only the first time
> That he visited a woman,
> Saw, the poor man, that it was necessary
> To enter Santa María,
>
> He won the lottery. (167)[4]

This poem is one of his "Letrillas satíricas," which were published after his death. A *letrilla* is a comic or mocking poem composed of short verses, akin in spirit to the English limerick. A verse that follows each stanza contains the main message of the composition and holds it together. In this case, Iglesias comments on the intervention of fate in the lives of different people: the man disappointed by the disdain of a young woman; the military man who wants to gain honor and ends up prematurely killed on the battlefield; the man with a little cold who asks for the help of the doctor, gets unnecessarily bled, and dies; the man who is cuckolded by the woman he thought was virtuous. In the section I just quoted, an inexperienced young man decides to gain knowledge of carnal desire and "visits" a woman for instruction. Of course, "visits" is a euphemism, because the visit is not of the courteous but of the courtesan kind. The refrain of the poem stresses that the man consequently wins a kind of questionable, inverted sweepstakes. In the same way that the soldier was looking for honor and glory in combat, the unwary seeker of pleasures gets *gálico* from his first visit with a prostitute and ends up in a long, passionate encounter with the treatment for *bubas* at the hospital of Santa María.

Torres Villarroel also mentions an institution in Salamanca named De las Dos Plazas (Of the Two Plazas), which was part of the Hospital de Nuestra Señora del Amparo, but located outside the walls of the town to avoid transmitting diseases like leprosy or *gálico* to the regular patients in the main hospital. This institution was run with the patronage of wealthy individuals in the city and with alms raised by some poor people living on the premises who also helped care for the inmates. During this time, in the spirit of what

Escuela Literaria Salmantina

The Literary School of Salamanca was a group of poets made up of Fray Diego Tadeo González, José Iglesias de la Casa, Fray Juan Fernández, Fray Andrés de Corral, Juan Pablo Forner, Juan Fernández de Rojas, Andrés del Corral, Ramón Cáseda, Pedro Estala, León de Arroyal, Salvador de Mena, Eugenio Llaguno y Amírola, Padre Alba, Gaspar González de Candamo, Antonio Tavira Almazán, and most notably, José Cadalso, Juan Meléndez Valdés, and Gaspar Melchor de Jovellanos. Both in their works and in their private lives, these poets demonstrated a strong faith in the power of friendship, a concept that was popular among the writers and other intellectuals of the Enlightenment. Through correspondence and other interactions, these poets shared ideas about the nature of literature itself, while also critiquing one another's work. Their poems have in common neoclassical features such as the search for a balance between the enjoyable and the useful (*dulce e útil*), the imitation of classical authors, and the use of archaic syntax. The members of the Salamanca school also employed pastoral themes in their works, as well as those of a sensual and amorous nature. In "Carta de Jovino a sus amigos salmantinos" (1776), Jovellanos proposed a turn away from the amorous and the pastoral, heading toward the use of moral and philosophical themes in eighteenth-century poetry.

historians have named "enlightened absolutism," King Ferdinand VI (1713–59) sanctioned several internal reforms in the country. The administrative mind behind these important changes was the Marqués de la Ensenada (1702–81), a successful commissioner who started as a minor manager of naval matters and became the architect of a large project to modernize the kingdom. In 1749 the crown initiated changes in the way beggars and paupers were handled by creating public hospices to feed and clothe them. This measure affected De las Dos Plazas, of which Torres Villarroel was a patron. Since the measure prohibited begging for alms, the helpers of the institution could not get the salaries that usually came from public solicitation. The relevance of the institution and the need to sustain the staff are strategically underlined by Torres to coincide with the goals of common good and organization imposed by the sovereign: "By the grace of God, there still remains an old and poor shelter outside the walls of Salamanca, which is the only welcome and remedy for all the poor people injured by leprosy, scabies, buboes, and other contagious afflictions, and the only refuge, and lodging for the pilgrims, passengers, vagabonds, and other wretched people, whom fortune and misfortune have in the world without even the sad coverage of a shack. [. . .] denied of compassion, lest the reeking poisons of their ailments add more pernicious infections to the feverish, and to those incapacitated by other less contagious afflictions, which are cured in its halls" (*Sexto trozo* 22).[5]

The tone used by Torres Villarroel here contrasts with that of Iglesias and with Torres's other more acrid writings related to *gálico* because its purpose is different. Torres's account of the institution's functions is part of a formal petition to the king: he wants the government either to allow these people to ask for alms for their sustenance, or to provide funds from the royal hospice to pay for their work. His agenda here is not to project an edifying and moral discourse, but to ask for the sovereign's help in funding a charity. The double function of the institution, as a place where those affected by contagious diseases received medicine and a place where the homeless could find a roof, is presented positively by Torres; at the same time, he stresses the importance of keeping these outcasts away from the arguably healthy, productive rest of the population.

During this time, when the monarchy wanted to centralize control through the benevolent yet tight implementation of organizational reforms like the one described above, one central discussion was the unification of public hospitals in order to make better use of available resources. Behind this seemingly innocuous move, which was initiated under Philip V, there was a struggle to gain control over public policy areas that had been in the hands of the church, such as health and education. In relation to this process of administrative hospital merging, there are two relevant writers of the period who discussed *gálico* and the hospitals where it was treated. In an entry on the city of Oviedo for the *Diccionario geográfico-histórico de España* (Geographic and historical dictionary of Spain), Gaspar Melchor de Jovellanos (1744–1811) cites in passing the hospital of "Nuestra Señora de los Remedios, para curación de bubas" (Our Lady of the Remedies, for the curing of buboes) (189). The *Diccionario,* an ambitious work of the Academy of History, shared the spirit of Diderot's and d'Alembert's *Encyclopédie* and involved many scholars. Nevertheless, only two volumes appeared, and Jovellanos's entry was not published (Olmedo Ramos 204). We know of this work, written in Gijón around 1795 during his time away from Madrid, from the publication of his correspondence with Carlos González de Posada in *Obras publicadas é inéditas* (Published and unpublished works) (1859). The government's hospital unification project is evident in this entry, when the author explains that Los Remedios and the hospital of San Juan were incorporated into the hospital of Santiago.

The other hospital reference appears in the writings of the renowned poet and playwright Juan Meléndez Valdés (1754–1817), author of "La paloma de Filis" (The dove of Filis), a cycle of *anacreónticas.* Meléndez Valdés combined his literary work with a public career that had been promoted by Jovellanos. The presence of *gálico* in the writings of Meléndez Valdés is not to be found in *jácaras* like those of Benegasi or Torres Villarroel; it is clear that he did not approve of that kind of writing from a discourse he addressed to the legal offices of the crown, titled "On the necessity of prohibiting the printing and sale of *jácaras* and popular romances, for [being] damaging to social norms, and on replacing them with other truly patriotic songs, which unify teaching and pleasure" (*Poesía y prosa* 665).[6] Rather, Meléndez Valdés's connection to *gálico* is to be found in the bureaucratic and compliant style of the reports he posted as executor of the unification of the hospitals in Ávila between 1792 and 1793, a task that drained his energy and affected his health because of the stern opposition of clerics in that city (Astorgano Abajo, "Los testamentos" 299).[7] In a letter to King Charles IV, on the throne between 1788 and 1808, Meléndez asks for a stern reprimand against the priests in charge of the hospitals who were not rendering accounts of their finances, and he petitions for the banishment of José Vicente de la Madrid, a representative of the bishop of Ávila, whom Meléndez accuses of not facilitating the process of unification and transferring of funds. Meléndez's tone in this report could not be more different from the terse and encomiastic style of his *Anacreónticas:*

> I have not been able to make this comparison with the books and journals of the Hospital of San Joaquín, because neither have I found in it such books of admittance nor any order to this branch, nor anything more than a few dirty notebooks without covers, which they would not have in even the most miserable tavern. [...] Nor do I send to Your Highness the compared states of the Hospital of God the Father, because since only *gálico* is cured there and in a limited period of forty days in spring, and since all the patients enter and leave on the same day, marked for the occasion by their overseer, there cannot be room for these differences as in the rest. But [...] their patients take exorbitant rations of five and even ten pounds of bread, one and two of mutton, and an *azumbre* and a half of wine [almost three liters]; such that the bakers, the shepherd, the water seller, and, it seems, everyone who went there, went only to eat and drink, and that they could, with room to spare, cut their current rations in half. (*Teatro y poesía* 495)[8]

Meléndez's reference to the Hospital de Dios Padre in Ávila, also known as Hospital de las Bubas, confirms that *gálico* treatment was conducted during the spring and gives the new detail that it lasted for forty days. The patients' diet is not in accord with that prescribed by doctors, who would have regarded mutton, bread, and wine as ill suited to balancing humors. In addition, after reading Torres Villarroel's description of the miserable state of those treated with mercury, one doubts they could eat or drink much; Meléndez was quite right to grumble about excessive food expenses. In her *Los hospitales de Extremadura* (2003), María Victoria Rodríguez Mateos corroborates this com-

Juan Meléndez Valdés

Juan Meléndez Valdés (1754–1817) is an emblematic member of the *afrancesados*, eighteenth-century Spanish intellectuals who were enamored with French culture and society. Because he supported the government of Joseph Bonaparte (1768–1844), Napoleon's brother, whom Napoleon established as king of Spain in 1808, Meléndez Valdés was forced to flee to France after the war of independence from 1808 to 1814. He held various positions in the government of Joseph I of Spain, in addition to being a poet, judge, and politician. Because he came from a family of the low nobility (*hidalgos*), Meléndez Valdés had a strong connection to the countryside, and poems such as "El filósofo en el campo" and "Los aradores" demonstrate a romanticized view of this part of Spanish society. Meléndez Valdés is also known for his *Odas anacreónticas,* poems that focus on the pleasures of life, such as "El amor mariposa," "La paloma," and "De los besos de amor." These poems, which seemingly deal with themes of an innocent love between the poet and his beloved, hide connotations of a more erotic, sensual love, as studied by Irene Gómez Castellano in *La cultura de las máscaras.*

---

plaint by describing the nourishment in similar institutions of the time: dry bread, broth, potatoes, and minced food (282–83).

The evidence of fraud at the Hospital de las Bubas explains why Meléndez Valdés did not have an easy time during the unification of hospitals in Ávila, particularly with the administration of the hospital for *gálico,* but the last will and testament of his wife, María Andrea Coca, in which she bequeaths twenty thousand reales to the Hospital General, shows that the couple remained very interested in the institution: "I order that to the General Hospital of the city of Ávila, for whose establishment my husband was commissioned by Royal Order, when he found himself judge in the chancery of Valladolid, and upon which he always looked with particular affection and interest, as much for the love he had for the poor, as for his worries, and even the illness that cost him the aforementioned establishment and merging [. . .] up to the quantity of twenty thousand *vellón* [billon] *reales* be given" (quoted in Astorgano Abajo, "Los testamentos" 300).[9]

If this bequest was in fact realized, the sizable charitable help should have made an impact on the hospital's many expenses in material and labor, including the constant use of coal in fumigation braziers. As a result of the soot, and the use of greasy and staining medicines, the rooms were fitted out with old mattresses and old bed linens that could later be thrown out or burned; as I discuss later, some people viewed the patients in the Hospital de Bubas as cases that were already lost, and thus had no problem giving as charity what they saw as equally lost—that is, things like mattresses that were useless and even infectious. At any rate, these gifts reduced the amount of money needed for furnishings (Rodríguez Mateos 282–83).

Fifty years before Meléndez Valdés's work in Ávila, Antonio de Ulloa (1716–95) and Jorge Juan (1713–73), two Spanish navy officers and scientists, had a more positive account of the treatment for *gálico* in a hospital run by the Bethlehemites religious order in Piura, today Peru. Back when relations between the French and the Spanish were amiable, Juan and Ulloa had been appointed by Philip V to be part of the French Geodesic Mission. The mission was organized by the French Academy of Sciences with the goal of measuring the length of a degree of latitude at the equator and assessing the exact shape of the earth. In addition to their scientific duties, Ulloa and Juan were to secretly report to the king the military, social, and political situation of the Viceroyalty of Peru. That their general assessment of the administration was as negative as that of Meléndez Valdés half a century later is attested by the unauthorized publication in London—under the baiting title *Noticias secretas de América* (Secret news of America) (1826)—of a confidential report they had produced for the Marqués of Ensenada. Included in the critical report was information on the rivalry between creole and peninsular Spaniards, the mistreatment of indigenous people by the administrators and priests, and the corruption of those in positions of power. The official report of Ulloa and Juan's trip was more scientific and matter-of-fact. Five volumes of a general account that included observations on geology, history, anthropology, customs, and geography appeared in Madrid in 1748 under the title *Relación histórica del viaje hecho de orden de su Majestad a la América Meridional* (Historical account of the journey accomplished by the order of His Majesty to the Southern America). It is in the third volume of this account where we find their record of the hospital in Piura: "*Piura* has a Hospital in the care of the Bethlehemite order. Although all kinds of diseases are cured there, it is famous for curing the *Morbo Gálico* because the quality of the climate contributes sensibly to its best cure. Those who are infested with this malady come to it from all parts; and in many it is experienced that, with less quantity of the specific remedy, compared with that usually applied in other countries, and without so much discomfort of the patient, the goal of reestablishing health is achieved (Juan and Ulloa 13).[10]

The subtropical location of Piura, south of the equator, and the dry desert climate offered the best conditions for curing the disease under the still-prevalent theory of humors. As was the case in many of the hospitals on the peninsula, including the one audited by Meléndez Valdés, hospitals in the American colonies were created and administered by religious orders with the help of patrons fulfilling their Catholic obligation of charity. It is unclear

The Geography of Hospitals

The ubiquitous presence of *gálico* meant the equally abundant existence of hospitals for its treatment on the Iberian Peninsula and in the Americas. A non-exhaustive list of these institutions reveals the geographical nodes where treatment was available: *Ávila:* Hospital de Dios Padre, also known as Hospital de las Bubas; *Lima:* Hospital de la Caridad (Hospital de San Cosme y San Damián), Hospital de San Bartolomé, Hospital de San Andrés, Hospital de Santa Ana, Hospital del Espíritu Santo; *Madrid:* Hospital de Nuestra Señora del Amor de Dios, commonly known as Antón Martín; *México City:* Hospital de San Juan de Dios, Hospital del Amor de Dios; *Oviedo:* Nuestra Señora de los Remedios; *Piura:* Hospital de Bethlemitas; *Salamanca:* Hospital Santa María la Blanca, Institución de las Dos Plazas; *Seville:* Hospital de las Bubas, whose official name was Hospital de San Cosme and San Damián; *Toledo:* Hospital de Santiago; *Talavera:* Hospital de San Bartolomé, formerly known as the Hospital de la Garriona, Hospital de San Lázaro; *Valladolid:* Hospital de la Resurrección.

---

what the "specific" remedy used in the Piura hospital was, but it is likely that it would be the same mercury or guaiacum used in Spain, and for that matter in the rest of the world. As is clear from Ulloa and Juan's description, the main difference in the supposed outcomes of treatment on the New Continent was that the warmth, dryness, or consistency of the climate expedited or facilitated the balancing effects of medical intervention.

According to Rodríguez Mateos, the yearly cycle of ointments and fumigations on the peninsula started in March. A priest, a physician, a surgeon, and the male nurses greeted the cohort of patients. After confession and communion, the treatment started (282–83). Spiritual help was offered to the diseased patients as they underwent the agonizing treatment with mercury or guaiacum while anticipating a horrible, imminent end that could look very much like the eternal punishment promised by the church.

In the same manner that *gálico's* painful symptoms were mitigated with opium and honey-laced theriacas, a palliative was necessary to assuage the terror of looming, certain, and interminable penance after death. With the goal of providing spiritual hope and relief, Father Manuel María de Arjona, a former priest of the church attached to the Hospital de las Bubas in Seville, published his *Exercicios de preparacion para la hora de la muerte que se practica en una de las distribuciones del santo retiro espiritual, en la iglesia del Hospital de las Bubas de esta ciudad* (Preparatory exercises for the time of death practiced in one of the offerings of the holy spiritual retreat, in the Hospital of Buboes of this city) (1805). The official name of this place in Seville was the Hospital de San Cosme y San Damián, which had been initially used for the treatment of the plague in the fourteenth century and then repurposed for *gálico* two centuries later. The imminence of death in such a place compels Arjona to urge sick people to reflect on the next step to come: "you know with evidence that you are a prisoner sentenced to death, even if you don't know when or how the sentence is to be carried out" (6).[11] Arjona compares the patient to a convicted prisoner facing certain death but with an uncertain time of execution. Like other diseases, *gálico* manifested itself in different ways and with various degrees of acuteness. For some patients, the disease would remain dormant for years; for some, its disfiguring and painful effects on face and bones would linger for a long time—compounded by the terrible consequences of the treatment with mercury; for others, death would come swiftly. Unlike many of the literary works that made fun of those affected by the disease, Arjona's chapter in the *Exercicios* entitled "Aceptación de todas las circunstancias de nuestra muerte" (Acceptance of all the circumstances of our death) is very telling of the sentiments produced by death in general, especially the fear produced by the terminal quality of *gálico:* "Take courage Christian and step forward to accept death with all the conditions that the Lord has prepared for you, whether he gives you a gentle illness, or whether [he gives you one] with cruel pains" (11).[12] Spiritual retreats for those confronting impending death, like the one described in Arjona's text, were usually a communal experience. This meant that the difficult experience of preparing to be executed by *gálico* was shared with others in the exact same situation, as Berco has shown in *From Body to Community. Gálico* hospitals in the Hispanic world at the time were inhospitable spaces, but the deliberate separation of their patients from other institutions may have also given those captives of their bodies the comfort and relief of being accompanied in their sorrows by their equals.

6

The Transformation of the Medical
Understanding of *Gálico*

In the second volume of his *Dissertaciones physico-medicas sobre varios curiosos assumptos de Medicina* (1758), Ramón Brunet de la Selva, "Priest, Member and Doctor of the Royal Society of Medicine of Madrid, and of the Village of San Vicente,"[1] included a treatise titled "Sobre las señales, prognostico, y curativa del Morbo galico, y su verdadero remedio" (About the signs, diagnosis, and healing of *Gálico,* and its true remedy). It summarizes the state of the discussion on *gálico* and the change of perspective in the medical understanding of the disease. I have already mentioned the way in which Brunet de la Selva lamented the growing publication of translations of French treatises to the detriment of the production of knowledge by Spanish doctors, a practice he attacks by claiming that Spain has already had as many and as excellent authors as other foreign countries, "but that they are forgotten by their own people, so much so that, without exaggeration, I can say to you, that those great men are, among us, dead twice over" (3).[2] This is the first treatise in Spanish in which an author clearly claims that *gálico* is incurable: "Gálico is incurable, and without doubt kills the patient when it comes to compromise any internal part [of the body]. [. . .] If it successfully creates a buildup of matter in any of the internal guts, which is what is called an abscess, it is irremediable" (148).[3] To accept the failure of medicine to find a solution to the problem is a radical claim for the time. Brunet's admission of the ineffectiveness of medicine to cure *gálico* goes as far as warning doctors to follow the advice of previous authors: either to avoid treating difficult diseases like this one altogether, or to continue the treatment while admonishing the patient and his family that the situation of the disease is so precarious that the natural and prompt outcome will be death: "this will repute him as wise, and will pardon the contemptible success of the healing" (149).[4] Brunet de la Selva considers almost all treatments nothing more than ways of postponing the outcome of the disease, "but these reliefs, after enduring a few contingencies, are not long-lasting" (155).[5] Brunet de la Selva is also different from the authors of previous treatises because he explains that *gálico* may not manifest itself with textbook clarity but can be hidden behind a number of other diseases, as "a traitorous enemy, who strikes the blow, and hides his hand, and his face" (150).[6] For him, *gálico* takes the shape of very dissimilar ailments, such as "gout of the limbs, hypochondria, kidney stones, canker, leprosy, salty phlegm, malign ulcers, inappropriate flows of the humors" (150),[7] and therefore all of these possible manifestations of the disease must be treated early on with mercury (150). The author represents a middle-ground position that considers *gálico* incurable but at the same time believes that it must be treated with mercury as the palliative of choice— that is, if the agony of mercury may be qualified as comforting.

Brunet de la Selva appears at this point as an author with a more objective vision of treating the disease, at least in a methodological sense, than his peers. He criticizes the voluminous treatises which other authors deem successful but which for him are untested prescriptions that may have been purportedly effective for only a few times as a result of chance. The author makes reference to the many printed books of the time that were packed with instructions for one preparation after another; rather than prescriptions, they could be called "recipes," since they did not provide a clear rationale for their active ingredients or dosage. The widely consulted works of the Portuguese doctor João Curvo Semedo (1635–1719) are good examples of this kind of medical publication; he combined elements of natural medicine with rudiments of the evolving discipline of chemistry in at least nine treatises of great renown in his country and beyond. Curvo's prominence is attested to by the already mentioned Suárez de Ribera, who based a book on Curvo Semedo's work entitled *Ilustracion, y publicacion de los diez y siete secretos del doctor Juan Curvo Semmedo, confirmadas sus virtudes con maravillosas observaciones* (Illustration and publication of the seventeen secrets of the doctor Juan Curvo Semedo, their virtues proven with marvelous observations) (1732). Curvo Semedo's work was so popular among doctors in Spain that it was selected by and translated into Spanish by Tomás Cortijo Herráiz with the enticing title of *Secretos medicos y chirurgicos del doctor don Juan Curbo Semmedo* (Medical and surgical secrets of the doctor Don Juan Curvo Semedo) (1735). This book contains preparations that could be confused with conjuring potions, such as this one to treat *incordios,* the inguinal *bubas* related to *gálico:*[8] "Take a pound of linseed flour, half a pound of finely shredded mature cheese, boil it all in a broth of pig feet, and make a poultice, and put it on the *incordio,* and know that it is a great remedy" (24).[9] Cortijo Herráiz offers the translation of several preparations of "agua antigálica" (anti-*gálico* water) crafted by Curvo Semedo, some of them with very persuasive names such as "Antigalico milagroso" (miraculous anti-*gálico*) or "Agua antigalica infalible" (infallible anti-*gálico* water). In all these remedies, the power of the medicine rests on its discursive presentation or its persuasive name, and not on the intrinsic characteristics of its ingredients: "This is the water with which great authors cured

Not the Same

Although there were no drastic changes or discoveries in regard to *gálico* during the eighteenth century, there were nevertheless steps toward a clearer understanding of venereal diseases. Until the first half of the century, physicians did not see the difference between syphilis and gonorrhea. Gonorrhea was also known as *purgación* or *purgación de garabatillo*. Many doctors believed that gonorrhea was a manifestation of syphilis, rather than a discrete disease. Even a doctor like Juan Manuel Venegas, in his *Compendio de la medicina* of 1788, claimed that if *gálico* was not cured promptly it would finally cause leprosy: "Corrompe los solidos, y causa la lepra" (223). In 1761, the Italian anatomist Giovanni Battista Morgagni (1682–1771) published his *De sedibus et causis morborum per anatomen indagatis* (On the seats and causes of diseases investigated through anatomy). In this treatise, which consolidated Morgagni's fame as the father of modern anatomical pathology by establishing the anatomical basis of disease processes, he explained that gonorrhea and syphilis had different origins and conditions. Nevertheless, Morgagni's observations did not take root. The confusion was not definitely cleared up until 1838, when the French physician Philippe Ricord (1800–1889) explained that the two diseases were different, and that in fact syphilis developed in stages.

---

the hopeless *gálico*. Curvo claims that he is an eyewitness of three persons in pain, so crippled that they couldn't turn over in bed, and with just this water they regained the most perfect health" (27),[10] and later on about a preparation against gonorrhea: "Whoever takes two ounces of sour lemon juice, mixed with two tablespoons of sugar, in the morning for five or six days without any other food, will stay free of gonorrhea, as is shown to be certain by an infinite number of experiences" (28).[11] The effectiveness of this type of prescription was based on or guaranteed by the name of the doctor who revealed the seemingly hermetic secrets of his practice, but there was no factual evidence of their usefulness.

This feature of the revealed secret is a key element in the understanding of *gálico* at the time. Similarly, the tension between revelation and concealment is a key element of our present interpretation of the written manifestations of *gálico*. I have explained how the disease was thought of as a creeping humor or acid that penetrated and unbalanced the body, temporarily appearing as *bubas,* only to hide once again and reappear as gummas, as well as a monstrous gnawing of the nose. Correspondingly, the only known remedies against *gálico* were guaiacum, sarsaparilla, and mercury, which were arcane in nature, with their curative quality hidden within and revealed only in the anticipated salivation and fever they produced. Like Curvo, those who purportedly knew the method to cure *gálico* held the knowledge of their medicine as a secret to be revealed only in the books they published, which were approved by the establishment. In turn, it is literature's double quality of hiding and uncovering, and the often hidden literary production of *gálico,* rediscovered only many years after the death of the authors, that presents an image of its presence in and influence on everyday life of the society of the time. Curvo's claim that the efficacy of his until-now-secret remedy has been proven by "an infinity of experiences" would have worked well within a vision of medicine that was in line with a Scholastic, rhetorical paradigm, but it is clear that Brunet de la Selva's view has been strongly influenced by the scientific method. His approach of systematic doubt demands that a rule be verifiable in most of the cases to which it is applied. If the cases adhere to clearly specified characteristics, and the rule is void only in a few of them, as a result of chance or exception, then the rule—or remedy, in this case—is a worthy postulate. But for Brunet de la Selva, in a jab that seems to be directed at medical authors such as the widely sold Suárez de Ribera or Curvo Semedo, the gathering of more and more recipes in thick volumes does not equate to effectiveness: "What wonders their authors tell us of them! What miracles they tell us they have attained with their application! It would seem to the inexperienced doctor upon reading this, that they have given him complete control over death. He takes up those arms, and when he thinks that he is victorious, he finds himself defeated, because that which seemed to him a sword is a spinning wheel" (152).[12]

For the author, instead of a manly, justice-imparting sword, the naive young doctor now holds a spinning wheel—the property of gossipy women stuck in old long-winded discussions without real outcome. The image of the distaff not only signals masculinity turned into weakness but also directly connects futile effort with inescapable death. In Greek mythology, the Fates (Moirai) decided on the length of every person's life, which was represented by a thread. A distaff, a measuring rod, and a pair of shears respectively symbolized their power to spin, measure, and cut short a man's life. The young doctors may have studied hard, but in vain, for the knowledge they had acquired from long treatises full of conjectures did nothing to prevent the moira Atropos from cutting too early the lives of those suffering from *gálico.* Instead of tangible cures, the newly trained physicians had to continue believing in miracles or in claims bordering on fantasy, and instead of maintaining the façade of warring conquerors of death, they had to face the reality of being continuously defeated by a disease known to Europeans for more than two hundred years.

Skeptics about medicine's ability to cure *gálico* were galvanized around the value of mercury as a remedy. The initial attacks called mercury a venom, as in the late 1730s dispute between Suárez de Ribera and the mysterious Bachiller Philaletes. By 1780 there had been few changes to this discussion, except for clearer and louder explanations of why mercury was not the best or only way of treating *bubas*, such as Dr. Vicente Ferrer Gorraiz's (1718–92) *Cartilla de cirujanos y manual para todos* (Handbook for surgeons and manual for all) (1780). Following the rising trend of translating and incorporating French works, Ferrer's *Cartilla* is in truth a Spanish version of work of the French surgeon Thomas Goulard, who practiced at the Military Hospital in Montpellier. Ferrer's treatise also contains some of his own claims, which in several instances are in frank opposition to the opinions of the original author. Goulard was known for the creation of a preparation called "white water" (*eau blanche*), made with lead oxyacetate, which was also known as "extract of Saturn." Regarding the use of mercury, Ferrer claims that "mercury has caused fatal consequences many times because of its poor preparation, because of being administered in excessive quantity, or because the sick persons are not prepared as is necessary. [. . . This treatise] will show how much it matters to humanity to banish the internal and external use of mercury in the curing of *gálico*" (163).[13] Ferrer calls for assessing "with greater circumspection" ("con la mayor circunspección," 164) all the remedies that contain mercury in the form of *solimán* (mercuric chloride). According to him, all medicines that include mercury in one way or another are "risky, and working upon the intestines sometimes can cause very dangerous colics, and if they come to infect the mass of the blood transmitting their action over the fibers of the most delicate viscera, they will cause terrible irritations, which are remedied with difficulty" (164).[14]

Ferrer mentions several preparations that contain this mercurial corrosive sublimate, including "the anti-*gálico* liquor of Visseman the famous English surgeon, the antivenereal liquor of Ricardo Hautesureq; that of the Baron van Swieten; the pills of Pablo Hartmanc; the anises of Mr. Keyser, my anti-*gálico* tablet, and preparations of the same class" (164).[15] The use of the precise names of these preparations marks an important point in the imbrication of medical discourse and commerce, because they are not named for their generic components or their ascribed properties, but rather after the proper names of their creators (that is, branded) to assure efficacy and purity. Commerce, and commercial advertisement of medicines, although incipient, began to have an important role in the understanding of the disease and the system of beliefs regarding its cure. By the second half of the nineteenth century, the branding and the commercial origin of medical products to treat *gálico* would become guarantees of their supposed effectiveness, especially if they were perceived as coming from places like France or England, which were considered centers of knowledge and progress. At the same time that Ferrer issues cautions about these brand-name remedies with foreign-sounding names, he recommends and guarantees as absolutely effective other remedies with equally commercially catchy names in which mercury is not used. Such is the case with Goulard's "extracto de Saturno," which features Saturn, another god-planet. From the time of the Romans, lead was also known as "Saturn," possibly because of the irritable quality of both the god and the metal. Ferrer maintains that this extract of Saturn "cures it all, as long as it is used wisely" (135).[16] He mentions the "Burgos anti-*gálico* syrup" (162), also known as the "Anti-gálico syrup of the Beinzas" ("jarabe Anti-galico Burgense") or "The Queen Bridge" ("Puente la Reyna," 164), which was created by an apothecary from Navarre named Mathias de Beinza. The principal component of this syrup or mixture is the "selected sarsaparilla of Honduras" ("zarza selecta de Honduras," 165), which had to be split and then broken into small pieces. Spaniards continued to believe that remedies based on American plants or animals were more likely to cure the diseases supposedly from that region.

The Hispanic world's transmission of medical knowledge regarding *gálico* started with the established treatises of authors such as Hippocrates, Avicenna, Galen, and their epigones, as exemplified by Juan Calvo's work. At the beginning of the eighteenth century, these texts were written in Latin and accessible only to a few practitioners of medicine. Over time, although the theory of humors remained prevalent, treatises started to be published in Spanish, using a kind of language comprehensible to doctors with less training who worked in rural areas. Translations and ideas from France were gradually published, as seen in Ferrer's work, but this knowledge from the other side of the Pyrenees produced a negative reaction from doctors who feared the decline of Spanish influence in medical treatments. This discomfort is voiced in Brunet de la Selva's claim that there were no medical authors in Spain, but only medical translators—the ones publishing an exorbitant number of repetitive treatises. The height of this dynamic can be seen in the Spanish translation of Jean Astruc's work. Besides his work on transmittable diseases, the French doctor is known for being the first person to apply exegetical methods of comparison to the study the sources of biblical texts, specifically the book of Genesis. Astruc was a professor of medicine at Montpellier and published his *De morbis venereis* (Of venereal diseases) in Paris in 1740. As was customary, the book was published in Latin, but it was also published in French the same year under the title *Traité des maladies vénériennes* (Treatise of venereal maladies). Thirty-two years later, in 1772, Felix Galisteo y Xiorro, professor of surgery in Madrid, published the Spanish edition of the book in four volumes under the title *Tratado de las enfermedades venereas*. From Latin to French to Spanish, Astruc's treatise became the most important monographic work on syphilis of the time. The fact that Galisteo translated and published it three decades after its first printing proves that the work was widely accepted, and that its ideas clearly summarized the latest advances in the understanding and treatment of *gálico*.[17] The translation demonstrates the increasing influence of French ideas in different areas of knowledge, from medicine to engineering and, more tellingly, from theology to politics, including the ideas of the *Encyclopedia* and the government.

When Astruc wrote *De morbis venereis,* new doctors generally believed that venereal disease was caused by the lack of good nourishment or a sudden corruption of humors. Astruc categorically claims that *gálico* is acquired only through direct contact between a healthy person and a diseased person (4). He also asserts that *gálico* may be transmitted from parents to offspring, a process that he terms "hereditary": "from the *father,* because the particles of the semen communicate the embryo, and the venereal virus by which they are infected: and from the *mother,* because by providing food to the fetus for the whole nine months of her pregnancy, at the same time it makes it [the fetus] participate in the sickness that she suffers [. . .] a father, who suffers this sickness, sometimes engenders children truly infected by it, and covered in ulcers, although the mother is healthy" (Astruc 5; emphasis in the original).[18] This observation counters the general view of women as the main vectors of *gálico* and points out that men are highly responsible for passing the disease to healthy mothers and their offspring. This observation would become especially important in the second half of the nineteenth century, when syphilis was interpreted as a menace to the future of each particular country.

The most important feature of Astruc's work and its translation into Spanish is that it reflects the dispassionate observation of phenomena which had slowly been taking place since Galileo Galilei; at the same time, it shows the way in which the knowledge of three hundred years about the disease was settling into verifiable facts instead of heated opinion. The desire to separate opinion from fact is visible in Astruc's contention that there is no such thing as catching *gálico* by touching the bedding, clothes, or kitchen utensils of a person with the disease. He goes against an idea first presented by Fracastoro in his *De Contagione et Contagiosis Morbis* (1546) that a disease can be acquired by touching a "fomes" or "fomite," that is, an inert object. Because there was an increasingly clear connection between unchecked sexual activity and *gálico,* the theory of contagion via a fomes for this particular disease was appealing to those who wanted their escapades to remain secret, but Astruc bursts their bubble by suggesting that "perhaps all these stories, too, are not more than inventions of the sick, who seek to hide their disorders with lies" (11).[19] In the spirit of the Enlightenment, Astruc is the first to state without beating around the bush that *gálico* also resulted from sexual intercourse between persons of the same sex: "one should also know about the abominable, and against nature, use between persons of the same sex; for in this last case, the person that is healthy acquires the sickness of one who is infected in the same way and even [acquires] a much more dangerous one (14).[20] Following the precepts of reason, Astruc begins to draw a line between social practice and scientific fact. Even though he qualifies this kind of sex as "abominable" in a moral sense, from the medical standpoint the process of contagion is no different from that of normative sex. Equally important, Galisteo y Xiorro's translation is faithful to the French original, and the environment in Spain was ripe enough for this type of assertion to be published without interference from the many institutions of vigilance.

When Astruc summarizes what is known about *gálico* at the medical level, he dismisses the theory of humors and adopts instead the theory of the disease as an acid or salt that enters the body and corrodes it. He expresses doubt about this explanation, however, and deems the idea of the acid more of a good explanatory image than a verifiable fact, "because it is not believable that such a pernicious and active venom could ever be engendered by the human body, it is instead a comparison that serves more to give some idea of the venereal virus, than to explain its nature with precision" (23).[21] He is more cautious about the idea that "the venereal virus is produced by small animals that swim in the blood" (26),[22] a theory already spelled out for the plague in 1646 by the German Jesuit priest Athanasius Kircher (1602–80). Astruc deems this theory a "chimera" and states that he will not even try to refute something that is "denuded of any reason" (26), but at the same time he devotes space to explaining it dispassionately, in very clear and logical terms: "But I will not stop to refute the opinions of those who believe that the venereal virus is nothing more than a numerous swarm of agile, lively, and very fertile, very small animals, that having been received one time quickly multiply, move frequently to different parts of the body, that sting, make holes in, and bite the parts to which they stick themselves, and in this way they inflame, eat away, and ulcerate; and finally, without any alteration of the humors, they produce the symptoms of the venereal disease" (25–26).[23]

It is important to notice that Astruc is still using the original meaning of "virus" as "venom," but the connection he makes with the theory of the disease as an acid or salt already incorporates the idea of an external agent that causes infection in the way we understand the word today. Even when he rejects the idea of microorganisms as producers of disease, he rightly considers that if this theory were correct, it would have revolutionary consequences, as indeed it did, and that it should also be applied to other transmissible diseases, such as pestilence, smallpox, rabies, scabies, and herpes (27).[24] The revolutionary upheaval adumbrated by Astruc would come about a century later with the emergence of the germ theory of disease epitomized by the works of Louis Pasteur (1822–95) and Robert Koch (1843–1910), but right now the author reasons that believing in the capacity of very small animals in the blood to

From Humoral Theory to Germ Theory

Although the tenets of the humoral theory of disease were still present in the everyday practice of medicine, by the first half of the eighteenth century they were under attack. Microscopic observation of plague victims' blood during the outburst of 1656 in Rome spurred the German Jesuit polymath Athanasius Kircher (1602–80) to claim that *vermes* (little worms) caused the epidemic. Kircher wrote about his observations in the treatise *Scrutinium physico-medicum contagiosae luis, qua dicitu pestis* (1658), making him one of the earliest proposers of germ theory (Fletcher 49). In his book *Les microbes organisés* (1878), the French biologist Louis Pasteur (1822–95) explained the connection between microbes and putrefaction, an observation that led to the investigation of particles as the cause of disease. In 1876, the German physician Robert Koch (1843–1910) discovered the relation between the aerobic bacterium *Bacillus anthracis* and the lethal anthrax infection, thus explaining the connection between specific germs and diseases as well as the mechanics of how disease travels from one host to another. The method of inoculating chicken with the weakened bacteria of cholera to immunize the animals was first developed in 1879 by Pasteur. This method is still in use today.

cause disease "would be a most egregious error" ("seria un grandisimo disparate," 27).

Although he attacks such theories, the scientific method is part of his thinking, and it pushes him to leave open the possibility of accepting them if someone were to produce verifiable evidence. He even mentions in some detail the quackery of a man named Boyle—not to be confused with the Irish-English chemist Robert Boyle (1627–91)—who in 1726 promoted in Paris the idea of particularly small animals in the blood as the cause of different diseases; in turn, these animals had natural enemies that could attack them "in the same way that hunting dogs destroy hares, or falcons doves" (27).[25] According to Boyle, his knowledge of each animal and its enemies through microscopic observations gave him the power of curing diseases. He used a rigged microscope that allowed him to show evidence of his claims, but ultimately it turned out to be, of course, a swindle. Astruc happily reports that the scam was revealed, but at the same time he laments that even very smart men from intellectual circles fell into the trap, because it was presented within the logic that states that if something can be proved using the scientific method then it may be acceptable: "These are the falsehoods that this astute, and shameless charlatan dared to present to the public in a century so enlightened, and instructed in the subjects of physics, as ours, and in a city like Paris, full of such able citizens" (30).[26] Still, the advanced, refined level of the swindler's claim shows how many changes there had been in the scientific understanding of transmissible diseases since the theory of humors. The charlatan was able to go very far among educated men precisely because he used instruments and arguments connected to advanced inquiries and mirrored the forward-looking spirit of science: it was a kind of fiction that was plausible, a discourse that although invented was believable, and a story rooted in factual science, more in line with stories published by Jules Verne one hundred years later about a submarine than with Cervantes's quixotic tales about windmills.

This kind of description, which functions inside a framework of plausibility, was used not only by swindlers like Boyle but also by Astruc himself. The professor employed it to explain to his contemporary readers how the virus that produces *gálico* enters the body and becomes a disease: "After having infected the parts of the body into which it was introduced, it penetrates the blood imperceptibly, which happens in my opinion in two ways, either by the circulation of the blood, which flows through the damaged parts, and picks up some of the virus as it passes through, or by the circulation of lymph, which, returning from these same parts, carries with it the blood to where it will deposit, through particular veins, many drops of this virus" (38).[27] Astruc's explanation of *gálico*'s communication through the body is as unproven as Boyle's attribution of the disease to little *gálico* animals in the blood. Yet, both explanations are equally plausible because they are based on relatively new knowledge that allowed for more room to interpret reality. Boyle, the charlatan, was making good use of previously acknowledged ideas such as Athanasius Kircher's 1658 discussion of "animalcules," and of important relatively recent technologies such as the microscope. Astruc, the physician of noblemen, based his explanation on William Harvey's (1578–1657) account of the circulation of blood and the production of lymph in his 1628 *De Motu Cordis* (On the motion of the heart). Boyle escaped certain imprisonment, and his work has long been lost in the annals of history. Astruc is considered a founder of modern biblical exegesis and the writer of a capital study on venereal diseases and syphilis.

The prevalence of Astruc's views and explanations in Spain is attested to by the fact that his translator, don Félix Galisteo y Xiorro, published an abridged version of the *Tratado de las enfermedades venereas* almost two decades later, in 1791. Galisteo reduced the four volumes of 1772 into a cheaper single volume, targeting both urban practitioners who needed factual information to provide treatment and rural doctors who "tend to lack books for lack of means, and the venereal disease [tends to] abound in the town for an excess of vices" (v).[28] Galisteo's prologue is relevant because he describes the state of medicine in Spain. For him, the discipline has gained social stature: it is now protected by the king and has become more open to the positive influence of theories and doctors from other countries, especially France. He claims that the role of translations in this process has been vital, and of course deems his own translation a good example of what can be achieved through the study and implementation of knowledge from other countries. In an article titled "Notas sobre la traducción científica y técnica en el siglo XVIII" (Notes on scientific and technical translation in the seventeenth century), Josefa Gómez de Enterría Sánchez places French writings as a long-awaited, almost messianic source of positive ideas and summarizes this moment of reaccommodation of knowledge in Spain: "In the second half of the century the modernization of surgery and medicine will be delivered in enlightened Spain; the translations of foreign bibliographies will be those which make this reality possible. [...] The intense activity developed regarding the translation by the brothers Juan and Félix Galisteo Xiorro, surgeon and doctor respectively, makes it possible for us to consider them as true translators of medical texts thanks to the numbers of the versions of treatises that they publish relentlessly between the years 1761 and 1807, with which they introduce to our country the latest advances of enlightened European medicine" (41).[29]

By the time Galisteo publishes his abridged edition of Astruc's work, the translator does not need to preach to the choir of possible medical readers the gospel of salvation written in France. Gone are the days when Latin was the language in which the most important works of science were written. French has taken its place: "The compliments are not necessary, nor is any recommendation for a work that is already so acclaimed, whose method is now followed by all the judicious physicians, and that has earned the fact that the Sovereign approves the choice made by the teachers whose role it is to teach this branch of surgery to use it in the new college erected in this court under his royal protection" (vi).[30]

The work of Astruc translated by Galisteo in relation to the understanding of *gálico* replicated the way in which ideas and knowledge from France were reappropriated in Spain, and consequently in the Spanish-speaking Americas. As the century reached its apogee, these French ideas became mainstream, which produced feelings of hope and change in some, and fear and revulsion in others. By the end of the century, the name of "*gálico*"—also known as *el mal francés* (the French evil)—represented the fears and hopes attached to the comings and goings of Spain's neighbors in the north. Not only did the French disease produce pustules in the skin of Spanish people at all levels of society, it also caused itching in relation to the reforms inspired by the French, which were appropriated, developed, and implemented by enlightened men such as Feijoo, Jovellanos, and Meléndez Valdés.

ᕲ 7

Naming the Disease: The French Malady

The connection between the disease, the menacing influence of French ideas, and Spain's economic and military rivalry with France stems from the Italian War of 1494–98. The first outbreak of syphilis in Europe supposedly took place when the French, led by King Charles VIII, took Naples from Ferdinand of Aragon in 1495. During this period, armies from Italy, France, and Spain had contact. The disease started claiming victims on all sides and acquired its multiple names from the enemies to which the disease was attributed. By 1498, under the leadership of "The Great Captain," Gonzalo Fernández de Córdoba, Spanish troops recovered Naples from the French. This military success boosted the animosity between the two nations and reinforced the Spaniards' labeling of the disease as *gálico* or *mal francés*. Gonzalo Fernández de Oviedo (1478–1557), who was secretary to The Great Captain during the Naples campaign, offers an early explanation of the connections between the disease and the meaning of France in the Spanish imaginary. Fernández de Oviedo is one of the first chroniclers of the Indies, and his writings are an important point of departure in studying descriptions of the New World, as well as an early source about the image and identity of the recently discovered continent. In the introductory paragraph of book 2, chapter 14, of his *Historia general y natural de las indias* (General and natural history of the Indies) (1535), the author complains about the waste of gold brought from the New Continent: "Because so much of the gold of the Indies has gone to Italy and France and even to the Moors and other enemies of Spain, and to all other parts of the world, it is fitting that since they have profited from our sweat that they should share some of our pain and misfortunes, because in everything, whether it be of gold or of labor, they should remember to give many thanks to God" (115).[1]

The chronicler is referring to the hefty amounts of gold taken from the New World. He does not mention, of course, that this gold was taken forcefully from the natives—for example, in the sacking of their camps—or obtained under duress, as in the case of the infamous ransom Francisco Pizarro received for freeing Atahualpa. Gold was also extracted from the Indians through slavery. The author sees with bitterness how the gains rendered by the enterprise of conquest and colonization of the new territories are undeservedly benefit-

Gonzalo Fernández de Oviedo

Gonzalo Fernández de Oviedo (1478–1557), a native of Madrid who first traveled to the Americas in 1513, published one of the earliest works on the flora and fauna of the region in 1535. His *Historia general y natural de las Indias* also details the discovery and conquest of the regions that correspond with present-day Mexico and Peru. What this collection of nineteen volumes is best known for, however, is its detailed descriptions of natural features unique to the Americas and never before seen by Europeans. Bartolomé de las Casas (1484–1566), a friar and a well-known defender of the rights of the indigenous people of the Americas, took issue with Fernández de Oviedo's representation of them in his *Historia general,* claiming that he saw them as being lesser than Europeans and made moral judgments about their customs and behavior. Nevertheless, the *Historia general* is recognized for the value of its catalog and its scientific descriptions of plants and animals, which were made before the procedures for such descriptions were standardized. Like many of the chroniclers of his time, Fernández de Oviedo lacked academic training as a scientist or a scribe. Chronicles such as the *Historia general* were valued at the time for the author's authority as a firsthand witness to the phenomena about which he wrote. Fernández de Oviedo was named "Cronista de las Indias" in 1532, and he held the position of *alcalde* (deputy) of the fortresses of Santo Domingo and La Española.

ing Spanish rivals. The gold of the Indies is spreading throughout the Old World, touching all strata of society and bringing opulence to those for whom he reckons it was not intended. The transitional sentence in Fernández de Oviedo's passage embodies a strange sort of generosity: "It is fitting that since they have profited from our sweat that they should share some of our pain and misfortunes." The structure of the chapter makes it initially difficult to understand what pain and what sweat he is referring to.

After this enigmatic introduction, the chronicler goes on to narrate what would become oft-cited references to the *bubas* disease. He writes about the "generous introduction" of syphilis to Europe by Columbus's crew after the second voyage, pointing to the infection's eventful trip, from the (most likely) violent sexual encounters with indigenous women to the crew members' ship berths, and after a few more close and itchy encounters to foot soldiers' cots in the Neapolitan campaign, and then to noblemen's chambers or the beds of churchmen. After several pages of this sort of description, it becomes clear that the pain and sweat Fernández de Oviedo wishes to share with the French, the Italians, and the Moors, whom he sees as "enemies of Spain," are those produced by *gálico.* Like the gold from the Indies, the disease has spread quickly without heeding the barriers of language or religion because it has the audacity to ignore the bonds of servitude to king, sultan, or pope. Very much like gold, it flooded the continent, and very much like gold it was minted to represent and establish exchanges, not of wealth and power, but of fear, weakness, and death. If gold had become the good treasure of the Indies, syphilis had become its hidden evil—the other side of the desired proverbial gold coin. With cynical tongue in cheek, Fernández de Oviedo affirms that even though the disease had been labeled in connection with other European powers, it was clear that its true source was beyond the Atlantic: "Many times while in Italy I would laugh to myself upon hearing the Italians speak about the 'French disease,' and the French call it the 'Neapolitan disease,' when in reality each would have described it correctly had they called it the disease of the Indies" (115).[2]

He chides those who have benefited from Spanish gold and admonishes them that with every dram of gold they hold there is a *buba,* a sore from the Indias—both the place and the indigenous women—and thinking about such painful retribution, he laughs. This antithetical logic explains why, in the first paragraph of the text, he states that "they should remember to give many thanks to God." For him, if the Italians, the Moors, and the French who benefited from the gold of the Indies were not going to thank God, in the end they would have to reckon with the divine. Protection from the pain of pustules and the anguish of induced fevers cannot be bought with a freshly minted coin.

The rivalry between the Spanish and the French intensified over time. The French were defeated at the Battle of Pavia in 1525 and their king, Francis I (1494–1547), was made prisoner. In spite of the many marriages between nobles from the two countries that were aimed at keeping peace during those years, the mix of disdain and fear between the two parties was never resolved. By the eighteenth century, with the change of dynasty from the Austrian Habsburgs to the French Bourbons, the ambiguous combination of deep cultural influence and profound rivalry was widespread. Following the crowning of Philip V, the Spanish court saw increasing numbers of French advisers and courtiers. As I explained above, the culture from France began to exercise greater influence, and soon many translations of French books started to appear. The upsurge of things French in the everyday culture of the Spaniards was rapidly connected to the spread of the disease that bore the French name. Since there were feelings of uneasiness toward the French, making their culture synonymous with the disease was an easy, almost automatic metonymic path.

Those who accepted, admired, or incorporated elements of French culture into their lives were easily labeled as diseased people, or as vectors of disease. Since prostitutes were thought to be the source of *gálico,* those inclined toward the French culture were accused openly or in a veiled way of having prostituted themselves. Such was the case with translators, who were often accused of being the cause of negative cultural contagion. One of the most important works of the eighteenth century, *Historia del famoso predicador fray Gerundio de Campazas* (The history of the famous preacher Friar Gerund de Campazas) (1758), written by José Francisco de Isla (1703–81), contains a radical criticism of translators of French texts, comparing them with the venereal disease. Through the voice of the sensible priest don Carlos, Isla complains about the increase of French words and grammatical structures in everyday speech in Spain and about the surge of bad translations and bad translators of French books. He affirms that "there is now a plague of translators; for almost all translations are a plague" (498).[3] His comparison goes beyond the old image of the plague as the representation of the most feared disease and jumps instead to the image of French ideas present in bad translations as parallel to the *mal francés*:

> What I say is that, in short, the bad, the perverse, the ridiculous, the extravagant, or the idiot translators are what have most principally contributed to the destruction of our language, corrupting our words as much as our soul. They are the ones who have given our poor idiom the French disease, for the cure of which will not suffice all the mercury prepared by the judicious pen of the elegant Fracastorius, *unicum illum Ulcera qui jussit castas tractare camenas* [the only one who made the chaste Muses get treated for their ulcers].
>
> These are the people who have so contrived that neither in our conversations, nor in our personal letters, nor in our public writings, can we see ourselves because of the French dust; I mean, that it seems as if they keep no other sand in their pounce pot than that of the Loire, the Rhone, or the Seine, they so unsparingly sprinkle all they write with gallicisms or French things. (497–98)[4]

For Isla, the disease of the body is a lesser evil compared to the disease of the spirit by which language is infected with foreign influences. As demonstrated by the creation of the Real Academia de la Lengua at the beginning of the century, purifying and anchoring the language of Spain was a task invested with great symbolic significance because it represented the soul of the Spanish people as unified and preeminent. The fact that the language was supposedly becoming more and more polluted with French words and grammatical forms meant that the strength of the Spaniards was being lost amid venereal and cultural disease, and in this instance for Isla the corruption of the language is equivalent to the corruption of the soul—a loss of Spanishness. Those touched by *gálico* could hope to be cured with mercury, but the disease of the Spanish soul, represented by a contaminated language and contaminating

José Francisco de Isla

José Francisco de Isla (1703–81) was a Jesuit friar who also served as a professor of philology and theology. Father Isla was forced to leave Spain in 1767 when the Jesuit order was expelled from the country. His most celebrated work is *Fray Gerundio de Campazas* (1758, 1768), which enjoyed immediate popularity upon publication of the first part, but was then banned by the Inquisition in 1759 for its criticism of priests and friars. In this work, Isla depicts the exaggerated preaching styles of friars, as well as their misuse of Latin, incorrect citations of sacred texts, obsessions with hygiene and with their own manner of dressing, and overall hypocritical behavior. This was an attack not only on the friars themselves but also on the general public for following unquestioningly their misguided and hypocritical teachings. This work is in part a social critique of eighteenth-century Spain, as well as a didactic manual on the art of composing and delivering a sermon. The humor and sarcasm used by Isla in *Fray Gerundio* does not take away from the seriousness of his challenge to men of the cloth, but rather makes for sharper criticism.

ideas, did not have recourse to a radical medicine that would expel the evil by means of salivation and sweat. For Isla, the ultimate result of the disease present in the Spanish soul is demise itself.

Isla is not against translations per se, but he disapproves of the rapid consumption of French texts that have not been processed and properly translated into Spanish. Instead, the translation must be a true reformulation of the foreign text into something that is in fact new because it is the result of processing and recasting the language, but the lack of rigor on the part of translators has become the weakness by which Spanish culture has become infected with a debilitating disease. While a medical translator like Galisteo saw translations as vehicles of progress and well-being, Isla's don Carlos places them at the same level as *bubas,* and translators at the same level as infecting prostitutes who have sold out to the French, and then sell themselves again to their fellow Spaniards. But Isla is very careful to aim his big guns at translators, not directly at French authors, French ideas, or French people. After all, one must remember, the ruling Ferdinand VI's father was French, and he was himself closely related to the French royal family. The French disease was too close for comfort, and rhetorical negotiation was something that Spanish authors knew how to do well, especially after many years of experiencing the watchful eye of the Holy Inquisition. Isla's popular *Fray Gerundio* voices concern about the presence of a French power that could not be defeated with the mere use of military prowess, as had been done historically. Recalling the military victories of the Spanish against the troops of their neighbors on the other side of the Pyrenees was not enough, because the influence of French ideas was entering the Spanish body, sneaking in behind pleasurable texts and lax translations in the same way that *gálico* infected the bodies of those given to corporal unchecked pleasures. The French influence, now connected with and named after the disease, was pervading everyday life. This fear of contamination is evident in Isla's account of a poor translation of a French book of dubious worth that had become immensely popular: "Which, although it is an inquiry among the wise to decide if it is more profitable or harmful, has nevertheless had a prodigious following. No library, public or private, no cell, no writing hutch, no parlor, nor scarcely a podium is to be found without it; insomuch that even the lapdogs play with it on the chairs" (498).[5] By mentioning lapdogs, Isla is indirectly pointing to the fact that even and especially women were being influenced; that is, they were being infected with the French disease through these translations, which punctured the gates of the private sphere.

Another iconic literary figure of Spain, Tomás de Iriarte (1750–91), agreed with the condemnation of French translations as a damaging influence. Especially known for his didactic *Fábulas* (Fables), Iriarte wrote several letters to his friend José Cadalso, the renowned author of the *Cartas marruecas* (Moroccan letters) mentioned above, about his views on what modern medicine should be. In one of Iriarte's letters of 1774, written in verse to his friend, who was away in Montijo in the western province of Extremadura, Iriarte tells him that he should not be jealous for not being at the court in Madrid. Iriarte criticizes the declining quality of education and the interests of high society there, the lack of elevated discussions in literary gatherings where the "Musas Españolas y Latinas" (Spanish and Latin muses) are absent (*Colección de obras* 3), and the dependence of Spanish scientific knowledge on advancements from the northern countries, especially France. In his opinion, the members of the new generation now occupying positions in the court had not had a proper education and were prone to the pleasures of leisure, to indolence, and to superficial knowledge. This slackness could be seen in the language used in regular conversation and in general publications. According to Iriarte, the new writers did not care about using a polished discourse, free of foreign constructions and poor wording: "They write it without rules or care; / They speak it by habit; / They do not respect its refined standing; / No one studies it; everyone corrupts it" (6).[6] Like Isla, Iriarte blames bad translators for the decline of the Spanish language, and the most poignant and clear way that he finds of attacking this decay is by equating foreign ideas and foreign linguistic influence from France to venereal French disease:

They are, oh Dalmiro, the perverse
Traitors of the language of their land
Doing unceasing war against it.
Oh! The just Apollo willing,
(I ask him thus in my poor verses)
That whatever they write in their life,
May remain, as archived in protocol,
In the back room of the most foolish bookseller;
That not even the candy makers may receive it,
That it is not even worth using for fireworks
or as carpeting in gloomy latrines!
Yes, clueless translators:
Let my anathema fall over you
Immoral Corruptors,
You, who have given the pure Castilian language,
a Gallic pustule,
leaving it with no healthy body part.[7] (Iriarte, *Colección* 7–8)

In a compilation of letters written by Spanish authors, Eugenio de Ochoa includes Iriarte's original letter, restoring two verses that were deleted when it first appeared. After the verse "In the back room of the most foolish bookseller," the two additional verses that add to the idea of putrefaction in the societal body of Spain: "That of them only the worms shall live / and eternal dust shall soil that property" (Ochoa 212).[8] The qualifications ascribed to the translators refurbish the image initially crafted by Isla and create a palette of signifiers connecting the French influence with ideas ranging from homosexuality to treason. Translators are idle, subservient, perverted, treacherous, corrupting, and bearers of disease. Iriarte believes that these carriers of the French disease have infected Spanish language, which is interestingly portrayed as a virginal woman. The translators have produced a venereal abscess—what was commonly known as an *incordio*—in the Spanish language's very reproductive center. As with the real *gálico,* this "Gálica apostema" has spread to the rest of the body. The symbolic consequence of this comparison is very disturbing, because from everyday experience it was clear that the result of acquiring the disease was almost inescapably death, and therefore the fear of those like Iriarte was that Spanish cultural prevalence was doomed to perish. The image of the purity of Spanish language and culture reflects the problem that resulted from the economic prevalence of the empire during the previous three centuries, which produced an impervious culture that lost strength by not opening itself early on to the renewal that foreign ideas could have brought. The virginal Spanish language may have remained pure, but in its perceived purity it also

Tomás de Iriarte

Tomás de Iriarte (1750–91) came from a prosperous aristocratic family, and as a court-ier in Madrid, he befriended the likes of Nicolás Fernández de Moratín and José de Cadalso. Iriarte belonged to the generation of Spanish intellectuals known as the *ilus-trados* (enlightened ones). He was an accomplished translator of French and Greek, as well as a playwright, musician, and author. He is most known for his didactic *fábulas* (fables), which fit within the conception of literature favored by the men of the Enlight-enment as being not only useful but also enjoyable (*dulce e útil*). Whereas the fables of Félix María Samaniego (1745–1801) were meant to be read by the children of the nobil-ity—the future heads of state—Iriarte's fables had a broader audience. Many of Iriarte's fables touch on the relationship between the people and their government. At the time, the Spanish government conceived of itself as a reign of *despotismo ilustrado,* or enlight-ened despotism. The king held absolute power, and made decisions supposedly for the good of his people, but without any of their input. In his fable "El jardinero y su amo," from his collection *Fábulas literarias* (1782), Iriarte toys with the idea that the people do not need to obey their leader without question, but instead have power themselves. The belief in the will of the individual was also part of Enlightenment thinking.

became weak and endogamous. This is why Iriarte laments that a country that used to be the producer of knowledge is now a passive, penetrated pupil: "Two centuries ago Master of the Sciences, / And in our century an apprentice to those from the North!" (*Colección* 4).[9] Instead of a slow change resulting from reasoned engagement with the advancements that were taking place in the other European powers—understandably avoided because those were the en-emies with which Spain engaged in continuous war—Spain experienced sud-den and continuous influence from France after the death of the last Habsburg king in 1700.

Iriarte's solution to the infection brought about by the bad translators of French texts is symptomatic of the helplessness he felt vis-à-vis the strong and continued prevalence of French ideas not only in Spain but also in the rest of Europe. The biggest gun he can produce to counter the bad influence of these translators is a curse that he hopes the just but also ineffective Apollo will back. He prays that the translators' books be consigned to a dark room in a book-store, and that the paper on which their translations are printed be deemed so filthy that not even fireworks or latrine mats are made with them. That Iriarte wishes to save the future of the Spanish ethos with a feeble jinx seems preposterous. Nevertheless, one important move in Iriarte's discourse is that he counters the idea of decay and decomposition represented by French influence with an attack that wishes similar decay and putrefaction on the vectors of this ideological disease. It is true that Iriarte is talking about the depletion of the form of the Spanish language and not of the French ideas themselves, but his condemnation and cursing of the disseminators of French texts strikes me as an ironic contradiction, knowing that Iriarte was accused by the Inquisition for being himself too prone to the ideas of French authors that were spread in Spain via the same kind of translations he had criticized; he was himself a translator of French theatrical works, and he had been official translator in a high office of the state.

Three decades after Isla's *Fray Gerundio* and five years after Iriarte's letter to Cadalso, Eugenio de Santa Cruz y Espejo (1747–95) published one of his most important texts, *El Nuevo Luciano de Quito o Despertador de los ingenios quiteños* (The New Lucian of Quito or Awakener of Quito's acumen) (1779), on the other side of the Atlantic. Espejo was born in Quito, a city deeply influenced by the church's power over education and political developments. He is considered to be an emblematic encyclopedist and an enlightened thinker, lawyer, and physician, and he embodies the learned individual who would provide the kind of understanding of his reality that would later be the basis for ideas of independence in the American Spanish colonies. The dialogues in *El Nuevo Luciano* aim to reveal and attack the lack of useful education in the Royal Audiencia of Quito. Espejo's style is not particularly refined, and his harsh use of satire, mocking tone, and derision underscores his goal of provoking immediate reactions among his readers. One of his main targets is the type of education offered by the Jesuits for fostering an unnecessarily intricate use of language; such affected language masked the lack of real knowledge among learned people in the colony.

The two main participants in Espejo's dialogues are Dr. Murillo and Dr. Mera. Murillo longs for the days when the Jesuits, expelled in 1773, were the almost exclusive providers of education in Quito. He represents a superficially educated man who masks his ignorance with pompous diction and stilted language that remind the reader of the sermons of Fray Gerundio in Isla's work. Aware of his deficient knowledge, Murillo is resistant to change and would prefer to block new sectors of society from gaining access to newly developed forms of training, an attitude that is further communicated by his name, which means "small wall"—that is, a small obstacle that may be surpassed with a more structured and forward-looking system of education. His opposite, Dr. Mera, whose name is connected with simplicity and good sense—*mero* in Spanish means "pure" or "plain"—defends ideas in line with the Enlightenment and attacks the perception that the education imparted by the Jesuits is complete and infallible. Mera quotes and supports ideas proposed by French authors, especially those of Dominique Bohours (1628–1702), a Jesuit priest who defended sophistication of the spirit without pretentiousness or artificiality. The portrayal of French ideas and their translation as a source of infection of the Spanish language and of Spanishness, which is so clear in Isla's *Fray Gerundio* for the peninsular case, changes its polarity and becomes positive when viewed from an American perspective by Espejo. The enlightened viewpoints brought from France are interpreted by this creole of the colony as a constructive influence that incorporates, among other things, the understanding that knowledge is accessible to all people, and that accessibility is the first step toward the improvement of education and the amelioration of the economic situation of the Spanish possessions on the New Continent.

When Mera defends simplicity as a balanced way of imitating nature and getting close to truth, he rattles Murillo, who immediately connects his opponent's ideas to French thinkers and tells him that some kind of bad fever is getting to him (20). Murillo sarcastically suggests that he does not want to tell Mera what kind of remedy to take, fearing that it would reveal the kind of disease that a cleric like Mera should not have. Mera responds that instead of beating around the bush, Murillo should tell him what is supposedly his ailment and what should be the remedy:

> *Dr. Murillo.* I will say or cognomen the ailment, if you, sir, chance to give me this
> permission; but I will not give you the specific antidote, because that would
> make you expel from your cavernous meatus the final spittle.
> *Dr. Mera.* As a doctor you do not need my permission to warn me of the disease
> and advise me of the remedy. Furthermore, it is already understood, Doctor,
> what it is. You want to advise the use of mercury.
> *Dr. Murillo.* Yes, Sir, a few metallic-mercurial unctions. (20)[10]

In this new formulation of the parallel between French ideas and the French disease, the pretentious doctor names the remedy, thinking that Mera will immediately feel defeated by his wisdom (*echar la última baba*) in the same way that a person with *bubas* suffers the terrible effects of the treatment with mercury. To Dr. Mera's simple question of why Murillo accuses him of being infected with the French disease, the ignorant doctor responds in the swollen, unnatural style that his opponent was criticizing:

> *Dr. Mera.* But where do I suffer from the French disease?
> *Dr. Murillo.* In all your intercostal bones, in all your visceral myologies, throughout your crimson lacteal substance, in all your mechanical body, and in all
> your intelligencial spirit. You are entirely full of the miasmas of the French
> disease, and gallicized in all the putrid breath you breathe. (20–21)[11]

Miasma

Murillo's reference to contagion through miasma shows his reliance on dated medical ideas. The word "miasma" comes from the Greek word for "pollution." For centuries it was believed that diseases were spread through poisoned air (miasma), usually the result of organic matter in the process of putrefaction. Other sources of miasmatic transmission included stagnant or contaminated water, enclosed quarters, and bad hygiene. With changes in scientific experimentation, including the use of the microscope, miasma theory was replaced with the germ theory in the second half of the nineteenth century as the explanation for contagion.

Espejo uses Murillo's reactionary discourse to ridicule a sector of society in Spain and the colonies that had become an uncouth mimicry without substance of the style of the Golden Age: "But come on, I can see that you are a legitimate son of the most grandiloquent poets, so that to say one thing you use more metaphors and allegories than all of them. As it is right now, to tell me that I am addicted to the French" (21).[12] Mera aims to debunk a now-exhausted approach to knowledge, but his effort is countered by Murillo's sweeping claim that any move toward change of the status quo is equivalent to foreign disease: "those like you want us to follow the fashion of their hair adornments, abandoning our curly quiff and our haughty cap; to follow their frigid nature, abandoning our meteoric lofty sublimity. That is how you have become frenchified. I will say again that you need some dribbling" (21).[13] Murillo equates change, balance, and moderation with frenchification and therefore with an infection of the mind that needs radical expulsion. His repeated effort to make his opponent "throw out the last bit of spit" (*echar la última baba*), or need to spit (*necesita babeo*), could even be interpreted as threatening Mera with the Santo Oficio, a place well-known for making life miserable for the accused and for wringing the last drop of "information" from those who visited their quarters.

According to Murillo's sweeping statement, Mera's inclination toward simplicity as a path to gaining knowledge is a coarse incorporation of French ideas without reflection—that is, a form of plagiarism (21). Mera assumes that his opponent knows what the French thinkers have said—the ideas he has supposedly lifted—and challenges him to prove it. Murillo's reaction is not to support his claim but to defend his ignorance with the excuse that he avoids readings that may damage his soul:

Dr. Murillo. Stop there, my Sir. May the Omnipotent Trinity not want that I see
nor read such Monsieurs. That would be to become an atheist, that is why I do
not want to indoctrinate myself in that damned language that makes everyone
heresiarchs. I shall not read them. But I have heard that they, and very much in
their lead Voltaire, hereticate more heretic than Arrio himself, say with heretical depravity that those poets ignored what they poeticized.

Dr. Mera. They have told you quite wrong, your grace. The first thing to warn
you of is (listen carefully so that this does not also end up being seen as French
plagiarized bricolage) that in every nation there have been literati with good
taste, who have spoken either against the corruption of poetry, or against the
abuse of it.[14]

With this defense of complete ignorance, Murillo is used by Espejo to epit-
omize deficiencies of the elite in Quito: they read only pious books, but not
the Bible; they label anything foreign, especially anything French, as heretic
or atheist; they know of the writings of the "enemy" not because they have
read them themselves, but because they have overheard somewhere a simplistic
and trite opinion of these works. What Espejo is criticizing in the archetype
of Murillo is what the Colombian critic Rafael Gutiérrez Girardot would call
"vignette culture" (*cultura de viñeta*): a watered-down culture, a copy of a copy
of independent interpretation; a clichéd, superficial reading that is accepted
and glorified by the status quo because it serves as a tool to maintain control
in the hands of the manorial elites (448). In the case of Espejo, his portrayal
is far more violent because those who want to have a firsthand approach to
new knowledge are immediately signaled as diseased, and worse, venereally
diseased.

But the proof that these ideas of the French Enlightenment were in fact
well studied and critically received in the American colonies, and not just
simply plagiarized, is that a few years later these notions would become the
seed for emancipatory movements on the continent. In America, this French
disease produced indeed a feverish reaction; in fact, it became a fever of
revolution and independence. One important instance of the effect of this
French disease was to come fourteen years after the publication of the *Nuevo
Luciano* by means of the translation of an inflammatory French document
in the Viceroyalty of Nueva Granada, adjacent to Espejo's Quito. Antonio
Nariño (1765–1823), a pro-independence member of the local elite in Santafé
(today Bogotá), translated and clandestinely published in 1793 the *Declaration of the Rights of Man and of the Citizen,* only four years after its signing by
the French National Constituent Assembly in 1789. This explosive document
was the most important outcome of the French Revolution, especially because

it claimed that there are universal rights in nature that supersede the power of a monarchic government. The Spanish Holy Inquisition had prohibited the circulation of the Declaration or of its ideas, and when Nariño's authorship was revealed, he was convicted of high treason and sentenced to prison. Nariño's translation was just the compilation in one document of all the ideas and sections of the Declaration that had already been circulated and discussed in newspapers and literary gatherings in Spain, in other words, the *mal francés* of the Declaration had already surreptitiously entered the Spanish body. What Nariño had done was to make the infestation public as a symptom in one of the faraway colonies — to use the image of *gálico* symptoms, as a pustule in a peripheral extremity and not as a centralized, say in Madrid or Salamanca, *inguinal incordio*. The texts in Nariño's translation defended individual freedom and equality before the law, the right to resist oppression, the right to honor the general will of an organized society and the self-determination of a community without distinction of its provenance, and more importantly, the freedom to express divergent opinions. There was reason for the Inquisition and the viceroyal administration to condemn Nariño as a dangerous vector of ideological infection in the colonies: the Declaration contained the dangerous seeds to philosophically justify their independence. The center of power in the Spanish metropolis, and its followers in the colonies á la Murillo, were right to fear the *mal francés* as an infection. On the other hand, the unsatisfied criollos in the colonies who felt the weight of their marginal position, such as the character Mera or the persecuted Nariño, would have seen this *mal francés,* not as a disease, but instead as a remedy for their situation.

Since peninsular writers remained unaware of the profound political outcomes brought about by the translations of French authors that were qualified as disease, their main line of attack continued to be the fear of the decay of the Spanish language. This is the case with Juan Pablo Forner (1756–97), considered to be one of the main figures of the Spanish Enlightenment and one of the most acid critics of his time. Published after his death, *Exequias de la lengua castellana: Sátira menipea* (Obsequies of the Castilian language: Menippean satire) (1871) attests to the preoccupation with the weakening of the language and its supposed imminent death already signaled by Iriarte. It is ironic that although Forner had a visceral aversion to Iriarte, he continues the same form of attack that the author of the *Fábulas* had adopted. In his introduction to the *Exequias,* critic José Jurado claims that the beginnings of Forner's work date back to 1783 (1), placing his attacks against translators of French books only four or five years after Espejo's in the colony of Quito and therefore confirming that the image of the metaphorical *mal francés* was already common. Forner's work is written in the manner of the Menippean satire, which combines poetry and prose and aims to criticize the attitudes of a distinct social

Juan Pablo Forner

Juan Pablo Forner (1756–97) was a Spanish writer of the eighteenth century known primarily for his satirical work and for his debates with other prominent literary figures of the time, such as Tomás de Iriarte. When a dispute arose between Iriarte and Juan Meléndez Valdés, a close friend of Forner, Forner lost little time in defending his friend by publishing *El asno erudito, fábula original, obra póstuma de un poeta anónimo* (1782), in which he presented a biting satire of Iriarte. This polemic between the two continued in their literary works. Conservative in his views on culture and literature, Forner defended the traditional Catholic values that were the foundation of Spanish culture and praised figures of Spanish humanism such as Juan Luis Vives. In works such as the *Sátira contra los vicios introducidos en la poesía castellana* (1782) and the *Oración apologética por la España y su mérito literario* (1786), Forner mounted attacks against claims made by the French and other European powers that Spain had made little or no contribution to developing the collective culture and literature of Europe. He resisted the influence of *afrancesado* intellectuals, seeking to maintain the purity of the Castilian language and its literature of the Golden Age. His *Exequias de la lengua castellana* (1782) is one of the most celebrated works of the eighteenth century, not only for its innovative revision of the changes introduced to the language that Forner deplored, but also for its criticism of his contemporaries and praise for authors of the Spanish Golden Age.

---

group. In this sense, Forner's satire wishes to present a stark landscape of a critical moment of Spanish culture as represented by its foremost product, language, with the intention of didactically and rationally correcting the mistakes he sees among the authors and publications of his time. The narrator of the text, a Licenciado Pablo Ignocausto, serves as a mask for Forner's critical task. Ignocausto's visit to Mount Parnassus, the mythical Greek place inhabited by the Muses, is guided by none other than Cervantes, the pinnacle of Spanish literature, who is leading the narrator to the peak of the mountain. They are on their way to take part in the funeral services of Spain, who is portrayed as a matron who lies dead after many assaults to her integrity. Although the Cervantes character thinks that his contemporaries had started the blows against the venerable woman, the worst attack happened in her last years, when she became infected by the "caterva engalicada" (*gálico*-infected horde):

> Apollo has now decreed this punishment upon the murderers of our language. Of them, he has specifically selected the half-French, because they are incurable and because they have caused the death of the respectable matron with the dirtiest and most foul smelling of diseases. They attacked her with furious desperation.

And, seeing herself already weakened—either from the horrible persecution that almost in my time the Gongorists did on her, or from the innumerable afflictions that she received from the *equivoquistas* and *conceptistas* that came right after, or from the immense and extravagant burden of adornment with which, believing it would make her more beautiful, she was weighed down (and they were close to suffocating her) by the preachers and novelists of this, your century—without champions, without advocates that would value her, she vainly resisted the insults of the *gálico*-infected horde and she let herself be raped as she could do nothing else. She became bloated, she contracted the disease that they spread to her and she aborted, finally, from the dreadful and forced union, a horde of clumps, spurious fruits of blindness and a hopeless fury. (126)[15]

The character of Apollo chooses to chastise writers contemporaneous with Forner as assassins, especially as "semigalos" (half-French)—that is, half-men who were neither wholly Spanish thinkers nor complete intellectuals from France. In Forner's eyes, they ravaged the body of the matriarch with their dirty, foul-smelling disease, which is an ideological duplication of the bodily venereal disease of oozing *bubas* and thick fetid spittle. Through the mask of Ignocausto/Cervantes, Forner thunders that these tainted assassins raped the Spanish language and infected her with their malady, that her body became swollen, and that she gave birth to monstrous clumps that do not even appear human. Forner's use of the image of *gálico* radicalizes French influence as a direct bodily attack on Spanish culture; his recounting of the gory details of rape, followed by the grotesque description of the product of such violence, is extreme in itself, but it is made worse when he identifies the source of this viciousness with the venereal disease, its connection with France, and the humiliating fact that the attack has come directly from Spaniards, with the French only incidentally to blame.

Ironically, Forner's image of the fall of Spain to foreign influence could be interpreted as an accurate account of what was to happen a few years later in far more tangible ways. The explosion of the French Revolution in 1789 sent shock waves throughout Europe and the Americas, and the monarchies of the Continent were afraid that the incidents in Paris could be replicated in their own royal cities and distant colonies. Charles IV became king of Spain only one year before the Revolution, and the first years of his rule were also marked by fear of a popular uprising. The initial social reforms implemented by his secretary of state, the Count of Floridablanca, were rapidly discarded in favor of strict control over public thinkers through the Inquisition and the blocking of any French influence. Gaspar Melchor de Jovellanos, the enlightened writer mentioned earlier in relation to the unification of public hospitals, was affected by the tightening vigilance of the crown; he had to leave the court

Gaspar Melchor de Jovellanos

Gaspar Melchor de Jovellanos (1744–1811) was one of the most highly regarded authors of his time. Educated in the spirit of the Enlightenment, Jovellanos was an accomplished economist, politician, essayist, and playwright. He held several administrative posts in the royal government, but was banished to his native Gijón when his friend and protector Francisco de Cabarrús (1752–1810) lost his influence in court after the death of Charles III (b. 1716) in 1788. The inheritor, Charles IV (1748–1819), feared a popular uprising similar to the Revolution in France and halted all reforms inspired by the Enlightenment. Both Cabarrús and Jovellanos suffered from the change of sovereign. Jovellanos was known as a strong proponent of literature that served a practical purpose, an Enlightenment concept. His "Informe de la ley agraria" (1795) proposed changes in Spain's system of land ownership and voiced the need for a stronger infrastructure of roads and other means of transport. Through works such as the "Sátiras a Arnesto" (1786–87), which criticized the indulgent behavior and lack of education among the Spanish nobility, he sought to provide a base of knowledge for creating a man of virtue. For Jovellanos, this *hombre de bien* was the key to a successful future for Spain. As demonstrated by his own writing, as well as his petitions to his colleagues, Jovellanos advocated for clarity in literary expression in opposition to the highly stylized, complex language employed by Baroque poets such as Luis de Góngora and Francisco de Quevedo.

---

in Madrid, having been banished to his home in Gijón. The king replaced Floridablanca with the Count of Aranda, who also fell into disgrace after failing to help keep the king's French cousin, the later-to-be-beheaded Louis XVI (1754–93), on his throne. Manuel Godoy, a young military man from Badajoz who had rapidly climbed the court's ladder, replaced Aranda. Enjoying the favor of Queen María Luisa, and later that of her husband, King Charles IV, in less than five years Godoy rose from being a member of the royal bodyguards to the position of prime minister. After the death of Louis XVI in 1793, Godoy broke the neutral position of Spain and led a somewhat successful campaign against the French, which ended with the Peace of Basel in 1795, a treaty that required Spain to relinquish its possessions on the island of Santo Domingo, although it managed to keep the peninsular Spanish territory intact. More important, this treaty distanced Spain from its English former allies and linked it tighter to France, creating almost a strategic dependency. The French influence on Spanish everyday life went beyond the ideas that seeped in through translations and started to filter into the higher echelon of the empire. One year later, with the Second Treaty of San Ildefonso, Godoy confirmed the alliance with France by declaring war on Great Britain. With this move, Portugal was left alone on the continent, with Britain as its only backup.

Meanwhile, the initial symptoms of revolutionary French influence that were present in Antonio Nariño's translation of the *Declaration of the Rights of Man* in Santafé de Bogotá became patently manifest in the plans for independence of Francisco Miranda (1750–1816), the Venezuelan revolutionary who envisioned a unified, independent monarchy comprising all the Spanish and Portuguese colonies on the continent. Miranda is considered the harbinger of the wars for independence that culminated in the independence of today's Bolivia, Ecuador, Peru, Colombia, and Venezuela under the leadership of Simón Bolívar. After taking active part in the events following the French Revolution—his is the only Latin American name inscribed on the Arc de Triomphe in Paris—Miranda gradually became disenchanted with the new system and was put in prison. He also grew apart from the procedures of the governing Directory, and after being freed he escaped a subsequent order of arrest by going to England in 1798. Miranda tried to get help from Britain to initiate the process of independence he had envisioned for the Spanish colonies. He visited Prime Minister William Pitt (1759–1806) and explained his plans for a kingdom led by a hereditary king (whom he called Inca, in memory of the ruler of the Peruvian empire), which would be administered by a bicameral system similar to that of Britain. According to Miranda's diary, Pitt is pleased to see that the plans are not to create a government similar to that of revolutionary France, but does not lose the chance to warn what Britain's reaction would be if that were the case: "Very good, he said to me; because if there was an attempt to introduce a system in the French style in the Country, I assure you (he intensely retorted) that we would prefer that the Spanish Americans would continue to be obedient subjects for a century under the oppressive government of the King of Spain than see them submerged in the calamities of the abominable system of the French!" (206).[16]

Pitt favors unjust oppression over any kind of government that does away with a sovereign monarch. For him, the system that the French had been trying to implement for the previous decade is somewhat monstrous and worthy of revulsion; in other words, the English leader prefers subjugation when the alternative is an experiment that deviates from traditional standards. Miranda responds to Pitt by using the already coined parallel between the venereal French disease and the perceived disease of the French political system, in part because of his growing difference from the political environment in France, in part because he knew by now that French material support was highly unlikely, and in part because of his diplomatic efforts to gain support for the cause. As he prods Pitt to offer help, Miranda exploits the image of the venereal disease, the fear of contagion, and the unavoidable consequence of festered sores: "Very good, I said, and it is precisely so as to avoid such a contagion, and take timely precautions against the Gallic influx, that we have thought to emancipate ourselves immediately; and to form an alliance with the United States of America and with England in order to unanimously combat (if it be necessary) the monstrous and abominable values of the supposed French Liberty!" (206).[17]

Well aware of the alliance between France and Spain against England, Miranda uses the idea of preventive medicine in hopes of convincing the influential British politician to back his campaign: if the Spanish colonies continue to be connected with Spain, they will suffer the same kind of contagion as the peninsula, with the French in their territory, but if the colonies manage to get liberated from Spain, they will side with the salubrious influence of England and the United States. Miranda suggests that, as with the venereal disease, the longer and more frequent the contact with the source of the disease, the more likely the contagion.

In spite of all his efforts for more than seven years, Miranda was given the runaround by the British. He left for the United States in 1805, and although he was well received by Thomas Jefferson and James Madison, they gave him no tangible help either because of the pacts of neutrality the United States had with European nations. Miranda left the United States in 1806 with the goal of initiating a process of liberation in Venezuela. After some victories in favor of liberty for his country and many defeats, in 1812 he was arrested by Simón Bolívar and handed to the Spanish Royal Army. He died in the Spanish prison of La Carraca in 1816.

Back in Europe, in 1799 the situation changed dramatically. Thanks to military and political aptitude, Napoleon Bonaparte (1769–1821) became first consul of France after a coup d'état. Napoleon wanted to cut all means of commerce between Britain and the Continent, and Portugal was the only remaining stronghold. Godoy was caught between his wish to maintain power in Spain and the constant pressure from Napoleon to tackle the British in Portugal. By 1801 the French-Spanish alliance had succeeded in dominating the Portuguese-British by land, but the crushing defeat in the naval Battle of Trafalgar in 1805 virtually obliterated Spain's navy. In spite of this heavy loss and the growing dislike of many sectors of the Spanish society, including Ferdinand, the heir to the throne, Godoy's influence over Charles IV did not dwindle. But Godoy's cozying up to Napoleon did not mean that the now emperor of the French was going to keep the promises of nonintervention in the treaties between both nations, especially when he felt that Godoy was likely to betray him. The terms of the treaties allowed for French troops to pass through and dwell in Spain. At the same time that Napoleon pledged to Godoy a principality of the recently occupied Portugal, he dismissed the pact and ordered his troops to invade the country. In the eyes of the populace, the French had entered Spain on the sly, as *gálico* had under the cover of more or less pleasurable encounters, and were now becoming painful *bubas* in the major towns along their path. Fearing for their lives and positions, the king and his entourage fled to Aranjuez, trying to reach a harbor that would allow them to arrive safely in Mexico, on the other side of the sea. Followers of Ferdinand rose up in Aranjuez, and the king was forced to abdicate in favor of his son, who became Ferdinand VII (1784–1833). Taking advantage of the turmoil and division, Napoleon's troops occupied Madrid while he schemed successfully to gain power over the whole peninsula. He called the two kings to Bayonne, ostensibly to solve their differences. Napoleon successfully maneuvered to get Ferdinand to return the crown to his father, having already negotiated with Charles for receipt of the crown in exchange for safety and money.

The situation enraged the people of Madrid. When the children of Ferdinand were summoned to Bayonne, there was a fierce public revolt on May 2, 1808, that ended in carnage. It is called the "Dos de mayo uprising," and the killing of common people by French troops sparked the sentiment of liberation across the country, leading to the War of Independence, or the Peninsular War. Napoleon imposed his brother Joseph on Spain as its new king on June 6 of the same year, but Joseph's rule was feeble, given the growing opposition of the people and the increase of attacks by the Spanish army, which wanted to expel the former allies turned invaders. The Spanish defeated the French army at Bailén in July, and by August 31 had broken the French siege of Zaragoza. Joseph had to flee Madrid, but not before he issued messages to the Spanish people, trying to gain their favor while threatening those who opposed him with reprisal. During his retreat, and the corresponding vacuum in Spanish royal power, five issues of the *Memorial literario o Biblioteca periódica de Ciencias, Literatura y Artes dedicado el Rey nuestro señor Don Fernando VII* (Literary memorial or periodical library of sciences, literature, and arts dedicated to our King Ferdinand VII) appeared in Madrid.[18] The journal had been published on and off in the years before the invasion. After being shut down by the French in May 1808, it reappeared on October 10 of the same year, after Joseph had fled the city and the French troops were gone (Larriba 2–4). The journal's main goal after its reappearance was to attack Joseph I and the French influence: "The French were the original subject of criticism that began to be published in *Literary Memorial* in the early issues; the French are and will be the target of our shots [. . .] and thus our periodical will be as always anti-French" (Larriba 41).[19]

By criticizing words with a French ring—the term in Spanish is telling: *afrancesadas*—that were being used by aristocrats who were publishing articles in favor of creating a transitional regency council, one of the writers in the *Memorial* hints at the possible inclination of some Spanish patricians to accept the rule of the occupiers. Under occupation, the slightest resemblance to anything French was rapidly criticized as harmful, even if the resemblance was not related to Napoleon but to Enlightenment ideas or the French Revolution twenty years before. As did authors like Isla or Forner, the writer of the *Memorial* article views someone using words taken directly from the French language, such as *alocución* (speech) (32), as a political traitor, or in the words of Eugenio Espejo's character Murillo, a *galiquiento* (tainted with *gálico*). The veiled attack on those prone to French principles becomes a humorous confrontation in a section of the journal titled "Variedades" (Varieties) where the author mocks the broken Spanish used by Joseph in his proclamations. The title of the text incorporates several elements of opposition to Joseph, especially "Pepe Botellas," a nickname alluding to his supposed alcoholism, and his Italianized jargon: "Sermon from Rev. Fr. Fr. Josef *Malaparte* (alias Bottles) predicated in Pagan, and translated into Sybaritic by the accompanying Father the Ex-Spaniard, Patriarch of the league. Put into arbitrary Castilian by a curious listener who understands a little about telegraphs" (38).[20] The allusion to the coded language of semaphore lines, a French invention of communication with light invented by Claude Chappe in 1792 and replaced by electromagnetic signals by the inventor Samuel Morse in 1837, further stresses the disjointed language used by the imposed ruler. The first sentences of the text describe the difficult and ambiguous situation of Joseph, crowned as king of Spain but not supported by the bulk of his constituents: "Spaniards, poorly did I begin! Vassals, poorly did I say! Demons, as no other title is fit for the *rebels,* how can you dare to raise arms against your both legitimate and well-accepted king?" (38).[21] He cannot rightfully call his subjects "Spanish," because the invasion and annexation amounted to making them French; he cannot call them "vassals," because they were certainly not bound to his will; he can only curse them as demons, but in truth they were rebels in the same way as those who twenty years before in France had risen against a monarch who had failed to listen to the needs of his people. Joseph is represented as a man who fails to accept reality, and as a babbling puppet of Napoleon.

The lampooning author jumps from the connection between the *mal francés* and the decaying use of language to the contagion with French ideas that some considered the root of the French military invasion, and then to the infection of every sector of society which would eventually bring Spain to its demise. The mocking of Joseph's discourse serves as a description of the gradual disease that is taking over the country: "My family will build the premeditated solid throne of Europe's redemption. It will make sure that everyone will attend to his or her own game, and woe be to you, if you get into making even one *pepitoria* [bird stew]! If you try it, what do I mean try?, if you only imagine it, allow me at least a *wing* to try it, that I swear to you on Bacchus, my tutelary god, that the *mal gálico* will do in your homes *what he usually does,* and you will not get rid of the plague even if you boast to have discovered the specific counter to its venomous influence" (38).[22]

The reference to the "pepitoria" is a play on Joseph's moniker, *Pepe,* and *pepitoria,* a Spanish dish made with the giblets, wings, neck, and other left-over parts of a chicken, goose, or duck. Joseph's continued retreat before his brother came to his rescue with the great army in October 1808 could well be understood as a *pepitoria*—a tearing apart of his pretensions of power, served to be eaten by the Spanish. This play on words reveals the code of subsequent sentences pronounced by the drunkard. The author of the parody puts in the mouth of the despised Pepe Botellas a threat clearly connected with the popular knowledge of *gálico:* if the Spanish were to go against the will of Napoleon, the disease brought by his army would enter their homes. Each person knew that once a man acquired the *bubas,* it was very likely that his wife would follow suit, and that their progeny would be infected as well. From their experience of everyday life with the disease, readers would also know that the remedies used by the physicians were simply ineffective, although excruciating. Using the image of the disease, the author of the parody represents mutatis mutandis what had happened in Europe with the ascent of Napoleon. Through piercing military invasion and sneaky diplomacy, the French presence, seen here as the French disease, had been able to penetrate most of Europe. In the same way that the traditional use of mercury had not been able to cure *gálico,* the old strategies of war had not been able to save most of Europe from the French invasion. Even if some physicians were experimenting on *gálico* with new remedies such as guaiacum or a specific kind of lizard, *gálico* was undefeatable once it had entered the body. Similarly, all military and political maneuvers had been to no avail in decisively opposing Bonaparte's might. The influx of the disease, the same kind of influx as the French invasion, is like a venom that will not stop until the victim has died in terrible pain. But at this point Joseph Bonaparte was not winning; the mocking tone of the parody points to the fact that at least the specific remedy of popular resistance successfully eradicated the military French disease, represented by the weak brother of the emperor.

Only one year later, in the city of Valencia, a text by Manuel Freyre de Castrillón (1751?–1820) appeared. The title of the work indicates that a connection between the French invasion and the disease has become established: *Remedio y preservativo contra el mal francés de que adolece parte de la nación española* (Remedy and protection against the French disease from which part of the Spanish nation suffers). The link is so strong that if a reader did not know that this text had been written by a Galician military man who describes himself on the front page of the work as "honorably included in Bonaparte's bloodthirsty death list,"[23] they might assume that it was a medical treatise and not a royalist, pro-church pamphlet. The goal of the tirade is the same as that of a prescribed medical treatment—that is, to craft a powerful medicine to purge the disease, followed by a regimen to avoid the patient's relapse. Freyre belonged to a party that defended Bourbon monarchical rule and the Catholic Church's influence. He was elected in 1811 as representative to the Cortes de Cádiz and years later was named secretary in the Holy Office or Inquisition, two posts that synthesized and supported his will to preserve the power of the monarchy and the church. In his pamphlet, he is not only against Napoleon, whom he calls "the greatest monster hell has vomited up" (3),[24] but also against the implementation of political ideas related to the Enlightenment, especially those connected with the elevation of the ordinary populace, the separation of church and state, and the secularization of society, which he rejects squarely as French and as harmful to Spain. He condemns the French as a whole nation that "boastfully, *à la French*, has bragged of being regicides, atheists, bandits and, in a word, Jacobins" (4).[25] Freyre laments the moment when all things French became fashionable in Spain, when "everyone read French books, or the deluge of frenchified translations that altered and frenchified our harmonious language and, worst of all, our customs and our ideas [. . .] and because of this vile knowledge the entire nation dressed, ate, walked, visited, coughed and sneezed *á la French*" (8).[26] The language of cultural influence as a disease that pervades all instances of social life is used by the author to remind the reader that the seemingly small things of fashion have turned into an infection of the very inner structure of society. The illness has blinded all social strata to the point that they cannot tell right from wrong: "Infected with the same spirit of inconstancy and vertigo, we have applauded and abominated with the same French enthusiasm the successive constitutions, parties, and leaders that, one after the other, rapidly followed and fell, enveloped in blood and carnage never before seen in the most frightening lawlessnesses in history" (8).[27] The main fear is that of contagion, a word that is repeated several times in the pamphlet and replaces the medical term of *comunicación* that was used in the early 1700s. The source of the contagion is the neighbors up north, whom he calls "pestilential neighbors" ("vecindad pestífera," 13). Following the medical logic for managing a contagious disease, the author defends a radical course of action that aims to obliterate what he considers the cause of the disease with the hope of returning the patient, in this case Spain, to the condition he or she had enjoyed before the infectious contact. Freyre mocks the many enlightened literati who used to say that Spain was backward and living in the past. In his opinion, after experiencing the bloody invasion of the French in his country, backwardness and stagnation are welcome ideals if they mean no further infection: "Happy Spanish gothicism, barbarity, and fanaticism! Happy with our friars and our Inquisition, which, according to French enlightenment, makes us fall behind other nations by at least a century! Oh! If only we could go back another two! That would mean distancing ourselves by three hundred moral leagues from France, seeing that we cannot physically separate ourselves from such contagious neighbors" (12).[28]

This first step is an internal purging that restores the state of things to the idealized time of Spanish economic and cultural preeminence in the world. For the second step, just as a physician would prohibit any sexual contact between a recovering *gálico* patient and an infected person—remember the graphic image of preventing a dog from eating its own vomit—the author advises actions to avoid further contact with French ideas: "Far from coveting French benevolence, let us all take any possible measures to eternally separate ourselves from this contagious and traitorous nation, from this cursed land where the holy hospitality so pleasing to God is violated" (12).[29] According to Freyre, in order to reject this "noxious vicinity, it is necessary to build a tall and thick wall that would separate the chosen people from these excommunicated Tatars" (13).[30] The proposed regime of isolation from the disease is radical. Freyre begins by proposing a core law banning any future alliance with France, a course of action he would like to expand by prohibiting Spanish kings from marrying French princesses or placing a Spanish prince in the French court. He also wants to prevent any French person from receiving a letter of naturalization in Spain and to confiscate the property of any person educated in France or any man marrying a French woman.

Beyond these measures for avoiding the mixing of French and Spanish blood because of the fear that such mixing could translate into a political or social debacle, Freyre is also especially against French books, which he thinks should be strictly censored, for the simple reason that "French philosophy necessitates precautions that go far beyond those that should be taken against yellow fever and all the plagues" (13).[31] For him, the French cultural disease is the worst of all maladies.

Freyre's image of infection by both book and blood would later become widely used during the second half of the nineteenth century, when others tried to explain a perceived exhaustion of European culture and the European system of values. This attitude is summed up many years later in an acerbic book by the Jesuit priest Juan Mir y Noguera (1840–1917) titled *Prontuario de hispanismo y barbarismo* (Handbook of hispanism and barbarism) (1908). Mir's claims serve also to synthesize the views of authors who unfairly labeled the eighteenth century as a period when Spanish culture merely mimicked French models, or as a hiatus when real Spanish thought had gone astray, or as a childish and even a gaudy aesthetic production. The author is writing when the *modernista* movement was at the heart of literary debate. *Modernismo* incorporated many of the innovations of French poetry in the second half of the nineteenth century and represented a radical departure from Romanticism. It is not a surprise that Mir attempts to trace the perceived decay of the Spanish language to its close contact with French literature, French ideas, and French military invasion, together with the abandonment of Catholic rigor during the eighteenth century: "there were not a few, Fathers Isla, Fathers Feijóo, Fathers Interián de Ayala, who, carried away by the pestiferous current, allowed Gallic forms in their writing" (lxxviii).[32] According to Mir, although these authors had been tainted with the French disease, they were redeemed by their connection to the Catholic Church (they were all priests) and their patriotism, which had empowered them to safeguard the Spanish language: "Thus the great secret of the Spanish language was made known, that is, that the causes that had come together to form it came together to maintain it as it was; I mean, religion in covenant with patriotic love; both causes joined their hands in friendship in the previously mentioned religious men, even though in some of them the frequent contact with those wounded with the French disease would spill the evil poison that put the health of the language in danger" (lxxviii).[33]

His despair about the contagion of the past leads him to his vision of a not good present and a worse future. Even great luminaries of the eighteenth century such as Feijoo or Isla had been too close, and for too long, in dealings with other authors sick with the French influence. The way in which Mir words the last part of this passage almost suggests that these authors had been too intimate with people who had spoiled the Spanish language. His accusation seems odd a century and a half after these authors had been in vogue, especially since Feijoo and Isla had directly attacked bad translations from the French during their own time. Perhaps Mir's harsh criticism is related to the fact that the French influence of the Enlightenment had produced a crack in the base of Spanish culture previously dominated by the clerical sector and the church. Isla and Feijoo had led the way to a rational approach to knowledge that was certainly detrimental to ecclesiastical primacy. After seeing the most recent works in literature, with their forms and language far distant from the qualities of the Spanish Golden Age, Mir feels that the battle against *gálico* in Spanish culture is beyond winning and finally gives up: "Blessed God! Keep on frenchifying, barbarizing, modernizing: anyway, this is the end; the Castilian language died of French disease; what is worse, it died foolishly, without hope of going on to a better life" (cxxxii).[34]

♒ 8

Naming the Disease: *Mal americano*

The xenophobia that prompted Spaniards to label syphilis as *gálico* or "the French disease" at the end of the fifteenth century, when soldiers of every provenance clashed in Naples, is the same that led them to connect the disease to the Americas. In a previously cited passage, Gonzalo Fernández de Oviedo recalls smirking at Neapolitans and Frenchmen who blamed each other as sources of the disease. The Spanish soldier and historian thought that "in reality each party would have described it correctly had they called it the disease of the Indies" (115),[1] with "Indies" (*indias*) referring both to the West Indies and to the aboriginal women who purportedly infected Columbus's sailors. Fernandez de Oviedo laughs at the Neapolitans and Frenchmen because he believes that the sources of so much pain and death are in fact the Spanish soldiers and the indigenous people of the recently discovered world.

Depending on an author's goals—to offend an enemy or to label a fear, for instance—the disease of the *bubas* shifted nationalities. During much of the eighteenth century, resenting the Bourbon dynasty, the French Enlightenment, and the Napoleonic invasion, the Spaniards and their colonies employed *mal francés* as their favorite nickname for what their enemies represented. But in parallel, the term *mal de las indias,* "disease of the Indies," was suitable for emphasizing the difference between colonies and metropolis, where the colonies represented a productive yet annoying appendage.

In a 1699 letter from Fray Pablo de Rebudilla and Fray Francisco de San José to their superior, these two Franciscan missionaries in what was then called the Kingdom of Guatemala lament how difficult is to access remote territories and how they have been frequently mistreated by the indigenous people they are trying to convert. They ask their superior to, "as immediately as possible, provide thirty men with their corporal, with arms, ammunition, and provisions, for our own protection and so that, out of fear of the mouths of fire (which they fear greatly) we can reduce them to villages, so that they live following the law of God, with good customs and Christian policy" (Léon Fernández 385).[2] To convince their superior about the positive outcome that would result from sending soldiers, cattle, and food, the friars describe the diseases they have been suffering from while trying to convert and baptize the people of these nations: "Your eminence would not get surprised of the trembling chins of the six priests that are supposed to be sent to Talamanca, in this holy province, even if they are of strong spirit, courage, and robust nature, because they know of my experience when I was there two years ago, and came away with *gálico* humor, from which I still suffer although somewhat better, and my companion came out after four years with quartan fevers, covered in pustules and blisters and with very bad humors; but with the people we will be able to open the paths to bring beasts and livestock for the sustenance and other reasonable provisions to conserve life" (388).[3]

The friars see that their missionary impetus is being thwarted by the rigors of nature in these distant territories, by the uncivilized inhabitants, and by the uncivil diseases that the uncivilized inhabitants have transferred to them. They have concluded that they can convert the natives only by containing them in pueblos, but Spanish military presence is needed for this. This coupling of the cross and the sword had been the main formula of conquest on the New Continent since the arrival of Columbus two hundred years before, and since the indigenous peoples feared the "mouths of fire" so much, it was normal to think that the formula was effective for evangelizing. For these priests, the indigenous population represented the lack of religion and the excess of a transmissible malady. For Fray Pablo and Fray Francisco, to convert is to control, and to Christianize is to cure the maladies of soul and body. But knowing as we do today that the main cause of a disease like *gálico* is sexual intercourse, the question arises: what were the convincing evangelizing methods of these friars such that they ended up with "*gálico* humor" while on their mission?

Spanish missionary efforts continued during the eighteenth century in the Mesoamerican region and as far north as California, where the Franciscan order established many posts under the direction of Fray Junípero Serra (1713–84). Father Serra's project followed the custom of conducting missionary work in tandem with a military presence. In 1768, he and sixteen other religious men went to what was called "Alta California" (high or north California) with Spanish troops that had been sent to conquer the region, but soon afterward, Fray Junípero clashed with the military superiors because of their managing of the expedition. The constant quarrel between the civilizing priests and the civilizing soldiers was resolved only when Viceroy Antonio María Bucareli (1717–79) endorsed the Franciscan priest. Viceroyal intervention did not block soldiers from transmitting *gálico* to the indigenous population in Alta California, as they had previously done in Baja California, leading to thousands of casualties. By the end of the eighteenth century, the most prevalent disease among Californian natives was *gálico*. According to J. S. Holliday, "the native population on the peninsula declined from 24,000 in 1697 to an estimated 7,500 in 1777, that loss due principally to European diseases" (9).[4] In a visit to the mission of Todos Santos, today Baja California Sur, Manuel

Espinosa de los Monteros comments on the bleak situation of the natives infected with *bubas:* "Everyone suffers from the French disease and thus they are always covered in sores, and not only do they not tell the Father of their illnesses, they also, clearly, resist being cured, even when the Father requests it. I saw and heard one who ended up having so many worms that, with a stick like an animal, the worms had to be removed. And such was the neglect for his own life that, if his pathetic state had not been noticed by accident, the worms would have eaten him."[5]

In the early 1800s, Franciscan priests in the Californian missions were asked to respond to detailed questionnaires about the geography and customs of their communities, and almost all of the reports attest to the impact of *gálico,* which had been brought to the region by the Spanish civilizing effort that had been initiated fifty years earlier. In 1812, the priests in the mission of Saint Francis, close to the harbor of San Francisco in Alta California, confirm the havoc wreaked by the disease: "The dominant disease among them is syphilis but it is quiet and hidden and from it arises a great number of illnesses. Some recover with sores. These live longer, although they do not easily recover. In others it strikes internally and they die sooner. Others succumb more slowly. The climate possibly acts unfavorably to this disease as it is damp and cold. When it becomes violently active, a bloody diarrhea finishes the individual" (Geiger and Meighan 79–80).[6]

The priests in the mission of Santa Cruz offer a valuable glimpse of how the indigenous people of this region dealt with death and the occurrence of disease: "To the present time we have not discovered if Californian Indians have any remedies to cure their diseases. When they are overtaken by disease, bereft of aid, they die, unless nature itself comes to the rescue. However, even for the baptized, death is little feared or not at all so they accept its approach with great indifference and die with the greatest tranquillity. At Santa Cruz we have no thermal baths but if such baths are available, as at Mission San Jose, the Indians use them for all their ills and diseases. What is in common use among them is the sweat house, which is built in the earth. A great fire is built therein and they sweat extremely much. Their prevalent sicknesses are pleurisy, sunstroke, and dysentery. These maladies strike the Indians in spring and in the fall. However, a still more common disease, and it is perennial, is syphilis" (Geiger and Meighan 78).[7]

Even though priests confirmed that Spanish soldiers had passed *gálico* to the native Californians, back in Spain there was a persistent belief that it was the Indians who kept infecting the Spaniards, based on the assumption that Columbus's sailors had brought the disease to Europe. Spain failed to recognize that many indigenous groups, like those in California, did not have the disease before the conquest, and that in fact the overwhelming number of natives succumbing to the disease was the result of their lack of immunity.[8]

An example of this understanding of *gálico* is to be found in a volume about California from a series titled *El viagero universal* (The universal traveler) (1799), by the Spanish writer Pedro Estala (1757–1815). Estala began this profitable set of writings by translating *Le voyageur François* (The French traveler), a series by Joseph de La Porte (1714–99) and other French compilers, but after the seventh installment he started finding material from other sources and adding his own perspectives, as is the case with the volume on California, then part of the Spanish territories in the New World. Estala is one of the important Enlightenment authors in Spain. Part of the Escuela Literaria Salmantina, he was a friend of Juan Meléndez Valdés, Leandro Fernández de Moratín, Juan Antonio Melón, and José Iglesias de la Casa.[9] Like many of them, he was a follower of French ideals; like many of them, he was called an *afrancesado* (frenchified person); like many of them, he participated in the government of Joseph I; and like many of them, he had to flee to France, where he died in exile.

Estala views the epidemic of the Indians as divine punishment for their uncivilized and unchristian insistence on attacking the European colonists: "This epidemic began in October of the year of 1788, and in that month they revolted, apostatized their Faith, rebelled against Spain, and killed the missionaries. And with the same order with which they showed themselves to be enemies of religion, they were attacked by the epidemic. [. . .] All of these circumstances show that this epidemic was a punishment from heaven; but whatever it was, for our purposes, the pustules that afflicted the Indians went on to form putrid wounds that appeared around the genitals, and this is the illness that has spread throughout this entire province: and although, as I said, the Gentiles are not afflicted, we see that as soon as they become Christians, a little while later they become disabled: this is the origin of the disease that here is called *gálico*" (131–33).[10]

According to Estala, the main problem is that these indigenous rioters had been baptized. They were Christians, as the French or the English were, but they had turned against those who invaded them. According to Estala, being Christians did not help them avoid contagion; in fact, it made them more vulnerable. In this sense, Estala's claims are ambiguous, since he believes that the natives were punished with *gálico* because of unchristian behavior, but at the same time suggests that becoming Christians had made them easier prey for the disease.

While some authors such as Estala understood *gálico* as an American disease transferred by indigenous people to Europeans, as well as a disease that the Indians deserved to die from because of their reluctance to become Christianized or their willingness to attack the civilizing Spaniards, other authors, like the similarly French-prone and enlightened Manuel José Quintana (1772–1857), believed that *gálico* was the just punishment of the conquerors for their violence against indigenous people. Quintana's teachers in Salamanca had been Juan Meléndez Valdés, Gaspar Melchor de Jovellanos, and Pedro Estala. In his *Vidas de españoles célebres* (Lives of famous Spaniards) (1807), Quintana revisits the core historical moment of the Spanish army's recovery of Naples, which Fernández de Oviedo had described in 1535. Although Quintana wants to praise the military and personal accomplishments of "El gran Capitán," he clearly stresses the terrible connection to *gálico*. For Quintana, the infection took hold when Ferdinand was king of Naples, around 1496: "It will always be marked in the notorious events of human history, not so much for the fortune of the occasion, but because at that time appeared the horrible and painful illness that began to declare the violence of its poison when this Prince had surrounded the castles of Naples. It was called the French disease because the first known to be ravaged by it were from that nation. America infected us with it as if in retaliation for our violence; and the following generations, attacked in the organs used for procreation and pleasure, have cursed and will curse the imprudence and recklessness of their forefathers" (231).[11]

Many things had changed in the perspective of Spanish intellectuals to come to this point where an important author like Quintana sees the conquest and colonization of the New World as intrinsically violent and morally wrong, and even accepts as fair a kind of natural justice that inflicts punishment on future generations. This outcome must again be credited to the Enlightenment, especially to the growing interest in societies that differed from the European. The publication of travelogues about faraway places, the description of other customs, and the understanding of the heterogeneity of the world sparked in thinkers like Quintana (albeit temporarily) the possibility of seeing the other as the self—that is, a level of empathy that only a philosophical and scientific revolution like that of the Enlightenment could have produced.

The scientific, rational, solidarity-seeking mindset is also seen in Quintana's enthusiasm for the vaccine against smallpox, a contagious disease that in English was named "smallpox" in contrast with syphilis, which was originally called the "great pox." The name in Latin for the viral infection is *variola,* a derivation of *varius,* meaning "spotted." As a consequence of the encounter between Europeans and Native Americans after the arrival of Christopher Columbus in 1492, smallpox killed millions of indigenous people. Infected Spanish soldiers led by Pánfilo de Narváez arrived in Veracruz in 1520. After infighting between Narváez's and Hernán Cortés's soldiers, the conquering throng brought the highly infectious disease inland. One of the main reasons for the fall of Tenochtitlán, seat of the Aztec Empire, was the extremely high number of casualties among the indigenous people, who had no natural immunity against it. A similar dynamic occurred when Huayna Capac, ruler of the Incan Empire, died in 1525, possibly as a result of the disease brought by the Spaniards. Inhabitants of the region fell sick from smallpox, and the disarray caused by the lethal infection facilitated their defeat.

The disease continued to affect thousands of people in Europe by the eighteenth century. Many of the survivors were left with heavy scarring from the blisters, and a high rate of people became blind as a consequence of the contagion. There are recorded instances of inoculation—the artificial induction of immunity—in Africa, China, and India as early as the tenth century. The inoculation with smallpox, known as *variolation,* consisted of the exposure to scabs from the sores produced by the disease. There were several methods of variolation: in Sudan, the arm of a healthy child was exposed to a cloth that had been previously wrapped around the arm of a child with the disease; in China, a special pipe was used to blow a small amount of powdered scabs up the nostrils of the healthy receiver. The first method of variolation explained in an European publication was the one used in the Ottoman Empire, when a letter written by Italian physician Emmanuel Timoni (1670–1718) to John Woodward was reproduced in January 1714 in the *Philosophical Transactions* of the Royal Society of England under the title "An Account, or History, of the Procuring the Small Pox by Incision, or Inoculation; as it has for some time been practiced at Constantinople." The method consisted of rubbing a small amount of pus from the sore of a diseased person into two or three small wounds made with a needle in the arm of the healthy patient (Timonius and Woodward 73). In the English colonies on the American continent, the important author and Puritan minister Cotton Mather (1663–1728) had learned about this method of variolation from his slave Onesimus, who was possibly from North Africa. Mather had also read Timoni's account, and when a hard outbreak of smallpox happened in Boston in 1721 he pushed for implementing variolation. Heeding his advice, Dr. Zabdiel Boylston immunized almost three hundred people, with only six of them dying. More than eight hundred in Boston who had not been inoculated died. This method did not take root in Europe until Lady Mary Wortley Montagu (1689–1762) campaigned for its use in England after her stay in Constantinople. Lady Montagu, who had survived smallpox (although she herself had not been inoculated), had her five-year-old son successfully variolated in Constantinople in 1718. In 1721, her four-year-old daughter was immunized under the observation of physicians of the royal court, which led to further trials, even with members of the royal family of England. The positive outcome of the method started a trend of variolation on the rest of the European continent and then in the colonies beyond the sea.

In Spain, many members of the royal family got infected with smallpox. After the death of his brother and sister-in-law, King Charles IV of Spain started variolation of his relatives. By 1798 a campaign of variolation of civilians started, and by 1800 there was a royal edict declaring a general availability of the immunization treatment. Spanish colonies in America also suffered greatly from smallpox, hampering the extraction of raw materials and the general production in those territories. According to the medical historian Francisco Fernández del Castillo, the king consulted with the Mexican doctor Joseph Flores, whom we will study further later on, about how to handle variolation in the colonies. Flores told the king to send two vessels with cows inoculated with cowpox, to employ the technique developed by Edward Jenner in England, in conjunction with young men being variolated arm to arm along the journey from Spain. Knowing of the great influence of religion in the colonies, Flores also advised having the church clearly and publicly support the plan, and the ecclesiastical institution organized the records of those who had been immunized (Fernández del Castillo 69). The king chose Francisco Javier de Balmis as the leader of what was to be known as the Real Expedición Filantrópica de la Vacuna (Royal Vaccine Philanthropic Expedition), which took place between 1803 and 1814 and was one of the most ambitious campaigns of medical care in the history of medicine. The expedition, supervised by Balmis and other overseers, reached all the Spanish territories in the Americas from Texas to Chiloé (in present-day Chile), as well as the Philippines (a Spanish possession at the time), the regions of Macao and Guangdong in China, and even the island of Saint Helena, the remote British territory where Napoleon Bonaparte was imprisoned and died in 1821.

In 1806, Quintana wrote an ode to the medical commission led by Balmis. Quintana starts his "A la expedición española para propagar la vacuna en América bajo la dirección de don Francisco Balmis" (To the Spanish expedition to disseminate the vaccine in America under the direction of don Francisco Balmis) with a heartfelt exaltation of America that signals ideals of liberation analogous to those of Antonio Nariño or Antonio Miranda:

> With blood are written
> In the eternal book of life
> The painful cries
> That your afflicted lips send to heaven.
> They cry out against my country, [. . .]
>
> Will they never cease? Are there not enough
> Three unhappy centuries
> Of bitter expiation? Now

Francisco Javier de Balmis

Francisco Javier de Balmis (1753–1819) was a Spanish military medic and surgeon who is most famous for heading the Royal Vaccine Philanthropic Expedition, during which he distributed and administered the vaccine for smallpox in Puerto Rico, Cuba, Venezuela, and Mexico, as well as in the Philippines, parts of China, and other islands between 1803 and 1806. Balmis traveled to the Spanish colonies for the first time in 1753, where he worked in hospitals in Havana and Mexico City and experimented with the use of medicinal plants to treat sexually transmitted diseases—treatments he would later bring back to Spain.

> We are not, no, those who on the face of the earth
> Dressed with the wings of audacity
> Flying over the Atlantic sea;
> Those that ripped you out,
> Bleeding, in chains, from the silence in which you laid. (*Obras* 5)[12]

He then praises Balmis for bringing Edward Jenner's vaccine to the other side of the Atlantic:

> I will fly; because a power sends me;
> I will fly; of the ardent Ocean
> I will face the raging fury,
> And in the midst of the infested America
> I will know how to plant the tree of life (*Obras* 5).[13]

According to Quintana, Balmis's vaccination commission was making amends for the three centuries of injustice America had suffered. In a fashion that almost seems to foretell the future, Quintana encourages Balmis to remain in America, where he can find the peace, liberty, and glory that the aging European continent cannot give him:

> In Europe no longer grows
> The sacred laurel to adorn your head.
> Stay there, where the peace,
> the beautiful independence, will have sacred refuge;
> Stay there, where finally you will receive
> The noble prize of your glorious action. (*Obras* 5–6)[14]

Quintana advises Balmis to stay on the New Continent because he thinks that it is there, and not in the exhausted Europe, where independence and peace will bloom in the future. In addition to the dynamism and hope present on American soil, Quintana also believes that scientific recognition will be found in the work from this region, which had been exploited and neglected for more than three centuries.

9 ∾

The Rejection of the Origin of *Gálico* as a Nucleus of Self-Identity in the Spanish Colonies

The triangulation of disease, scientific advancement, and the construction of commonality is clearly visible in the particular case of *gálico*. The dispute about America as the source of syphilis galvanized an effort to differentiate the colonies from the Spanish metropolis. The discourse of differentiation was not carried out exclusively in literary texts, as we tend to believe, but also through textualities more related to reason, practicality, and scientific spirit as a result of the Enlightenment mood in the Spanish colonies. A discourse that has been interpreted as a point of departure, almost as the genesis of Spanish American selfhood, is that crafted by the glorified Cuban author José Martí (1853–95).

Literary criticism has turned Martí into an example of what James W. Loewen defines in his popular *Lies My Teacher Told Me* (1995) as *heroification,* "a degenerative process (much like calcification) that makes people over into heroes. Through this process, our educational media turn flesh-and-blood individuals into pious, perfect creatures without conflicts, pain, credibility, or human interest" (463–64). A case in point is the use and abuse of Martí's essay "Nuestra América" (Our America) (1891), which is usually hailed as a foundational text in the crafting of an independent Latin American identity. A second instance is the much-anthologized "La agricultura de la zona tórrida" (The agriculture of the torrid zone) (1826), by Andrés Bello. The quoting of a single verse brings to mind its canonical resonance: "The living scarlet bustles in the leaves of your cactus plant, / surpassing the purple color of the Tyrian sea-shells."[1] Enrique Anderson Imbert praised the poem as new and innovative because of "that abundance of images, that enthusiastic impetus in the description, that pride in the American fruit and its indigenous name" (250).[2] But Bello's pride in the fertility and uniqueness of the New Continent's plants, his descriptions of them, and his use of their indigenous names were already common, perhaps not in literary works, but definitely in scientific texts.

These occurrences may be decalcified by using "searching for the foundation of the foundation." I claim that a movement toward self-definition in Spanish-speaking America was already fully fledged by the end of the eighteenth century in relation to ideas of disease and remedy. The idea of "nuestra América" that we ascribe solely to Martí, and the references to autochthonous products as instantiations of self-definition we see in Bello, had already appeared in essays related to the development of medicine and a cure for *gálico*. These essays were published more than a century before Martí's essay, and over four decades before Bello's publication of his *silva* (a form of Spanish poetry written in lines of eleven and seven syllables) in the *Repertorio Americano*.

The four main books I study here—from 1780, 1782, 1785, and 1788—were written between the 1776 U.S. Declaration of Independence and the start of the French Revolution in 1789. These texts are arguably not direct consequences of the revolutionary struggles that we tend to view as precursors of Spanish American independence. Rather, we can see them as examples of an intellectual debate parallel to the Enlightenment.

The seminal work in the discussion of the French disease as a point of departure for the creation of commonality vis-à-vis Europe is *Storia antica del Messico* (Ancient history of Mexico), written by Francisco Javier Clavijero (1731–87) and published in Italy in 1780. In the second volume, Clavijero included nine "dissertazione" dealing with miscellaneous topics related to Mexico. In the last of these essays, titled "Su l'origine del malfrancese" (About the origin of the French disease), Clavijero writes: "I must dispute not only with Mr. de Paw, but with almost all the Europeans, among whom the opinion is quite widespread that the venereal disease owes its origin to the New World, a recourse that the European nations took, as if in a common agreement, after having blamed each other for the space of thirty years for the origin of such a shameful disease" (465).[3]

Clavijero's goal is to prove that *gálico* did not originate on the American continent.[4] He explains that for many years after the appearance of *malfrancese*— the term used by the Italians—medical authors never connected the disease to the New World; on the contrary, they blamed it on their enemy, on prostitutes, on the shocking tactics of war (such as feeding human flesh to enemy troops, or adding the blood of lepers to the wine the enemy was to drink), or on sexual contact with women with uterine diseases, with none of these causes related to Americans (466). Strictly following the rhetorical rules of the time, Clavijero backs up each of his assertions by citing multiple authorities and various sources. He theorizes that the disease could have been "communicated" to Europe from other regions where it is endemic, such as the "interior provinces of Africa situated on either side of Senegal" (467),[5] calling on the authority of Andrea Thevet, a French geographer. He also suggests that the venereal disease is native to the island of Java (his source is Andrea

Francisco Javier Clavijero

Francisco Javier Clavijero (1731–87) was a Jesuit priest born in the Spanish colony of New Spain (now Mexico). The works of Descartes, Newton, and Feijoo influenced this member of the Ilustración Novohispana generation. With this knowledge base, along with a deep love for his homeland, Clavijero became one of the era's strongest defenders of the indigenous Mexican population. He dedicated much of his time to teaching indigenous students in the Jesuit schools, an activity facilitated by his knowledge of Náhuatl. Clavijero worked in this arena until the expulsion of the Jesuits in 1767, when he was forced to move to Bologna. He was also a historiographer, and his most influential work is the *Historia antigua de México*. It details the cultural history of the region before the arrival of the Spanish, beginning with the Toltecs and continuing until the sixteenth century. It was not only a work of history but also a means of dispelling the European notion that indigenous peoples were lesser human beings and advocating for their rights.

Cleyer, "protomedico de la colonia holandesa de la isla de Java") or Amboina or the Molucas, or seen by Magellan's sailors in Timor (his source is the Spanish chronicler Antonio de Herrera y Tordesillas) or in China (as told to the French doctor Jean Astruc by the priest Pierre Foureau), where it was considered a very old disease (468), and he questions how is it possible to blame exclusively the American continent when it is clear that the disease could have been communicated by other nations with which Europeans had had continuous and direct commercial exchanges.[6]

Clavijero also considers the possibility that the disease could have appeared in Europe "senza contagio" (469)—that is, not through contact with other peoples, but rather by first developing in a particular individual already in the Old World. Clavijero criticizes the lack of logic displayed by Astruc, who attributes the origin of the disease to the diet of indigenous people in Española, a diet that supposedly lacked cassava and corn and was instead composed of spiders, worms, bats, and other vermin. Clavijero also criticizes Astruc for arguing that the hot weather in regions such as Española affects the blood of indigenous women, who supposedly produce menses that are very acidic and almost virulent and therefore prone to generate a malady such as the French disease. Clavijero heaps scorn on Astruc's theory for being based on very uncertain premises: "Here we have Mr. Astruc's entire argument supporting his system for the venereal disease, completely full, from beginning to end, with falsities, as I aim to demonstrate; but supposing that all of it is true, I maintain what I have said before, that what he refers to on the island of Haiti could have happened in Europe" (471).[7] Clavijero counters Astruc by reminding the reader that, for example, European men ate rats, lizards, and animal excrement when their continent was ravished by war, and that in Europe there have likewise been immoderate men and lecherous women, and acrid seminal fluids and virulent menses that could have caused the disease on the Old Continent.

Although Clavijero's argumentative purpose is initially to debunk what he considers fallacious claims by respected authors of the time, such as Oviedo, Astruc, and Cornelius de Pauw (whom I will discuss further in my reading of Sánchez Valverde), his ultimate goal is to render a more accurate and positive representation of his own country, which is called here not by the colonial name of *New Spain* but by the name *Mexico,* with its indigenous resonances. The crafting of this positive commonality is done by means of what I call "engagement through differentiation," a form of negotiation with the preponderant European mode of knowledge that allowed for a better positioning of the discourse produced by authors born in the colonial New World, even as they employed the European modes of knowledge in which they had been trained and from which they could derive agency. This type of engagement through differentiation, and the wielding of rhetorical arguments, characteristic of the European discourse in vogue—in this case exemplified by the use of irony and disdainful humor—are patent in Clavijero's positioning himself against another author, one who had conjectured that the origin of the French disease was to be found in sexual relations between indigenous peoples and primates of the Cercopithecidae family (i.e., Old World monkeys):[8] "Before concluding this article I cannot help but mention the ridiculous and absurd opinion of Dr. Juan Linder, an English writer, regarding the origin of the venereal disease, so that the full determination to discredit the Americans in this regard may be seen. That extravagant naturalist argues, then, that this contagion originated from the union of the Americans with female satyrs or great cercopithecidae. Fortunately for the inhabitants of Haiti, there were no cercopithecidae there, big or small" (475).[9]

Clavijero's attack on Linder's spurious theory is aimed at showing that the English author is using the disease as a vehicle to brand a certain group—specifically the natives of Española, but implicitly all indigenous people and all those born on the American continent—as sexually aberrant and therefore less human.[10] Clavijero's work represents one of the first and most scholarly discursive moves to differentiate the Spanish colonies from Europe. What makes Clavijero's *Storia* an important signpost in this process of differentiation is that he avoids any direct political comment. The possible political reading comes, nevertheless, from his wish to prove via scientific argument that the negative label of the French disease cannot be ascribed to America. By showing that the disease is not American, he also aims to establish that America is different from Europe, and perhaps better than Europe. The inferred corollary of this kind of reasoning is that the colonies are clearly self-reliant.

Clavijero's *Storia* became increasingly read as a reliable source for the history of Mexico and for information related to America. He forcefully debated with and corrected the opinions of European scholars such as the influential Scottish historian William Robertson (1721–93) and the Dutch philosopher Cornelius de Pauw (1739–99), who had been deemed authorities on the subject of the New Continent, but whose statements Clavijero showed to be unreliable and even untrue.[11] The Mexican author confronts an incomplete and skewed construction of the history of the New Continent and gives precedence to what Anthony Pagden calls autoptic authority, "the privileged understanding which those present at an event have over all those who have only read or been told about it" (51). This type of agency is also present in the historical account of the conquest of Mexico by the Spanish soldier Bernal Díaz del Castillo, for example. The impressive circulation of Clavijero's work is apparent from the translations of his *Storia* into German in 1790 and into English in 1807. Although the first Spanish translation appeared only in 1844, his influence on other American authors is manifest. For instance, Antonio Sánchez Valverde (1729–91) radicalized Clavijero's implied discourse of the Spanish colonies' singularity. Sánchez Valverde, a defiant, insubordinate priest born in Santo Domingo, is considered by critics to be the first Dominican writer. Sánchez Valverde uses Clavijero's dissertation on the French disease as the basis for his far more forceful discourse. His strategy is to translate sections of Clavijero's treatise and then add stinging information and criticism of his own. To avoid repetition in my treatment of both texts, I signal which ideas or details Sánchez Valverde extracts from Clavijero's work.

The title of Sánchez Valverde's second book, which was printed in Madrid, presents a powerful discourse of differentiation: *La America vindicada de la calumnia de haber sido madre del mal venereo* (America vindicated of the defamation of having been the mother of the venereal disease) (1785). This spirit of self-determination is also evident in the challenging tone of his discourse. Like Clavijero, his goal is to prove that America is not the source of *gálico*, but Sánchez Valverde also wants to prove that America is the source of its cure. In the same spirit and style as European authors, Sánchez Valverde develops a complex hermeneutical criticism that aims to destroy the arguments of his enemies. The most important features of Sánchez Valverde's text are his methodical references to contemporary works of science, especially those of Jesuit priests and French authors related to the *Encyclopedia,* such as Montesquieu, and his insistent pride in his homeland, which he accompanies with a growing reactive discourse against Europeans in general, and in particular against Spaniards who deemed the *americanos* as lesser beings, or as savages. His strategy is

Antonio Sánchez Valverde

Antonio Sánchez Valverde (1729–91) is a key intellectual from the island of Hispaniola. Born in Santo Domingo into a family of high social and economic status, he graduated with degrees in theology (1755) and law (1758). He earned the title "abogado de los Reales Consejos" while living in Madrid from 1763 to 1765. Ordained as a priest, he preached throughout the region and became known for delivering controversial sermons, which caught the attention of ecclesiastical authorities. He was forced to flee to Haiti in 1781, and later to Madrid in 1782, where he spent time working on *El Predicador,* a collection of sermons published that same year. Valverde is also known for his *Idea del valor de la Isla Española, y utilidades que de ella puede sacar su monarquía* (1785), which detailed the natural features of the island and possible ways that the Spanish could make use of its natural resources and agricultural products. This work also delves into the history of the island and its commerce, from the beginnings of Spanish domination leading up to the current state of Hispaniola's economy. Although it focuses on the economic promise of Hispaniola for the Spanish, *Idea* could be considered a precursor of the works of Alexander von Humboldt in the nineteenth century, in its cataloging and recognition of the uniqueness of the plants and animals native to the region of Spanish America. Sánchez Valverde's most controversial work is *La América vindicada de la calumnia de haber sido la madre del mal venéreo* (1785), in which he disputes the belief widely accepted by European scholars that syphilis originated in Spanish America, and specifically on Hispaniola. He disputes the opinions of the doctors of antiquity on the origin of the disease, presenting a defense of the island and portraying it as having more to offer—economic potential, unique flora and fauna—than its reputation as the place where venereal disease supposedly began.

---

one we already know from other subaltern colonial texts—namely, the power derived from knowing names, places, and events firsthand, and from giving extensive details that are lacking in the discourses of the status quo.

Following Clavijero, one of Sánchez Valverde's main targets is the widely read *Historia general y natural de las indias* (1535) by Gonzalo Fernández de Oviedo (1478–1557), a book and author I discussed earlier. Sánchez Valverde claims that Oviedo's story of the New Continent as the origin of *gálico* is a tall tale that has become "a widely generalized concern that can deter European commerce and settling in Hispaniola," to the point that he sees it "necessary to dispel, using principles as well as solid and undistortable reasoning, a myth that is so damaging to the development of that island" (3–4).[12] The author's annoyance with the historian from Madrid is later summarized in a blunt statement of rejection that labels Oviedo "the first slanderer of the Island of

Haiti" (lxi).[13] In addition to debunking Oviedo's account of the origin of the disease, the author also lambasts those who have gone along with what he deems Oviedo's cock-and-bull story. A case in point is his heavy criticism of Cornelius de Pauw, who, as I mentioned before, was also attacked by Clavijero. De Pauw was a well-known Dutch philosopher who contributed to the French *Encyclopedia,* worked in the court of Frederick the Great of Prussia, and for many years was considered a true authority on the New Continent. De Pauw offered sweeping statements about the Spanish colonies that became common preconceptions about the continent: "The Europeans who pass into America degenerate, as do the animals; a proof that the climate is unfavorable to the improvement of either man or animal. The Creoles, descending from Europeans and born in America, though educated in the universities of Mexico, of Lima, and the College of Santa Fé, have never produced a single book. This degradation of humanity must be imputed to the vitiated qualities of the air stagnating in their immense forests, and corrupted by noxious vapours from standing waters and uncultivated grounds" (18).

Sánchez Valverde attacks de Pauw's claim that *gálico* originated in the West Indies by showing that the European author was nothing more than an ignorant outsider: "We cannot easily ignore the Prussian Philosopher Paw, who used up ten years conducting philosophical inquiries on the Americans: labor he would have saved himself by taking at least a year to tour those lands. This Wise Man, like the others who share his views, waste a lot of paper and time investigating the causes of the origin of *gálico* in the West Indies, raving or lying" (lv).[14] His critical characterization of de Pauw's careless claims echoes the annoyance expressed by Clavijero, who five years earlier had portrayed the scholar as "Mr. de Paw, that enemy number one of all of the New World, that great investigator of the American filth" (474).[15]

Sánchez Valverde follows Clavijero in seeking an equalization of the hemispheres by revising existing histories. When Astruc or Oviedo or de Pauw declares, for example, that the indigenous peoples of America were prone to unbridled sex, Sánchez Valverde counters that the truly unbridled sexuality was historically that of the Europeans, the excesses of the Roman Empire being a case in point. As he translates Clavijero's dissertation, Sánchez Valverde goes a step further by showing that the arguments of these scholars were fallacious at best and tendentious in general: "What do these contradictions mean, other than that these systematic authors paint the Americans with the colors they find more convenient? When they want to qualify the apathy or insensitivity of those men, they say that they are most frigid; but when they try to discredit their customs or charge them with the origin of *gálico,* then they claim that they are extremely lecherous" (xxxii).[16] When authors like Astruc claim that the weather or the food in the New World is conducive to the emergence of *gálico* and consequently that the disease must be native to that region, Sánchez Valverde uses syllogisms to show that the very same conditions could be or have been present in Europe, and therefore the disease could also easily be ascribed to that area instead of the New World. The best way that the author finds to equalize the accepted discourse about the savageness of America and the American origin of the disease is by crafting a countering discourse that uses the same kind of persuasive tools. That is why Sánchez Valverde develops a complex hermeneutical criticism—a reading in between the lines that aims to destroy the arguments of his enemies, but also incurs the risk of the over-interpretation and exaggeration they are guilty of.

Nevertheless, by using the same rhetorical arsenal, the author from Española puts his own discourse on the same level as that of the Europeans who enjoyed international acclaim for their opinions. Sánchez Valverde takes care to point out that many of those opinions were not based on the Europeans' own direct observations. The fact that he is from the New Continent places him in a better position because he can claim a direct, factual knowledge that someone like Oviedo, Astruc, or de Pauw cannot: "I now disregard the errors of the Spaniard, of the French man, and of this Wise man from Berlin [. . .] among whom one can find, not only a notable difference, but a clear contradiction between the three, taking into account the latter two never saw lizards; and the first, if he did see any, could not identify the species and wrote about them from what others told him" (xxix).[17] Sánchez Valverde uses rhetorical arguments to prove that Astruc contradicts himself when he says in one part of his treatise that eating iguanas is the *cause* of *gálico* and later states that eating iguanas is a *remedy* against *gálico*. He employs the same approach to oppose de Pauw's assertion that all the inhabitants of the Indies have vitiated blood. According to de Pauw, Americans are more prone to degeneration because they eat lizards, which reinforces their natural inclination to develop syphilitic buboes. Sánchez Valverde debunks this attempt to link diet to buboes on the New Continent by attacking de Pauw from the inside—that is, by highlighting the contradictions in the Dutchman's text. For example, de Pauw claims that the inhabitants of southern Asia eat the same type of lizards as the inhabitants of the New Continent; he also informs his readers that only in Americans does such a diet produce *gálico*. Sánchez Valverde dwells on the incongruity: "A very peculiar thing that, the same species of lizard, when eaten in the Indies, is the origin of the venereal disease, according to Pavv, but it is an antivenereal in south Asia, where it produces different effects, and it cannot be the same in the Indies, as confirmed by those who have been there" (xxxi).[18] After restating that eating iguanas is the remedy and not the cause of *gálico,* Sánchez Valverde condemns de Pauw's lack of direct observation—a basic failure in any medical pursuit of the time. In a more obvious fashion than those of his predecessor Clavijero, Sánchez Valverde's arguments support his more political goal of crafting a sense of common identity for the region where he was born, and that is why he strategically accuses de Pauw of prejudice: "I cannot believe that Mr. de Pavv is an ignorant: but I am persuaded that in his brain there was certainly an anti-American seed, which unhinged and corrupted him when he was writing about those countries and their inhabitants, or that he wanted at all costs to console Prussia for its lack of colonies in America" (xxxi).[19]

As I will soon show, Sánchez Valverde has the same goal as the Guatemalan doctor Joseph Flores of crafting a discourse of engagement through differentiation with Europe, and he similarly points to the nature and the natural products of the New Continent to construct a sense of equality between the hemispheres. The generosity of the soil and the great harvest of all sorts of products serve to illustrate the potential of this region and the growing understanding of its self-sufficiency in economic terms. A proof of this realization in Sánchez Valverde's treatise can be found in a footnote related to his attack on de Pauw, where he agrees with the European scholar—only to strike at him later—about the youthful quality of America. The passage is all the more remarkable because of its literary quality: "She seems to be a beautiful, and robust maiden, and Europe, a frail and sterile old lady. America offers everywhere you look beautiful charms of green, and most leafy forests, that in both January and May and all the year are dressed and hanging with fruit. [...] The favored Europe, in order to show for three months some graciousness, spends nine in the most arduous pregnancy, arid, prickly, and dry as a skeleton. That land produces and grows with no more labor than spreading the seeds: this one, old as she is, needs to be encouraged with thousands of perseverant actions" (lxx).[20]

This florid praise of America as a fertile young woman brings me finally to the previously mentioned Joseph Flores. In a treatise circulated between the publications of Clavijero and Sánchez Valverde, Flores discusses the singularity of the Spanish colonies by emphasizing engagement through differentiation in the way that he depicts the unique curative flora and fauna of America and the use of native curative methods that surpass in their effectiveness those of erudite European doctors. On the title page of his *Específico nuevamente descubierto en el reyno de Goatemala, para la curacion radical del cancro, y otros mas frecuentes* (1782), he lists his academic affiliation as "of the guild and faculty of the Royal University of the mentioned Guatemala, his Fatherland."[21] There is overt pride in having studied at an American university and in the fact that he was born in "his Fatherland" (*su Patria*), Guatemala.[22] Flores is essentially addressing the public in the Spanish metropolis, underlining his goal of asserting commonality as a Guatemalan vis-à-vis his peninsular counterparts. In the introduction, he indirectly attacks what he perceives as the disdain felt by the people in Spain toward the colonies: "In the fertile countries of this America the Indians not only find their food, dress, furnishings, and everything they need to conserve the robust health they enjoy, but among the natural products they discover remedies that are as simple as they are effective to cure illnesses that until now have taunted the medical art and its wisest professors. So that, if we did not disdain learning from these simple people, and tried to treat them with friendship, we would discover specifics more important than the most eloquent essays, or the most curious discoveries of anatomy" (1).[23]

The inhabitants of "esta América" can lead bountiful lives without external help, and in spite of their supposed simplicity and backwardness they can provide solutions to problems that continue to affect Europe. He states that highbrow words—that is, Spanish or European discourses—are just empty sounds if they cannot counteract a disease, and that specific remedies known from customary practice by the indigenous people can actually cure what doctors trained in universities on the other side of the Atlantic cannot. Flores is presenting here an acute criticism of dogmatic medicine, which saw organizing observations as more important than trial and error—that is, experimentation. At the time, barber-surgeons and other empirical practitioners were considered inferior to doctors trained at universities in the Scholastic method. To bolster his argument, Flores includes the idea of "specifics more important than the most eloquent essays" from a French book published in Paris in 1741 by Gilbert Charles Le Gendre, *Traité historique et critique de l'opinion* (Historical and critical treatise on opinion). The part of the French argument that Flores uses is not that about the source of a specific remedy as self-defining, but instead the theoretical claim that a specific remedy is more valuable than an abstract six-hundred-page dissertation. In other words, the author himself crafts the *political* claim, while he uses the *scientific* claim to engage with previously sanctioned knowledge, in this case the French medical milieu where most of the advances in medicine were being made at the time.

The strategy of persuasion developed by Flores in his book is very different from the one I discussed above in examining other medical texts from the peninsula during the same period. His narrative of cure involves highly plotted stories and stories within stories that transfer his authority to the voices of multiple narrators. He starts with the true account of D. Joseph Ferrer, a Catalonian residing in Guatemala who has a cancerous ulcer on his face. European medicine has no remedy for his disease and he is near death. He goes to the priest of the Iglesia de la Candelaria, Father D. Joseph de Eloso, to prepare for his departure from earth into heaven. But the priest remembers the case of an indigenous woman in the town of San Juan Amatitan who was covered with buboes, the tumors that appear in the first stage of syphilis. The priest recalls that the woman had been begging for money. Although she was married, her husband was not with her because she was infected with *gálico*. When the priest decided to send her to a white doctor to be cured with Western medicine, the people of the town told him that there was no need for that, because they had their own medicine: eating the raw meat of a local kind of lizard. The Catalonian accepts the unorthodox treatment suggested by the priest and is cured, to the surprise of Western-trained doctors: "Mr. Nicolas Verdugo, Professor of Surgery, who had attended to him, and however many had seen corrupted not a small part of Ferrer's face, could not help but admire the quick restitution to his natural form" (4).[24]

From this web of narrations, Flores draws the idea of "domesticating" or "Westernizing" the indigenous cure. With that goal in mind, instead of advising patients to eat the raw lizard as the natives do and "to make the remedy less unpleasant, while imitating the method of the Indians," the author devises a new preparation in which he rapidly covers fresh pieces of lizard meat in wafers, then a normal form of European administration of medicines, "as quickly as possible so as to take the freshest meat possible, according to the Amatitaneco method" (6–7).[25] What is relevant here is that the author offers *lagartijas* (lizards) as a replacement for mercury—virtually the only treatment against *gálico* known to his colleagues—and its negative outcomes: "The heat, sweat, and salivation make it clear that the lizards are an advantageous equivalent of mercury. It is not necessary to take the scrupulous precautions as are needed with the mineral; nor is there any concern about the results" (11).[26] According to the medical ideas of the time, copious sweating, profuse salivation, and high fever helped expel the cause of the illness, bringing back to equilibrium the humors of the patient. Flores claims that this specific American remedy was far better than mercury, its European counterpart, because it would produce the same kind of high fever without requiring cumbersome mercurial preparations. The American remedy surpasses the effectiveness of the European both because of its simplicity—all you have to do is to eat the raw or "wafered/medicalized" meat of this particularly beneficial reptile—and because of its potential to cure diseases besides *gálico*, such as rabies and smallpox: "In these animals there can be found an excellent vermifugal, an antihydrophobic, and the specific against the smallpox that the celebrated Boerhave thought could be found in a certain composition prepared with antimony and mercury" (11).[27] Flores is following a medical inductive method in which the cure of one illness can be transferred to the cure of another illness, one with an analogous humoral structure: "This knowledge can open doors for us to many experiences, that can be tried with other animals eaten in the same way" (11).[28] Flores is even more attuned to the general ideas of the scientific method, and states that to collect more accurate information related to the effectiveness of the lizards from Amatitan he has started raising six of them in the Real Hospital "to examine their life, their genitals, their reproduction, and conservation, with the purpose of sending them live to the Royal Office of Natural History, and that Europe may participate in such a precious discovery" (12).[29] The political element is that now it is the observation and application of knowledge from the New World that is going to save the Europeans from disease, turning on its head the deep-rooted idea that the colonies were the ones passively receiving and passively taking advantage of knowledge haughtily provided by the Old World.

Twelve years after the publication of Flores's treatise, and ten years before Francisco Javier de Balmis became the director of the Real Expedición Filantrópica de la Vacuna (Royal Vaccine Philanthropic Expedition), Balmis published a book that defended the ability of agave and begonia, two American plants, to treat *gálico*. The storyline in Balmis's text is very similar to that of Flores. The author explains that in 1790 don Nicolas Viana, a criollo (an American-born person of Spanish and indigenous descent) from Pátzcuaro in Michoacán, revealed a cure for *gálico* to the Real Tribunal del Protomedicato, which regulated the medical professions in the Spanish Empire. Viana had learned about the medicine, which did not use mercury, from "an Indian woman, the last one of her family, who had used it since ancient times in Acapuacáro" (1).[30] The title of Balmis's treatise, *Demostración de las eficaces virtudes nuevamente descubiertas en las raices de dos plantas de Nueva-España, especies de ágave y de begónia, para la curacion del vicio venéreo y escrofuloso, Y de otras graves enfermedades que resisten al uso del Mercurio, y demás remedios conocidos* (Demonstration of the effective virtues newly rediscovered in the roots of two plants in New Spain, species of agave and begonia, for the cure of the venereal and scrofulous vice, and of other grave illnesses that resist the use of mercury and the rest of known remedies), shows how traditional indigenous knowledge was displaced by authors like Balmis who reframed and incorporated it as Western knowledge. The medicinal value of the American plants is presented as "nuevamente descubierto," that is, as "discovered anew" or "rediscovered," meaning that previous customary knowledge from the indigenous people in Mexico became real only through its reiteration by the sanctioned voice of the European scientific man. In this process, the knowledge of the plant's curative quality was displaced from the nameless indigenous woman— the true initial source—to the named but voiceless criollo with no professional credentials, and then to the published book of Dr. Balmis that reinforced his scientific authority.

This dynamic of "discovery" or "rediscovery," terms that in a strict sense really mean falling under a Western gaze, is one of the main features of the encounter of Europe with the New World. The much-debated use of the term "discovery" to qualify Christopher Columbus's arrival in 1492 is emblematic of the equivocal nature of the narration of a Western individual meeting a non-Western fact. In 1911, while in Peru, Hiram Bingham (1875–1956), a Yale University lecturer, was brought by Richarte, a local farmer, to the Inca ruins of Machu Picchu. The place, regularly known to the farmer and to children who played on the site, acquired its iconic eminence only when Bingham, thanks to his status as an American Yale scholar, brought it to international attention. A visitor to Machu Picchu today may find commemorative plaques at the entrance of the site celebrating and thanking Bingham as the "scientific discoverer" (*descubridor científico*) of the ruins. The term "scientific" here is synonymous with acknowledged knowledge—that is, Western knowledge.

According to Balmis, once Viana approached the Protomedicato in the capital city of New Spain, the medical regulators put in place a protocol of verification, showing that the rational ideas of the scientific method had taken root among the physicians in the colony.[31] Viana first administered the cure to a small group of *gálico* patients in the Hospital de San Juan de Dios under the vigilance of the hospital's doctor and surgeon, as well as the nurse priests (2). When the results of this monitored test were positive, Viana requested permission to use and sell his remedy, but the judges of the medical tribunal, even after the good results of the cure, decided that further trials should be implemented on a larger scale under rigorous monitoring (3). Under the patronage of the church, the Protomedicato called for a board composed of important figures of society to set up experiments with Viana's medicine. Among those invited were the principal people of the city, members of the Protomedicato, doctors and professors of the Hospital de San Andrés, and employees of the hospital. Viana was to implement his cure in twelve men and six women. After a good outcome was also achieved with these patients, the Protomedicato asked for further trials among a larger group: "Forty men and twenty women, affected to almost all degrees by the venereal disease" (4).[32] During all these trials, the only person involved in the cure was Viana, and the supervising physicians limited themselves to observing the process and results. The outcome was again very positive, and several of the doctors lauded it, stating that it was indeed a great find that should be used instead of mercury. Others nevertheless asked for further evidence because this remedy could mean "changing and even banishing, if it were possible, the use of Mercury, established in all Nations" (5).[33]

This is at the end of the eighteenth century, and the discourse that sanctions medical knowledge now puts experimentation and observation as benchmarks to verify efficacy. In his treatise, Balmis states his approval of Viana's adherence to the experimental method by identifying it under the rubric of empiricism, a title that would have been clearly negative eighty years before. Nevertheless, although the cure had been tested by using experimental benchmarks—"in spite of the *empiricism* with which it had been administered up until then, and although it was given on determined days in equal doses to all the sick, without distinction based on age, sex, or temperament" (6–7; emphasis in the original)[34]—the Viana's cure is not accepted until it conforms to the control provided by the institution that holds power over medical knowledge. This is the reason why after the verified success of the remedy, the ruling institution of the church and the Protomedicato decided that the technique should be used in the hospital, but this time administered by doctors who had the knowledge and who, after "well-thought examination, modify, simplify and organize in good method the new medicine" (6).[35] Viana was displaced from his position as the one holding knowledge and was replaced by officials who theoretically knew how to contain it under the parameters of sanctioned medicine. The key term used by Balmis here is "good method," meaning the control of received knowledge within the parameters of European viewpoints, a move very similar to that of Flores in finding a way to make the cure with lizard meat palatable and acceptable to a European public.

It was this good method that Balmis sought to follow upon his arrival in New Spain as chief surgeon of the Hospital General de San Andrés. The Spanish physician recognized the criollo's achievement, but criticized what he considered a lack of medical knowledge: "It is not my aim to criticize or censure Viana's empirical practice: it is easily seen that his lack of method and the disproportionate formulas that he used are direct consequences of his lack of medical knowledge: but what is worthy of admiration is how this man achieved with his methods such happy cures" (11).[36]

To rationalize Viana's practice, Balmis simplified the medicine and calibrated the doses given to *gálico* patients. he began by eliminating ingredients he considered superfluous, leaving those he deemed simple and effective. To this effect, he discarded the use of roses, which he thought would not help the patient to sweat profusely, and snake meat, a component that "modern doctors"—a French Mr. Vitet in particular—understood as glutinous and nutritious, but not actively curative (12). He similarly discarded the use of senna, anise, and colocynth because their purgative properties did not help directly in the destruction of the "*virus venéreo*" (13; emphasis in the original). Once Balmis isolated begonia and agave as the two therapeutic components, he applied himself to creating a system of treatments that differentiated between the gender, age, and body type of each patient in the Mexican hospital. Balmis combined the use of American plants with traditional European techniques of medicine administration, such as bloodletting, enemas, purges, as well as mixing the plants with opium or *quina* bark and presenting them as powders or granules, or in solutions of water.

The supposed effectiveness of the treatment—according to Balmis, 234 *gálico* patients had been cured with the method in Mexico (18)—moved the members of the Protomedicato to urge its use by "Professors of the Kingdom for the cure of *gálico* for the good of humanity, for its low cost, simplicity, safe usage, and short time that it is used in the treatment" (18).[37] Alonso Núñez de Haro (1772–1800), a powerful man who was the archbishop and had briefly been the viceroy of Mexico, recommended the implementation of new trials with the plants, but now in Madrid, the seat of the Spanish crown in Europe. Six months later, in January 1792, Balmis left the colony for Spain with 1,150 kilos of agave and 345 kilos of begonia.

With the backing of the Protomedicato and Núñez de Haro, Balmis's method was welcomed by the king. The positive reception of a potential remedy for *gálico* was predictable, especially because it would mean the end of a disease that had killed multitudes in the last three centuries. The positive economic outcome of holding a monopoly on the production of the specific plants, something similar to what had happened with the wood of the guaiacum tree since the sixteenth century, would have been the delight of any emperor. Balmis knew the importance of the "rediscovery" of the remedy and strategically placed himself at the center of the revelation of its curative qualities. The commercial potential of the two plants did not escape his otherwise altruistic reasoning: "The love that I profess to humanity; the distinguished confidence that I deserved from Your Excellency; the desire that encouraged me (just like this wise Prelate) to be useful to my Nation, creating a new branch of active commerce for the consumption of these roots, that only grow in that Kingdom, and many other important advantages for humanity; compelled me, without judgment, to happily accept the commission to transport to Europe the medicinal knowledge of these plants, at the cost of many dangers and annoyances, and thousands of other discomforts" (19–20).[38]

New trials, this time under the monitoring of court physicians, took place in the Hospital de San Juan de Dios, the Hospital General, and the Hospital de la Pasión in Madrid (21). One of the members of the overseeing board, Bartolomé Piñera y Siles (1753–1828), was not that enthusiastic or convinced about the medicinal value of the plants and very early into the trial published a treatise attacking the outcome of Balmis's regime. It is not clear whether Piñera's barrage was a the result of personal animus against Balmis, a rejection of a common medicine used by people he considered uncivilized, or simply an unbiased assessment of what he saw during the trials in Madrid. In the end, as we know, the begonia and agave treatment as a specific cure against *gálico* failed. Balmis, on the other hand, succeeded in his career as a physician. He was named personal surgeon and personal doctor to the king, received a degree as physician from the Real Universidad de Toledo, and later became the director of the royal vaccination expedition. One of the plants he used for the treatment of *gálico* was named after him: *Begonia balmisiana*. Neither the criollo Nicolas Viana nor the nameless indigenous woman who introduced the remedies to the colonial medical elite enjoyed such an honor.

Flores's exposition illustrates the process of engagement through differentiation I mentioned before, and which here aims to link his appropriation of indigenous knowledge to mainstream European knowledge.[39] This mode of relation is, of course, not simple. From one side, this dynamic is complex because, as explored at the beginning of the book in the discussion of the poem by Benegasi and his bowel movements, disease invests the subject with power, and disease is the source of her or his authority. The poor diseased indigenous woman stands at the same level as the diseased Spanish man. From another standpoint, by using a strategy of multilayered narrations, Flores is able to give authority to his voice and to his claims, but at the same time he cedes his own authority to his characters—the diseased Ferrer, who is from Catalunya; the parish priest, Joseph de Eloso, who recalls the indigenous cure; and the surgery professor, Nicolás Verdugo, who verifies the positive outcome of the treatment. They have real roles of authority in the colony and can attest to the efficacy of the American product because of their rank and because they are either Spaniards or closer to the status of the authoritative Europeans than the indigenous or the poor in the colony. In this sense, Europe continues to be the standard by which the efficacy of an American product is measured. Following this logic, the importance that Flores sees in his study is related to its capacity to answer questions or quandaries posed by Europe, here represented by the quest of the famous Dutch physician Herman Boerhaave (1688–1738) to find a cure or an effective treatment for smallpox. Another layer of complexity is added by Flores's choice of terminology and his citation of French medical sources, which reveal the use of a more modern scientific language than that of the peninsular texts of the time. These characteristics are compounded by the pervasive influence of French and English scientific discourses in Flores's text, instead of the traditional Spanish one.

Sánchez Valverde's fight to prove that America was not the source of *gálico* was to be continued by other important Spanish American figures of the eighteenth and nineteenth centuries. Both Fray Servando Teresa de Mier (1765–1827) and Andrés Bello (1781–1865) researched and wrote extensively to argue that Europeans had brought the disease to America. Bello's work on *gálico* was not published until after his death, but it is clear that during his time in England between 1810 and 1829 he was interested in analyzing texts to prove that the disease did not originate on the New Continent, and that for him, rejecting attempts to cast the colonies as the source of the French disease was a key component of his agenda to claim autonomy for America.

In the sixth volume of Bello's *Obras completas* the editor explains that "there was especially one point in the history of medicine that caught Bello's attention and about which he did a lot of research during his time in England, though, unfortunately, he did not have the time to put it together, much less publish it. That point was the origin of syphilis" (xxxvii).[40] In his manuscript, Bello holds Clavijero's work in high regard, calling it "the interesting and erudite dissertation on the *Origin of the Venereal Disease,* composed in 1780 by the Mexican ex-Jesuit Don Francisco Saverio Clavijero" (xliii).[41] This reference makes me believe that the notes and citations in Bello's manuscript are in fact based on Clavijero, and not necessarily the result of Bello's direct assessment of the primary sources. Like Clavijero, he uses the strategy of revealing "the contradictions that can be seen in the authors that have studied this subject" (lxiii),[42] similarly exhibiting his annoyance at the lack of serious research behind the claims of European authors: "I cannot help but mention here an example of the flippancy with which those who maintain that syphilis was brought from America to Europe have acted" (lxiv).[43] Like Clavijero, Bello was especially interested in tracing sources in order to show the contradictions of those ascribing *gálico* to the New Continent. He mentions de Pauw as an unreliable source—"Cornelio de Pauw, indeed a glib writer, and given to arguing paradoxical theses, composed his work to demonstrate that the indigenous race of America was much inferior than those of the old world" (xli)[44]—as well as Robertson, whom he criticizes for following the opinions of Astruc and de Pauw.

What differentiates Bello's notes from Clavijero's is that he uses a rhetorical move similar to that of Sánchez Valverde when tackling these authors. For example, he quotes parts of the Scottish historian's book to stress the New World's right to oppose the conquering rulers by seeing *gálico* as a sort of retribution: "By passing it to their conquerors, they most abundantly avenged the abuses that had been done to them" (xli).[45] He employs this argument as ammunition to attack Spanish rule and to justify the processes of autonomy that he very much supported.

Fray Servando Teresa de Mier, an important figure in the campaign for Mexican independence, was also invested in the cause of self-rule on the New Continent and in proving that *gálico* was not an American disease. The incidents in Teresa de Mier's life, especially his recurring imprisonment for religious and political reasons, prove that he was an active critical thinker, constantly opposing ingrained ideas, defying the establishment, and defending autonomy. Teresa de Mier's arguments on *gálico* form part of an unpublished volume he wrote while in prison in San Juan de Ulúa, in Veracruz, where he was held prisoner by orders of Viceroy Apodaca in 1820. The volume, titled *Idea de la constitución* (Thoughts on the constitution), was an examination of the legal corpus that had been promulgated by the Spanish monarchy before the French invasion and that he interpreted as clearly establishing Spanish colonies as autonomous regions associated with the metropolis.[46] The author hoped to address the Americans' lack of representation in the Cortes de Cádiz, which he had attended in the assembly's initial stages.[47] When Teresa de Mier realized that the Cortes would not provide fair treatment of the colonies, he moved to London in 1811, where he befriended Bello.[48] There is no textual evidence that the two men shared their ideas about the origin of *gálico,* but it is relevant that all these authors were aware of the topic's potential ability to bolster statements about selfhood and autonomy for the colonies.

Teresa de Mier's discussion about *gálico* is consigned to a section titled "Nota 2," with the subtitle "Sobre el origen del gálico o mal venéreo" (On the origin of *gálico* or venereal disease) (315). He supposedly wrote these notes for inclusion in a reprint of his work, but the publication of neither a short treatise in Veracruz nor a longer volume in Havana took place. Following a line of attack that can be traced back to Clavijero, Teresa de Mier argues with de Pauw, but the main difference between his discourse and that of his predecessors is an increased level of acrimony that mirrors his despondency over Europeans looking down on Americans. The targets of his ire include the Spaniards in the Cortes de Cádiz, whom he came to loathe for not treating Americans as their equals: "There was an unknowing one named Paw who was born in Prussia; but he must have written his *Investigations on the Americans* only beyond the polar circles; otherwise it would not have been possible to write with such utter and absolute ignorance of the Americas and all their things: even though he says he worked there for nine years to compile his material" (295–96).[49]

One of the scholars with whom Teresa de Mier continuously debated was Pedro Estala, the Spanish writer I have already discussed. Estala said that the deadly outbreak of *gálico* among the natives of California was their punishment for not being Christians. Teresa de Mier claims that in "Letters from Tulitas Cácalo-xochitl [a text that is now lost] I caught five hundred lies in what [Estala] wrote about Mexico, beyond the innumerable absurdities and contradictions" (319).[50] He also argues that Estala used de Pauw's *Investigaciones sobre los americanos* in his *Viagero Universal* to attack Americans in general, and Teresa de Mier in particular, for having broadcast evidence of his shoddy scholarship: "From it he extracted many lies and absurdities that, bothered by me, who had refuted him, and prodded by don Luis Trespalacios, a mountain simpleton, vomited against the Mexicans this don Pedro Estala, *universal voyager,* who has not gone farther than the cloisters of the Piarist School" (297).[51]

In addition to restating Sánchez Valverde's objections to the lack of direct observation on the part of European authors who underestimated those on the New Continent, Teresa de Mier also follows his lead in attributing the source

Fray Servando Teresa de Mier

Fray Servando Teresa de Mier (1765–1827), a priest, writer, and orator, was born in the viceroyalty of New Spain into an upper-class criollo family. Teresa de Mier famously delivered a sermon in 1794 in which he claimed that the Virgen de Guadalupe, an important religious and cultural icon for the residents of New Spain, had appeared first to Saint Thomas the Apostle and not in 1531 to Juan Diego—an indigenous man, canonized in 2002 as Saint Juan Diego Cuauhtlatoatzin. For this challenge to accepted historical and religious beliefs, Teresa de Mier was sentenced to exile in Spain and prevented from preaching. Throughout his life, he would go on to be jailed, and escape successfully, seven times. Teresa de Mier's support of revolution and independence for Mexico is visible not only in his many writings—among others, "Cartas de un americano al español" (1811–13), "Historia de la revolución de la Nueva España" (1813), and, in collaboration with José María Blanco, *El Español,* a pro-independence newspaper published in London—but also in the military campaigns in which he participated, such as in Soto la Marina in 1817 when he was captured, imprisoned, and tried by the Inquisition in Mexico. Following the establishment of independence, Mier served as a representative of the Second Constituent Congress, and in 1824 signed the Federal Constitution for the United States of Mexico.

of the lie about the origin of *gálico* to Oviedo: "But the Europeans, far from agreeing that we also owe the venereal disease to them, have taken for granted, with their elegant babblers Paw and Raynal, that it was from America that this fateful gift came to them, carried on Columbus's ships. But this voice has no other origin than the authority of Oviedo, enemy and tyrant of the indians, in his false and loathsome *History of the Indies*" (315).[52]

The attacks against Estala, de Pauw, and the French writer Abbé Raynal (1713–96), in conjunction with his disdain for Oviedo's history, serve Teresa de Mier well as he triangulates his criticism as part of a combined effort among Americans to believe in their own authors and their own ways of thinking. Years later, Andrés Bello stated the call for intellectual autonomy in very clear terms years n his 1848 "Modo de estudiar la historia" (Method of studying history): "Bernal Díaz will tell you much more than Solís and Robertson. Interrogate every civilization in its own works; ask every historian for his sources. That is the first philosophy we should learn from Europe. Our civilization will also be judged by its works; and if it is seen as obediently copying from Europe, even when it is not applicable, what will be the judgment a Michelet or a Guizot will make of us? They will say: America still has not shaken off its chains; it follows in our footsteps blindfolded; in their works, you cannot breathe their own way of thinking, there is nothing original, nothing characteristic; it mimics the forms of our philosophy, and you cannot grasp its spirit. Its civilization is an exotic plant that has not yet sucked up the juices of the land that holds it" (7:125).[53]

This increasing sense of selfhood is already present throughout Teresa de Mier's body of work, and can be seen in his acknowledgment of Sánchez Valverde's scholarly proof of *gálico*'s non-American origin. In recognizing this source of pride, he uses the possessive to indicate that the author from Española belongs to this tradition of autonomy and dignity: "But our Sánchez Valverde, from Santo Domingo, wrote against Paw in his erudite dissertation on the origin of *gálico*, a thorough demonstration with the monuments of history" (316).[54]

Shifting to a more scientific perspective, Teresa de Mier incorporates into his discourse the possibilities of other forms of contagion, perhaps in line with enhanced knowledge about the spread and cure of smallpox. He must then concede that syphilis may have been present on the New Continent in a similar stage or form to what materialized in Europe: "I do not deny that in some part of our immense America could there have been the venereal disease, even though the Indians are the least susceptible to it; because as Fracastoro asserts, this seems to be one of those diseases that covers the entire globe, and it is as the price paid to all excesses in all cases. Perhaps there was this disease in Mexico in the same way that there were flies, like those that were brought to the islands on Spanish boats; but it is evidently false that it was carried to Europe from America. Precisely, Peter Martyr d'Anghiera tells that the Indians from the islands waged war against the Spaniards for having infected their women" (318).[55]

Notice that he is not agreeing that the disease was brought to Europe from America; he says only that there could have been a local presence of the disease on the New Continent, and that the occurrence of *gálico* in Europe could have been the result of a European outburst. This form of argumentation allows him to refute negative discourse about his motherland while remaining open to the new medical theories that he knew would come. On a scientific level, he seems to be appreciative of medical advancements in Europe, as exemplified by his hopeful tone about a cure for *gálico* coming from that region of the world: "Thank God that just as knowledge of the vaccine has come to us from Europe, whence smallpox came, we are going to receive the cure, or at least the prevention, for *gálico*" (318).[56] Nevertheless, he also clearly refers to the schism between the colonies and the metropolis at the political level. This is another instance of what I have argued is a discourse of engagement through differentiation.

Clavijero, Sánchez Valverde, Bello, and Teresa de Mier, all major figures in the process of solidifying the Spanish colonies' sense of self-determination and self-worth, and all preeminent authors in the history of Latin American letters, used the controversy about the origin of *gálico* to circulate an ethos of differentiation from the Spanish metropolis. The rhetorical dispute with medical, philosophical, and historical authorities allowed them to press for that impetus of differentiation while preserving channels of engagement with the prevalent modes of knowledge in Europe. While the content of these four authors' works does not change much—from the initial argument posed by Clavijero in 1780 to the claims made by Teresa de Mier as late as 1821—the dynamic in these texts is one of increasing antagonism felt by these authors toward those who fallaciously attempted to put down the peoples they considered worthy of respect and representation.

In addition to their crafting of an idea of selfhood by debunking the American origin of *gálico* via rhetorical arguments, that idea of selfhood was also galvanized via the presentation of the New Continent's abundance of soil and the richness of its other natural resources, and the envisioning of economic ventures that could provide tangible support for the future of the region. In this gradual establishment of associative difference, it was important to show facts to demonstrate that America was indeed the promising source of a cure for *gálico*. Historically, the most important remedy from America against *gálico* was guaiacum, also known as *vara de Indias* (stick of the Indies). Chips and slivers of this tree were generally used to prepare a beverage that, in line with medical treatments of the time, produced humor-expelling sweat and salivation. This beverage was called *agua de palo* (wood water), and although it was initially administered on its own, over time doctors prescribed it as a medicine to be mixed with other ingredients.

A similar concoction used from very early on in Europe was made from sarsaparilla, or zarzaparrilla (*Smilax ornata*), a vine found in Central America, and not surprisingly called *agua de zarza*. Sarsaparilla was listed as a treatment for syphilis well into the beginning of the twentieth century. As I have discussed before, sarsaparilla was the American remedy mentioned by Francisco de Quevedo in his humorous and scatological poem titled "To Marica the moocher" and by Benegasi y Luján in his mocking poem about Anastacio Pantaleón de Ribera's illness and death. The effectiveness of these remedies was largely believed to depend on the specific place where the plants were found, and that is why an author like the surgeon Juan Calvo insists in his *Cirugia universal* (1703) on using sarsaparilla brought from "Honduras, which is the best, and the one that produces the best effects" (553), a claim backed eighty years later by Vicente Ferrer Gorraiz in his *Cartilla de cirujanos* (1780), where he states that the "Anti-gálico syrup of the Beinzas must be prepared using selected sarsaparilla of Honduras split and then broken into small pieces" (171). The economic importance of the American continent's natural products, especially the sarsaparilla vine, is evident in Father Joseph Gumilla's *El Orinoco ilustrado* (The learned Orinoco) (1741), a product of his prolonged work as a Jesuit missionary in the regions of Orinoco, Meta, and Casanare in Nueva Granada (present-day Colombia). The priorities of the Society of Jesus and of the Spanish crown—balanced between economic interest, desire for knowledge, and religious zeal—are mirrored in the equally polygonal subtitle of Gumilla's book: "Natural, Civil, and Geographic History of this Great River and Its Mighty Watersheds: Government, Practices, and Customs of the Indians That Inhabit It, with New and Useful Information of Animals, Trees, Fruits, Oils, Resins, Herbs, and Medicinal Roots: And Above All, There Will Be Found Unique Conversions to Our Holy Faith, and Cases of Much Edification."[57] Among the many catalogs of peoples, animals, and plants, and the precise mention of geographical features, Gumilla comments on the presence of sarsaparilla by connecting the fecundity of the distant Orinoco region with the needs and desires of Spaniards and Europeans, who, after all, are his target audience: "In the rivers *Chire, Tate, Punapuna,* and many others from those plains, can be found the much celebrated *sarsaparilla,* proven remedy against *gálico*" (279).[58] The celebration and approval of this American plant as a cure for the feared disease foretells the differentiation that will slowly turn into a clear and radicalized sense of selfhood—that is, one in which the emphasis in the sentence "our zarza *for you* to use" would shift to "*our* zarza for you to use."

I have mentioned other American remedies such as sassafras, brought especially from Florida to Europe to treat *bubas* (Astruc, *Tratado* 90), or milk extracted from the root of the now seemingly extinct *mechoacán.* In his *Arcanismo* (1731), Suárez de Ribera explains that *mechoacán* had been brought to Spain from Mexico and Peru and was known for its purgative properties, as well as for its effectiveness in treating *bubas.* Another medicinal plant believed to cure all symptoms of *gálico* was a fern from Central and South America called calaguala (Pérez Bravo 13). The name of this plant was derived from the Quechua *Ccallahuala* (for more information on this plant, see the sidebar "Calaguala," on p. 67). I have also commented on the tortoise meat found off the coasts of America, which was commonly used by buccaneers to cure their *gálico* (Astruc 102), but which had to be fresh for the treatment to be effective. During previous centuries, the lavishness, variety, and effectiveness of remedies from America were exclusively utilitarian in purpose. It is only during the last third of the eighteenth century that these qualities are connected to a sense of belonging. The prospect of Spanish America presenting a specific cure for *gálico,* which would benefit humanity as a whole while offering worthy materials for the conformation of selfhood among those living in the Spanish colonies, reinforces this germinal stage of differentiation.

Botanical Expeditions

The royal chest was always in need of more resources. After the drastic reduction in the production of silver in the Potosí mines around 1712, and needing to keep the cogs of the largest administrative apparatus of the time moving, the Spanish crown was invested in measuring, cataloging, and appraising the worth of its resources across the Atlantic. Material need coincided with a growing scientific interest in Enlightenment thought, particularly in the connection between natural resources and wealth developed by François Quesnay (1694–1774) in his *Maximes générales de gouvernement economique d'un royaume agricole* (1758), and in the realm of botany, spearheaded by the taxonomical efforts of Sweden's Carl Linnaeus (1707–78), whose system of binomial nomenclature inspired those who wished to inscribe into the annals of scientific history the flora and fauna beyond the European sphere. As in the case of Balmis's *Begonia balmisiana,* scientific nomenclature was also a way of gaining a place in posterity. The creation of botanical expeditions to explore, gather, and organize natural wealth fulfilled in part the need to assess and manage colonial possessions. The three main botanical expeditions took place in the Viceroyalty of Peru (1777–1811), the Viceroyalty of Nueva Granada (1783–1817), and the Viceroyalty of New Spain (1787–1803). These expeditions included the participation of botanists, mathematicians, painters, astronomers, and geographers in a task that took several years to complete and offered young scientists from the colonies an opportunity to see the riches of their regions and the place of importance they had in relation to the rest of the world from a scientific and material viewpoint.

This progressive sense of self is exemplified by Dr. Flores in Guatemala, and also appears very distinctly in the 1788 *Compendio de la medicina: Ó medicina practica, en que se declara laconicamente lo mas util de ella, que el autor tiene observado en estas Regiones de Nueva España* (Medicine compendium: Or practical medicine, in which the most useful that the author has observed in these regions of New Spain is briefly stated), by Dr. Juan Manuel Venegas. Like previous authors, Venegas generates knowledge in the colonies to produce effects in the metropolis. In a veiled criticism of the Bourbon king and his viceroys, he laments the lack of doctors in Mexico and offers his book as a temporary but practical solution, giving remedies to regular people in the colony (x). There are several characteristics of Venegas's treatise that place his work within a spirit of knowledge that is kin to the eclectic reception of the Enlightenment in the Spanish colonies. One of them, also present in Flores's *Específico,* is the increasing incorporation of scientific advances in countries other than Spain. Like the other authors I have been discussing in this section,

Venegas appreciates and appropriates the nature and history to which he feels he belongs, as can be seen in the localization of his discourse in New Spain.

Another instance of the author's enlightened quality is his self-satisfaction in writing the book in plain language, making it understandable to the general public, a quality that reverberates with the idea of the social function of knowledge. Although Venegas's goal is medical, the texture of his writing exemplifies a transitional scientific discourse that mixes narrative nuance and a more rational discourse based on a systematic use of numbers and measures to convey efficacy. His definition of *amor venéreo* (venereal love), for example, shows that his training as a doctor combined traditional medical knowledge and secular humanism: "Venereal love is defined so: a desire to be in union with the beloved thing. The poet paints it like a smooth fire in the bones, or a hidden wound in the heart: *est mollis flamma medullas. Interea & tacitum vivit sub pectore vulnus* [the flame devours the tender heartstrings and deep in the breast lives the silent wound]. The cause is the desire to possess a delectable property. Those who fall in its webs suffer deceptions, faintness, sleeplessness, and fever; they believe their suspicions, the impossible does not terrify them, neither are they contained by difficulties, they are not persuaded by advice, nor does the mind constrain them. They are blind to reason: *quid deceat non videt ullus amans* [love never suffers itself to be under any restraint from decency]. Ovid" (292).[59] Venegas's description is part of his discussion on *pathemata animi* (passions of the soul) that can be cured with medicine; the other three allegedly curable passions are fear, wrath, and sadness.

In his task of synthesis, an emblem of the colony-metropolis relationship, Venegas interweaves formalized knowledge, coming from Spain and the rest of Europe in the form of printed books, with empirical knowledge, which he has obtained from practicing medicine among creoles and indigenous people. In the production of knowledge, Venegas's in-between position seeks to balance the old and the new forms of understanding the world and deriving knowledge from it: "In this little work I make an effort so that the public may have in a small volume, not only the most useful things that can be found dispersed throughout many books, but also what I have observed in our America, frankly stating everything that I have experienced to be the most beneficial for the sick" (x).[60] The heated dispute between empirical and academic doctors, which resulted in tome after tome of rhetorical hodgepodge in Spain, finds a completely different outcome in America, where authors like Flores or Venegas respectfully listen and learn about traditional remedies (especially from *curanderos*), for the very simple reason that such medicines are at times effective: "As brilliant and great the number of philosophical, chemical, and botanical books that adorn the libraries may seem; and as exquisite and tasteful as the discourses given by learned physicians may be, in spite of the display of pompous voices in the board meetings, and of the erudite dissertations, a wretched old woman, a poor peasant, or a stupid Indian frequently taunt them with the effective use of a disparaged medicine" (xi).[61]

Furthermore, regarding the rationalization of nature—a pursuit that had reached its pinnacle with the taxonomical work of Linneaus in his 1758 *Systema Naturae*—Venegas points out how ineffectual it can be when medical science does not know how to identify or apply the virtues of particular specimens. For Venegas, that was the important service that empirical practice could perform, and more specifically the service that could be derived from the indigenous empirical practice that was so abundant on and deep-rooted in the New Continent: "If we present a strange plant to the most accomplished botanists, they would never give us the slimmest light with the *Systema* to assure us in the uses for which we should apply it" (xi).[62] In addition to defending this unconventional, nonformalized type of knowledge, Venegas insists on the economic potential of aboriginal products, and that the Old Continent should be thankful to America: "America is the wealth of all-powerfulness, and the earthly paradise that enriches Europe, not only with its precious metals, but also with its many most noble vegetables, in woods, roots, plants, fruits, saps, balms, etc. [. . .] Let it be an example the *Quina* and the *Xalapa*. These indigenous drugs, which, in many cases, are undeniably preferable to the most precious remedies, do not show their virtues as commonly on the American soil itself as much as it is experienced in the northern regions and cold countries of Europe" (xiii–xiv).[63]

Venegas's claim is a counterargument to a European view, such as that of Pedro Estala, which held that the quality and quantity of riches extracted from the American colonies would not pay for all the negative consequences of colonization. For authors like Cornelius de Pauw, the New Continent was a misshapen grouping of feral territories, populated by savages and generating unbearable diseases. Venegas's treatise addresses this kind of negative preconception. He argues that America is *both* the source of riches sent to the Spanish metropolis *and* the place where all sorts of invaluable remedies in the form of plants and animals could be found. This knowledge makes the doctor from New Spain proud of his autochthonous yet privileged position, away from the peninsula. In Venegas's text, there is a consistent naming with local words—for example, the common use of the term *garabatillo* instead of gonorrhea (150)—and he persistently refers to natural American remedies and methods together with European procedures and preparations. To cure syphilitic buboes, he not only lists mercury but also adds that *incordios* can be dissolved by applying the "lightly roasted and split stem of the *tapona* prickly pear nopal cactus" (*Opuntia robusta*) (50);[64] or by using tequesquite, the grey salt extracted from Lake Texcoco; or "fine powder of *chichicamole*" (*Microsechium helleri*), a cu-

Cinchona

Quina (*Cinchona officinalis*) is a tree in the Rubiaceae family, native to the Andes. It is known in Spanish as *cinchona, quina, cascarilla;* in Quechua as *quarango* (Jarcho 207); and in English as Peruvian crown, Peruvian bark, Jesuit's bark, Loxa bark, Pale bark, or Countess's powder. The tree is the source of quinine, a very effective remedy and prophylactic for malaria, as well as an efficient antipyretic. The Quechua population knew about the medical properties of the *quinaquina* tree (in Quechua, *kina kina*) for many years before the Europeans learned about its use, using it as an antifebrile, and as a muscle relaxer to halt shivering from the cold. After the introduction of malaria to the continent by the European conquest, it was used as an antimalarial. The main legend about *quina* is that the powder, procured by a Jesuit magistrate, cured the Countess of Chinchón from a serious tertiary fever, after which she distributed it to the populace and took it to Europe. However, there are enough historical inaccuracies in this legend to make its credibility more than suspect, as Saúl Jarcho discusses in great detail (6). *Quina* was brought to Rome in 1631 and spread from the Iberian Peninsula across the continent over the course of the next decades. It was not until 1751 that the Spanish crown decreed *quina* as worthy of intense interest and study, perhaps because its efficacy goes against Hippocratic and Galenic teachings about the treatment of fevers, as it was hot and dry and thought to retard the expulsion of morbid matter, the opposite of accepted treatments for fever (Jarcho 6–7; Ruiz López, *Quinologia* 5–6). Indeed, its adoption throughout Europe was relatively slow, with rates of use falling below what could be expected based on clinical trials and royal endorsements. The importance of *quina* for humanity can also be measured by the fact that an image of the tree is part of Peru's coat of arms.

---

curbitaceous plant (see fig. 6); or the root of pegapega (*Desmodium incanum*) (see fig. 7); or "agave mead"; or copaiba tree balsam (*Copaifera*), an American remedy for *gálico* that became prevalent during the nineteenth century (see fig. 8). There is even an antivenereal made with hot chocolate. From this inventory of native medical ingredients and local products to the stanzas of Bello's "The Agriculture of the Torrid Zone," which extol the rural area versus the urban, there is only one little step. In the prologue of Venegas's treatise, his powerful praise of the natural remedies found in his country is striking, but his designation of the region that is the source of these remedies is even more surprising: "And thus, not having planned to write the Natural History of these Kingdoms [. . .] I am content with proposing the most effective medicines, which I have experienced as being the most beneficial in *this, our America*" (xiv; my emphasis).[65] Venegas's vision of the present and the future of the continent—

Figure 6. Chichicamole (*Microsechium helleri*). (Courtesy of the Hunt Institute for Botanical Documentation, Carnegie Mellon University, Pittsburgh, PA, Torner Collection of Sessé and Mociño Biological Illustrations)

"*esta nuestra* América"—is a formulation *avant la lettre* of Martí's famous homonymous essay, even though Venegas's agenda does not contain the radical divorce with the European or North American episteme we find in Martí's. Venegas is proposing "engagement through differentiation" with Europe and its ideals of progress, while Martí seeks a radical differentiation that will help protect the acquired yet still feeble status of self-government.

These authors used *gálico* to situate authority on people previously deemed as peripheral. The appropriation of enlightened ideas turns the locus of knowledge on its head, and the colonies are now the ones producing knowledge that affects the metropolis. The localized colonial provenance of plants and animals used to cure diseases such as syphilis began to foster a sense of commonality, identity, self-sufficiency, and difference from the imperial center.

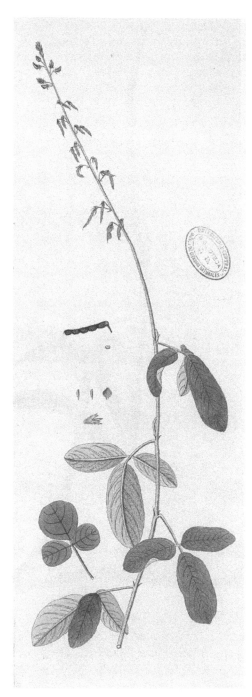

Figure 7. Pegapega (*Desmodium incanum*). (Biblioteca Digital del Real Jardín Botánico, CSIC, Madrid; © RJB-CSIC)

Figure 8. Copaiba (*Copaifera*), William Woodville, and James Sowerby, 1790. *Medical Botany,* vol. 3, p. 137. London: Printed and sold for the author, by James Phillips. (Peter H. Raven Library/ Missouri Botanical Garden)

Throughout this process of presenting the New Continent as the answer to a disease of global proportions, the authors portray elements of what we rather loosely may call the Enlightenment. There is a discourse of reason represented in their measurements, methods, and generalizations. There is an enlightened economic defense of agriculture as a source of wealth that echoes the work of François Quesnay. There is a promotion of useful knowledge as a relevant instance of the Enlightenment. There is the eclectic presence of encyclopedic authors, philosophers, and physiocrats, as well as English thought and even U.S. ideals of self-governability. But this brand or incarnation of Spanish American Enlightenment is above all the strategic use of ideas to support assertions of self-worth from a subaltern position. In other words, here in the eighteenth century, and later in the nineteenth century, this dynamic is not necessarily that of an *adoption* of Western ideas, or of the Enlightenment, but rather a deliberate *adaptation* of such ideas—products of the dominant status quo—in order to reorganize them or to remanufacture them into new meanings to back the agenda of differentiation, providing elements to counteract the feeling of being "less than."

Along these lines, and considering positions others have taken about the origin of *gálico* and its links to changing literary and political discourses, I beg to differ with the prevailing interpretation of the eighteenth century—generally conducted under an ill-defined lens of the Enlightenment—as an almost infantile preparation for the independence movements and nation building that were to come almost miraculously around 1810. Instead, it would be more accurate to assert that those who made public their ideas in Spanish America at the time were simply setting in place revised forms of engaging with their natural interlocutors by means of a clear differentiation. This study of the prolegomena of independence via the assessment of the discourse on *gálico* points to the hypothesis that those revolutions were the result of a conjunction of circumstances, such as the vacuum of power, the pressure of unfair taxation, and the rampant disdain the authorities exhibited toward their subjects. But before that conjunction of circumstances, all there was a need of engagement through differentiation.

This drive toward self-worth was connected to the rejection of the idea of the New Continent as the source of *gálico* and to the lushness of the American soil, and is present, clear, and continued use in the medical, literary, and political texts I have studied, but there is no doubt that this disease was also a literal, common *mal americano*. The relocalization of both the origin of the disease and the autochthonous curative products was an unmistakably ideological move by those unable to deny that, in America, the negative consequences of the disease at the economic and social levels were as rampant as in Spain.

10 ❧

José Joaquín Fernández de Lizardi's Diseased Characters

The portrayal of *gálico* as the outcome of damaging yet accepted practices in Spanish American colonial societies takes literary shape in three of the best-known works by the important Mexican writer José Joaquín Fernández de Lizardi (1776–1827), whose *Noches tristes* I have alluded to before. His father was a modest physician in Mexico City, and Fernández de Lizardi was consequently familiar with the dynamic of *gálico* and the way it pervaded all levels of the social texture. By the last third of the eighteenth century, the city had around 150,000 inhabitants, and Lizardi's texts provide an effective way to understand the great differences among social levels and the complex web of social exchanges that occurred there. The title of Lizardi's most important work, *El Periquillo Sarniento* (*The Mangy Parrot*) (1816), signals the idea of contagious disease, its relationship to social problems, and the role of humor as a form of cathartic or purgative treatment.[1] The text, considered by some critics to be the first novel written in Spanish America, begins with Periquillo, the bedridden protagonist, retelling his life as a boy who strayed from the right path. Through the picaresque narration of his wrongdoings, Periquillo wants to teach his children about the negative results of keeping bad company and the dangers of the world. His exploits also include time spent as a servant-secretary to D. Cosme Casalla, a pettifogger known among the prisoners and others who sought his services as "Escribano Chanfaina" (Notary Offalstew), a moniker that both resonates with his real name and reflects his inclination to stir up shady business. Chanfaina is on one occasion confronted by an honorable lawyer, D. Severo Justiniano, whose own name may mean "uncompromising justice." In his diatribe, Justiniano summarizes the social disease represented by this kind of dishonest and ignorant functionary: "You, and other notaries as driven by passion and malice as yourself, are to blame for the fact that the common people, who are rarely correct in their judgments, view this noble profession with dislike and even, I would say, with hatred. [...] Isn't it a pity, then, that through their fraud, stupidity, and petty thefts, a handful of rascals should besmirch a profession that is so laudable for society?" (*Mangy* 246–47).[2]

Chanfaina is old, venal, corrupt, arrogant, miserly, and a swindler. Lizardi condenses and transfers these qualities to the shyster's body as the presence of *gálico* and the hideous effects of radical attempts to treat it. These are especially visible in relation to Chanfaina's face and mouth: "he spoke with a nasal twang, and splattered spittle all over whoever was listening to him, because the French disease and the mercury treatment had left him without teeth or uvula; he was hardly generous; and on top of all these fine qualities, he had the laudable one of being extremely jealous" (*Mangy* 250).[3] The lack of teeth, the missing uvula, and the twangy voice—all marks of a body touched by the venereal disease—are used by Fernández de Lizardi to create a veritable image of the rot within the colonial administrative apparatus. In his view, Chanfaina's dribbling on the common people who seek help within the bureaucracy of the New Spain's viceroyalty makes them willing or unwary vehicles of contamination amid the rampant disarray of governmental affairs.

Notary Offalstew is not the only corroder of the social fabric in relation to *gálico*. Periquillo himself deceives people when he decides to become a quack doctor. To make a good living, he must appear to have undergone university training. Because New Spain lacked an effective system for licensing physicians or enforcing stated regulations through the Protomedicato, the practice of medicine by fake doctors was rampant. The shortage of doctors in the colony allowed unprincipled individuals such as Periquillo to take advantage of the unsuspecting or the gullible. A priest with whom "Dr." Periquillo is conversing summarizes the situation of the people in the colony who live far from the main urban centers: "I am speaking in general, and only against bad physicians—empiricists and charlatans who abuse this precious and necessary art, which was bestowed upon us by the Author of Nature to ease us of our pains" (*Mangy* 295).[4] Fearing that the harsh comment is a veiled attack against himself, Periquillo rushes to fill the resulting space in the dialogue with all the superficial information and trumpery he can muster in order to create a smoke screen around his deception. The portrayal of bombastic and obscure language to deceive the public had been one of the central and most effective stylistic features of Isla's *Fray Gerundio*. Lizardi's caricature of medical training, through Periquillo's recitation of his spurious qualifications, allows us to trace a contour of the medical profession's presence in the colony. Here is just a sample of the parody: "'But I'm not, sir,' I broke in; 'I'm not one of those; I know what my obligations are, and I have been examined and approved *nemine discrepante,* unanimously, by the Royal Protomedicato of Mexico; I know what all the branches of medicine are: Physiology, Pathology, Semeiotics, and Therapeutics; . . . I know how many humors man has, and their names, such as blood, bile, phlegm chyle, and gastric juices . . . I can call illnesses by their proper and legitimate Greek names, such as ascites, anasarca, hydropho-

José Joaquín Fernández de Lizardi

José Joaquín Fernández de Lizardi (1776–1827) was a writer and politician in New Spain (Mexico), known for his *El Periquillo Sarniento* (*The Mangy Parrot*) (first published in installments in 1816), one of the first novels in Spanish America. Although Lizardi vacillated in his political views—chastised by rebels for his support of the royalists and at the same time persecuted by royalists for his criticism of the colonial government—his belief in the ideals of the Enlightenment never waivered. In his newspaper *El Pensador Mexicano,* Lizardi attacked the colonial administration, including the educational and legal systems, the economy, the Catholic Church and its priests, the medical organization, and even the doctors themselves. Lizardi believed that the way to improve the social and economic status of the viceroyalty was by perfecting the functioning of these institutions. He was eventually imprisoned for expressing his opinions, but continued to write while in jail, although moderating his judgments to avoid further retribution. His critical stance is also visible in *El Periquillo,* where Lizardi's *pícaro* (rogue) finishes school, although feeling that he has not learned anything of value. The character also poses (convincingly) as a doctor and uses fake Latin terms and phrases to dazzle the family members of a sick man, tricking them into believing that he is cured. Although it was a work of fiction, the invective against priests, doctors, and government officials and the author's views on slavery caught the attention of censors: the fourth installment of the novel was banned. The complete novel only appeared posthumously, in 1830. Lizardi also wrote fables in the style of Samaniego and Iriarte, although with a deliberate Spanish American touch, such as in the use of animals unique to the region as characters. Fernández de Lizardi is considered one of the foundational writers and intellectuals of Mexico and Spanish America.

---

bia, cancer, pleurisy, venereal disease, chlorosis, cachexia, podagra, paraphrenitis, priapism, paroxysm, and a thousand other illnesses that the foolish common folk call dropsy, rabies, the French disease, aching sides, gout, and the other usual nonsense'" (*Mangy* 295–96).[5]

Periquillo acknowledges the power of the "Real Protomedicato," the administrative tribunal that was part of the royal state apparatus and that in principle was to judge the competence of those practicing medicine.[6] Of course, he could claim to have the unanimous approval of the board without being trained in medicine. Outside a major city, there was nobody monitoring such claims, nobody to detect the lie, and using a fistful of fancy words would be good enough to reassure even the village priest. Periquillo's fake lecture also shows that although there had been many advances in medicine, the traditional understanding of humoral balance was still very much in place, and the treatment of ailments was still imbued with an age-old interpretation that could be traced back to Hippocrates, Galen, and Avicenna. Furthermore, what he calls "simplezas," or the unsophisticated language used by common people to name diseases, actually yields a very good list of the frequent ailments a doctor would find in colonial society, and it is clear that *gálico* occupies a prominent place among these familiar medical conditions. More interestingly, with the exception of priapism, *gálico* is the only disease on Periquillo's list that is related to unbound sexuality. To cure such disease, a quack doctor—and perhaps those trained, stamped, and approved as well—could only use two things: on the one hand, a concoction with mercury, guaiacum, or *palo de indias,* or perhaps a lizard or a cactus plant; on the other, a lot of fancy-word ammunition.

According to Fernández de Lizardi, the economic success of both quack and trained doctors depended not only on such verbal outpourings but also on restraint. As Periquillo says, the practitioner must act in such a way that if a patient's condition worsens, he can blame the disease itself, rather than admitting fault for administering a too-radical treatment. Since most diseases were rationalized in terms of an imbalance of humors, most doctors, unlike the more pragmatic surgeons, were satisfied with a regimen of bloodletting, purgatives, and fever inducers, which led to changes that were dramatic enough to reassure both the patient and the relatives that the disease was being addressed, but controlled enough that the sickly were not sent too quickly to the grave. Andrés, Periquillo's apprentice, observes that many of the victories against maladies were the result of "chiripa" (*Obras* 2:22), a gambling term that means that the player won because of luck and coincidence, rather than strategy or knowledge. Nevertheless, Periquillo proudly claims that he can cure all diseases and that he can teach Andrés to become the most successful of (quack) doctors: "Let 'em bring on the apoplectics by the thousands, and just see if I don't raise them all *ipso facto* from the dead—and not just apoplectics: bring on lepers, psoriatics, syphilitics, gouty men, women in labor, folks with fever, people with rabies, and every ill patient in the world. You did a pretty job of it, yourself, but you have to make sure your fingers don't move so fast, and that you don't stick the lancet in so deep; I wouldn't want to see you cut somebody's artery. But as for the rest, don't worry: by my side, you won't come out of this a mere barber, you'll be a physician, a surgeon, a chemist, a botanist, an alchemist, and if you please me and serve me well, you'll even get to be an astrologer and a necromancer" (*Mangy* 281).[7] These stark yet poignantly witty characterizations allow Fernández de Lizardi to reveal the problems that everybody in his society knew about but which, as with *gálico,* everybody chose to hide or to overlook. On another level, his text, which was to appear as a serialized, accessible, and popular leaflet, functioned as a slowly administered purgative, made palatable with humor and ridicule as it drew forth the disarray afflicting its readers. That the purgative was rather effective is clear from the fact that Fernández de Lizardi's *El Periquillo Sarniento* was censored by the administration it portrayed.

Fernández de Lizardi's novel *Noches tristes y día alegre* (Sad nights and happy day) (1818) also included a reference to *gálico* as social commentary. As I mentioned above, when discussing the treatment of *gálico*, the application of messy ointments and purgatives made necessary the use of old mattresses and pillows, which were burned in a bonfire afterward. The treatment of *gálico* in the American colonies was similar to that in Spain, perhaps with modifications such as the one described by Dr. Juan Manuel Venegas in his *Compendio*, where the treatment includes a dose of antivenereal chocolate made with ground snake bones: "The patient will be placed naked in the sun until the body has heated up a lot. Then he will be settled in the bed, he will drink very hot chocolate, and he will be wrapped up as much as possible, staying very still for a few hours, during which time the spittle will break out, and copious sweat" (227).[8] Unlike in Europe, where patients were confined to a heated room, colonial patients were placed outside so that exposure to direct sun would make them sweat and salivate. The use of old mattresses and bedcovers is brought up in comments made by Lizardi's character Dorotea to the priest Joaquín. The devout woman criticizes the practice of donating dead patients' clothes and bedding to the hospital: "In other places they have the holy devotion of sending to the San Lázaro hospital the clothing and mattress of the person who died of consumption, of *gálico,* or from another malignant and contagious illness, and they say they send that pestilence to the miserable sick *out of charity.* Wretched! The sick have to suffer and endure much already with their bad humors, is it necessary to poison their blood more *out of charity?*" (*Noches* 94).[9]

That people considered it acceptable to give contaminated goods to those who were already sick shows their disregard for and lack of solidarity—a basic component of a progressive society—with those in worse conditions. The priest Joaquín condemns this social conduct to an even more radical degree, accusing such people of trying to deceive God: "This is not alms, nor could you call it charity, but miserliness, evil deed, hypocrisy. This is to want to deceive God and buy his compassion with trash" (95).[10] This not-so-charitable charity also reveals in part the deficiencies of the health system in Mexico. The willingness of hospitals like San Lázaro to receive donations that could worsen the condition of their patients points to the lack of funding and the inadequacy of the colonial administration.

Like other texts imbued with the traits of the Enlightenment, the literary production of Fernández de Lizardi aims to reveal and underline the common problems of a rapidly transforming society that he saw as riddled with inequality and lacking clear moral principles. This need for moral instruction is at the core of *La Quijotita y su prima* (The Quijotita and her cousin) (1818–19), a novel in which the author again uses an unexemplary life as a vehicle for presenting appropriate ideas of edification. While Pomposa (also known as Pomposita) is spoiled by the absence of her mother in early childhood and by her lax upbringing in general, her cousin Pudenciana is a feminine role model who was parented skillfully by doña Matilde Contreras and don Rodrigo Linarte. For the author, the negative fate of the youth in New Spain starts when well-off women refuse to nurse their babies and instead hire wet nurses. Pomposita's mother, doña Eufrosina Contreras, is supported by one of her friends when she decides to avoid breastfeeding: "Because breastfeeding finishes women, and in the end it is not in fashion nor does this kind of thing belong with the people of our class, but with the poor and ordinary people" (*Obras* 7:17).[11] Fernández de Lizardi emphatically rejects this idea by linking the custom of hiring wet nurses to the contagion of *gálico*. Another friend of Eufrosina narrates without remorse the death of one of her children, whom she had given to a sick nursemaid: "But I was able to get away with my wish of having him nursed by a black woman as rebellious as the devil and I believe with *gálico,* because of signs that the boy died half rotten within a few days, and from then on my husband is careful to look for robust nursemaids for his children" (7:18).[12] The author further stresses his disapproval by linking the disease to a hired black woman who nursed the baby. The social disease of mothers unwilling to fulfill their maternal duty is thus transferred to a marginal diseased and racialized body. The fact that the nurse is black becomes a way for Fernández de Lizardi to instill a combination of fear and disgust in his readers, overtly defending breastfeeding by mothers but tacitly disparaging the Afro-Mexican component as a source of "retobado" (rebellious) contagion. It is indeed this undesirable and despicable disease that ends Pomposita's days. Encumbered by the bad example set by her superficial mother, the one who would not breastfeed her when she was an infant, the pretentious young woman stumbles down the ladder of life, losing her riches, marrying a fake nobleman who is in truth a rogue and an assassin from Cádiz in Spain, turning to prostitution, and becoming infected with the terrible disease: "On top of an incurable *gálico,* as was made clear by the mouth and nose ulcers and the sores on her legs, she had a voracious fever from which she could not escape" (7:529).[13] The awful disease serves Fernández de Lizardi as a quintessential representation of what could happen to the fabric of society in New Spain if his calls for renewing moral rule and education were not heeded by his contemporaries: "In the midst of the most furious pains and agitation, assisted by the priests of the Camilian order, who had been called, she entrusted her soul to the Creator, leaving a pathetic and sobering example and reprimand to the thoughtless women that follow the same ideas and behavior of the unhappy Pomposa" (7:529).[14] As an infant, Pomposa had escaped the putrefaction and other horrors of syphilis because her wet nurse happened to be free of the disease, but the weak education she had received from her parents finally brings about the same outcome: she dies as a prostitute, overtaken by *gálico*. Fernández de Lizardi seems to be telling us that if Pomposa had followed her assigned role as a virtuous, obedient, home-loving woman, her reward would have been the one that her cousin Pudenciana enjoyed—that is, the reward of many healthy children, an orderly home, and a life devoted to family and God.

Gálico, its treatment, and its consequences conform to an arc of meaning in relation to the creation of an autonomous identity for the Spanish colonies. The same ideas continued vibrating during the process of independence and preoccupied the budding nations. The menace of the disease unfolded as a somber harbinger of what was to come for these nations, societies, families, and individuals. The anxiety resulting from this gloomy possibility was exorcised by principled discourses of the kind written by Fernández de Lizardi; the picaresque quality of a text like *Periquillo* does not make it less prescriptive. The other way to confront the threat of disease was through humor—sick humor.

> 11

Sick Humor

The prevalent eighteenth-century medical theory explained *gálico* as an imbalance of the four vital elements or humors: phlegm, blood, black bile, and yellow bile. The good mood or good humor of the patient was to be brought back into balance by expelling the bad humors produced by the disease. The doctor, whether a real one or a quack like Fernández de Lizardi's Periquillo, sought to restore proper harmony by bleeding the patient, administering remedies that would produce heavy salivation and sweating, applying treatments that would bring out or tone down humidity, prescribing a certain diet, or advising the patient to dwell in a particular climate to restore equilibrium. In the case of *gálico,* as I've explained before, specific remedies such as mercury, guaiacum, or lizard meat were used to expel the predominant humor, which was usually related to the humidity of phlegm. The term *humor* we use today to describe something that produces amusement or hilarity is related to the Galenic theory of humors, which dates back to the ancient Greeks. In this sense, good humor was to be seen as the result of balanced humors, and humors are balanced through a constant tuning of the humoral flow by expulsion, ingestion, and reaccommodation.

By applying a regimen of *palo santo* or sarsaparilla, the physician aimed to bring out a substantial amount of the imbalanced humor of the patient with *gálico;* the medicine was used to make apparent what was hidden inside the diseased body. In other words, the medical treatment was aimed at helping make present the unrepresentable. The humorous representation of *gálico* follows a similar dynamic to that of the medical treatment in the sense that, even by using radical medicines that produced violent reactions, it aims to reveal what is usually hidden and to represent what otherwise would be unrepresentable or out of bounds. In the same way, humor about *gálico*—this sick humor—served as a pressure-relief device that allowed for the normalization of fear and as a way of handling the overwhelming presence of an overpowering disease that affected all levels of society.

Throughout this section, I intend to study a wide array of humorous forms related to *gálico,* from the use of obscenity, innuendo, and double entendres to gallows humor—the kind that makes fun of situations that are otherwise terrifying, such as disease, death, and imminent disaster—as well as epigrams, intricate wordplay, and satire. I begin by analyzing different levels of humor in a particular early eighteenth-century poem, an approach that will allow me to introduce reflections on the use of humor in relation to society, and continue by interweaving other examples from the Spanish-speaking world.

As I showed in the section on Francisco Benegasi y Luján and his mocking poetry on the death by *gálico* of Anastasio Pantaleón de Ribera, the humorous representation of the disease in the Hispanic world at the beginning of the eighteenth century stems from the discursive strategies developed by key writers of the Spanish Golden Age, such as Góngora and Quevedo. A contemporary of Benegasi, Juan del Valle y Caviedes (1645–97), was born in Porcuna, Jaén, and divided his career between writing and working as a mine administrator in the Viceroyalty of Peru. His most celebrated work is a collection of satirical poetry known today under the title of *Diente del Parnaso* (The tooth of Parnassus). His poem "A una dama que por serlo paró en La Caridad" (To a lady who being one ended up in La Caridad) is an illustrative instance of dark humor as a tool of societal control of behavior that diverges from the hegemonic discourse.[1] Through analysis of a few stanzas—the poem has a total of twenty-eight—I aim to follow the representation of *gálico* in Valle's poem. I will specifically trace the use of humor and how this type of humorous representation articulates a masculine fear of women that unfurls in the shape of repulsive or scatological imagery as well as in a disparaging view of females who own their body and their desire. Although I will work more deeply with the poem "A una dama que por serlo paró en La Caridad" (hereafter "Que por serlo"), I will also incorporate comparative analysis of an earlier poem by the author with a very similar structure and identical theme, titled "A una dama que paró en el Hospital de la Caridad" (hereafter "Que paró").[2]

"Que por serlo" presents a clear affinity with the work of Francisco de Quevedo, especially his poems on women with gálico, such as "Tomando estaba sudores" or "A Marica la chupona," which I have already discussed in relation to the work of Torres Villarroel. But the name of the woman mocked by Valle y Caviedes is not "Marica" but "Belisa," an anagram of the name "Isabel." This anagram can be traced back to Lope de Vega (1562–1635), who used it to refer to his wife, Isabel de Urbina. Valle y Caviedes is most likely using this name because of the seductive qualities of the main character in *Las bizarrías de Belisa* (The gallantry of Belisa), one of Lope's final plays, in which the young woman flirts continuously with several men. Belisa's maid, Finea, scolds her for her fickleness and warns her of the bad outcome that her behavior may bring her:

> So much disdaining lovers
> so much undoing marriages

> so much of making of the ears
> diamond earrings
> it is clear that it would bring
> the chance for Love
> to avenge your tyranny. (*Bizarrías* 1)[3]

From the beginning of his poem Valle conveys that women's fickle behavior results in terrible punishment. In this case, the consequence she deserves for doing what she wanted to do with her body is getting it anointed with mercury to treat her *gálico,* and suffering the terrible treatment in the hospital of *bubas.* This idea of expiation is already present in the first stanza of the earlier "Que paró," which reads: "Purging her faults / was Anarda in the hospital / because the sins in this life / and in death must be purged" (vv. 1–4).[4] But in this case, the idea of spiritual atonement is even clearer because Valle plays with double meaning of the word "purge" (*purgar*). In one sense, the word relates to medically causing the evacuation of the bowels or the expulsion of a harmful substance in the body—the original Greek meaning of the cathartic—and in the other sense, it relates to the reparation of guilt via spiritual or bodily mortification. The latter is the main idea at the core of the transitional condition of purgatory—the purging place—in Catholic dogma, a state in which moral transgressors purge their sins through suffering before reaching divine forgiveness and promised heaven. With dark humor that verges on gallows humor, Valle indicates that the physical purge at the hospital is only the beginning of the spiritual purge in purgatory and that the disease Anarda acquired for her loose sexual behavior has marked her for certain and impending death, a prelude to the terrible punishment she will endure until the end of times.

The multiple layers of signification condensed in just a few verses in this poem show how prevalent the traits of Baroque *conceptismo* still are in an author in the New World such as Valle y Caviedes. One good example of this polysemic conceptual interest lies in the multiple meanings of the word "charity" in the opening stanza: "Taking the anointments / is Belisa in the Caridad [charity] / because charity is the exchange / for the charitable one" ("Que por serlo" vv. 1–4).[5] The first level is about location. The hospital where Belisa is taking the *unciones,* simply mentioned here as "La Caridad," was founded in 1562 in Lima, in one of the main squares of the city, currently known as Plaza Bolívar. The hospital stood near the Church of Santa María de la Caridad and for that reason was known with the same name. Its real, original name, however, was Hospital de San Cosme and San Damián. The institution was led by the hermandad (Sisters) de la Caridad and intended for the exclusive treatment of women, especially those with no resources.[6] In Spain the name "Antón Martín" represented the connection to the treatment of *gálico,* but the name might not have meant anything to a inhabitant of the colonial city of Lima. "La Caridad," however, did represent with clarity the final, horrific consequences of *gálico* in the Peruvian setting: only sick or despondent women, in need of public charity, would end in such a place. The second level of charity is that offered by society to the unworthy Belisa in obeyance to *charitas,* one of the three Christian virtues, which consists of loving God over all things and loving others as you would yourself. Valle adds even more complexity because his use of the word "caridad" can be also understood as the alms or material help given to someone who needs it—"because charity is the exchange / for the charitable one"—in the sense given in the dictionary at the time as "the alms and help given to someone: and is specially called so by those who ask for it, or receive it" (RAE A 1729, s.v. "caridad").[7] This means that the charity of the hospital protects and serves Belisa as a compensation for her own charity. But her charity functions at a skewed level. Through his *conceptista* play of words, Valle indicates that Belisa's charitable character is sexual, and that she not only gives herself to anyone who needs or asks for it but also presents herself as needing and asking to be given sex from anyone.[8] As a result of this distorted form of charity, she ends up receiving the material charity of the Hospital de la Caridad.

With the use of this kind of language, which reveals meaning by hiding meaning, an author of colonial Lima such as Valle y Caviedes not only expresses judgment against a particular feminine behavior but also plays with the fire of Catholic dogma by equivocating the meaning of a chief theological virtue that is supposed to be the greatest perfection the human spirit may attain. He equates the charity that reveals human love for God and mankind with the loose offering of sexual favors that he sees as corrupting the society of Lima. It is clear that if Valle were to be interpreted by a zealous reader of the religious institution, taking *unciones* by the side of Belisa would have been a better choice than ending in an interrogation at the Tribunal del Santo Oficio de la Inquisición, whose well-visited building, with its own kind of sweating and pained sighs, was located in the same square as the Hospital de la Caridad.

Once in the hospital, and well into the treatment, Belisa's body reveals the effects of mercury: "like silkworms / she threads spittle from her mouth, / because going around with two cocoons / is something she has not yet forgotten" ("Que por serlo" vv. 37–40).[9] The most apparent of these outcomes is that of heavy salivation, which we already saw in the character of "Don Babilés" in Torres Villarroel's work. The metaphorical connection here is different because the humorous description of the disease is now connected to unbridled sex, and therefore it now belongs to the realm of obscenity. The dripping slobber coming out of her mouth is compared with silk threads coming out of silkworms. Her mouth has become a space of linked sexual associations: it starts being compared to silkworms and then with silk in the first two verses, and by the third verse the linked image is that of silk cocoons. The obscene allusion is related to the meaning of the word *capullo* in Spanish, which can be understood as cocoon. The word is also used, however, as a vulgar word for a man's foreskin or phallus, indicating that until recently, Belisa was accustomed to having two penises in her mouth, performing fellatio, a non-sanctioned form of sexual exchange during this period.[10] The allusion jumps from oral sex to the image of threads of semen coming from the two penises, reinforcing as a result the connection between unrestrained sexual activity—two partners and their seminal fluid—and punitive consequence in the form of pain and humiliating slobbering. Besides the phallic indirect reference to cocoons, Valle uses a military musical reference by claiming that she used to go around many "pífanos" (fifes) and that, as a painful consequence, she now has numerous "parches"—a polysemic word that means both the skin of the drums in the military drumline and the medical bandage or dressing used to cover suppurating wounds or syphilitic blisters: "because the one going around with fifes / is committed to drum skins" ("Que por serlo" vv. 59–60).[11] The excess of her sexual exchanges is also connected to the euphemism of a pipe or water spout (*caño*), which references the many penises she used to serve, to the point that sweat or water would come out of her face: "she would run so many pipes / that water would come to her face / to spill over the pot" (vv. 62–64).[12]

This retaliatory attitude expressed by the poetic voice is a thread that can be followed throughout the lengthy poem in multiple forms. In all cases, the humorous burst comes from the mocking tone resulting from the feeling that justice has been served. This exemplary punishment of a woman who did not operate under the ideals of modesty and constraint ensures that moral rule prevails. In that way, in the stanza that reads "The billet-doux have become / pharmacy envelopes, / and the continued help / is now the price of other syringes" (vv. 93–96),[13] the brief written messages from lovers or customers she used to receive have become transmuted into small envelopes containing medicine to cure her ailment, and the money or "help" (*ayudas*) she used to receive for her sexual favors is now to be spent on the other type of *ayuda,* which in this case is that of rectal enemas. The syringes that are now used on Belisa's body for medical purposes are the punitive transmogrification of the syringe-shaped penises of her lovers, who used to penetrate her when she was healthy, perhaps anally, as a clyster does now that she is sick. In the earlier "Que paró" poem (vv. 37–40), the retribution of the "billetes" or love messages she wrote to many lovers is the treatment with the content of "papelillos" as in the later "Que por serlo" poem, with the difference that now the medicine will purge

Jeringa

Nowadays the term *jeringa* is used almost exclusively to denote the hypodermic needle, a device invented in the nineteenth century. But before that, a jeringa was the "instrumento con que se echa la ayuda"—that is, the tool for giving enemas, a common albeit uncomfortable treatment used to evacuate the lower bowel, thus speeding up the goal of balancing the patient's humors. The uncomfortable and humiliating treatment was so common that the derived verbal form *jeringar* was used to signify "bothering."

from her bones all the bad behavior she committed as a woman who writes, and who writes expressing desire.

A similar opposing pleasurable cause and painful consequence disguised under the robe of obscene language lies in another stanza where Belisa is described as used to "pedir," which is a euphemism for having sex, and more exactly for expressing the desire to have sex: "The custom of asking / is imitated by her own pain / because in a repeated 'ay!' / she goes night and day" ("Que por serlo" vv. 65–68).[14] The poetic voice tacitly rejects the fact that a woman like Belisa dares to express sexual desire and to respond verbally to pleasure with an interjection of enjoyment, and therefore her behavior is punished with the parallel agonizing sigh produced by the continuous pain of the disease. The implied rebuff of Belisa's sexual behavior is laced nevertheless with the appeal of titillation, that is, the hidden pleasure afforded by seeing or imagining a sexual act. Valle intentionally incorporates this arousing component to further stress its negative consequences; such is the case in a stanza describing Belisa's sexual appetite and her mastery at engaging with fully erected penises: "She was always triumphant over all / who had them the stiffest" ("Que por serlo" vv. 101–2). Although covered with the sweetened veneer of humor, the dictum is that unsanctioned manifestations of pleasure can only result in pain. Nevertheless, in a later stanza, the moral objective in Valle y Caviedes poem loses its humorous traits—mockery, obscenity, double entendre—and pronounces with clarity an agenda of social conformation to established rules: "Love charges with pains / the loans he made her with affectionate tickles / so she is paying with tears / the debt she acquired in laughter" ("Que por serlo" vv. 25–28).[15]

Valle's humorous use of veiled obscenity and equivocal meaning takes advantage of the fact that the obscene is a constant part of the use of language and of the ordering of the world. All readers or listeners immersed in the particular context can recognize obscenity and its meaning when they hear it or

Many Names for the Unmentionable

Sex and disease are inescapable realities, but society prefers to keep them in the private, even intimate realm. Still, their presence is so constant that to solve the tension of naming the unmentionable, each society crafts allusive terms or euphemisms to refer to them. Death, bodily functions, and physical difference are other areas of social life expressed through euphemisms. As with the sexually transmitted disease of *gálico,* sexual intercourse was ripe for indirect language. The list is extensive, but here are some of the names for copulation, in alphabetical order, I found while reading texts linked to *gálico* in the eighteenth century. The profusion of names shows, on one hand, the level of interest and preoccupation with sex at the time and, on the other, the difficulty of tracing the presence of the disease and topics related to sexuality in literary texts: *acostarse, agarrar, cepillar, clavar, coger, culear, empernar, encamarse, fajar, folgar, follar, fornicar, pedir peinar, tirar, tomar, trincar, tupir, yacer.*

read it. The author knows that the public will avoid recognizing obscenity or will pretend not to hear it unless the reader or listener is in a context where the obscene is temporarily accepted—either in a safe private space or in spaces of public enjoyment, such as feasts or rowdy social gatherings. But the fact that a poem such as Valle's is embedded in a bracketed space akin to that of the carnival underscores the way it benefits from the dynamic of the suspension *and* underscoring of social mores. The direct attack on the type of person represented by Belisa aims at putting to shame the real persons who could be qualified in that particular context as similar to her, thus reinforcing accepted behavior and humorously mortifying those individuals in public. This proves that in fact the obscene is not outside the social pact, but actually a participant in the reinforcement of that social rule.

As in early Greek theater, obscenity and allusion serve to bring onstage what is customarily kept offstage in our culture. It exposes what should be hidden. In this sense, obscenity, allusion, and humor share with humoral medical treatments the aspiration to reveal and to produce catharsis. I use the term catharsis in its original sense of purgation or purification; a cathartic is a component that speeds up the process of defecation, a substance that accelerates the evacuation of noxious matter from inside out. The medium of the obscene is an explicit verbal reference to activities or parts of the body deemed to be off-limits in a specific social context. Such explicit expression through language is also deemed to be off-limits. Almost always, these parts and these activities are related to the sexual realm. As can be seen in several instances I have included in this discussion on *gálico,* because of its revelatory dynamic, because of its capacity to expose the unmentionable, because of its enigmatic power of revelation, obscenity runs together with and is kin to poetry.

Obscenity is a voice of the limit, of the possibility of radical transgression and the challenging of order. It is a voice that is acquired through social interaction and resides in each individual in a society, but at the same time, it is a voice that society prefers to keep concealed or temporarily isolated. It is perhaps because of this quality of inevitable but uneasy contact with the very basics of our bodily experience that obscenity is related to the scatological, a feature that is often evinced by the use of humorous language, as can be traced in the representations of *gálico* or other diseases related to intimate sexual activity. As with poetry, obscenity provides a language to name the extraordinary or the bewildering, to name what produces wonder beyond normal, accepted discourse. But, as poetry and as seen in several of the texts broached in this study, obscenity ultimately maintains the structure of the accepted, the productive, the well-behaved, although wrapped with a sense of joy, humor, and impish catharsis that blurs the limit of the acceptable and the unacceptable, between the accepted and the perverse.

In Valle's poem, in the verses in which obscenity is more clearly revealed, such as those alluding to Belisa performing fellatio on two men at the same time, the feminine subject is presented with an animalized and animalizing language. In order to exercise control over the actions that are considered contrary to the moral rule, it does not suffice to hint that this woman's harrowing disease is the price she must pay for her unsanctioned past pleasures. The control is enhanced by placing her and her out-of-line experience in the realm of objects or animals that must be restrained. Belisa's unbridled sexuality is connected with the image of her being saddled as a pack animal that sweats under its cargo: "The sweat blanket will not be unexpected / by one who has made herself saddled so many times, / an irritation that in the sore / is hitting her right in the middle" ("Que paró" vv. 61–64).[16] Beyond the expiation of her sweaty sexual activities through the sweats of the mercurial treatment, the obscene reference is related to comparing a saddle sore (*matadura*), proper of an animal that is repeatedly mounted, with her vagina as an open wound continuously bruised in sexual intercourse. Valle also uses this type of language, bordering on the scatological, in his portrayal of the signs of rampant *gálico* and the effects of treatment with mercury. Instead of a direct description of the ailments, as seen in medical treatises, the humorous scatological allusion produces an effect of amplification aimed at rousing hilarity and intensifying the sense of moral condemnation of the subject.

After four to six weeks of treatment with mercury, some of the side effects included substantial damage to the patient's gums, loss of teeth, and complete loss of the uvula, which resulted in a characteristic twangy and raspy voice.

Valle makes use of the double meaning of the word *campanilla* in Spanish, meaning both "uvula" and "small bell," to comical effect, which is compounded by the scatological materiality of that body part being split as if it were a bell broken by the powerful strike of the clapper: "They say that her small bell [uvula] / is helplessly falling, / or is being split by the blows / of so much clappering to and fro" ("Que paró" vv. 65–68).[17] In a similar way, the author parallels the sores in Anarda's palate with the idea of desire or enthusiasm (*gusto* means both "taste" and "desire" or "enthusiasm"), indicating that the pain of the wounds in her mouth was what she wanted with her conduct, or that the sores in her mouth are what she asked for: "It seems she is asking / the sickness out of pleasure / as they come quite to her measure / the sores in her palate" ("Que paró" vv. 73–78).[18] This dynamic is replicated in the "Que por serlo" poem, making fun of the fact that the disease, which is acquired as a result of a desire of the flesh (as opposed to the spirit) and through the flesh (as a result of sexual intercourse), results in painful tumors in the bones of the patient—"There is no bone liking her well, / because this damned sickness / even if acquired through the flesh / in the bones is always released" ("Que por serlo" vv. 77–80)[19]—or in the equivocal allusion to her lack of luck (not having a good star) because of the many "luceros" (bright stars), which was a euphemism for syphilitic wounds on the face: "She laments her good star / because she is in danger of bright stars" (vv. 33–34).[20]

This abjection of the feminine is connected to the scatological—semen, perspiration, pustules, ulcers, raw wounds—and is opposed to the poetic idealization that would instead have described her lips as made out of coral, or that would have compared her teeth to pearls, or that would have compared her body with that of a goddess or an innocent shepherdess. However, while here we can see a condemnation and an attack on women in general, and on sexualized women in particular, the festive, out-of-bounds mood that frames the poem also reveals the clear and present knowledge that the poetic voice has of this reality, of the feared sexually transmitted disease, and of the at once desired and feared women of this kind as a source of pleasure and pain. The poetic voice is actually speaking from his literal experience "in the flesh"—it is clear that it is a masculine voice—because otherwise he would not know how to impart a moral dictum to his readers or listeners, or would not be able to hint that *gálico* is cured in La Caridad, or that the treatment of choice for this sexually related disease is mercury. The poem presents a mix of contempt, repulsion, and subsequent vengeance because, after a second reading, what one can gather is that the poetic voice is perhaps reacting after having been rejected by a woman like Belisa. In other words, instead of publicly singing the desire for the woman who has rejected him, he has chosen—cowardly so—to use negative obscene language as escape. Still, what this shows is that any practice that remains intimate and private cannot be considered obscene. Obscenity needs witnesses; it needs a presence from outside; it has to be exhibited, performed, staged to produce certain effect at the social level; it needs an outside from the referenced. The common knowledge of the broken moral rule expressed in the stanzas represents to a certain point its acceptance; it normalizes the impure exchanges because the public does know what they are about. On the other hand, through scornful humor, this kind of representation emphasizes a moral matrix of vigilance. It is in this renewed tension of testing the limits of acceptance that the obscene shows how related it is to its more lyric-poetic counterparts. The fact that Valle's readers or the listeners of his festive poetry could clearly understand, and even memorize, an obscene poetic representation shows how pervasively capable obscenity is of surpassing social and academic strictures. The titillation produced by the sexual allusions in the poems serves as an inducement to think twice about the meaning of the verses and the consequences of the actions that are described in each stanza. The knowledge of the multiple layers of meaning in many of the words, in conjunction with the laughter that springs out of that recognition, functions as a vehicle to advance Valle's social agenda of containing feminine roles and as a warning to male readers of the danger of the venereal disease.

One of the most extreme forms of testing the limits of acceptance is the imbrication of humor, obscenity, and scatological references, especially in relation to sexual practices. The scatological imagery produces in the reader or listener an immediate reaction of revulsion, which results in the implicit rejection of the represented subject. For example, continuing the double image of sweat as a result of active sexuality and as an outcome of the treatment with mercury ointment, Valle presents bodily fluids as the unnatural and repugnant manifestation of Anarda's conduct: "Sweating light and heavy / in the front and from behind / not being rare that in her trysts / her underwear would stick to her" ("Que paró" vv. 17–20).[21] Anarda is portrayed as having repeated *bureos*—an illicit form of entertainment, party, or amusement (RAE A 1726, s.v. "bureo")—as being accustomed to her underwear clinging to the front and back of her body because of the sweat resulting from her merry activity. Valle also tacitly alludes to her being familiar with having seminal fluid sticking to her intimate clothing and her skin after having sexual intercourse in different positions. Valle's discourse demonstrates that these disgusting images are in fact representations of the fear of women's bodies and of their corporeality linked to palpable desire. The tangibility of a sexual body in characters such as Belisa or Anarda is also a representation of a binary of destruction and seduction, a binary with which men, who recognize their own finitude and the fact that they could also end up in a hospital like that of La Caridad, find it difficult to grapple. Attached to that apprehension there is also recognition of female physicality and therefore recognition of the physicality and finitude of the male body, the acknowledgment of the difficulty of recognizing his own desiring sexuality and the fear that *gálico* could and would produce the same effects on his own flesh.

From a different perspective, this recognition of shared finitude means a different understanding of femininity. Women are not only seen as idealized representations but also perceived as flesh and bone in the same manner that men, in this case represented by the poetic voice, are bone and flesh. Thus it could also be read that the poetic voice reveals the envy or resentment of not being able to claim to have as active an amorous life or sexual bustle as Anarda and Belisa, an ambivalence that results in a complex mix of revulsion and deep attraction to their comportment. As a result, these scatological features, conjoined with the elements of obscenity and humor, not only serve as the contours of a standard of moral behavior for women but also function as a standard of masculine behavior, serving as a warning that what happened to the sick women will also happen to men. In other words, if Valle uses the animalizing image of Anarda as a saddled pack animal, he tacitly recognizes that if the mount falls, the riders mounting it will undoubtedly fall as well, and suffer, with it, a painful death.

In a time when Spain was still at peace with its French neighbors, and the French disease was not yet synonymous with the invasion of the Napoleonic troops, the French reference to the disease, even in military terms, was not yet politicized, as it would be by the last quarter of the century. This happens, for example, with the disease playing the part of French troops attacking the stronghold, represented by Anarda, and employing military tactics to penetrate the garrison she represents: "A French harm is warring her / such a military froggy [French] / that besieged Fuenterrabía / and breached through the slums" ("Que paró" vv. 21–24).[22] Valle refers to Fuenterrabía or Hondarribia in the Basque country, a town on the border with France. The women of the town were famous during the Thirty Years' War (1618–48) for not surrendering to a French siege in 1638. In the suggestive double meaning, the author depicts Anarda being vanquished after a siege of Fuenterrabía—here meaning her vagina through the scatological allusion to a spilling spring or fountain— and finally entering through the "arrabal" or slum in the suburbs, but which in another sense means buttocks, indicating that Anarda was penetrated from behind, leaving her with the French disease.[23] In other instances, the meaning of the French disease is humorously unfolded as a synecdoche of geographical location and abasement: "She has a French ailment / so much of the son of these provinces, / that he was born in the city / they call of Picardy [lewdness]" ("Que por serlo" vv. 105–8).[24] Here, Valle plays with the word *picardía*, which can mean both the northern region of Picardy in France and the lack of sexual pudor both of the feminine subject in the poems and of her masculine counterpart, who is also representing the feared contagion. This terminology indicates that Belisa is not credited with having a sexual relationship with a foreign partner, which could be viewed as positive, but is described as having a coarse and local filthy disease. This is especially emphasized because, at the time, the first meaning of *picardía* was that of low action, meanness, vile acts, fraud, or wickedness and as "dishonest or shameless action" ("accion deshonesta ò impúdica," RAE A 1737, s.v. "picardía").

Valle's humorous discourse makes as much use of double meanings as possible, and jumps from the allusion to foreign references and remote geographies to the localized knowledge of the colonial environment. In the same way that in the last third of the century authors such as Joseph Flores and Antonio Sánchez Valverde would employ their direct experience with products of the New World to craft an identity of self-worth and autarky, in the early 1700s Valle overhauls the common meanings of mercury in the treatment of *gálico* and connects them with the exploitation of mercury and silver in the Viceroyalty of Peru. According to Lohmann Villena and Reedy (Reedy xiv–xv), Valle was involved in his youth in the production of mercury (*azogue*) in the cinnabar-rich mines of Huancavelica, located southeast of Lima at an altitude of about four thousand meters. Given that the exploitation of cinnabar was one of the main resources, the terminology related to mining and processing silver was well known in the region.

The production of *azogue* was of capital importance in the extraction of silver in the mines of Peru and in the immensely rich mine of Potosí, in today's Bolivia. The area of a silver mine was divided into *estacadas* (stockades) or *estacas* (stakes), which were soil sections assigned for exploitation and marked with stakes. It was difficult to separate the silver particles in the soil from other minerals in the ore, but in the sixteenth century a new method of separation of the precious metal, known as "amalgamation" or the "patio process," was developed in New Spain and used in the mines of the New World. The technique and process to purify silver with mercury was known as *beneficio*, meaning "improvement" or "purification," and consisted in adding mercury to the pulverized soil. Treading on it and stirring it with shovels accelerated the chemical reaction of ore, mercury, salt, and water, a practice known as *repaso*, which lasted up to three months. The resulting amalgamation heap (*torta*) was thoroughly washed to obtain the *pella*, a mass composed of only mercury and silver. The *pella* was sifted in bags made out of sailcloth, and the pure silver remaining in the bag was the much-desired *piña* or silver cake. Valle uses mining and metallurgic terminology to make fun of Anarda and Belisa's situation. Since mercury was used to treat *gálico*, the two women become distorted representations of silver, which in this case is not the coveted pure metal but the despised disease. Through this mutation of meaning, Anarda is "benefi-ciada," although not much improved, with *azogue,* and trodden upon with the ointments applied by her unqualified doctor: "Like silver [ore] with mercury / is benefiting [purifying] her / a bad doctor by *repasos* [treading process] / of kneading and more kneading" ("Que paró" vv. 5–8).[25] In her turn, Belisa has so many stockades, not of silver ore but of *gálico* blisters, that she can compete with all the mines of the New World. In addition, she has received such a strong treatment with mercury that the poetic voice presumes that her doctor is set to extract a precious silver *piña* out of her mushed-up body: "By pure mercury he presumes / that he will make her silver cake / her who has more stockades / than all of those in the Indies" ("Que por serlo" vv. 81–84).[26]

One of the most cryptic stanzas of "Que por serlo paró" can only be under-stood today by those with a good knowledge of the business and production of mercury in Spain and its colonies at the time: "It is the vengeance for the swindles, / if to her lovers she would say / that they should give their soul, whose mercury / Huancavelica avenges" ("Que por serlo" vv. 89–92).[27] The apparent complexity must have been easily resolved by Valle's peers, who or-dinarily dealt in the cinnabar market that reached as far as the Viceroyalty of New Spain, in today's Mexico. Belisa used to ask her lovers to "give their soul" ("el alma den," v. 91), and the poetic voice mocks the victims for falling for her swindle ("estafa"), because in return they were tainted with a bodily disease that can only be cured with great quantities of mercury. In a second level of meaning, Valle is playing with the words "el alma den," which can also be read as "el Almadén," which is the name of the most important cinnabar mine in Spain, located in the Castilla-La Mancha region and with a history of extrac-tion dating back to before the tenth century. The play of words brings a new meaning because the great production from Almadén is put in competition or rivalry ("lo venga" [avenges it], v. 92) with the prolific yields of quicksilver from Huancavelica. While Belisa's lovers, who give her their soul, are cheated and repaid with local mercury to try to get healed, Huancavelica is put at the center because of its importance in the health of the Spanish crown's treasure, purifying its silver and feeding its imperial power.

The structure of the stanzas in Valle's poems can be understood as a bi-polarity that unfolds at multiple levels, contrasting the before and the now, pleasure and pain, unbridled sexuality and unbearable affliction. At the center of this tension is, of course, the dynamic of sex, but especially a dynamic of excess, as illustrated by the image of Belisa servicing "dos capullos" at the same time, or the plural form of the "jeringas," "pífanos," and water pipes. At the same time that this excess is condemned, it also becomes a powerful center of attraction to forbidden practices that afford pleasure, therefore produc-ing images that hesitate between scandal and acceptance. Valle y Caviedes's perception of this kind of behavior, which straddles between the private and the public realms, is managed through his use of a language that is also excessive, a language of the humorous, the abject, and the obscene—the latter two forming a dyad that tries to give narrative structure to the underlying fear by means of images of revulsion. The poetic voice does not signal perceived improper behavior through the simple iteration of the moral law "You shall not have more than one legalized, accepted, sexual partner," but rather with a type of radical language that answers with tangible verbal sarcastic excess, as if it were the only way to neutralize Belisa and Anarda's disapproved action. Such language condenses the before and after, the pleasure counteracted by horrible displeasure. This language is used therefore as an equalizer, in fact as a form of punishment of the behavior that is deemed to be against the society at large. The disapproval could have been aimed at men who sought excess, but here it is tightly connected to the fear of this type of woman, who at the same time acted in the terrain of the private and the public, under and against the rule of the moral law.

As I will show in texts such as Nicolás Fernández de Moratín's *Arte de las putas* (ca. 1770), or in Samaniego's "Las moscas" (The flies) (1781), this hidden fear represented as scatological disgust is later transformed into sets of preventative measures for men in order to foster a recognition of their own finitude and physicality, to impel them to contain their own sexuality, and to find ways of exercising and fulfilling their sexual desires without risking being touched by the disease.

In the Peruvian author, the obscene language runs parallel to the abject description of disease. The awful drooling from the use of mercury is stitched to the image of ejaculating penises close to Belisa's mouth, and therefore disease, especially a disease with epidemic features on both sides of the Atlantic, becomes an incarnation of justice, of equalization after breaking the moral law. A contemporary reader may be surprised at the use of this kind of language by an author of the early eighteenth century, but at a time when these texts were known not through compiled, arranged editions but through highly socialized exchanges, such as public recitation and *tertulias* (social gatherings), passed from one hand to the other amid hushed laughter, these poems functioned very much in the same way that a woman like Belisa functioned. Like Belisa, these texts were shared and enjoyed by many, spreading judgment in the same way that Belisa's lovers spread *gálico*.

This straddling quality is important for understanding the power of humorous or mocking poems related to sexually transmitted diseases because it helps to show how the normalization of the codification of language functioned at the time. Valle's poems use epigrammatic humor that goes hand in hand with *conceptista* elements. Epigrammatic humor is brief and cryptic, the kind of humor that needs time and effort to be understood. The epigrammatic element here is related to the uncovering of multiple meanings of the same word, a *conceptista* feature that Lope de Vega interestingly described to be much favored by the "vulgo" because the "vulgo" "thinks that he is the only one who can understand what the other is saying" (*Arte Nuevo* 97).[28] This type of humor supposedly veils meaning, and in this way it is connected to the realm of the private. But at the same time, the excessive, invective, abject, gallows humor explodes in its baseness in the realm of the public because all of us, like it or not, accepting it or not, have sufficient knowledge to understand its meaning. In order to understand the meaning of the text, the reader has to be initiated in the meanings of both high and low culture, in the words used both in the bedroom and in the hospital, in the seedy bordello and in the well-provided bookshop. The reader has to know what the Hospital de la Caridad is, and what kinds of disease are treated there. The fact that the reader knows all these double entendres makes the poems even more powerful because it means that he or she could be the next one in the hospital, by the side of Belisa, drooling as a result of the treatment with mercury. Then, at the same time that this is a punishment to women like Belisa, it is in its double meaning an underscoring of the fear in men and in orthodox society.

Valle y Caviedes retools the scatological interest of his predecessors of the Spanish Golden Age in order to pass judgment on the everyday reality of the Viceroyalty of Peru. Like Góngora and Quevedo, Valle y Caviedes approaches the crude reality of the body by using oblique references and the qualities of allusion in poetry. The result is humorous but at the same time sobering because it shows, on the one hand, the limits of the human body in contrast with man's longing for idealization and, on the other, a disdainful view of colonial feminine roles. The fact that Valle y Caviedes used *gálico* and its symptoms as a medium to obliquely reveal his opinions concerning the public sphere helps the contemporary critical reader position private and public reality in coordinates of place and time. He transmutes the horror of the pustules of syphilis into visceral humor, inscribing literarily the pain of the buboes, the horrible outcomes of the cure, and the disfiguring consequences of the disease through the waggish revelation of reality, making the dreadfulness more human and more present. The Peruvian author's sobering humor points to the here and now, to the tangible disturbing reality as embodied in the experience of syphilis. This kind of humor that tests the boundaries of the acceptable is also a kind of soothing medicine, a purgative of sorts, palatable only because its acrid flavor is masked by a type of wordplay that reveals by hiding, hides by revealing, and uncovers through allusion. Obscene language and unrefined imagery served as a vehicle to portray the fear and the need of containment of disease around the topic of syphilis, and for that reason these messages mir-

José Iglesias de la Casa

José Iglesias de la Casa (1748–91) was a poet of the Escuela Literaria Salmantina (see the sidebar on p. 92), who studied at the Universidad de Salamanca and received holy orders in Madrid. As a member of this literary school, where he was known by the nickname "Arcadio," Iglesias wrote, as did other poets such as Meléndez Valdés, poems with pastoral themes, as well as amorous poems and *anacreónticas*. Iglesias is most known for his satirical works and has been given the honorific title of being one of the best Spanish satirical poets, second only to Francisco de Quevedo. He composed poetry of many genres, including *letrilla, romance, égloga, apólogo, elegía*. Multiple volumes of his poetry were published after his death and were subsequently banned by the Inquisition.

rored multilayered beliefs about prostitution, feminine and masculine roles, and medical practices.

I have pointed out how the obscene and scatological mockery of Anarda and Belisa is almost always related to the bodily signs of *gálico* and its treatment: buboes, chancres, bone tumors, drooling, or loss of teeth and uvula. This use of the raw physicality of the disease for humorous effect remains present during the rest of the century, but the goal of providing implicit sets of moral rules and edification for men becomes more important as time progresses. A turning point in the target of mockery can be seen, for example, in José Iglesias de la Casa's "Epigrama LXVIII," written in the late 1780s. The main characteristics of an epigram are brevity and wittiness. Epigrams are festive, humorous, and clever in character, and because of their concision they have a cryptic quality, with their meaning being revealed only after some moments of reflection and deduction. The author presents in this epigram a female character who is not the object of scatological mockery on the part of the masculine poetic voice. Quite the opposite: Inés is now the one who mocks the signs of syphilitic decay in the body of a military man:

> Inés found out that an Official,
> much maimed by *gálico,*
> had ordered that in his house
> they should pour salt on nothing.
> And she said in laughter: I do not understand
> how salt could cause anger
> in this one, who on more than one side
> is quickly rotting away. (34)[29]

The source of humorous effect lies in the different uses of salt. The reduction of the use of salt in the diet of diseased persons was usually recommended in order to manage the function of the kidneys, the organs in charge of purifying the blood and expelling waste from the body. This is the reason why the officer, who is very sick with *gálico,* orders that "they should pour salt on nothing," an instruction that can be understood as prohibiting the use of salt in his food, but more comically it can also be taken as prohibiting his servants to put salt *on him.* Inés's jeering comment relates to the other use of salt as a long-established method of curing meat. By wrapping meats in salt, or by brining them in a highly concentrated saline solution, it was possible to preserve them from putrefaction for extended periods of time. The lack of effective refrigeration methods made salt curing one of the most commonly used methods of food preservation at the time. Inés laughs at the officer, indicating that since he is rapidly putrefying—remember that *gálico* or its treatment causes decaying blisters and the loss of nose and nose septum, teeth and uvula—he should actually allow his servants to put salt on his meals and even on his own body in order to preserve his disintegrating flesh. This female laughter acquires a new meaning because the revelation of fear now touches directly the skin of someone like a military man, usually considered the epitome of manliness and self-reliance. The pervasive nature of the disease could at first be blamed on women who negotiated sexual favors, but the men who sought such favors from ill-reputed women equally felt the results of sexual exchanges. This understanding of *gálico* as a problem of individual men or women would not change radically until well into the nineteenth century, when it became a preoccupation about family and nation. Nevertheless, as I will show when discussing urban and public policy during this period with relevant figures such as Francisco Cabarrús in Spain, the need to control the spread of this disease was of the utmost importance for the well-being of city dwellers, society, and the economy.

The humorous projections of *gálico* on the urban space can indeed be traced through the century in multiple forms. For example, as I discussed before in relation to a short piece by Francisco Benegasi y Luján, the author playfully names a street by connecting the French disease suffered by a passerby with the remedy of sarsaparilla brought from the New World: "Where is he going, the one who has / the ailments of France? / . . . To the Street, they say, / of the Zarza" (119).[30] Humor and *gálico* are also used in "Breve diseño de las ciudades de Guayaquil y Quito" (Brief sketch of the cities of Guayaquil and Quito), by the Jesuit priest Juan Bautista Aguirre (1725–86), a biting portrayal of the Andean city and its society. Aguirre, who is considered one of the most notable Ecuadorian poets of the eighteenth century, subtitled this work "A seriocomic letter written by the author to his brother-in-law Don Gerónimo

Juan Bautista Aguirre

Juan Bautista Aguirre (1725–86) was a Jesuit priest, writer, and teacher from present-day Ecuador. He lived and worked in Quito until 1767, when the Jesuit order was forced to leave Spanish America. Aguirre moved to Italy, where he stayed for the remainder of his life. His teaching methods reflected the ideals of the Enlightenment in their emphasis on reasoning and scientific processes. Scholars have noted the influence of Baroque authors like Góngora in his work, such as in his "Décimas a Guayaquil," an ode to the Ecuadorian city. In this poem, Bautista Aguirre lists numerous elements that hold the promise of riches for the city (emeralds and pearls, among others). There is also an emphasis on the abundance of agriculture not only as a source of commerce but also as a source of pride for the people of this region. Aguirre wrote poetry with a varied thematic range, including religious, moral, amorous, and mythological compositions.

Mendiola, describing Guayaquil and Quito,"[31] and draws comic material from the perennial rivalry between the high-mountain seat of the Royal Audience of Quito and the entrepreneurial coastal city of Guayaquil. The author uses acerbic language to criticize the scarcity of food and the abundance of diseases in Quito. He describes Guayaquil as "beautiful city / garland of America, / lovely emerald of the earth / and of the sea a precious pearl" (vv. 31–34),[32] but of Quito he says, "Brother, in this Quito / many die of abscesses / of buboes, ulcers, and phlegms, / but no one dies of indigestion . . ." (vv. 271–74).[33] According to the Ecuadorian scholar Ximena Romero, the difficult economic situation in Quito at the time was largely due to the depletion of the silver deposits of Potosí that reduced the purchasing power in Lima and therefore affected the textile production of Quito (26). One would suppose that if the production of *azogue* from Huancavelica was not used as extensively in the purification of silver from Potosí, then its main purpose would have been to treat the scores of patients of *gálico*, especially in Quito, if one is to follow Aguirre's assertion that many there died of abscesses, buboes, ulcers and phlegm, all signs of the French disease.

Another sign of a sexual ailment, a *potra*, a testicular hernia or testicular cancerous tumor, is humorously used by Aguirre to describe the miserliness of the sedan chairs used to transport people through the narrow streets of the city: "seeing the broken seats / and the splintered boards, / I said: they may well be chairs, / but I'd take them for colts" (vv. 177–80).[34] The jumps of the palanquin, and the lack of cushioning, produce the comic effect of imagining the rider, in this case the author himself, having his testicles crushed as if he were riding a colt (*potro*); but in a second meaning, the plural of the word, *potros,* relates to hernias in the scrotum that result from a heavy blow to the testis. The author uses humor to expose the failure of administration in the city, and to show how sexually related diseases, parasites resulting from lack of hygiene—he writes extensively about the ravages of lice—and the signs of syphilis mirrored the negative social traits that he saw in Quito. Even if Aguirre was not very fond of the city, he taught there until 1767, when he and all the Jesuits of the land were expelled by the decree of Charles III. Aguirre had to flee to his beloved Guayaquil, and from there, like Clavijero, he left to exile in Italy, where he died in 1786.

An alternate humorous reference to *potras* is found in Diego de Torres Villarroel's theatrical *entremés* (interlude) titled "El médico sordo y el vecino gangoso" (The deaf doctor and the twangy neighbor), first published in Valencia in 1765. Torres Villarroel, whom we have studied before in this volume, takes advantage of the comic possibilities of the lack of understanding between the two characters in this short play. The doctor cannot grasp what his diseased neighbor says because he is hard of hearing, but also because his disease makes him have a twangy, rough voice, a characteristic sign of *gálico.* The neighbor complains to the doctor that he has gotten a new "empanada" (2), which is usually a culinary term for a turnover but here has the more disgusting sense of a bubo near his anus, a growth that does not let him walk without pain. The doctor misunderstands *empanada* for *papada* (double chin), and tells him he should not worry because his countenance is just fine, with no trace of illness. The sick neighbor has to explain again that what he has is a *potra* the size of a sieve or strainer in his tailbone: "That, after my ills has sprouted on me / on the spinal marrow of my butt / a *potra* that's bigger than a sieve" (2).[35] Even with this clarification, the doctor errs in his diagnosis, claiming that it is a "nitrous flatulence" (2) to be cured with a purge. The neighbor is surprised by the doctor's opinion because what he feels is not light air but something as heavy as lead that gives him "congojas infelices" (miserable pain), a new word that the doctor confuses with *lombrices* (pinworms) and continues to pontificate that it cannot be intestinal worms because otherwise the patient would be feverish, with diarrhea and vomiting (3). The string of verbal confusion continues, and the doctor misunderstands "bueno es eso" (that's a good one!) with *sobrehueso,* the term for a tumor on the bone, also known as a gumma, and gives a bookish explanation that it cannot be an exostosis because in that case the pain would be higher and the consistency harder because of its "material resinoso" (resinous matter) (3).

This humorous use of equivocal language and the mockery of overblown but empty language in Torres Villarroel are akin to the work of his contemporary, the previously studied Jesuit man of letters José Francisco de Isla. The first part of Isla's most important book, *Fray Gerundio de Campazas,* appeared in

Entertaining *Entremeses*

An *entremés* is a brief, one-act theatrical work that is comical and may be satirical in nature, and that was presented on stage between the acts of the main play. These works, written and performed in the theaters of sixteenth- and seventeenth-century Spain, treated everyday themes—for example, discussions among neighbors or arguments between parents and their children. One of the principal writers of *entremeses,* Luis Quiñones de Benavente, clarified the formal qualities of the genre by stating that they were only to be written in verse. Other prominent authors of *entremeses* include renowned names such as Lope de Rueda, Miguel de Cervantes Saavedra, Francisco de Quevedo, and Pedro Calderón de la Barca.

1758 and rapidly became a bestseller that influenced many writers at the time, perhaps including Torres Villarroel in his *entremés* of the deaf doctor and his twangy diseased neighbor. In the second chapter of *Fray Gerundio,* the main character takes a stroll with Fray Blas, a priest who does not believe in crafting solid sermons based on direct interpretation of scripture and aided by the judicious reading of the Fathers of the Church. Instead, Fray Blas advises Gerundio to use grandiloquent forceful language that will either awe or confuse, or both, the listeners of his homily. Instead of a simple title, the friar advises as one of his rules of thumb to make sure that the title is "always a jest, either by being bombastic, or funny, or highly specialized, or for some little pun," as for example "Dolorous Obsequy, Funereal Invocation, Bereaved Epicedium" (313),[36] which was used for the funeral rites of a blue-blooded nun and could have been replaced by more current and understandable words not taken from pedantic dictionaries.

In the same fashion that he recommends that Gerundio say "taciturnities of the lip" ("taciturnidades del labio," 315) instead of the simple word "silence," Fray Blas tells the novice to obfuscate biblical passages to produce wonder and admiration on his parishioners: "Take pains to never say *Aaron's rod,* because that could be judged as the staff of some village mayor; by saying instead *the aaronitic rod,* you bring to mind the rod of the Indies [guaiacum], and enrich the imagination" (316).[37]

In his essay "Aspectos de la visión de América en los ilustrados" (Aspects of the view of the Indies held by Enlightenment thinkers), Javier Yagüe Bosch interprets this passing reference to a product coming from the New World, guaiacum, as the evocative path to imagination and possibility represented by everything related to the land beyond the Atlantic (642). Although this view is plausible and useful, Fray Blas's reference to the Indies is ambiguous and requires further interpretation. I would add to Yagüe Bosch's reading the possibility of understanding the mention of guaiacum as something that, even if it requires imagining something removed from the context of the homily in the church, is not far from the immediate experience of churchgoers. I believe that Isla refers jokingly to the raising of the imagination, not because the sermon would bring the parishioners to think about the miraculous nature of the Israelites' flight from Egypt, but because *palo* or *vara de Indias* was a known remedy against a disease that touched many a family in Spain. Isla knew that many of his readers would be familiar with the treatment with guaiacum in their own bodies or in those of people they knew well, and that they would laugh—and worry at the same time—at this disparate connection, therefore stressing how detrimental it was to Spanish society to continue fostering this type of superficial, equivocal, and deceitful use of the sermon, which instead should have been used for the real edification of lay Catholic worshippers.

The fissure between sanctioned language (the kind one would expect to hear in the context of the homily or read in the enlightening book) and the language of the street (the kind used in a base conversation about unsanctioned sex) is spanned by the power of allusion through which Aaron's staff becomes a door opening the imagination to the remote Indies, or a reminder of a terrible disease that could be caught just a few steps away from the church after a furtive exchange with an infected lover or a prostitute. But allusion in this sense only functions as a vehicle to say obliquely what cannot be said directly. Direct language related to sexuality and venereal disease could be found only in the more and more formal discourse of medicine, as we have noted before, or in the language of obscenity, which could only be accessed in hidden, humorous, unsanctioned discourse. In the following pages, I intend to study paramount examples of such shady representations, written by two most enlightened authors who nevertheless produced texts that remained concealed for a long time because their content was out-of-bounds: Nicolás Fernández de Moratín's *Arte de las putas,* written before 1777, and José María Blanco White's "El incordio: Poema épico-gálico en un canto," written between 1806 and 1808, while he was living in Madrid. I will finish the chapter by studying Félix María de Samaniego's "Las moscas," one of his fabled fables, which viewed under a traditional light seems to be just another moralizing text, but under a somber light refers to the outcomes of contagion with *gálico.*

12

Moratín's *Arte de las putas,* or the Distorted Art of Avoiding *Gálico*

Moratín's *Arte de las putas* was well known in lettered circles, but it only circulated through manuscript copies. Its first printed edition did not appear until 1898.[1] Until then, an edict of 1777 by the Inquisition court had forbidden its publication and circulation, stating that it was prohibited in its entirety, even to those with special license to read forbidden books, "by dint of its being full of false propositions that were scandalous, provocative of inappropriate things, injurious to the state of Christianity, blasphemous, heretical, and with the flavor of atheism and polytheism" ("Edicto").[2] The reasoning of the edict shows that for the ruling system the main problem had to do not so much with the theme of indulgent sexuality and the practice of prostitution as with the anticlericalism that Moratín shows in the text, for example, when he presents a friar as the debauched inventor of the condom (2:142–202), or when he accuses a priest of infecting a prostitute with *gálico* after having anal intercourse (3:119–20).

The purpose of this "arte," as *ars* or skill and method to fulfill sexual desire, is not what made this text subversive in the eyes of his contemporary censors. Perhaps because it is still in a early state, critical work on this text has overlooked why and how the author discusses his craft and knowledge of satisfying sexual drive.[3] But if one approaches this text from the viewpoint of someone who understands the dynamic of disease, it is clear that *El arte de las putas* is not just a text where sexuality and obscenity are represented—this would not have been new, since we know of similar texts, such as Félix María de Samaniego's *El jardín de Venus* (ca. 1780)—but that in fact its main goal is to function as a manual for containing prostitutes and as a problematic self-serving instruction booklet to prevent being infected with *gálico*. The overarching aim of Moratín's work is to present a didactic treatise on the economy of masculine sexual desire. I do not intend the meaning of didacticism as a positive and constructive term under current standards, but in its broadest sense of teaching how to accomplish a certain goal. In other words, here I understand didacticism as free from moral subjectivism. In this regard, for example, a manual teaching how to cheat the tax system of a country is still didactic, even if it does not necessarily mean that the purpose of the text is legal or acceptable. For this reason I differ from Garrote Bernal's position in the introduction to his edition of the text, where he claims that the text is not didactic because otherwise it would not have been prohibited (26). I concur, rather, with David Gies's early signaling that the situation is quite the opposite: the text is a manual against the grain to teach how to avoid *gálico,* and its didactic aim in this regard is clearly stated at the beginning of the first canto: "If the sweetness of my poem were in fact / able to affect the horrific and vile / *gálico,* and could achieve its extinction / that indeed would be for my poem quite the feat" (1:119–22).[4] Moratín also emphasizes this instructive goal at the end of the poem, as if bracketing its purpose by addressing the imaginary pupil and reminding him of the positive outcome of following his art: "Oh, whoremonger, who my muse / led to this outlandish height / by new paths that others have not plowed, / did not abandon my good purpose!" (4:1–4);[5] an idea immediately reinforced by invoking the instructive qualities of Apollo: "but if Apollo to the wretched mortals / wished to teach something useful through my lips" (4:8–9);[6] and ultimately blaming those who criticize his task as morally shortsighted: "In this you must study night and day, / because it is seen as wrong because they want it to be so" (4:15–16).[7]

The economy of fulfilled desire in the *Arte* functions under the premise that masculine sexual desire is a natural occurrence. Under the aegis of scientific observation, the author sees that having sex is as natural as any other bodily function. Following a logical sequence, he argues that the penis's functions of urination and ejaculation are equal and natural: "the spilling of urine, the task / comes to be almost the same and through the same thing, / and no one is affronted by an action that is so unavoidable" (1:535–37).[8] If the penis is used to urinate, and urinating is a natural function that must not be hindered, the other function of the penis, that of having sex and ejaculating, is correspondingly natural and therefore should be allowed. Consequently, it is only natural that the satisfaction of sexual desire by the male participants of his social group is to be fulfilled expeditiously and at low cost. Moratín explains that in order to satisfy this sexual urge, some men—there is no instance where female desire is broached in this poem—resort to masturbation, a practice spurned by the author as "brutal appetite" (1:89) and as "squandering loss of the vital substance that can produce life" (1:97–98). Masculine sexual desire is also satisfied through the sanctioned marital relation, one that the poetic voice approves and presents as an ideal but difficult situation that his teachings would like to preserve:

> Not hollowly do I wish to break
> the ties that bind together a marriage:

may the magnanimous and robust neck suffer
its yoke, as heavy as it is just,
and he will avoid the horror of my lessons. (1:44–48)[9]

But in practice this is not the norm, especially because some men do not have the money to enter into matrimony and others—those related to a religious institution or those dependent on their parents—cannot get married without permission (1:49–52).

Even those who may have the possibility of release of their desire with their spouse may find it impossible if their wife is "fantastically insolent" (1:55) because she is confident that the binding quality of marriage will protect her and allow her to "tyrannically seize the authority of the man" (1:56–58). Moratín follows this logic with a defense of the legal dissolution of marriage: "Of so many misfortunes liberated / would be humanity, if this contract / were to be annulled if its conditions were violated!" (1:59–61),[10] an idea with clear connection to the changes of enlightened secularization already in place in the court of Frederick II of Prussia, who sanctioned a divorce law in 1752, and which would also operate in France after the Revolution of 1789.[11] The poetic voice claims that since in his context the "system" (1:68) will not change, it is acceptable that he aims to establish his own system, one that would give release to the completely natural sexual impulse of men: "And it not being possible to impede / that for which nature sometimes clamors, / justly or unjustly, unavoidable / is the quenching of love's ardent flame" (1:99–102).[12] This proposed system is that of prostitution, which of course already exists, alive and well, but which presents two major hitches: it is expensive, and, as one might guess, *gálico* is also alive and well. Moratín's three cantos are indeed a proposal to regulate and diminish the negative outcomes of satisfied sexual desire in men through prostitution. The why and how of the *Arte* is exclusively connected to the management of these two obstacles, as clearly stated at the beginning of the first canto:

If the excessive outlays
that ruin the lascivious youths are moderated
and venereal contagion is exiled
from the ardent groins, and the marriage beds
are made safe, then future
fruits of blessing may be expected for sure . . .
the lesser harm should be
suffered so as to avoid greater harms. (1:135–46)[13]

The defense of regulated prostitution is presented then as a contribution to the future of Spain. If the price of the service of prostitutes is reduced, the wealth of nonaffluent young men will not be affected as heavily, and therefore the country's economy will improve. If the spread of *gálico* is contained, the future of the country, represented by healthy offspring, will be bright and flourishing.

The beginning of the second canto states clearly that the *Arte* has been written for men of the same social status as the poetic voice but who only have moderate economic means. According to the poetic voice, for a wealthy man there is no real skill needed to procure healthy prostitutes, because with money "for you all the skirts will be lifted / of any female whosoever" (2:6–7),[14] and the poem's lessons will not apply to him. Instead, the instructions are dedicated to "he who, for lack of resources, says that he is in litigation / and expects to eat both well and cheaply" (2:9–10),[15] a euphemism for having cheap sex with a variety of healthy women. These two goals of controlling prices and *gálico* are to be solved discursively in the poem by the formulation of a geography of containment, whereby the poetic voice didactically identifies the hubs of prostitution in which the source of sexual release is to be found. Criticism on Moratín's poem has tended to see this mapping of prostitution as a somewhat festive and humorous view of the unsanctioned habits of Madrid's society, but it is clear that the charting of these women as a wealth of sexual products is equally intended to serve as a cartography of control and vigilance: only what is charted can be monitored.

> It would be easier to count every light
> of the starry globe, or all the sands
> of the sea that bathes from the Indus to the Moorish shore,
> than for me to count up all the girls
> that there are in Madrid. (3:95–99)[16]

The abundance of sexual product is first stated in terms of locations where prostitutes can be found (gates, streets, plazas, portals, entryways, stores, water fountains, promenades, creeks, inns, carriageways, bridges, parks, forests), and reinforced by the wide array of nicknames that describe the sexual skills or physical qualities of the prostitutes to be found in these places. In this regard, the main lesson taught by the poetic voice to his understudy is to find women with "a good slit and a good ass, / firm breasts and flesh, but healthy" (3:481–82),[17] with variations on the attributes that make them desirable or amusing: the breasts big as cushions of la Ramona (2:342–43); the small breasts together with the big thighs of Carrasca (3:41), or the uneven ones of Benita (3:133); the red lips of la Poderosa "with her carmine mouth bathed in laughter" (3:146);[18] or the deep vagina of Pepa la Larga (3:104–5). This list of sexual harvest also includes Belica, who, according to the poetic voice, exchanged sex for sonnets written by the author, "And as I continued to recite them / the incontinent and dissolute female / became electrified by pure lust" (3:146),[19] and who according to David Gies may also have infected Moratín with *gálico* (*Nicolás* 100).[20] The result is a catalog of women as goods and merchandise to be quantified, assessed, described, and organized as part of a productive economy, a dynamic very much akin to the discourse derived from the expeditions to study nature and people in faraway places, such as James Cook's British expedition to Tahiti, New Zealand, and Australia (1768–71), later mirrored by the botanical expeditions to New Spain and New Granada propelled by the Bourbon administration, which took place just a few years after Moratín wrote the *Arte*.[21]

At the same time that this geography of containment describes the wealth of women and "where to find the most abundant supply" (2:301) as material and economic prospects, the element of vigilance is equally localized when the poetic voice refers, with proper name and location, to women who have been touched by *gálico* as resources not to be tapped. In this way, the author locates "la Catalana de la calle de Hita," who passed the disease to an inattentive man (2:132–34); or Juanita, close to the Real Panadería, explaining that she used to be very attractive until she got infected: "What a treat you were before / you started tenderizing loafers [cheaper clientele] / that fitted you with disgusting buboes, / and have left you, used up in a doorway!" (2:334–37);[22] Teresa Mané, who only four days before had been discharged from the Antón Martín hospital where she had been treated (3:43–44); "Tiny, to whom Padre Angulo / gave blennorrhea in the ass" (3:119–20);[23] Lavenana (a character I will discuss later), who when very young had sex with the poetic voice for two pesetas, and who later became very sought after by clients at a high price, only to end up spreading "purgaciones" (blennorrhea), a mucous genital discharge that can be related to gonorrhea or syphilis (14:20–33). In the fourth canto, the author describes a woman nicknamed "la Cafetera" (the Coffeemaker) whose trade is to serve as go-between and who washes the rags used by those with blennorrhea, and whose two sisters and sister-in-law the author recommends avoiding because they are a "podridero" (rotting place), "and they get hold of the member of anyone they see / and are most dexterous in making it stiff, / and later they plague anyone who gets into them" (4:157–60).[24] Moratín uses a double meaning of the word *diestra,* which in one sense refers to being skilled and in the other means being right-handed, alluding to the ability of these women to arouse men with their hands. The author also uses the double meaning of dexterity to describe the "refined Fausta," a woman who got badly infected right after arriving in Madrid. After learning the hard lesson ("escarmentada"), Fausta avoided having sex with men, becoming "like an old or ugly whore; / and so you became, by dint of exercise, / the most dexterous of all humans"

¡Puñetas!

The word may be shocking because of its coarse ring. Although in the present day it is generally used as an expression of surprise or annoyance, or as a dismissive farewell, it is indeed a remnant of the longtime practice of performing sex with the hand to avoid venereal disease and pregnancy. In Francisco Sobrino's Spanish-French dictionary of 1705, the definition is exclusively connected to the sexual practice: "Puñeta, hazer la puñeta, *Faire sortir la semence du membre par plaisir*" (To make the seed of the virile member come out for pleasure). The term is connected to the shape the hand makes, forming a *puño* (fist) when giving sexual pleasure to a man. As is the case with Moratín's Fausta, the ability to perform hand jobs was a skill appreciated by men who feared infection through genital sex, although here it also supposedly helps the prostitute dodge becoming reinfected with *gálico*. The fact that the poet joins the sexual practice and the fear of contagion suggests that this type of sex was not as sought after as other types of encounters, and that it was also less profitable. The name *puñeta,* and the practice of *hacer puñetas,* with its present meaning of asking someone to get lost or to engage in a purposeless activity, are connected to the belief in the unproductive and negative quality of masturbation (RAE 2001, s.v. "puñeta"). The word *puñetera,* initially connected solely to a sexual practice or a service performed by prostitutes, has evolved into a derogatory adjective that qualifies something as being empty, infertile, or disposable.

(3:121–27).[25] Moratín is referring to the practice of hand masturbation, used by this particular prostitute as a way of avoiding contagion with *gálico,* but which according to the poetic voice is a procedure mainly used by women who are considered older and less attractive. The enlightened don Nicolás jeeringly refers to the knowledge and ability acquired by Fausta by comparing it with the skill of sanctioned trades or professions such as that of a painter, a jeweler, a cobbler, or perhaps a poet and dramatist, and mockingly raising her to the level of universal mastery. It is from this disjuncture, which otherwise is clearly offensive, that the humorous element arises in Moratín's verses.

The sneering tone in the description of Fausta's cautious attempts to avoid infection with *gálico* masks the poetic voice's hovering terror of acquiring the terrible disease, an idea defended by Gies when he proposes that Moratín himself feared contracting venereal diseases (*Nicolás* 46). I agree with this reading. As I have discussed before when dealing with the idea of humor, obscenity, and scatological discourse, what lies at the bottom of a text that dwells on the portrayal of raw instances of a sexuality that otherwise would remain in the private sphere is a coded, allusive construction of language that represents latent fear. This is precisely the case in the passage in the *Arte* where the poetic voice narrates the encounter between a priest and a syphilitic prostitute as the origin of the condom, perhaps the most scatological episode of the four cantos. The obscenity is further stressed by the compounding fashion in which the author presents this particular highway prostitute's vagina, listing all the symptoms of the French disease which he describes with coarse detail:

> instead of a sovereign beauty
> one encountered a putrid female member,
> full of buboes, some burst,
> others still maturing, others mature,
> standing above, the sore-covered clitoris,
> without labia and bald in patches;
> droplets from the seventh anointments
> with scars, grime and moles,
> of reeking breath and corrupted pus;
> dirty from patches, gummas, and warts,
> numerous and abundant purgations,
> that inundated the crotch with plague
> smearing with matter the creases
> of the filthy (swinish), blackened gut. (2:161–74)[26]

A putrefacted vagina, buboes in different stages of growth, an ulcered clitoris, severed labia, scars, mucous discharge, wounds, gummas, warts, pus, and a vulva dark in color and compared to guts are more than enough features to provoke fear masked as disgust. This accumulation of manifested disease causes in the reader a fearful revulsion and, in consequence, a sympathetic view of the solution by containment proposed by the poetic voice, especially when this fix still allows for a continuation of current sexual practices for men.

The emphatic description shows that *gálico* was a reality, and as a reality it produced not only fear but also an abundance of opinions to explain it. The incomprehensibility of and inescapability from the subject of fear is provisionally resolved through its narrativization and theorization. The *Arte de las putas* opens a space in which medical debates and pseudoscientific opinions that mix traditional understanding and innovative interpretation are examined, trying to find real solutions to a real occurrence that produced real fear. Moratín is not immune to the need to apply such rationalization to the etiology and manifestations of *gálico,* and his opinion in the long poem reflects the state of popular beliefs about the disease. A reading of the text from this perspective shows that by the end of the eighteenth century, Moratín still believed that all humans had the potential or rudiments of a disease like *gálico,* but that only in some people—those prone to develop it—will the disease become manifest. This is, of course, the theory of inherent disease we have already discussed when studying the work of Francisco Suárez de Ribera, the author of *Arcanismo anti-galico, o Margarita mercurial,* who claimed that a "seminio" (seed or seedling) of an ailment like *gálico* is already in the body of mankind as a punishment from God for original sin, and that the disease is communicated, unchained, or made active by the venereal act or other similar causes, and also as a manifestation of divine wrath. This theorization of the origin of the disease gives cause to the poetic voice to allege that the practice of "encabronamiento" (cuckolding) is not practical or effective:

> Many will ponder the rare excellence
> of cuckolding, which preserves one
> from venereal infection. Such are errors
> of the masses; such are your humors
> that, though you may be with a woman free from *gálico,*
> your lymph will be corrupted by scalding,
> for the disposition is in all of us. (2:115–21)[27]

For Moratín, given that the seed of *gálico* is already present in everyone, having a longtime lover is not a guarantee that the disease will not be unchained if the person is prone to develop the disease anyway. As an instantiation of the truth of this logic, the poetic voice comments on women who go to the taverns to get free drink and food, and who have sex with many men, including those infected with *gálico,* and still do not get the disease: "who go to the freeloaders of the taverns /—covered in lancings and bandages, / with every Antón Martín between their legs—/ and they pull it out cleaner than a sword" (2:123–26).[28]

The reappearance of the name Antón Martín, the hospital where people received treatment for *gálico* in Madrid, stresses the belief that these women have sex with men who are clearly syphilitic but remain unscathed. Moratín further stresses his theory of inherent disease a few verses down when he says that "Mange, as well as the plague and the pox / don't stick to many who are present, and no one else gave it to the first" (2:127–29),[29] which is the same logical inference of doctors like Suárez de Ribera, who argued that the first person who had a disease could not have received it from someone else, corroborating that the first case of any disease was necessarily inherent, and therefore asserting the inherent quality of all diseases in all cases.

Also following a medical understanding of venereal diseases that came from the previous century, Moratín defends the idea that if a man acquires *gálico* all that is necessary to avoid its development is to simply refrain from any sexual contact: "But if your cock should chance / to show by misfortune small purgations, / observe hard abstinence and be consoled / for it is impossible that the disease should take root" (2:220–23).[30] For him, the hasty repetition of sexual encounters after the first sign of the disease dooms the sick men to forfeit recovery. This idea had already been manifested in the definition of "buba" in the *Diccionario de autoridades,* the first dictionary published by the Real Academia in 1726, which stresses that the first Spaniards acquired the disease because of the frequent sexual exchanges they had with indigenous women: "from the dishonest exchange that they repeatedly had with the women of those new regions" (RAE 1726, s.v. "buba").[31] For the poetic voice, the practical outcome from these theorizations of the spread of *gálico* is that men should not exercise abstinence for fear of getting infected (2:229–35), and that they should only abstain from sex if they see the first signs of blennorrhea, a logic that one could summarize as "do it as you can, as much as you can, only until you can't."

It is relevant here that Moratín's humorous and obscene text is imbued with a contrasting use of language and knowledge of a higher level. The crude language employed to describe the diseased prostitute I just mentioned has been preceded by a clear summary of the physiology of the masculine erection and ejaculation that, although foreign in a text of this sort at first sight, resonates with medical treatises in its accuracy, clarity, and power of observation:

> The overheated blood is roused . . .
> in a robust and ardent young man,
> in an old man, in a cleric or a monk,
> and the glop, being expelled by the kidneys,
> goes down by means of the most thin channels
> to engorge the hanging testicles,
> the flexible muscles extending,
> and the human instrument becoming clogged with blood,
> rises swollen to the belly button,
> filled by the abundant semen,
> which, bursting to get out, proves
> to be poisonous if being detained,
> according to the knowledgeable Hippocrates of Cos. (1:472–84)[32]

This straightforward discourse stresses the didactic quality of the poem as a whole. It also reinforces the idea that the writing of the learned elite at the time sought to be direct and useful—regardless if it was a high-brow moral discourse or a humorous manual to avoid *gálico*—therefore encompassing the double-sided quality of Janus. Although the aim and structure pursue clarity and practicality, the discourse on *gálico* in Moratín's poem shows an ambiguous mix of long-held beliefs—such as the theory of inherence or the promotion of the disease as a result of repeated sex—and forward-looking discussions that were radically changing the understanding of medicine and science at the time. This ambiguity is apparent not only in literary works but, as I have shown, in contemporaneous medical texts. One inclusion of up-to-date scientific debates in the *Arte* is the argument that a disease like scabies originated from animalcules that came in contact with the human body, a discussion included in Feijoo's discourse "Lo máximo en lo mínimo" (The greatest in the smallest), published in 1736 as part of his *Teatro crítico universal* (7:16). In the *Arte,* when the priest is about to have sex by the side of the road with a terribly infected prostitute, he immediately recalls the current discussion on the origin of diseases from tiny worms or insects. What the priest says to himself is clearly a reformulation of the argument Feijoo developed in his *Teatro crítico* forty years before:

> if the buboes are a living multitude
> of tender and minute insects,
> as modern physicians believe,
> because mercury kills every creature,
> I want to avoid their communication,
> by making a shield of holy clothes. (2:187–92)[33]

It is evident that the author makes use of excessive language for his humorous purpose. His method is to create intervals of rather approachable affirmations, followed by a shocking apex that disorients the reader and drives the humorous release. It is this kind of excessive language, especially in connection with the institution of the church, which had the poem prohibited by 1777. In this particular instance, the terse outline of current scientific dialogue is disrupted by the risky inclusion of the skull cap, a holy garment, used by the lascivious friar as a shield for his penis while penetrating the diseased woman.

The scientific theorization of the transmission of diseases—which would later become what we know as "germ theory"—is used rhetorically by Moratín to introduce the idea of condom use, an important component of his proposal for containing *gálico,* which he jokingly attributes to the friar but which he also says may well have been the devil's invention. This hints that one or the other are just the same thing, as a way to denounce the corrupt practices of the clergy: "The inventiveness of a monk / gave a happy start to this ruse, which could only be the invention / of a monk or of the devil" (2:142–44).[34] In the raucous mythologization of the birth of the condom—the sexual encounter of the cleric and the prostitute, the use of the cap that indicates his status as a man of God, and the scatological final punch line of the friar putting the garment back on his head, smearing his face with semen—we can observe a secularizing thrust pulsing in the substratum of the text. Yet, from another viewpoint, perhaps more important to Moratín, he seeks a strategy to normalize and foment the use of the prophylactic technology, which had already arrived in Spain from England and France, and which he repeatedly advises the man who wants to become an "expert whoremonger" ("experto putañero," 2:130) to use. The poetic voice states that his advisee should have as many new sexual encounters as he wishes, but repeatedly insists that he should always use a sheath, instructing that "in this way, go abuse yourself from the copse to the house; / but I want to make you safe from everything, / facilitating the use of the condom" (2:139–41),[35] and later, almost closing the second canto, reminds him of the miseries awaiting him at the hospitals where *gálico* is treated if he does not "arm" himself: "I assume that you go out always armed / with a condom, your constant companion, / and in this way you will not dirty the hospitals" (2:372–74).[36]

By the last third of the eighteenth century, condoms were of common use in London and Paris. Their main initial purpose was clearly to prevent the transmission of *gálico,* and only later were they welcomed for their added contraceptive advantage.[37] Nevertheless, as early as 1714, Spanish diplomats may have been familiar with the use of condoms made out of a lamb's intestinal membrane. According to Amy and Thiery, "The first organised and large scale sale of skin condoms may have taken place in Utrecht, in the Netherlands" (5). The authors explain that a large number of diplomats and their entourage arrived in the city for the peace talks that ended in the Peace of Utrecht. The treaty would bring the end of the War of Succession of the Spanish throne that began with the death of Charles II, *El hechizado,* the monarch who, according to some, died from syphilis, and with whom I started this book. The political map of the world changed drastically after the treaty, which introduced the idea of a "balance of power" in Europe. The talks leading to the treaty started in the spring of 1713 and continued into 1715. Men from all the involved nations—Britain, the Dutch Republic, France, Prussia, Portugal, Savoy, and Spain (who took most of the losses)—arrived in the city, together with their sexual drives: "The local sex workers could not meet the demand. . . . Venereal diseases spread explosively. But soon it became known that a means of protection could be purchased from a shop at the corner of the Beguine convent" (5). The means of protection was of course the use of skin sheaths, crafted by a woman who was a condom merchant, and who was also willing to impart to the prospective users a full theoretical-practical course on their use, she being the teacher and the subject used for the practices. Amy and Thiery explain that "some Englishmen brought the devices back to their country and shortly thereafter skin condoms were being manufactured and sold in London as well. Britain's capital became the international centre in the trade of condoms" (5).

The Craft of Condom Making

Amy and Thiery quote an informative explanation of making condoms from the sheep's cecum (blind gut), from the second edition of Robley Dunglison's *New Dictionary of Medical Science and Literature* (1874): "The caecum of a sheep, soaked for some hours in water, [is] turned inside out, macerated again in weak alkaline ley [lye], changed every twelve hours, scraped carefully to abstract the mucous membrane, leaving the peritoneal and muscular coats exposed to the vapour of burning brimstone, and afterwards washed with soap and water. It is then blown up, dried, cut to the length of seven or eight inches, and bordered at the open end with a riband. It is drawn over the penis prior to coition, to prevent venereal infection and pregnancy" (5). The original edition of 1844 reveals further information about condoms by listing euphemisms for the contraption: "*Baudruches, Redingote Anglaises, Gant des Dames, Calottes d'assurance*" (181). Other names in French were *peau divine* and *chemisette,* while "armor" or "French letter" were used in English. Supplementary sources mention condoms made out of fish bladders, but none, to my knowledge, mentions a condom made from a cap, like the one described by Moratín. Rubber condoms debuted in the middle of the nineteenth century, thanks to the process of rubber vulcanization developed by Thomas Hancock (1786–1865) and Charles Goodyear (1800–1860).

It would not be far-fetched to claim that Spanish diplomats also brought samples of the device, or at least the knowledge of its form and use. What is clear is that by the time Moratín writes his poem, Madrid has a decent supply of condoms brought from France and England. Unfortunately, it seems that there was no domestic industry for making condoms in Spain at the time, unless the mythical one of the friar's cap counts.

Moratín credits Englishmen with refining the friar's prototype: "then the most keen Englishmen, / the philosophers of the century, have polished it, / and have reduced it to a fine membrane" (2:206–9).[38] By calling them "the philosophers of the century, " he is using an equivocal label, since the reader does not know whether he is referring to their skillful crafting of condoms or to the nation in general.

From Moratín we also know that there was a practice of preserving the sheaths in almond oil to keep them fresh (2:210–11). I will add that the oil would also keep them supple, given that lamb intestines harden when they become dry. According to Amy and Thiery, in order to make condoms flexible before intercourse, the user had to soak them in milk or tepid water (4). If the use of almond oil to preserve them was a Spanish development during

Moratín's time, it indeed would have been a great accomplishment. Oiled or not, from the *Arte*'s verses we can gather that men in Moratín's circle would provision themselves with condoms that came either from England or from France. If they had the chance—or the obligation, if they had been banished from court—they could also get their condoms in Montpellier, where they were sold by the bundle: "Y en Montpellier se venden a paquetes" (2:215).

Also instructive in Moratín's manual are his insights on the gray market of condoms in Madrid. He mentions that condoms can be bought "in the stores of Pérez and Geniani" ("en las tiendas de Pérez y Geniani," 2:216), a reference that needs further development. Geniani was an Italian merchant located at number 13, Calle de la Montera.[39] During the eighteenth century, Montera was one of the most important strolling lanes in Madrid, flanked on both sides with stores of all types. Geniani's specialty store was an active place where people of the upper crust of Madrid's society acquired imported goods, especially jewelry and housewares. An entry in the *Calendario manual y guia de forasteros en Chipre* (Manual calendar and guide of outsiders in Cyprus) (1768), a satirical piece attributed to José Cadalso (1741–82) and dated during the carnival of 1768, suggests that Pérez's and Geniani's stores also served as centers of animated discussion and gossiping. In a section titled "Juvileo" (Celebrations), Cadalso offers a list of places where he would meet companions: "Wednesdays and Saturdays during Carnival in front of the Royal Library, and any day of the year in the Puerta del Sol, Calle Mayor, the houses of Geniani, Pérez, Lumbreras, Tarsi, Larus, Vallejo, Gallinas, and others of the same class and station" (*Obras* 77).[40] In 1772, the future duchess of Alba received from her fiancé, the future marquis of Villafranca del Bierzo, "a repeater watch of gold, enameled and adorned with diamonds, which was purchased in Geniani's house at a price of 18,000 *reales*" as one of her engagement gifts (Nicolás Martínez 3).[41] *Il mentore perfetto de negozianti* (The businessman's perfect mentor), a publication of 1794, indicates that in Madrid the main "[m]erchants of jewelry and trinkets . . . [are] Geniani and Perez" (Metrà 379),[42] the same stores mentioned by Moratín. *Il mentore* was an Italian publication with relevant information for those doing business of all types in the main commercial cities in Europe; it included names of the main industries, coin exchange rates, weight values, main banks, and, of course, the leading specialty stores.

The most telling document of the significance of Geniani's store is a canvas by the master painter Luis Paret y Alcázar (1746–99), finished in 1772 and titled *La tienda del anticuario Geniani* (The store of the antiquarian Geniani), which is currently housed at the Museo Lázaro Galdiano in Madrid (see fig. 9).[43] The scene shows the interior of the store, where a couple of wealthy patrons are conducting business. While the lady is assessing a beautiful hairband, the gentleman is getting some coins from his small silk bag. To the side, a nursemaid is holding their baby girl. The background shows the wide array of products sold by Geniani, and its ornateness demonstrates the preeminence of foreign objects and fashion. From top to bottom, and from left to right, the viewer can identify jugs made out of precious metal, fine dishware, elegantly framed paintings, a very large porcelain vase and small crystal containers, as well as silk lady's gloves. Framing the scene, fashionable brilliant fabric and small mats hang on a cord that traverses the upper right corner of the store. The way that Paret has arranged these last items clearly aims at showing the store as a theater stage, the fabric and mats functioning as makeshift drapes, and the shelves holding exquisite French porcelains behind their glass doors as the backstage. This interpretation is further supported by the fact that three masks crown the composition, one of them clearly theatrical, and the other two of the kind used in soirees and parties to protect one's identity. The reference to mask and disguise in Paret's painting stresses the porosity and seemingly ambiguous discrepancy between public enlightened ideas of balance and reason and private practices related to enjoyment, excess, and the superfluous. Irene Gómez Castellano has studied this apparent imbalance in depth. In her insightful *La cultura de las máscaras* (The culture of the masks) she shows how the framed moments of pleasure—represented by sensual and frivolous poems by members of the Escuela Salmantina, or by Goya's tapestry vignettes of aristocrats pretending to be peasants—functioned as a release mechanism whereby the authors offered a nonsanctioned form of criticism, expressed their inner desire, or projected themselves with alternative identities.

This dynamic is also present in Paret's depiction of Geniani's store. In the framed space of the store, the wealthy young couple purchases items that outwardly represent refinement and status, but at the same time this apparent harmony, this excess of adornment, masks the unstable reality of other disrobed excesses. In this visit, the young man is producing coins from his purse to pay for his wife's headband, or for the French fancy laces that rest by the side of the golden clock. One or two days later, when the store would be less crowded, following the didactic lessons of the poetic voice in the *Arte,* this very same young man, perhaps modeled after someone in Moratín's circle, may have come to purchase English and French condoms. In one of the many boxes shown in Paret's canvas, I imagine, rest neatly packed sheaths that were supposed to protect the young man from the feared *gálico.* Condoms are then a commodity that functions within the same dynamic as luxurious imported goods. Even if hidden and used in the private, even furtive, realm, the condom still belongs to the dimension of novelty and the portrayal of social status. The condom is not yet coded as an object that procures common good—

Figure 9. *La tienda del anticuario Geniani,* Luis Paret y Alcázar, 1772. (© Museo Lázaro Galdiano)

such as the practice of variolation to prevent smallpox—but one that provides bourgeois convenience, comfort, and luxury, like a fancy headpiece or a gilded clock would do.

The condoms could be discreetly bought in this fancy store at a high price ("if you pay well for them, and with discretion," 2:217)[44] or slyly commissioned from a secretary of an embassy ("and by means of the secretaries of the embassy, / which other nations send to ours," 2:218–19),[45] that is, at exclusive places where only a small bracket of society had access. But the prostitutes could be found in the lower level of the street, even in the darkness of a doorway and, following Moratín, at the cheapest possible price. If the condom did not perform its fancy function, and the prostitute was so poor that she had acquired *gálico* from one of her many clients, the diseased, poor and rich, ended up in the rather equalizing space of the Antón Martín hospital, or suffering the universal consequences of the treatment with mercury.

Contagion—or rather, "communication"—was a reality, so much so that an author like Moratín writes a whole didactic poem proposing ways to stem it. For those touched by the disease, the author also has some advice: find a good doctor and endure the treatment with cinnabar, which the author calls "red vermilion":

> But if by chance your health is ravaged
> by the sows who have it with worms
> and whose nethers reek in the summer,
> Urbina, Juan de Dios and Talavera,
> (surgeons with much experience
> on the groins of dissolute young men)
> will slice you with delicate hands,
> and the fumigations with cinnabar
> will tear up the tenacious lice. (4:161–69)[46]

While at this end of the spectrum, once the disease has been acquired, the poetic voice instructs the advisee to go to the doctor and suffer his fumigations, purges, and bloodlettings, in the preventative main thrust of his poem Moratín insists on the use of the condom. He even goes so far as to forward public policy, one more instance of his proposal of control, that would require prostitutes to offer condoms to their clients, stating that such is the practice in England: "and the whores of London are fined / if they do not offer trays of condoms, / which they have brought from China" (2:212–14).[47] Along the same line of precautionary public policy ideas to stem *gálico,* the author praises the idea of organizing a guild, which he says had been proposed by the prostitutes in Barcelona: "It is known that they have offered a project / to the Ministry, by which they would oblige themselves / to furnish the court with fish / and fresh healthy meat" (4:235–38).[48] The association would self-regulate and offer clients a steady cohort of young and healthy prostitutes. But that was not all; the quantity of prostitutes and the prices for their services would be regulated—"who will serve the public for low prices, / and with so much affection and abundance, / that there will never be a lack nor will / the insatiable courtly lust be able to complain" (4:239–42)[49]—and they would also commit to pay a levy for exercising their profession, the only proviso being that the guild be composed exclusively of Catalonian women: "and with this pact they oblige themselves to pay / a larger levy than the Jews did in their day" (4:249–50).[50] According to Moratín, the proposal fell through because the prostitutes from Madrid opposed it vehemently, perhaps concerned about the competition, and the government gave in, alleging the protection of free commerce (4:251–67). Still, the author sees an organization of prostitution that would reduce the amount of diseased prostitutes as practical and progressive—he does not mention what to do with the constant flow of diseased clients, though—because it would contain them in certain areas of the city and would arbitrate low prices. It is clear that, for Moratín, such an arrangement is not feasible in the short term that the sexual urgency of the *putañeros* requires, and he laments what he sees as the negative consequences of the implementation of an economic system akin to the laissez-faire that had been initiated in France in 1754 by King Louis XV. The main goal of the laissez-faire doctrine was to promote wealth and trade through free economic competition. As applied to the realm of prostitution in Madrid, Moratín argues that this "letting be" hampers control, allows for the spread of *gálico,* and grants prostitutes regulation of the price, making the market for sex more expensive in some cases, and very badly paid in others:

> Also, around the barracks,
> roam the most novice whorers
> the poorly paid whores of the soldiers,
> because in Madrid there are more than a hundred brothels
> given that there is not a single one that is allowed
> as it happens in other cities, which do not lose
> for that: and you, Madrid, would lose nothing
> but would, by doing that, cause much less scandal. (2:314–21)[51]

Moratín's immediate proposal to fulfill the three goals of getting young, healthy and low-priced women to satisfy men's sexual needs is practical, although disturbingly twisted. The main preventative method in the *Arte* is the procurement of a constant flux of young women, usually from the countryside or the lower economic strata of Madrid, which the *putañero* was to use for a maximum of two encounters and immediately dispose of. The poetic voice claims that his pupil must understand that if the goal is to gratify his sexual drive, he must get rid of the idea of finding professional prostitutes that charge higher prices only because of their alluring external appearance. He claims, furthermore, that in fact the expensive professional prostitutes were humble women at first (2:258–59). Instead, the advisee should locate the easier prey of simple women—he uses hunting terminology, "you'll take what you hunt" ("llevarás lo que caces," 2:246)—not minding their humble dress, but thinking only of their flesh, an idea he expresses with disconcerting poetic accuracy, instructing that "you'll see that these tatty ones, / are pearls mounted in vile lead" (2:256–57),[52] and later that "many times, / beneath a rustic and crude dress, / you'll find Titian's Venus, / like a good drinker in a bad cape" (2:280–83),[53] an indication that he rounds up in the last canto with great precision, warning the pupil to "trade in the beautiful ones for the healthy" (4:140).[54] Moratín's discussion on beauty here is a reiteration of the ambiguous nature

of enlightened ideals in the Hispanic world. In clear agreement with the enlightened mood that examines the deceptive way in which our senses give us
information about the world—an idea I discussed in relation to Feijoó's "Lo
máximo en lo mínimo"—the poetic voice recommends to his apprentice to
look beyond external beauty and adornment and to seek true naked beauty;
only in this case, this nakedness is all too awkwardly literal: "Take her to the
room, and if her clothes offend / your sight, then clothes out, and stark naked / like a yearling ewe, put her in the bed" (2:277–79).[55] The reasoning
for his advice to put health over beauty rests on the true goal of the poem of
fomenting sensual and sexual satisfaction, even in compounding excess, over
the fleeting quality of beauty. But masked by this idealized notion of the transitory nature of beauty is a conception of beauty as irrelevant and even as disposable. As long as the resources the man uses to satisfy his sexuality change
constantly, his health will be unspoiled. The concept of beauty is replaced by
that of disposability, and the long list of women and places where they can
be found in "abundant supply" ("provision abundante," 2:301) is just a way to
chart where to find the raw material resources and how to make the most out
of them while at the same time avoiding the disease: "And after all, everything
in Madrid, when night comes / gives to an upstanding man a thousand female
doorkeepers / who, though poor, assume not that *gálico,* / is harbored in their
groins" (2:402–5).[56] In order to find information about the type of woman
who might be his easy prey, the instructor of the poem allows the *putañero* to
feign friendship with corrupt court clerks and notaries,

> for their news is worth a fortune.
> You will save time, silver and gold, and yourself from ills
> if you know how to find the recently arrived,
> who do not ask for much nor are worn out, for they as yet don't have
> corrupted health nor corrupted habits. (4:115–19)[57]

Moratín is against the practice of *encabronamiento,* or having a mistress for a
prolonged period of time, perhaps because he feels it gets expensive in the long
run. Although he advises the reader to deceive the targeted underprivileged
women by promising to keep them as lovers, he insists that there should only
be a maximum of two encounters in order to avoid larger expenses:

> our art does not permit enjoying one woman
> more than twice—even if she were
> the graceful and funny Saturnine—,
> unless she were to give it up just because she wanted to,
> for then there is no risk, if there's no expenditure. (2:94–98)[58]

Nevertheless, he grants that, in order to keep the flow of sexual encounters brief but constant, a good investment is to find a go-between woman. A procurer of this kind would help with the legwork of identifying young women fitting the characteristics given by the *putañero*. That is the case of la Pepona, the poetic voice's middlewoman who does the rounds to find new candidates for her employer, as she explains:

> The Sol inn, the one of Zaragoza,
> and Barcelona, and the inn of Ocaña,
> I went around to all of them; for there is where one appreciates
> the goods recently arrived to Madrid,
> because the old stock is all spoiled. (3:433–37)[59]

It is clear that Moratín presents the engagement with younger women from outside of Madrid as a prophylactic method against *gálico* (if one can give it such a name). In spite of its possible effectiveness, the outcome of such practice is desolating because the fluctuating satisfaction of sexual desire, even if healthy, does not necessarily translate into the satisfaction of a pleasurable life. Two hundred and fifty years after this text was written and circulated, and with the unfair advantage of perspective that such a passage of time offers, one wonders if there had not been *gálico,* how a masked text by someone like Moratín would have looked.

➤ 13

An Epic Chant to the Syphilitic Bubo

Another relevant work of a hidden nature, but written by an otherwise lauded man of letters, is the poem titled "El *incordio:* Poema épico-gálico en un canto" (The *incordio:* An epic-gallic poem in one canto), by the Sevillian thinker José María Blanco White, né José María Blanco Crespo (1775–1841). In the following pages, I will refer to the author as "Blanco," given that the poem was written between 1806 and 1807 when he was still in Spain and had not yet acquired the English name of Joseph Blanco White.

The main source of criticism on Blanco's poem is Antonio Garnica Silva, who in 1987 published the first transcription of a manuscript copy, apparently the only copy we have, held in the library of the Hispanic Society in New York. I use the more established version of the poem in Garnica's edition of the complete poetic works of Blanco, *Obra poética completa,* published in 1994. In this edition, Garnica provides a transcription of handwritten notes added to the manuscript, which offer important insights on the treatment of and beliefs about *gálico* at the time. Garnica has also published *Escritos autobiográficos menores* (Minor autobiographical writings) (1999), the translation of a group of original manuscripts written by Blanco as thoughts on his life which indicate that he himself had acquired syphilis and that the poem is indeed autobiographical.[1] In addition to this autobiographical source, Antonio Rafael Ríos Santos explains in his doctoral dissertation that the correspondence of 1806 between Blanco and his father shows that the author was sick, very likely as a result of *gálico,* a piece of information that helps to date the poem to that year (207).[2] The poem was written in Madrid, very soon after Blanco left the stifling environment of Seville that instigated his heterodox criticism of Catholicism and social strictures. Blanco was supposed to be in Madrid only in transit to Salamanca, and his residence at the court was not lawful, but he used the argument of his ailment to buy time in the city. He also sought the help of the influential king's favorite, the prime minister Manuel Godoy (1767–1851), to gain permission to remain in Madrid. According to Antonio de Campmany, the poem helped Blanco gain the favor of the *valido* (favorite),[3] but with the arrival of the French army some months later, this relationship, which was purely practical on Blanco's side, made him suspicious in the eyes of those in Godoy's circle.[4] This tension, together with the French military presence, was

José María Blanco White

José María Blanco White, originally José María Blanco Crespo (1775–1841), was born in Seville, the son of a merchant of Irish descent who was also the English vice-consul in that city, and María Gertrudis Crespo y Neve, a devout Catholic who encouraged him to become a priest. He is known for his work as a representative Romantic writer in Spain and England and also, later in life, as a prominent theologian of Unitarianism. Soon after his Catholic ordination in 1799 he had a crisis of faith and in 1805 left Seville for Madrid, where he became preceptor of the Infante Don Francisco de Paula. Prime Minister Manuel Godoy had given the position to him, but he lost it soon afterward, probably because he no longer had the backing of the king's favorite. In 1808, with the beginning of the War of Independence against the French invasion, Blanco returned to Seville, declared himself a patriot, and edited *El semanario patriótico* (1808–9), a publication that favored autonomy and attacked the court's corruption. Nevertheless, his criticism made him unpopular even among the patriots, and he left for England in 1810. In London he founded *El Español* (1810–14), in which he supported the political changes toward autonomy in Spanish America. At this time he met Venezuelan Andrés Bello, whom he invited to contribute to the journal and introduced to his circle. Blanco is known in the English Romantic movement for his poem "Night and Death," which was dedicated to Samuel Taylor Coleridge (1772–1834) and appears in several anthologies.

one of the reasons why Blanco finally left Madrid and went back to Seville. Political and religious incompatibility would soon compel him to leave for England, never to return.

The poem is composed of fifty-one *octavas reales* (real octave or *ottava rima*), a poetic structure usually connected with epic themes. This formal feature stresses the aim of the comical title of the poem, disguised as a heroic account. Blanco's humorous choice of the epic genre reveals his keen use of the strategic power of presenting a removed account that refers directly, nevertheless, to immediate reality. Mikhail Bakhtin states that "the epic world is constructed in the zone of an absolute distanced image, beyond the sphere of possible contact with the developing, incomplete, and therefore re-thinking and re-evaluating present" (15–17). As I will show, the use of humor, of the epic discourse, and of the distortion of mythical mores serve Blanco as a way of voicing a radical critique of the prevalent Catholic discourse and of an established social structure that sanctimoniously negated sexuality. This humorous epic reevaluates the actuality of the real and present disease of *gálico;* it shows how this malady revealed the unsanctioned sexual exchanges between social classes and indicates the ubiquity of these hidden relationships. Once the epic account is over, the fact of death and the reality of being vanquished by an inglorious bubo become drastic reminders of the futility of appearances in Hispanic society on both sides of the Atlantic.

The poem is structured as a story within a story. At the first level, a masculine poetic voice, diseased with the first stages of *gálico,* has an *incordio* (inguinal bubo). At a second level, this character is brought, in his dreams, by the goddess Iris to a warped kind of Olympus. She presents herself in the shape of an old, ugly, witchlike woman dressed as an *alcahueta*—the go-between character already visited in the study of Moratín's *Arte.* Iris tells the protagonist that he has been summoned to Olympus to be introduced to the Love deity. Upon arriving at a palace, he finds out that a licentious Love god has dethroned the conventional childlike representation of Eros. Once transported into this newly established court, the poetic voice is introduced to the "Archi-incordio" (Archbubo), who laments the impending doom of his regime thanks to the arrival of a powerful medicine that is curing all those infected with *gálico.* But at this point, the main character is awakened from his convalescent sleep by the pain of his own, tangible *incordio.*

The poetic voice starts by refusing the Muses' inspiration. The Muses are the rulers of liberal arts and of the sciences, but he tells them that they should leave him alone and instead take good care of the "pegazo" of their brother: "Stay on your mountain, demure, / taking care of your brother's pegapus (5–6).[5] The term *pegazo* does not appear in dictionaries, but it is clear that it is related to the idea of contagion present in the word *pegadizo* (contagious), therefore hinting at an acquired venereal disease. Blanco crafts a double entendre derived from a play on words. According to Greek legend, the nine Muses had been born from four springs on Mount Helicon. These springs had been created when Pegasus, the fabled winged horse, touched the ground with its hoofs. The name in Spanish for this mythological creature born from Poseidon and Medusa is Pegaso, which makes the humorous connection with its homophone related to contagion. Athena was said to have caught Pegasus and after taming it presented it to the Muses, a relation that makes the goddesses of inspiration familiar with the horse that also represents high-flying imagination. The result of the humorous confusion devised by Blanco is that Pegasus had syphilis.

By using commonplaces related to poetry (muses, gods, myths) and then attacking them, Blanco is exercising a form of secularization in poetry, one that moves away from classical topics and becomes more interested in a personal, individual experience of the poetic voice out in the world: "What do I want with muses or Apollo: / To sing about an *incordio* I am enough by myself" (7–8).[6] This experience of the world through the sensations perceived by the indi-

¡Eres un incordio!

The *Diccionario de Autoridades* defined *incordio* (bubo) as a "a tumor that solidifies in the groin, usually the product of *gálico* humor. It derives from the word *cuerda* [cord], because of the many cords that conjoin in the place where it is formed" ("tumor que se congela, y forma en las ingles, procedido regularmente de humor gálico. Derivase del nombre Cuerda, por las muchas que concurren à la parte donde se forma"). Torre y Balcárçel explains that buboes must be "brought up" or "helped" by rubbing them with cow's fat or with a cupping glass. If the pustule appears to be easy to treat, only a "thin" fomentation is needed, but "if the humor is rebelliously not coming out, for the same reason it will not mature properly, and then a stronger plaster must be applied to it" ("si el humor està rebelde en salir, por el mismo caso serà malo de madurar, y entonces se aplicarà emplasto mas fuerte," 16). If the pustule remained difficult to bring up, then it was necessary to conduct a bloodletting to help the body get rid of poisoned blood. Once the pustule appeared, it was to be opened immediately with a lancet to let the expulsion of the corrupted blood take place, and then followed by another bloodletting to purge the "humores viciosos" (vicious humors). Torre quotes Andrés Alcazar: "Opening an encordio before it matures completely and keeping it open for a long time preserves against the French disease" ("Abrir un encordio antes que se madure perfectamente, y tenerle abierto mucho tiempo, preserva de mal Frances," 16). Inguinal buboes are extremely painful, to the point that an affected person may limp while walking. This persistent and excruciating pain is behind the still-common saying "¡No me incordies!" or "¡Eres un incordio!" which accuses the person of being as nagging and impossible to get rid of as the inguinal pain produced by an *incordio*.

---

vidual already marks in Blanco a kinship with Romantic ideals. Nevertheless, without much Romanticism, the masculine poetic voice prefers the Ninfas del Barquillo (nymphs of El Barquillo Street) to the praised Muses: "And if it is that one must perforce have muses, / Come, come, oh nymphs of Barquillo Street, / Who do not stop for scrupulousness nor excuses" (9–11).[7] According to mythological stories, the Muses were related to or blended with the image of water nymphs, the beautiful young female deities of nature who are usually portrayed as singing, dancing, and exercising their sexuality with great freedom. Nicolás Fernández de Moratín also mentions El Barquillo Street in his *Arte* as a good place to find prostitutes:

> You are well to trade also with the great house
> to which Jácome Roque gave his name,
> and entering in her, you will not leave hungry.

Tócame Roque

The tenement of Jácome Roque was razed in the 1850s. The lively social interactions within its crowded quarters were depicted by the Spanish neoclassic playwright Ramón de la Cruz (1731–94) in his *sainete* (comic sketch) *La Petra y la Juana o El casero prudente o La casa de Tócame Roque*. The character of Juana is a young woman dressed as a *maja* who entertains several suitors at the same time. Cruz was influential in the theatrical life of Madrid, and his comedies of manners were popular. It is likely that Blanco was familiar with Cruz's piece because the dramatist had died in 1794, at least twelve years before the writing of "El incordio." In 1886, the Sevillian painter Manuel García y García, known as "Hispaleto" (1836–98), finished *La casa de Tócame Roque,* which he based on Ramón de la Cruz's piece. De la Cruz's description of the place and the situation between the characters of the tailors, Petra, Juana, the *alférez* (second lieutenant), and the widow are mirrored in Hispaleto's painting. The clothing of the characters, mostly young women, shows the fashion of the second half of the eighteenth century. It is possible that the "nymphs" sung by Blanco would have dressed in this way.

> The neighborhoods of Barquillo and Leganitos Streets,
> lower Lavapies and high Maravillas
> send by the thousands their girls
> with limes and hazelnuts as a pretext [*achaque,* which also means disease];
> tasty grass for lustful appetites. (2:306–13)[8]

At the corner of El Barquillo Street and Belén Street in Madrid was the "casa de Jácome Roque," mentioned here by Moratín, a large raucous tenement for poorer families, famous for its scandals and fights. This place was also known in popular lore as "casa de Tócame Roque" [lit., house of touch me, Roque], a name with sexual implications very likely related to the exchanges that may have taken place there (see fig. 10).

Related to this urban geographical representation of sexuality and disease in the colonial environment is Ruth Hill's nuanced discussion, in *Hierarchy, Commerce and Fraud in Bourbon Spanish America: A Postal Inspector's Exposé* (2005), of the cryptic meaning of the final passage in Alonso Carrió de Lavandera's (1715–83) *El lazarillo de ciegos caminantes* (1775). The riddle is related to the rivalry between Lima and Mexico City, the seats of the viceroyalties of Peru and New Spain, and revolves around the meaning of the letter *p* repeated four times in relation to the city of Lima. In Lavandera's story (484), the four *p*'s are at first sight understood as meaning *Pila, Puente, Pan,* and *Peynes* (fountain, bridge, bread, and a location in Lima named "Los Peines," or

Figure 10. *Casa de Tócame-Roque,* Manuel García Hispaleto, 1886. (© Photographic Archive Museo Nacional del Prado)

"The Combs," an unfinished beautification project initiated by Viceroy Amat in what is today the Paseo de Aguas). These four things are what make Lima surpass Mexico City (Hill, *Hierarchy* 41–70). Following Hill's detailed reading, this first, literal interpretation explains the rivalry in terms of the administration, wealth, and urban organization of each place, but a more in depth study reveals the double meanings, many of them sexual in nature, which Carrió used to criticize the high ranks of the administration, especially the viceroy Manuel de Amat y Junient (1707–82), who had been placed in power by the Bourbon monarch Charles III.

Hill uncovers the meanings of these words related to the topography of Lima, as for example the bridge entering the city (65), and Lavandera's advice to be careful there with the mulattas who "will put you in the harp, which is the same as getting the cords treatment, with which they punish discreetly" (Lavandera 388).[9] Lavandera is playing with the meaning of *cuerda,* which in argot meant the torture used by the Inquisition and the legal system to seek a confession by using a cord to stretch or to hang a person from the arms

(Chamorro, s.v. "cuerda" 288).[10] Hill shows that this "discreet" punishment with cords is connected to the supposed etymology of the *incordio,* since the *gálico* bubo is made out of "cords" or veins and nerves (65). Hill also shows that this idea of strings and harps was already present in the work of another Peruvian author, Pedro Peralta y Barnuevo (1663–1743), in his *Dialogue of the Dead: An Academic Trial* (Diálogo de los muertos: La causa académica) (1725). In one passage, a character named "A new shadow" ("una nueva sombra"), visits the kingdom of death straight from the Viceroyalty of Peru. He has a book given to him by Mercury himself and is ordered to cross the Lethe, the river of oblivion, to put this book together with others equally inspired by *gálico* (Peralta 18–19). Hill illustrates that Peralta displays the same racialized criticism of mixed mulatta women in Lima as vectors of the corded disease which one finds in Lavandera: "and the Mulattas already have him over de cords of the harps by the side of D. Pantaleón and Juan Puerco" (Peralta 19).[11] In her footnote, Hill does not quote the last part mentioning Pantaleón and Juan Puerco (65n26), but we can add that this Pantaleón is very likely the infamous *gálico* victim Anastasio Pantaleón de Ribera, whom we discussed at the beginning of this book. The strings of the *incordio* link Madrid with Lima and Mexico.

In another point relevant to my discussion, Hill explains that Los Peines, a street connected to the famous Alameda (43), and the main bridge entering Lima are used by Lavandera to indicate the scandalous relations of the viceroy with prostitutes and women of the lower strata of society, a behavior followed by other members of the privileged class in Lima—including the military (47–48)—who also used these spaces to initiate their unsanctioned relationships. Hill demonstrates that Lavandera is critiquing the erasure of difference among social strata in Lima, a preoccupation that we can also see in Cabarrús's ideas to preserve the health of the Spanish court in Madrid.

Following Hill's interpretive path, I would like to add one more possible decryption of the *Peynes* tangle. There is a connection by familiarity and etymology with the word *empeyne*—the same type of connection that allowed contemporaneous readers to understand humor between the lines. The interpretation unfolds in this way: One meaning of *empeine* is etymologically related to *peine* as a tool for brushing hair; the word comes from the Latin *pecten,* meaning "pubic hair," and by extension the lower part of the abdomen: "the lower part of the belly in the groin" (RAE 1780, s.v. "empeyne").[12] Thus, the cryptic "Peynes" in Lavandera would refer to the groins and, more pointedly, to the fame of the feminine sexual organs of Lima's women. The other meaning of *empeyne* is related to disease: a skin rash similar to ringworm, also known in English as impetigo, highly contagious, which appears in the form of red eruptions on the face that could be confused with *gálico* sores. The fame of

Lima would reside in the diseased sores of those promenading in the Alameda and the adjoining Los Peines. By extension, the cryptic letter *p* may refer to "putas" or prostitutes with *gálico*.

Through Sam Krieg and his research on the sensorial representations of Lima in the eighteenth century, I learned that about thirty years before Blanco's poem was published, Fray Francisco del Castillo Andraca y Tamayo (1714?–70), a Peruvian cleric from Piura known as "El ciego de la Merced," had written a satire that also connected prostitution to a particular neighborhood and *gálico*. His poem, titled "Conversación de unas negras en la calle de los Borricos" (Conversation of some black women on Borricos Street [the Street of Donkeys])," uses the fictional chat as a vehicle to criticize the hidden exchanges of multiple actors in everyday Lima. Castillo's text is highly bigoted and portrays Afro-Peruvians as being a hindrance, having a negative presence, connected to practices against religion, and foul-smelling or loud. In this particular case, the characters are described as boisterous gossipers in the middle of Borricos Street. Like many of the streets in the old city, specifically in the Rímac area, Borricos disappeared around 1862 when small alleyways were razed to create bigger streets known in Lima as *jirones*. The conversation among the women is precisely about what happens in the many narrow, dark streets of these neighborhoods. The poem's opening speaker, a woman who is lighter in color and states that she is not "negra mina" (black from Mina, today Elmina, in Ghana; v. 10), fears that the badly kept walls of the alleyways will crumble and bury her, or—even worse—that the death of the soul will be upon those walking in the backstreets where evil things happen if justice does not come to close them down (v. 39). A louder gossiper, who is described as "más ladina" (lit. "more Ladina," suggesting that she is more of a scoundrel, or perhaps darker; v. 48), interrupts her to claim that the alleys she has to go through near Belén, a neighborhood close to present-day Plaza de San Martín, are worse, and she compares their narrowness to that of a *jeringa,* the tool used to apply rectal enemas, as discussed before. The connection between the clyster and the muck that it expels from the pointed end leaves no doubt about the criminal activity Castillo saw as taking place in these streets, especially killings and robberies (vv. 85–100). The third participant is depicted as "una Sabá" (v. 104), a comparison to the biblical Queen of Sheba that indicates she is darker than the other two chatterboxes. She claims that it is indeed not in a narrow backstreet but in an open alleyway that leads to the main square that many sources of evil, in the form of prostitutes, can be found. The street she mentions is "[Callejón de] Petateros" (v. 113), known today as Pasaje de José Olaya, on the south side of the Plaza Mayor de Lima. Not surprisingly, the presence of prostitutes is rapidly connected to *gálico,* and the street is compared to a cylinder or barrel where the disease is manufactured:

Fray Francisco del Castillo Andraca y Tamayo

Fray Francisco del Castillo Andraca y Tamayo (1714?–70) was a Peruvian cleric of the Orden de la Merced (Order of the Blessed Virgin Mary of Mercy) and was also known by the nickname "El ciego de la Merced." He became an important literary figure in colonial Lima. His works includes poetry, plays, and translations, with his plays being the most well known. Of these, only twelve have been preserved—five of which are full-length dramas and seven are shorter works, such as *sainetes* and *entremeses,* brief theatrical pieces that were comical in nature. Fray Francisco del Castillo composed numerous works in praise of figures of the nobility of his time, such as his benefactor don José Perfecto de Salas. Another notable work is the play *La conquista del Perú* (1748), which details the events of the conquest of the Incas, based on the writings of Del Castillo's compatriot, the Inca Garcilaso de la Vega.

It is the pocket of Hell,
the Devil's little pouch
since what counts about the people
who frequent it is what they didn't have
it is a barrel where
gálico is refined and redressed
and buboes
run like water in a basin;
everything there is straw
where no one sleeps nor even dozes
and at night there are more
petites than mattresses by day.
And though gossipers may judge
that which is warned truthfully,
for holidays in hell,
more than tents are pitched.
There is where, at all hours,
to Venus is sacrificed,
by means of her dreadful
filthy priestesses. (vv. 121–40)[13]

Castillo's double entendres, wordplay, and allusions, which are similar to those of Torres Villarroel and Blanco White, were easily decoded by his public but are today somewhat difficult to understand. Nevertheless, it can be gathered that on this street "petates" (mattresses) are crafted during the day, but at night it is populated by "petites," a French word used to mean small women or prostitutes (vv. 131–32); it can also be understood that on this street, everything is related to the type of "pajas" (straw) used for bedding, but in fact nobody sleeps here because these *pajas* are more related to sexual encounters or masturbation (vv. 129–30); in this trade fair of the devil, instead of tents being set up ("tiendas tendidas," v. 136), the ones being stretched out or laid— another meaning of the word *tender* (the infinitive form of *tendidas*)—are the prostitutes. This section of the poem closes with four verses dubbing the prostitutes as "inmundas sacerdotisas" (filthy priestesses) in the cult of Venus (vv. 137–40).

The poem continues by comparing these "portaleras" with the mythological Furies (the Fates or Moirai) and harpies, because they are killing and dooming Lima's youth (vv. 140–48). The name *portaleras* (doorkeepers) was also connected to the prostitutes' custom of standing next to doors to offer their services to passersby. The gossiper speaking at this point in the poem turns into a moral orator, lamenting the way in which unsuspecting men were lured to eventual death by making contact with these women in the narrow space of this street, which she calls "the vile frontier of an ungodly war" (vv. 157–58). She also claims that these women and their customers are the ones filling up the hospitals of the city, including La Caridad—also mentioned by Valle y Caviedes—Santa Ana, San Andrés, San Bartolomé, and Espíritu Santo (vv. 159–69). According to Castillo's character, going to the hospital would be of no avail because the suffering of those "touched by the venom / that tyrannically kills" (vv. 163–64)[14] will be alleviated only by death itself. Castillo's black conversationalist also claims that the only cause of death by disease in Lima is the *gálico* spread by the doorway prostitutes, because indeed the city enjoys a "benigno clima" (benign climate) (v. 172).

After heavily criticizing the existence of "callejones" (alleyways) in Lima as places where anything good that enters them comes out bad, another chatterer in the group claims that many women in other alleys are sick with *gálico:*

> Epilepsy is born in many
> due to these alleyways,
> and it is wounding, because their mothers
> are wounded by *gálico*
> and almost all of the
> wet nurses have the same
> disease, in their breast
> with which they have paid for their lust. (vv. 356–63)[15]

Mothers are sick, and the wet nurses who feed the children in Lima are also wounded by *gálico*. The disease is the result of the relaxation of customs regarding matrimony, the easy communication between those who seek secrecy in these unguarded places, and the liberty with which men and women go about freely in the geography of the city, which leaves space for unchecked lascivious behavior.

In contrast to Castillo's acrid criticism, the narrator of Blanco's poem likes the street nymphs and in fact prefers them over the mythological ones because they are not aloof, do not require the poet to call on them with great rhetorical armament, and will give their attention to any man with a coin in his hand (13–16). The humorous effect of secularizing mythological characters is further intensified when the women in El Barquillo are addressed as "deidades verduleras" (greengrocery deities) (17), a reference to their lowly, rugged demeanor, but in this case also seen as positive for their unrefined strength and liveliness. He asks these reconditioned muses to bestow upon him a happy chant in the style of a bolero—a popular singing and dancing Spanish musical style—that he may sing in praise of the Antón Martín hospital, the institution to treat *gálico*. The poet states that this chant will sing the story of the most ferocious *incordio* in man's memory (23–24), but warns that he will not start by telling its source or cause, that is, the unmentionable circumstances whereby he caught the disease: "Yet I daren't say its name, / for that is to go against Horace, who says, / that one should never start with the egg" (25–27).[16] Blanco claims to follow the Horatian classical lesson of avoiding telling an epic tale from the very beginning of events, but instead starting the story in the middle of the plot. Horace exemplified this dictum in his *Ars poetica* with the remark that "Nec gemino bellum Troianum orditur ab ovo" (403), claiming that the epic poet should not start singing the Trojan War by retelling the story of the twin eggs from which Helen of Troy and Clytemnestra were born. But Blanco is humorously using the double meaning of *huevo* (egg) in Spanish as one of the vulgar words for a testicle or for coitus, indicating that he will not start his epic chant by describing the poetic voice's genitalia and the image of the sexual encounter where the testes play a role. Furthermore, he claims that his audience of "deidades aguerridas" (warmongering deities) (38) does not need an explanation of the sexual origin of *gálico* because they are so highly experienced in having intercourse that they "are sick and tired of knowing so much about it" ("de saberlo estáis podridas," 54). This is a new ambiguity derived from the double meaning of *podrido* as "rotten" (the putrefaction of *gálico* chancres) and as being sick and tired of the repetition of a single activity (their frequent sexual encounters).

This humorous mixing up of the classical poetic imaginary with ordinary and absolutely physical sources in order to craft a new textuality reveals a profound challenge to long-established and rapidly deteriorating modes of ordering reality. The source of literary creation is now literally upside down, and instead of singing the praises of a cerebral and idealized understanding of sexuality—that is, hidden, unfulfilled sexuality that is redirected to other purposes considered more constructive—the poetic voice is praising physical, overt, naturalized sexuality that is expressed as an impulse to be fulfilled. This dynamic of debunked past ideals replaced by a new, secularized state of affairs is also present in the next part of the poem, when Iris carries the poetic voice to a section of Olympus that has been taken over by a veritable revolution. This is not too different from what happened in France over two decades before Blanco wrote this poem, which resulted in the beheading of King Louis XVI and his consort, Marie Antoinette. In this case, the one that has been overthrown is the pudgy, playful, naive, blind Love, whose rule has been taken over by a sensuous, sanguine avatar who aims only at bodily, pleasurable satisfaction. Iris explains to the poetic voice, "You will not see that winged boy / Called Love by the poets / That naughty boy, that cunning one / With a blindfold and a load of arrows" (121–24).[17] As an ill-behaved child, Love has been sent to the *escolapios* to be raised with stiff discipline. Francisco de Goya was also raised by the *escolapios,* the Order of the Poor Clerics Regular of the Mother of God of the Pious Schools, which was known for its goal of teaching poor children and young people. But with the childlike Love banished from court, the temple is now filled with people, "racket and shouting" ("gresca y gritería," 145–46), to the point that the poetic voice compares it to a bullring (147–48). The floor trembles and the now-ruling Love appears thundering: "With a *fucking hell* pronounced in such a wild voice / that I could not doubt that he was a god" (159–60).[18] The fact that this new god marks his arrival with the vulgar word that means both "fucking hell" and "dick" shows that this new ruler of love is the penis and sexual desire. Contrary to the previous representation of Love, the new one is not naked. The way that his dress, speech, and demeanor are portrayed locate him as being from Jerez de la Frontera, in the Andalusian south of Spain, a region stereotyped as populated by genial, sensuous, vivacious, happy-go-lucky, and lazy inhabitants: "Without a doubt he was descended from *guiferos:* / he was adorned in dress from Jérez, / with a menacing air and breathing wildly" (180–82).[19] The description of the new Love as being an offspring of "guiferos" makes reference to men who use a type of bodkin knife, directly related to illegal or criminal activities proper of the riffraff, and also to the trade of selling giblets and blood in the slaughterhouse, a profession usually associated with violence and criminality.[20] The new Love explains to the poetic voice that his dress is proper to his trade (191), and that it also shows the type of devious and fleshly relationships that are under his empire (194). His trade does not deal with the usual obstacles of idealized love—anxiety, jealousy, and resentment—because those are now cloistered in a monastery (193–96). The pains derived from this kind of love are not the traditional pains of disdain and mystery, but are instead truthful and straightforward in their own way, "Since here, although not clean, loving is clear" (197–200).[21] This love results from a frank negotiation that does not involve sentiment, and if there is pain, this time of the physical kind, the diseased lover must have "a manly chest and constant soul" and suffer the lessons of this new love's military discipline ("pecho varonil y alma constante," 209–12), a reminder of the epic quality of this humorous poem. All of the physical sufferings in the name of this new kind of bodily love (blennorraghia and buboes) are nothing but a light guerrilla skirmish to prove his bravery: "Defeating that riffraff that before you / you see of warts, sores, blennorrheas, / Is such a small thing, so simple, / That it is like defeating parties of guerillas" (213–66).[22] This transmogrified love is sharper than a fox—in Spanish, the word for fox, *raposa,* is always a feminine noun—and he does not use the usual amorous arrows to hunt those that are to be bound in rhapsodized infatuation, but instead he uses "another thing" ("otra cosa," 127–28), an obscene reference to his penis, an image that shows Blanco's definition of a kind of liaison that dwells in lively exultation, foreign to the "foggy exhortations" ("arengas muy difusas," 13) of unfulfilled postponement, and indeed trying to create a space for the fulfillment of a (male) basic sexual urge. Of course, we have already seen this move to explore the features of sexual desire as both idealized and naturalized fact in the unpublished work by Moratín. To this we must add that such naturalization is frequently presented in obscene or scatological language, which is precisely the case with Blanco's description of the Archbubo's leading role, for which he uses a whole epic octave of raw allusions:

> His thick face was a motley
> of purple and carmine, and badly embroidered
> so capriciously varied
> that I could barely make out his features.
> His clothing was embroidered with miters
> with sashes, crosses, keys, and cords;
> Then vividly it ended
> in a curly fringe that trimmed it. (233–40)[23]

The characteristic groin swelling of *gálico* is depicted as a personage with a fat shapeless face, tumescent colors, and "costurones," a term used to denote a badly tailored thing but also the scar tissue over a blister or a wound. His dress is "embroidered" with miters similar to those used by bishops to show their religious dignity, but here it is actually referring to *gálico* blisters with raised borders that make them look like the dignifying hat. The decorations, religious medals, laces, and crosses that embellish his dress are in fact allusions to the ulcers, inflammation, fistulas, and suppuration proper of this type of painful engorgement. The shapeless character is further described as surrounded by a curly fringe of hair, an image that connects directly with the tonsure of a friar. Blanco uses all of these references to hint daringly and dangerously at the diseased body of the Catholic Church. The author deeply criticizes these institutions of power by conjoining obscenity, scatology, and humor.

The extreme secularization of classical aesthetic conventions is nothing more than the demythologizing of knowledge structures that had long been in power. Blanco continues to use this method of dispelling the shroud of mystery and fear that is pervasive in the Catholic Church when the Archbubo recounts his story as a ruler over the body of men, and gloats over the way he was able to establish a relationship with a Catholic clergyman. The "místicas consultas" (mystical exchanges) (276) between the priest and a sanctimonious woman (*beata*) result in his contagion. This is a very aggressive statement by Blanco against a principal point of Catholic dogma. The superficial prayer and everyday mass of the hypocritical woman, together with the exterior representation of the priest's purity, hides the reality of unsanctioned relationships that have tainted her with *gálico,* which in turn she has passed to the priest, who also was not supposed to be infected in his position as abstinent man of God. The radical and daring demythologization of dogma is brought one step further when Blanco represents the *incordio* as imparting blessings to the parishioners: "And thanks to their good condition [high social class] / very soon I saw myself imparting blessings" (279–80).[24] The pervasive challenge to the dominant religious doctrine is even more radicalized when the Archbubo, incarnated in or constitutive of the priest, becomes a pope, ruling over the world from the Capitoline, one of the towering hills of Rome, which here stands as an image of the power of the Vatican. Hidden in humor, the attack on the foremost figure of the prevalent doctrine is a dicey statement by Blanco:

> Soon I found myself dressed in purple.
> Oh time when I saw myself decreeing laws!
> I saw the world so surrendered to my will,
> so confident in my supreme knowledge
> that with a parchment, I split the world. (284–88)[25]

If dogma states that the pope is infallible, that he is also the representative of God on earth, and that his religious standing has binding political consequences, the fact that he is sick with *gálico* means that everything that he says,

establishes, and sanctions is touched by *gálico* as well. Such diseased papal ruling of the world is instantiated by the poetic character of the Archbubo in his
claim that he himself was part of the verdict of the partition of the world, a
reference to the *Inter caetera* papal letter patent of 1493 that divided the new
land discovered by Christopher Columbus between Castile and Portugal. The
pope who promulgated the bull was Alexander VI, the infamous Rodrigo de
Borja or Rodrigo Borgia (1431–1503), known for the profligate quality of his
papacy and for having several children despite being a priest—among them
Cesare Borgia and the ill-reputed Lucrezia Borgia, both of them serving as
inspiration for Macchiavelli's *The Prince*. Cesare acquired syphilis in his early
twenties, and by placing the syphilitic bubo in connection with the pope,
Blanco is stating that the disease was always close to a papal stronghold that
was open to unsanctioned sexual exchange.

Blanco also places the *incordio* at the center of the protracted negotiations
of the Council of Trent in the second half of the sixteenth century, a series of
meetings aimed at healing the schism between Protestants and Catholics, and
including the participation of the major political powers of Europe at the time.
Blanco blames the negative qualities of *gálico* as the reason why the Lutherans
had such a large prevalence among Germans at the time (289–96), and the
person who made notes on Blanco's manuscript says that the interruptions
of the negotiations were the result of the ravages of *gálico* among the German
Lutherans. The note also gossips that "[i]n the Ministry of State they keep a
letter from the envoy of Spain that says that the pope has a sore on his dick. In
those times, they spoke plainly" (232n, v. 292).[26] This, of course, is a comment
that stresses the great presence of the venereal disease in the higher echelons
of the church.[27]

Blanco represents *gálico* as a physical and moral disease that had permeated
the religious and political ruling class. The poem traces the spread of *gálico*,
starting with its supposed origin in the Indies with the "primitive pustule /
that the distinguished Columbus brought to Spain" (249–50).[28] Upon its arrival in Europe, *gálico* is so powerful, young, and active that it gains great favor
in court and dwells near "the great Ferdinand" (256), that is, King Ferdinand II
of Aragon and Castille, known as "the Catholic," who received Columbus in
Barcelona in April of 1493. The author of "El *incordio*" intimates that the royal
family who founded what has been considered modern Spain after the expulsion of the Moors and the Jews had also tinged it with the disease, and that
perhaps Spain itself was marked by *gálico* from its inception. After this passage,
Blanco portrays the *incordio* as going to Granada and converting the Moors
(263–64), and from there to "becoming" a pope (273–88), as I have discussed
before. But the *incordio* is also shown by Blanco to be present among people
of lower strata, always aiming, not always successfully, at reaching higher posi-

tions and functioning as a mobile menace by bridging social differentiation: "I frequented many places, ministries, / antechambers, salons and promenades, / I kept guard in the palace for many days / but without achieving my ultimate desire" (313–16).[29]

The most relevant example of this quality of *gálico*'s moving from one place to the other is the description of the way in which the *incordio* is finally able to gain access to the aristocracy in Spain through the sexual relationship between a lowly page and a high noblewoman (321–22). As with Moratín, Blanco reveals the unsanctioned relations between social strata that were supposed to be separate. While in Moratín's poem the equalizing center of high-class *putañeros* and lower-class women is the bracketed space of bordellos and streets—the "casa de Tócame Roque" is a case in point—in Blanco's poem the equalization is the result of the sexual linkage between the lower classes that serve the aristocracy and their masters. At the same time that the author reveals these unsanctioned relations, he also states that such intermingling has debilitated the power of the disease. The poetic voice explains that after the noblewoman got infected from the page, she herself passed it to a "lacayazo" (a big, strong liveryman), who in turn practiced the recommendation to stop having sexual relations altogether as a way to halt *gálico:* "The brute, in order to get rid of that louse / took me to inhabit a garret" (327–28),[30] a situation of containment that is seemingly proving to be effective:

> Despairing in this situation
> I waited for the first one to arrive
> to escape with them. I relied on this evildoer
> with the faith of a gentleman
> and instead of liberating me he has battled
> to the point of turning me over to a fierce enemy,
> Such a strong and powerful enemy
> that I barely dare to name him. (329–36)[31]

Blanco's implication from the depiction of the stoic liveryman is that it is the popular class, and not the fickle aristocracy, that has the strength to oppose and halt such a pervasive situation of indolence, and that it is in a modest garret, and not in a sumptuous chamber, where *gálico* is finding its nemesis. The author offers a stark criticism of those in positions of control in society: the corollary of portraying the liveryman as the only one capable of resisting the urge to continue having sexual relations, and the only one trying to find a remedy to his ailment, is that the nobility in its unchecked excess and slackness is not able to limit or contain itself and will indeed perish by its own fault. *Gálico* is not only *gálico;* it is also a representation of sloth that must be expelled.

While the *incordio* is becoming weakened by the self-discipline of the likes of the liveryman, "of manly mien, though wild" ("de traza varonil aunque salvaje," 326), it is also being tamed by the power of science, represented here by the creation of an effective remedy. Blanco shows that, with historic perspective, *gálico* reveals the weakness of any type of instituted knowledge: over time and as a result of accrued experience, any system of ideals and ideas may be debunked and replaced. The author humorously recounts that the initially all-powerful *incordio* was able to fool the most eminent doctors: "But later, hungering for the accolades / of the sciences, I pursued university studies, / I confounded the most sublime of doctors / and made them say a thousand foolishnesses" (265–69).[32] With keen intelligence, he also reveals how particular groups are kept in power through printed discourses that purport to contain the truth. The printed iteration of the understanding of *gálico* makes it into a mirage that is believed by society at large.

This fabricated illusion is maintained by a machine composed of writers and other public figures, of men who offer their opinions, and of professionals of medicine and knowledge. It is only as a result of time and irrefutable experience that this illusion is reinvented and presented anew. According to the poetic voice, it is in this way that lettered and professional circles maintain their arbitrating positions, a criticism presented in the poem by using the double meaning of the words *dar trabajo* as "to give a job or a profession" and "to give trouble" in the second part of the stanza: "I gave jobs [troubles] to many writers, / that they have not transmitted to these ages. / And so pricked in my honor, I birth / my works in print now every day" (269–72).[33] *Gálico* has given lettered men a job to continue writing the never-ending printed production that sustains them, but Blanco is also saying that many writers (including himself) have suffered *gálico* and *incordios*—experiences that inform their writing, but because such unsanctioned content could not be published openly, we do not know about it. But there is one more twist in the last two verses of this stanza; by claiming that he sees a constant production of writings inspired and informed by the *incordio,* Blanco is referring to its meaning as "French disease," that is, as the strong influence of French culture on the work of the many writers who derived their sustenance from the state, and whom we know as the *afrancesados.*

Later in the poem, the new ruling Love claims that science has made progress, and that *gálico* is to be tamed by "Fierabrás," a new kind of medicine that resonates with the mythical "Bálsamo [balm] de Fierabrás" in *Don Quixote.*[34] The qualities of this new remedy—obviously the result of a mix of magic and medicine in the poetic voice's dream—make it the best choice for those with the disease:

My followers will have in it
an aid most sweet and sure;
not in that god from Almadén, terrible and hard
cruel prosecutor of loves.
Perhaps they will have some small hardship
but they will suffer joyfully their pains
and full of confidence in Fierabrás
standing firm they'll say: a *incordio* [nuisance] more or less. (385–92)[35]

The person who annotated Blanco's poem claims that this medicine was an antisyphilitic mixture prepared by a "D. Antonio Fernández" and that "it has marvelous effects on various illnesses, particularly the venereal, which it cures with an admirable softness" (232n, v. 345).[36] The same note explains that patients who were thankful for the curative properties of the mixture had given it the name "bálsamo de Fierabrás." The mixture referenced by the gloss, and very likely the remedy that Blanco praises in the poem, is composed of the "píldoras mercuriales" (mercury capsules) devised by don Antonio Fernández, a doctor from Madrid who worked as "Cirujano de la Real familia, y Pensionado de mérito de S. M." ("Surgeon of the Royal family, and Pensioned for merit by His Majesty," iii). In his *Reflexîones sobre las calenturas remitentes é intermitentes* (Thoughts on the remittent and intermittent fevers) (1805), Fernández comments that he is honored to give further explanation about the use of mercury in the capsules he devised "which by dint of their common benefit have merited the powerful welcome of your Eminence" (vi).[37] The author laments that ignorant people believe that the capsules are only effective against the morally dubious *gálico*, knowing that they also have positive results in "pertinacious dysenteries, in malign anginas, and other illnesses" (79–80).[38] Fierabrás is soft and safe, contrary to the harsh traditional treatment with mercury, represented here under the name of "dios de Almadén," referring to the famous cinnabar mine of Castilla-La Mancha that competed with the Huancavelica mine in Peru (as discussed above in relation to the work of Valle y Caviedes). After a little initial pain, the faithful followers of sexual pleasure, who until now had to keep themselves in check because of the devastating consequences of *gálico,* could continue fulfilling their amorous desire. The Archincordio is tamed by a dreamed medicine produced by science, meaning that the twilight of *gálico* as a powerful ruler is the victory of reason, and therefore the victory of naturalized sexuality. The Archbubo and his cohort of lesser *incordios* are obviously crestfallen at the arrival of this medicine that will stop their influence.

The new Love demands that the Archincordio give the name of the medicine at once, claiming, "I am about to burst here with you!" ("Que estoy por reventar aquí contigo," 340), a funny remark about "bursting" as being fed up with someone, but also as the literal bursting of the accumulation of pus inside a bubo. When the Archbubo finally utters the name of the medicine, all of his legion of lesser *incordios* start screaming, asking Love to do something against the "insolencia" (insolence) of Fierabrás (351). If this dreamed Fierabrás is as effective as it seems, it will affect the vast economic network of *gálico*. The medicine would debilitate not only the buboes but also "the great council that surrounded it / composed of doctors, hospitallers, / monks, gravediggers, apothecaries" (358–60).[39] A monk who chants using twisted dog Latin from dogmatic texts pleads to the lecherous Love, requesting him to "then turn your eyes to us" ("*Ad nos ergo oculos tuos converte,*" 365), which is a formula usually employed to address the Virgin Mary in prayers: "Turn then, most gracious Advocate, thine eyes of mercy toward us." It is clear that Blanco, like several other authors we have studied in relation to *gálico,* is playing with dogmatic fire. The monk goes as far as to threaten to accuse Fierabrás of being a Jansenist (368), a movement within Catholicism opposed by the Jesuits, who linked it to the ideas of Protestant Calvinism. The absurdity of accusing a valuable medicine of being a heretic, although hilarious, is used by Blanco to reveal how the power of instituted religion was able to squash constructive ideas using a discourse of fear and difference. The witty commentary also shows the increasing differences that Blanco had with institutionalized Catholicism and marks the beginning of his turn toward the Anglican Church and later toward Unitarianism.

The economic cycle of *gálico* described by the author encompasses pages, liverymen, prelates, noblewomen, young priests like Blanco himself, the nymphs of El Barquillo Street, the doctors and the helpers at the hospital, the apothecary who prepares medicines, the friars who receive money for their prayers when someone is sick or dies—like the one in Moratín's poem who uses the alms to pay a highway prostitute—and finally the gravediggers, who also sustain themselves after burying someone, even if it is "de secreto." If the imagined medicine were to work, this economic cycle would be greatly disrupted. All the wasted effort in dealing with the disease would be rechanneled to other, more worthy, productive activities, and this is in itself a projective structuration that seeks common good. But the secularizing thrust that informs Blanco's poem brings with it a revolutionary consequence in regard to intimate relations as well: the invention of a medicine of this type, in the same way that the condom functions in Moratín's work, would liberate people from the fear of death that was used by the religious institution to preserve its rule as sanctioner of social exchanges. In this dream, the overthrower Love has no problem with allowing the effectiveness of Fierabrás taking place and bringing an end to the Archincordio. This would mean that his naturalized form of love could be practiced without restraint, reason enough to threaten to castrate the "most reverend clod" ("reverendísimo camueso," 373) if he does not shut up: "I do not know Latin, nor Jansenism, / but I'll know how to castrate you right here and now" (375–76),[40] and to admit that he himself will drink the medicine from now on as a preventative companion:

> I will set Fierabrás up at my side
> and with him my kingdom shall have a thousand advantages
> I will command a cask of sacred liquor
> to be preserved among my treasures
> and instead of bland nectar and ambrosia
> I'll drink a bottle every day. (379–84)[41]

At this moment, there is a lot of noise and confusion. Old Iris, who was escorting the poetic voice, comes with the news that thousands of soldiers are coming their way, followed by the powerful "Mercurio y Olivares" (400). Mercury, we know, is the harsh medicine that was still in use to combat *gálico*. In his *Farmacología quirúrgica* (Pharmacology of surgery) (1819), Joseph Jakob von Plenck explains that "Olivares" was an "anti-venereal concoction" ("Tisana anti-venérea," 426) prepared with sarsaparilla, lime, guaiacum, and coriander. The medicine was to be taken for twenty to thirty days. The recipe also explains that it "works for venereal pains, ulcerated bone spurs, hardened tumors, and scrofulas. There will always be found in Madrid a person selling this infusion in secret and for a good price" (427).[42] But it was all just a dream. The poetic voice's real pain from the real bubo awakens him from his reverie and makes it clear that the project of radical secularization is only that, a project, but one that at least is devised and projected.

The overtly physical and sexualized language of Moratín's and Blanco's poems was muffled by the fact that the texts were aimed at a restricted circle of readers. This imbalance can also be seen in the opposite way, namely, that it is thanks to their limited intended public that these texts could engage head-on with the undeniable reality out there, and with the persistent presence of unfulfilled desire in a highly regimented society. The concealed quality of these texts allows a glance into titillating appeal without being identified. There is a didactic aim in these texts, but the purpose of shaping moral corollaries is not necessarily part of their goals. The haziness of the moral imperative, that is, the dwelling in the primary sensual stage, does not necessarily mean a lack of the highly enlightened purpose of the advancement of a common good. Although imbued with the will of individual satisfaction, in his stanzas Moratín's text suggests relevant proposals of public policy—even if we do not agree with them today—such as the creation of monitored prostitution districts in major cities, or the implementation of prophylactic measures as exemplified by the idea of consistent use of condoms. More importantly, Moratín's and Blanco's poems state a clear recognition of a public health concern that was beyond the strictures of moral rule, as was the case with the celibacy of priests, the sacredness of matrimony, monogamy, or the distinction of classes, and that could be tackled or relatively controlled by nonclerical policies. Equally permeated by the pursuit of individual fulfillment of pleasure, Blanco's text points to the need for liberalization of the government, for the restraint of the ecclesiastical institution in regard to affairs of state, and for the debunking of the tradition of Catholicism in Spain. On another level, Blanco's poem reveals a growing hope in the power of science in general, and especially in medicine, to provide mankind with solutions to a pervasive disease such as *gálico,* in the same way as it had already done with the method of variolation implemented in Europe and later in the Americas. The amoral, even immoral texts do reveal a desire for common good.

14 ❦

Samaniego's Sticky Fable

Blanco's and Moratín's texts are clear examples of masked representations of the desires and interests they and their peers understood in their context. But this is not the only way of carrying out such representation. Not having a visible disguise in this masked play may also be a way of hiding a substratum of vibrant challenge to traditional institutions, only that in this case its strategy of representation is to be revealed in public, in plain sight. A textuality of this sort is "Las moscas" by Félix María de Samaniego (1745–1801), a brief apologue or rhymed fable that takes advantage of the understanding of the fable as a tool for the dissemination of prevalent moral values to discuss the idea of sexual desire as a natural occurrence and of disease as the consequence of a lack of measure in dealing with such otherwise normal desire. Nevertheless, the fact that Samaniego's fables have been widely anthologized, canonized, and institutionalized as the condensation of a set of moral values has blurred the presence of nonnormative features in the writing of the author from Álava. The normative understanding of Samaniego's established apologues is so pervasive that they are still being employed as a pedagogical tool to instill values in new generations of children in Spanish-speaking countries. Nevertheless, I will show that, at least in this apparently innocuous instance and in many other riskier writings, their interpretation may bring an obverse or complementary axiom of carnal desire as natural, although susceptible to being ill-fated.[1]

In an early essay, Emilio Palacios Fernández pointed to the need to understand the nuance of morality in Samaniego's fables, especially if we take into account that the genre straddles the realms of cultured and popular society ("Caracterización" 169). A typical understanding of the fable is that it is a brief narration in which the actions function as an example that sheds light on an aspect of human conduct. We also tend to understand that the light shone on human experience is encapsulated in the form of a moral dictum, which in Spanish has the revealing name of *moraleja*. The interpretative problem we may fall into is understanding the *moraleja* as an arbitration of what is good or bad in a moral sense. But this light does not necessarily have the capacity of resolving such an arbitration because it is only that, a light that allows the reader to read more clearly and with better definition in order to apply her or

Félix María de Samaniego

Félix María de Samaniego (1745–1801) was a Spanish writer and a member of the *ilus-trados* (Enlightenment thinkers; lit. "Enlightened ones"). This generation of intellectuals sought to restore clarity and concision to Spanish literature, as a reaction to the previous Baroque works that were characterized by the use of complex metaphors and intricate language. Many of the *ilustrados* believed that literature should serve a moral purpose, as exemplified in Samaniego's collections of *fábulas,* the first of which was published in 1781. He entered into a debate with Tomás de Iriarte, another *ilustrado,* who claimed to be the first Spanish *fabulista,* although Iriarte's first collection was published a year later. Samaniego founded a school for the children of the Spanish nobility and used his fables to teach lessons on morality and to instruct the future noble classes on the ways in which they would one day govern the nation. Like Aesop, Samaniego used animals as the characters in his fables to make them more universal and accessible to his primarily young audience while also presenting important lessons for the human realm, masked as the interactions between animals in order to avoid the appearance of social criticism. For example, his fable titled *El león y el ratón* (The lion and the mouse) details an encounter between a rat, which represents a commoner or a lower-class individual, and a lion, representing the king and the nobility. This fable, written in verse like most of Samaniego's work, cautions the nobility to treat the members of the lower class with respect, for many nobles feared the power of the masses to overthrow them. This seems to conflict with the contemporary idea of *despotismo ilustrado* (enlightened despotism), whereby the ruling class held absolute power, irrespective of the interests of the lower classes.

---

his inferences to their contextual reality. Palacios Fernández explains that, in the same vein as Jean de La Fontaine (1621–95), Samaniego is not interested in forging a system of moral conduct, but in portraying the rules of everyday, practical wisdom: "It is, then, a moral without definition, naturalistic, terrestrial, without religion. It is a utilitarian moral, and is frequently instinctive. It places man at the level of the animals, in a fight for survival with life itself. . . . The instinct of conservation dominates over many sentiments of Christian morality" ("Caracterización" 189).[2]

This practical trait of the apologue uses emblematic animals to represent "facts" that would instruct people on how to follow proper social conduct. But this representation among the brutes required a codification of the meaning of each animal in order to help carry the didactic moral principles as represented unequivocally by each one of them. Following Aesop, it is understood that a fox represents cunning, a dog represents loyalty, and a bee represents industry. In other cases the emblem may shift, as is the case of the lion, which sometimes represents generosity, other times tyranny, and other times wise sovereignty. Despite this codification of the meaning of the animals, it is not necessarily the case that the roles and characterizations are always the same— as is the case with the lion—or that there could not be an underlying meaning that goes against the grain of the typical interpretation of the apologue. In another essay, Palacios Fernández indicates that even from the moment Samaniego chooses one topic over another he is already taking a path embedded in his ideological affinities, and he claims that "Samaniego takes up the tradition of the fable in a personal and critical way. If the themes passed through the filter of his inventiveness, he had more reasons to control the morals" ("Las *Fabulas*" 96).[3] This means that Samaniego's fables are not rigid, and that the characterizations of the animals they contain may be hiding other layers of meaning.

This nonconforming avenue, which is in tension with more orthodox apologues, is clearly shown by Samaniego in the texts of *El jardín de Venus*. In a study on eighteenth-century ethics in Spain through the literary work of Samaniego, Juan Alfredo Bellón Cazabán explains that "if we want to understand correctly what was the literature of the *Fábulas* and what was its role in the totality of the eighteenth-century literary production" we must take into account that even if the texts in *Jardín* show a clear dissent from the thematical norms of moral literature, they are nevertheless their necessary complement (8).[4] Bellón Cazabán illustrates this shifting possibility of interpretation between the widely known *Fábulas* and the obscure *Jardín* with the image of the flip sides of a page or the head and tail of a coin. The image is functional, but it does not encompass the permeability and connection between the two discursive modes, which operate as communicating vessels. I prefer to continue with the image of the masks because it allows us to understand that what we have here is a dynamic of uncovering, covering, exaggeration, and astute mechanisms to say without saying and to mark silences while screaming out loud.

Samaniego's apologues are indeed coded language, and the openly presented *moraleja* at the end of the fable is not necessarily the main goal of the text; it may be in fact a decoy or a mask that signals to other elements that can be gleaned by the public. Still, no matter whether in the risky *Jardín* or in the instructional *Fábulas*, the main impetus that informs the author is concentrated in the poem that opens his repeatedly reissued fables: "That in these verses I attempt / to give you a topic / that instructs while delighting" (*Fábulas* 2).[5]

In a volume that deals with syphilis and ever-present fleshly encounters, a possible route of analysis would be to mine the images of sexuality in Samaniego's *Jardín*. Nevertheless, this strategy would not be fruitful for me.

Although there are myriad sexual references expressed with direct or obscene language, and facetious references to some diseases, there are no allusions to *gálico*. In fact, in the four poems of the *Jardín* that deal with sickness — "Las entradas de Tortuga" (The entries of Tortuga), "La postema" (The abscess), "La receta" (The prescription), and "La medicina de san Agustín" (Saint Augustin's medicine) — the remedy is always to have more sexual intercourse, or to have sexual intercourse with a bigger penis. In other words, the ethos of these poems is one of the celebration of life, instead of one of careful regimentation to preserve it. In addition, I am more interested in uncovering the hidden signals of contentious representation dispersed throughout an apparently innocuous text. In what follows, I will show how the enlightened goal of *enseñar deleitando* (teaching enjoyably) is offered by Samaniego thorough a re-signification of fabulistic canonical traits and through the layered presentation of hidden truths, which are nevertheless in plain sight in the widely anthologized "Las moscas":

> To a comb of rich honey
> Two thousand flies flocked
> and they died for their gluttony,
> their feet imprisoned in it.
> Another, within a cake,
> buried his *golosina* (gluttony).
> *And so, if well examined*
> *the hearts of mankind*
> *perish in the prisons*
> *of the vice that rules them.* (*Fábulas* 15–16; emphasis in the original)[6]

Although presented in the extremely synthetized structure of ten octosyllabic verses, the poem shows with clarity that there is no denial of the object of desire, and no denial of the desire for the object. The beehive, which is the object of desire, is qualified as having plentiful and delicious honey, two characteristics that imply that it is only natural that such an object would be desired. Such normalized or naturalized desire is further stressed by the large number of desiring subjects (flies) that would like the satisfaction of their desire. It is not just two or ten flies that would like to repeatedly taste the honey, but two thousand, which by all means qualifies as a crowd and consequently, in the terms of the anthropomorphism of the fable, indicates that this is a pervasive tendency of the society Samaniego intends to address. The flies are not flies; they are the representation of the "human heart" (v. 8), and the desire for honey and the action to taste it are part of that condition.

Another outcome of this relational rhetorical construction of the fable is that the hive is not only a hive and its honey. The traditional understanding of the apiary and the honey as positive and productive images is subverted in order to become a representation of titillating objects that can bring doom to humankind, especially to men. This understanding of the honeycomb as a source of pleasure is substantiated in a definition of *panal* (beehive) in the dictionary of the Real Academia published in 1737, which shows the evocative power of the word: "It can be taken metaphorically for any thing whatever that delights the tastes, or that includes in itself special softness and delight" (RAE 1737, s.v. "panal").[7] The interpretation of the hive is then related to the satisfaction of desire and the pleasure of the senses, and stresses that the problem formulated by Samaniego in his fable is one of the degree of such satisfaction. This connotation of the word *panal* fell in disuse and does not appear in the dictionary after 1822; but from this subverted angle contemporaneous to Samaniego, the apiary stands for the place where the desired object of rich honey is to be found. The physical structure of the beehive, with the packed alcoves, the buzzing sound, and the many active bees, resembles the structure of the urban setting, and within that space the kind of intricate tenements described by Blanco and Moratín as the places where they procured women to satisfy what they saw as natural desire, and which they knew would be easily identified by their limited reading circle. Samaniego and those in his circle also very likely visited these buzzing places at times when they were not writing edifying stanzas. In this way, the apiary becomes a place like El Barquillo in Madrid, the bees become the representation of the many women sung by Moratín in his *Arte*, and the honey is the abundantly satisfied sexual desire.

There is one more implied outcome of this subversion of the positive image of honey and hive, not because of the bees, but because of the flies. While the traditional interpretation of the apiary image is one of bounty, organization, and labor, the interpretation of flies is always related to decay and death. Flies do not dwell in honey; they settle and relish in excrement. The outcome of this warped image is that the desired object of unbridled sex is somewhat positive, or that this supposed honey alluded to in the poem is in reality dung, or that all of us who like the richness of honey are nothing but flies.

The interpretation of the first four verses of "Las moscas" can lead us to another route. If the metaphorical meaning of *panal* was anything that pleases an appetite ("qualquier cosa que deleyta el gusto"), it can also be understood as a woman or, even more objectifyingly, a vagina visited by many men-flies who consequently died in it, caught in the bitter honey of a sickly venereal disease. According to the apologue, liking honey, or visiting places such as the neighborhoods of Leganitos and El Barquillo, or liking having sex with women was not the problem because that is what one or a thousand flies, one or a thousand men, are bound to be fond of by nature. The sticky point is that of the flies being *golosas* (gluttonous). Again, the contemporaneous definition of *goloso* in the *Diccionario de autoridades* (1734) states that it is a person "inclined to eat without necessity, and who seeks out exquisite delicacies, paying more attention to taste than to the good maintenance of the stomach. Formed from the name Gula" (RAE 1734, s.v. "goloso").[8] This means that the doomed flies end up stuck in the honey or in the venereal disease because they frequent this sweet locus to satiate an unbalanced desire not directly connected to sustenance, instead of attending to a basic natural need. They do not die for having honey, but for having too much of the same honey. The *moraleja* between the lines of the apologue would be, not to refrain from sticking the legs in the honey, but to do it with measure, which is the same impetus that Moratín develops as a distorted method in his *Arte*. The outcome of this veiled dictum is to avoid the concentration of many flies in just one place, an idea that stresses the preoccupation with the spread of *gálico* because of only one vector, for example a popular prostitute being visited by many clients. As we have studied before, Moratín proposed to counteract this risk by advising his fly brethren to have sex with many newly found sexual partners who had no previous experience in sexual commerce.

Perhaps the most cryptic passage of this apologue is in the sixth and seventh verses: "Another, within a cake, / buried his *golosina*." The two lines are disconnected and encapsulated, and are only linked to the rest of the poem through the rhyme with verses seven and ten. The assertion does not relate to the previous idea of many flies attracted to honey, and instead is related to a particular fly that "buried his *golosina*." Our present understanding of the word *golosina* would make us think that the verses depict the awkward image of a fly sticking a piece of candy or a treat in a cake or pastry. A perusal of the handy *Diccionario de autoridades* of 1734 may give us some keys and, as I will show later, a reminder that the Spanish language has been greatly impoverished in the last two hundred years, especially in relation to sexual overtones. As mentioned before, the word *golosina* is derived from the Latin terms *gula* or *gula inordinata,* or gluttony, one of the capital sins. It is used as an adjective connected to the idea of an unchecked appetite for unnecessary things that are not needed for nourishment. The other sense is that of a substantive to name a delicacy that pleases the senses but does not give sustenance. A metaphorical sense, more proper for interpreting Samaniego's apologue, indicates that *golosina* is the "unruly or slovenly desire or pleasure for a inedible thing" ("deseo ò gusto desreglado de alguna cosa, que no es comestible"). Things start to get more interesting: one of the entries that has completely fallen in disuse reads that *golosina* is the "base vice—or sickness—of sex" ("vulgar achaque del sexo") (RAE 1734, s.v. "golosina"). With these definitions in mind, the image becomes less awkward in meaning, and more awkward in its implications: the fly that shoves its desire, or its genitals, into a pastry that represents a woman—or more plausibly a vagina, since in Spanish there is a profuse usage of confectionary terminology as sexual slang: the vagina is referred to as *bollo, bizcocho, galleta, pastel,* and *roscón,* among many others—visited by too many of his fly brethren will certainly perish in the inescapable prison of gluttony and venereal disease.

⟫ 15

Gálico, Prostitution, and Public Policy

As I have shown, at the ideological level the Spanish *ilustrados* were not necessarily against men attending to a natural sexual desire, even if this meant the frequenting of prostitutes. In contrast, reputable public figures like Feijoo or Moratín were against masturbation as a way to deal with sexual need because they deemed onanism unnatural. This tension is the main reason prostitution was silently tolerated as a necessary evil, even though sporadic raids served to appease both residents of areas like Lavapiés—where the number of prostitutes may have made them too conspicuous—and the conscience of those entrusted with the moral health of Spanish society. To use the image of the fly in the Samaniego poem we just discussed, the problem was with going to the honey pot too many times or more frequently than naturally necessary, thus breaking the boundary between necessity and pure pleasure; that is, the problem was with being *goloso* or gluttonous.

Similar to the controversial logic of control that we see in our own day with narcotic substances, the answer offered by public policy authorities to the spread of *gálico* was not to curb the number of men having sexual intercourse with prostitutes but to focus on controlling the women. Francisco Gregorio de Salas (1729–1808), a priest, a member of the Academia de San Fernando, and a friend of Leandro Fernández de Moratín, further clarifies the image of the *goloso* as sexually overindulgent and his connection with the prostitute or, as he euphemistically calls her in the title of the following poem, "Una mujer de mala vida" (A woman of the bad life):

> She is an inhuman harpy,
> poison to the licentious
> *punishment for the gluttonous*
> and the ruin of healthy people;
> a monster that eats without wanting to,
> a ring for every hand,
> scourge of easygoing men,
> everyday thing for two,
> the census of San Juan de Dios
> and the fortune of surgeons. (531; my emphasis)[1]

As in Samaniego's apologue, overindulgent sexual satisfaction is both the enticing product and the source of death: "poison to the licentious / punishment for the gluttonous." The author also makes clear that this lethal punishment for the featherbrained man is not abstract, but a real and present manifestation that can be tangibly quantified in the tally of the patients at the San Juan de Dios hospital—a place that we know was almost exclusively dedicated to the treatment of *gálico*—or in the painfully measurable amount of money paid to the physicians who administered always elusive cures for the disease.

The extent of this reality of *golosos,* prostitutes, and unbridled indulgence in some of the streets and districts of Madrid and other cities was very noticeable by the last quarter of the century. In 1798, during his tenure as a district attorney in Madrid, the iconic writer Juan Meléndez Valdés complained to the king about the rampant proliferation of vice and street prostitution in the "great capital city": "In this great capital, where misfortunes commonly abound at every step, and everywhere you find the objects of the most shameful prostitution; where imprudent corruption, free and brazen, walks unchecked, insulting public virtue and decency; where, notwithstanding the severe vigilance of your Highness, frivolity, leisure, misery, and unspeakable seduction offer ever new and newer victims unto vice; where a thousand wretches pass through these streets day and night, offering to everyone their dirty, venal favors; where, finally, it is so easy—would that it were not!—to sacrifice the depraved to his sensuality and lustful debauchery [*desenfreno*]" (*Discursos* 74).[2]

This condemnation is part of a group of legal documents by Meléndez Valdés that appeared in 1821, several years after his death, under the title *Discursos forenses* (Forensic studies). One of the most important ideas in this fragment is represented by the words *desenfreno* and *sin freno,* which are among the phrases that appear most frequently in the whole volume. They literally mean "unbridled"—that is, the lack of self-control to stop a certain behavior. The repetition of this idea pleads for the creation of more measures to stem the irrepressible impetus of virile passion in the country. It is evident that Meléndez Valdés, Jovellanos, and Moratín share the same line of thought: that control—a restraining device—was necessary.

Five years before Meléndez wrote this legal document, Count Francisco de Cabarrús had also pointed to the need to deal directly with a rampant reality that nevertheless remained suppressed: "And what a poison, my friend, the one that hides equally among the roses of beauty and the least mistakable signs of modesty and virtue, and which, infecting entire generations, tends to sleep and then become more concentrated in the innocent, who, all unknowing, shelters it, and will propagate it, until, thriving with yet more fury, it will print the shameful signs of a atrocious degradation on their faces and external members!" (67).[3] Although the author had been discussing how to stop smallpox in Spain, his discourse slowly veers to a disease directly linked to the way the country was dealing with the dynamic of sexuality, matrimony, celibacy, and bachelorhood. Advanced for his time, Cabarrús defended divorce as an approach to help preserve functional matrimony, which was for him the best way to put a halt to what he called "asqueroso libertinage" (disgusting licentiousness) because it reduced the number of unsanctioned relations that helped spread physical and moral disease. The poison that hides among the beautiful roses described by Cabarrús is not that of smallpox, but the same syphilitic "veneno de licenciosos" that Salas mentions in his poem about the woman who takes the wrong path in life. This venom, communicated from one person to another, is rapidly infecting a whole generation of young men, and it is even more lethal because it is being propagated in the hidden realm of unregulated prostitution. Smallpox was difficult to control, but it was not connected to extramarital sexual relations. *Gálico* was far more insidious because its solution required moral reform, going beyond basic hygienic measures.

The main document in which Cabarrús presents his ideas on an enlightened public policy for the country is a book titled *Cartas sobre los obstáculos que la naturaleza, la opinion y las leyes oponen a la felicidad pública* (Letters on the obstacles by which nature, opinion, and laws oppose public happiness). These letters, written by Cabarrús to Gaspar Melchor de Jovellanos between 1792 and 1793 but not published until 1808, tackle governance, finance, and engineering. The letter that deals with the regimentation of prostitution, titled "Sobre la sanidad pública" (On public health) is regarded by some critics as a major document about hygienics in Spain, and it is where I found the passage I quoted above. Like Moratín and Samaniego, Cabarrús believes in the natural character of sexuality and has the practical sense to understand that measures to control licentiousness—managing celibacy, implementing divorce, renewing the positive outcomes of matrimony—will take a long time to produce meaningful effects. This same practical sense is the one that he invokes in his proposal to contain *gálico* with the same rigor as his proposal to contain smallpox: "It is necessary to wage the same war on venereal diseases as on smallpox, and I shall risk my ideas on this subject" (73–74).[4]

Cabarrús's idea is to stem the spread of *gálico* by reopening and regulating *mancebías* (brothels) in major urban settings. As in his other practical projects, such as for building bridges and drawing regional maps, the main goal is to create a strong administration that will further the common good. In the following paragraphs, I will offer a summary of the count's proposal, and I will develop a discussion of its multilayered meanings and consequences.

Each *mancebía* was to be regulated by a *regidor* (supervisor), aided by a military squad, and guarded by sentries in the main streets who would also make sure that there was no street prostitution. It is clear that Cabarrús, public

Cabarrús

François Cabarrus (1752–1810), also known by the name Francisco Cabarrús Lalanne, and later as Conde de Cabarrús, is usually remembered for founding the Banco de San Carlos, the first Spanish bank, in 1785. Cabarrús was born in Bayonne, France, to a merchant family. At the age of eighteen his father sent him as an apprentice to several cities in Spain and finally to Valencia, where he married the daughter of his employer.

In addition to creating the Bank of Spain and the Real Compañía de Filipinas—an enterprise that held the monopoly of commerce between Spain and Asia—Cabarrús is known for devising several engineering projects to improve Spain's means of communication and to catapult its economy toward greater success. In keeping with the mood of the Enlightenment, Cabarrús believed in strong interventions by the state to foster changes in the social fabric and in the economy. His wealth and his ideas brought him close to the powerful counts of Aranda, Floridablanca, and Campomanes, and to Gaspar Melchor de Jovellanos, to whom he wrote the *Cartas sobre los obstáculos que la naturaleza, la opinión y las leyes oponen a la felicidad pública,* which includes his project on the control of prostitution.

At the peak of his influence, he was accused of contraband and illegal currency negotiations, and he was imprisoned in 1790. Two years later he was freed by Manuel Godoy, a favorite of Charles IV, and trusted with several public positions. By 1803 he was counselor of state for Charles IV.

With the arrival of Joseph Bonaparte in 1808, Cabarrús's knowledge of Spanish finance and his French background led to his appointment as minister of finance. He died in Seville and was buried in its cathedral. Later, he was accused of collaborating with the French, and his remains were disinterred and thrown out of the church.

---

administrators, and the city's well-to-do people were preoccupied with prostitution taking place in the streets. It seemed sufficient, convenient, and proper to keep this commercial exchange behind closed doors and out of entryways. Each prostitute would be assigned to a particular brothel. If a woman was found working on the street, outside an assigned zone without permission, she would be sent to the closest regulated brothel and, depending on the gravity of the "offense," punished accordingly. All sexual workers who went outside the brothel, like those who went to the theater with a patron or on their own, had to display some kind of sign of their profession (a yellow feather was Cabarrús's choice). Each *mancebía* was to be monitored daily by a doctor "of the greatest integrity, and with a remuneration that would make them inaccessible to any seduction whatsoever [. . .] and under the same penalty of deportation they would have to report, without losing an instant, on any who should find herself infected [. . .] to the point of taking the sick one to the hospital destined for such object" (76).[5] These doctors were also to be in charge of setting personal hygiene standards for each prostitute. Sick prostitutes were to be quarantined in an isolation hospital and, if they had become infected for the third time, were to be deported to the colonies (75). Any complaint of contagion from a prostitute by a client was to be taken as reliable, with the caveat—in order to deter wrongful accusations—that the denouncer was to be quarantined as well.

The *mancebías* were not a new thing in Spain. They had existed on the peninsula as regulated places for sexual commerce since the thirteenth or fourteenth century, but they had been officially closed since 1623 when, after an arduous campaign by the Jesuits, Philip IV issued a *pragmática* (royal edict) with the title *Prohibición de mancebías y casas públicas de mugeres en todos los pueblos de estos reynos* (Prohibition of brothels and public houses of women in all the populations of these our lands), which was reinforced in 1661 with another *pragmática, Recogimiento de las mugeres perdidas de la Corte, y su reclusion en la galera (Capitulos de reformación)* (Seclusion of the fallen women of the Court, and their seclusion in the *galera* [Chapters of reformation]). So while Cabarrús was not proposing something that had not been tried before, the count shifted the administration of prostitution away from the ecclesiastic institutions and the priests, who aimed to save the souls of the prostitutes, and moved it to the government and the doctors, who sought to save bodies and corporal health by stopping the advance of the *morbo gálico* (Jiménez Salcedo 136). The laws on prohibition in the seventeenth century had not reduced the business of prostitution, and by the middle of the eighteenth century there were more than seven hundred registered brothels in Madrid alone. According to regulations published in 1714 and 1749, any woman found prostituting herself would be obligated to work in regulated institutions. Such regulations treated prostitutes in the same fashion as beggars and, of course, negated the reality of their labor (Jiménez Salcedo 136). The tangible presence of prostitution, promulgated by men with the ever-present demand for sex, was undeniable. This made the intent of regulation swing from complete eradication to a more pragmatic regimentation, exemplified by Cabarrús's proposals for tolerating a controlled practice of prostitution.

According to Juan Jiménez Salcedo, Cabarrús's letter benefits from previous works on the regulation of prostitution, such as Rétif de la Bretonne's *Le pornographe* (The pornographer) (1770) in France, and Bernard Mandeville's *Modest Defence of Public Stews* (1724) in England. Although Bretonne's recommended regulation was developed with a more quantitative focus and much more minutiae, he and Cabarrús both believe that prostitution is the main culprit in the propagation of *gálico* and, therefore, that addressing it is the first step toward controlling "the shameful contagion that assaults the universe": "Prostitution has not, indeed, produced the shameful contagion that assaults the universe: but it propagates it; it is the repository, the impure impetus always reborn" (Bretonne 45).[6] Bretonne's interest in controlling the disease is evident in the last part of *Le pornographe*'s subtitle, which is not usually quoted in references to the book. It clarifies that the treatise is "geared to the prevention of the diseases produced by the public activity of women"[7] — a phrase that in fact would be a good summary of the goal Cabarrús expressed in his letter on "public health" to Jovellanos.

One of the main problems for Cabarrús was precisely that the activity of these women was public: it had become so pervasive and open that it was increasingly difficult to distinguish public from private women, especially if both appeared at times as equally demure "roses of beauty" ("rosas de la hermosura," 67). Indeed, as brilliantly studied by Carmen Martín Gaite in her *Usos amorosos del dieciocho en España* (Amorous practices of the eighteenth century in Spain) (1972), the institution of matrimony in the eighteenth century had become more and more a matter of social appearance, and it was progressively normal for men in the higher echelons of society to frequent and support women other than their wives, including women from inferior socioeconomic circles, such as actresses.[8] Cabarrús conceives of the yellow feather as a way to control this feared lack of differentiation, and to counteract how prostitutes in the higher end of the business could be easily mistaken for women from the higher strata of society, who dressed in the same kind of lavish outfits and who gradually wanted to reproduce the attitude of the lower-strata *majas* as well.[9] Cabarrús has seen this himself and states that the yellow feather will be very useful "so that in the promenades and the theatres, these women should be recognizable" (76).[10] As we can observe, the reformer's problem was not only the contagion of *gálico* but also the homogeneous appearance and access to similar ways of dress — a crisis of socioeconomic roles.

The conundrum that Cabarrús aims to tackle connects the complexity of intimate relations to hidden and overt dynamics and to the crisis of social stratification in the main cities of the kingdom. All three elements are present in Leandro Fernández de Moratín's cryptic diary from 1804, which documents his more-than-familiar relationship with the actress María García, whom he later dubs "Calipigia" — that is, "the one with the shapely buttocks." For example, on November 24, 1804, he records that he was "at Mariquita García's, with whom we fooled around, kissed" ("chez Mariquita García, cum quam scherzi, bassia," *Diario*). Just one day before, on November 23, he had been enjoying a similar game with a street prostitute: "Streets; with a little prostitute on Jesús Valis street, we played" ("Calles; chez quaedam meretricula Jesús Valis street: lussimus").[11] A few weeks later he went to a light theater piece

with Paquita (Francisca Gertrudis de Muñoz y Ortiz), whom he was slug-
gishly courting, and her ever-watchful mother: "With Paquita and Mother,
box seat, Comedy" ("Cum Paquita and Mother, palco, Comedia," Jan. 3, 1805).
This behavior—of an individual simultaneously exchanging intimacies with
multiple women from multiple tiers of society—pervaded the social group to
which Moratín belonged, and illustrates why Cabarrús's preoccupation with
discerning difference was not unfounded. His ideas were pragmatic after all,
even though it is clear that to him the prostitutes were not flesh and blood,
but merely numbers and disposable materiality. For Cabarrús, marking prostitutes with the humiliating feather would force higher society to differentiate between types of women. Even so, both syphilis and prostitution acted
as equalizers: anyone could be infected, no matter their social stratum, and
underprivileged women could look like those deemed honorable. (See my discussion of Goya's *Ni asi la distingue* below on p. 262.)

In addition to the feather's semiotic yet demeaning isolation of its wear-
ers from legitimate society, Cabarrús proposes more tangible penalties for
women who did not submit to his organization of prostitution. If a woman
was caught selling sexual favors without being assigned to a regulated brothel,
or carrying out business in a district different from the one assigned to her, the
penalty could be as light as consignment to the brothel and as severe as deportation to the colonies: "Merely for the fact of exercising this dreadful trade
without the authorization of the police, she would be exposed to a gradation
of penalties, from consignment to the brothel, which would be the first, to
deportation to the colonies, which would be the gravest" (75).[12] A few pages
later it becomes clear that deportation to the colonies, the harshest punishment, would be reserved for women who had to be treated for the third time
for the venereal disease in the special hospitals of containment planned by
Cabarrús: "Finally, the women who, being cured and declared healthy of the
contagion two times, should need a third treatment, would be unpardonably
transported from the clinic or hospital to the colonies, under the conditions
demanded by the population of such [colonies], and of which I will speak sep-
arately" (78).[13] According to Francisco Vásquez García and Andrés Moreno
Mengíbar (62), Cabarrús's idea of sending reoffending prostitutes and other
people considered beyond hope to the colonies came from his familiarity with
the work of the influential Italian legal theorist and criminologist Cesare Beccaria (1738–94). In his book *Dei delitti e delle pene* (*On Crimes and Punishments*) (1764), Beccaria said that it was less onerous to send criminals to se-
cluded penitentiaries than to try to change them in the metropole. Beccaria
and Cabarrús had witnessed the use of exile as a punishment by the Italian
and Spanish legal system, respectively; both were also aware of convicts being
sent to English colonial penitentiaries. In this sense, Cabarrús's proposal to

exile offenders was not new, but merely a reformulation of previous measures with a different purpose in mind. Banishment to the colonies plays an important role in Cabarrús's logic of control and containment, and his text makes evident that he favored, more than anything else, a dynamic of differentiation and exclusion in which the colonies, physically removed from the metropole, were seen as places where inconvenient excess could be disposed of, and from which useful excess—wealth in the form of silver and gold, raw material, and valuable products—could be extracted.

In his previous discussion of the management of smallpox Cabarrús had proposed that any landlady or physician in charge of dealing with the contagion who failed to report a person or family that had acquired the disease should endure the consequence of "the death penalty, or at least penalty of lifetime banishment to the colonies [. . .] should be] irretrievably ruled" (63).[14] Notice that on Cabarrús's scale only execution—that is, expulsion to another world altogether—tops the penalty of banishment. The colonies are just one degree below obliteration. Later, in his discussion of *gálico* and prostitution, the semicapital punishment of exile is proposed for men who have knowingly acted as hustlers for their wives. More forgivingly, if the husband did not know about his wife's sexual commerce, he is to be granted a divorce and permission to marry again (75–76). *Gálico* was to be controlled by clearly tagging its perceived vectors and placing them in circumscribed spaces, but if those soft forms of differentiation were not effective, the next step was to physically remove the unwanted element and consign her or him to a faraway space, applying a radical separation from what was deemed relevant or necessary. The colonies' condition of ancillarity—the word "ancillary" comes from the Latin *ancilla,* meaning "maidservant"—was in fact part of the reason why their representatives so actively pursued recognition and equal treatment in the Cortes de Cádiz in 1810. Their bitter awareness of their status also energized their search for a discourse of self-value and autonomy, as we saw earlier in the strong need of Clavijero, Sánchez Valverde, Flores, and Teresa de Mier to prove that the New Continent was not the source of *gálico* but instead the place where the natural cure for the disease would be found. Finally, this understanding of metropolitan disregard for the colonies brought about, in part as a well thought out project and in part as the result of fortuity, the successful independence of the region.

The separation of the colonies from the Spanish metropole would only happen two decades after Cabarrús wrote his letters to Jovellanos. The count's project is embedded in a context in which control of the colonies—or of the peninsular territories, if one does not want to go that far—was still unhampered. For Cabarrús, the problem of *gálico* and prostitution was analogous to that of a difficult disease such as smallpox, and much more pressing than

Cortes de Cádiz

The Cádiz national legislative assembly was prompted by the Napoleonic occupation. The abdication of Charles IV in favor of his son Ferdinand VII in 1808, and the following transfer of power to Joseph Bonaparte, resulted in a power crisis on the peninsula and in the colonies. Regional gatherings, known as *juntas,* met to discuss Ferdinand's renunciation of the throne and the military advancement of French troops. The assembly was inaugurated in Real Isla de León (present-day San Fernando), adjacent to Cádiz, in September 1810. Cádiz was one of the few redoubts held by Spanish troops. Assembly leaders considered moving the Cortes to the American continent if French pressure became overwhelming. One of the main concerns of the peninsular juntas was the imminent separation of the American colonies as a result of the power vacuum. Perhaps for this reason, the Cortes aimed to include delegates from beyond the peninsula, avoiding separate chambers for nobility and clergy in favor of proportional regional representation.

The underlying goal of the Cortes was to craft a new social pact in the form of a constitution. Representatives from America wanted this accord to recognize their territories as provinces, pushing for an autonomous voice for each region, decentralization of the metropolitan power, and self-regulation of the administrative system, which was to include the appointment of individuals not born in Spain to provincial high posts. These aspirations displeased participants who did not see the colonies as equal to the metropolis. Only between 21 and 28 percent of the deputies in the course of the Cortes were American, and several of them merely held positions as alternate assemblymen. Only two representatives from the Philippines attended the inauguration. Teresa de Mier, the Mexican liberal thinker discussed in this study, participated in the Cortes as an auditor, but left disillusioned by the lack of support for American autonomy.

---

governance of the colonies. Furthermore, expulsion from the metropole was a threat a social reformer in Spain could have in the toolbox, and for that reason not much different from quarantine or the regimentation of military garrisons, which Cabarrús saw as important strategies to halt the spread of the disease. Soldiers and officers were known for unrestrained, less-than-safe sexual encounters with prostitutes and other women wherever they were stationed— a proclivity leading to the pustules of *gálico.* This deadly combination is dramatized in the humorous "Epigrama LXVIII" by José Iglesias de la Casa: when a diseased officer asks his cook not to put salt in his food, the poetic voice quips that salt would indeed be a good thing for someone whose flesh is rotting. Moratín comments in his *Arte* about the abundance of prostitutes near the military garrisons in Madrid. Cabarrús incorporates into his proposals what he has learned about recent successful medical methods to manage contagious diseases and defends strict quarantine as paramount in the control of *gálico:* "The regiments must perform an exacting review of the clothing of their soldiers, and at the least indication of contagion, remand the infected, not letting them leave until they should be cured" (77).[15] This call to monitor military personnel demonstrates Cabarrús's practical sense; he aims to control the vectors that are controllable (e.g., prostitutes and soldiers) and does not spend energy on formulating modes of control over social sectors that will not easily respond to regimentation (e.g., men who did not depend on an institution or organized group). The idea of imposing hygienic rules on the military is a first step toward recognizing that a large part of the problem with *gálico* was not the prostitutes but the men who frequented them while at the same time having sexual exchanges with other women, including their own wives. It would not have been easy to check and monitor someone like Moratín, who in a matter of days had sexual relations with an actress and a prostitute while courting an upper-class woman, but the disciplinary structure of the military did allow Cabarrús to think about procedures to break the cycle of disease which were very similar to those he had already proposed for the *mancebías.* Nevertheless, direct campaigns to educate and control the common man as a fundamental vector of the contagion of syphilis would not happen until one hundred years after Cabarrús wrote his letters.

Cabarrús shows that, given the circumstances in large cities like Madrid, a campaign of instruction or an appeal to religious or moral zeal would not yield fruit. He envisions the possibility that controlling prostitution through the creation of *mancebías* would in the long run cultivate social awareness of a common good—that is, an ethical understanding of the balance of desire and pleasure: "Allow, then, that the attempt be made to diminish the risks that accompany this inevitable disorder, and perhaps you will realize that the precautions demanded by public health will come out in benefit to the customs themselves" (75).[16] But Cabarrús's proposal is only that—a possibility. From the start, he knew that the main obstacle to implementing it was the double standard—the proverbial mask discussed by Gómez Castellano—which on the one hand realized the natural quality of sexual exchanges, but on the other hand acted as if sexuality, including *gálico* and prostitutes, was not part of social life. Cabarrús rightly uses the word "timorato" (sanctimonious) (74) to name those who turn a blind eye to the reality of sex as natural, of prostitution and its clients as a fact, and of male chastity as an unrealistic goal for bachelors, widowers, or soldiers; women, of course, are not part of this relaxed understanding of sexuality. Moratín and his father (the literary reformer Nicolás Fernández de Moratín), Jovellanos, Meléndez Valdés, and Cadalso all engage in this double standard whereby poetic and narrative characters function as people without bodies in accepted literary works, while vibrant corporeality and sensuality are hushed into texts to be read in secret.

The growing contagion of *gálico* and its linkage with prostitution inspired more policymakers to craft systems of control. Just a few years after Cabarrús wrote his letters to Jovellanos, other authors wrote letters and treatises in the same tone, offering rational solutions of containment. Two cases in point are the *Cartas sobre la policía* (Letters on policing) (1801) by Valentín de Foronda (1751–1821), an economist and diplomat from Álava, in the north of Spain, and the "Medidas propuestas por D. Antonio Cibat para contener los progresos de la sífilis" (Measures proposed by don Antonio Cibat for the containment of the progress of syphilis) (1861), written by the Catalonian military doctor Antonio Cibat (1750?–1811) in 1809. Foronda's letters, written to the royal counselor Pedro Cevallos, whom he dubs the prince of the quixotic, imaginary island of Barataria, discuss only briefly the regulation of prostitutes through *mancebías*. As with Cabarrús's ideas, Foronda's proposal is derived from and analogous to the containment of smallpox. Like the other medical treatise authors we have discussed before, Foronda imagines *gálico* as a punishment for the discovery of the New Continent (28–29) and blames prostitutes for the spread of the disease, to the point of calling them "murderers . . . of whole generations" (30). What makes Foronda's proposal unique for the purpose of this study is that he explicitly considers the containment of diseased prostitutes in specialized hospitals as a *prevention* of the continuation of the disease (31).

Cibat's ideas on the control of prostitutes as carriers of *gálico* are more developed, but his hygienic discourse was not published until well into the nineteenth century, when some regulations had already been implemented. Although most of his contemporaries may not have known the text, it presents features that help us to understand the problems the reformers were confronting, and the speculative solutions they were discussing with their peers.[17] Like Cabarrús, whom he may have read, the doctor from Girona begins by proposing the creation of houses to gather small groups of prostitutes under the direction of experienced and principled women. Each woman is to officially register with and dwell in one house, and Cibat recommends strict measures to prevent changes of address.

He also calls for medical monitoring of each prostitute through the use of a "cartilla sanitaria" (health record) in the form of a booklet to be updated weekly. This health certificate had to be placed on the worker's headboard as a way to prove her fitness to the client: "A printed note of health signed by the professor charged with visiting them, stuck to the headboard of the bed, which will serve as a patent or witness of safety for herself and her clients" (point 3; qtd. in Guereña 24).[18] Because of the etiology of *gálico,* and especially the fact that transmission clearly involved both men and women, Cibat includes in his discussion at least a minimal regulation for men. One of his nineteen points indicates that prostitutes were to check the health of clients and refuse their services if they suspected a possibility of contagion, "to not hand themselves over to them if they should find them to be sick" (point 19; qtd. in Guereña 24).[19]

Even though these measures were not enacted, even though they were devised to stop the spread of a lethal disease, their portrayal of women as instruments to be made sanitary strikes us as dismissive and neglectful of women's feelings: one of the biggest gaps in the study of *gálico* during this period is the virtual absence of written sources showing the perspective of women, especially prostitutes, on the hovering presence of the venereal infection in their everyday life.

Like Cabarrús, Cibat does not forget that the implementation of these regulations has a cost. The payments for the physicians who were to examine the prostitutes and the treatments in specialized hospitals—harsh, prisonlike institutions for the "indecent" prostitutes and very comfortable spaces for those doing their trade with "dignity"—were to be funded by weekly dues collected from the healthy working prostitutes and the house director. In Cibat's mind, if the houses of prostitution were clean (in his opinion, maintaining hygienic conditions was the best measure against contagion), if the woman who directed each small group of prostitutes fostered the reading of appropriate books, and if the coworkers learned how to govern a house or other skills, then the clients and society at large would benefit.

But by the end of the eighteenth century the ideas of Cibat, Foronda, and Cabarrús had not found fertile ground for implementation. Their proposals of creating *mancebías* and geographically controlling prostitutes, which had also been developed by Moratín in his *Arte de las putas* several decades before (albeit literarily and somewhat humorously), were either shelved or hidden, reflecting the failure of numerous Spanish enlightenment projects. The sheer overproduction of unviable schemes is criticized by José Cadalso in letter 34 of his famous *Cartas marruecas,* where the character Nuño converses with a "proyectista" (planner) who dreams of an oversized canal system that would cross the peninsula and divide the country into four regions endowed with redundant administrative institutions, quadrupled expenses, and separate goals. The project becomes even more ridiculous when the man explains that the royal court would move its administrative seat from corner to corner according to the seasons. Irritated, Nuño sarcastically suggests that the *proyectista* should also think of building four asylums, where foolish planners would be confined. In a less fictional instance, one of the most ambitious and impracticable projects of the eighteenth century in Spain was Charles III's plan to populate the region of Sierra Morena, known at the time for being the stomping ground of outlaws and highwaymen. The king entrusted the project to the Peruvian-born *ilustrado* Pablo de Olavide (1725–1803). Olavide brought to the region about six thousand Swiss, German, and Flemish Catholic settlers who were supposed to work exclusively on agricultural endeavors. Despite the investment in and relative initial success of the project, however, it never achieved its grand purpose. In regard to the treatment of *gálico,* none of the ideas of the authors I have mentioned (not even the use of condoms, which had been defended by Moratín) took hold until a century later. Their era's measures were not preventative but mainly punitive, such as the raids against prostitutes in the streets of Madrid, Cádiz, and Seville, and their confinement to *galeras.*

To be sentenced to a *galera* should not be confused with *remar en galeras* (rowing in the galleys), the forced servitude of convicted felons in royal vessels, which was common during the sixteenth and seventeenth centuries. Before 1665, the authorities had tried to deal with prostitution by supporting reeducation efforts in the so-called *casas de arrepentidas* (houses for repentant women).[20] But the number of women in the trade was so high that in 1665 the Consejo de Castilla (Council of Castille) decided on a blanket solution: the mayors of larger cities were to punish women practicing street prostitution by herding them into *galeras,* which were *casas de corrección* (reformatory institutions) or penitentiary buildings, where other criminals were confined (Morel D'Arleux 134).[21] As stated by Moratín in his *Arte,* the imminence of raids and *galeras* was feared by prostitutes and lamented by their clients: "And the beautiful Gertrudis, a carpenter / so dexterous in all her art of fondling, / of whose benefit the *galera* now deprives us" (vv. 167–69).[22]

Two decades after Moratín wrote his poem, Francisco de Goya used his artistic skills to illustrate the reality of prostitution and the consequences of raids and *galeras.* Goya's paintings and etchings share the dark humor, grotesqueness, and criticism of social mores we find in Moratín's *Arte.* In what follows, I will discuss the link between Goya's famous *Caprichos* and *gálico,* which has not been pursued in detail by art critics. It offers a more nuanced understanding of this group of etchings, and I will show how the presence of the disease hovers over several of the images, confirming that it was a pervasive source of fear in sexual relations and that it was the driving force of the punitive measures against prostitutes.[23] By giving order to and commenting on Goya's etchings, I will analyze the fate of young women who ended up in prostitution, from the moment they decided or were convinced to enter the trade, either on their own or with the help of a procuress, to their imprisonment in *galeras.*[24]

Goya worked on his *Caprichos* between 1797 and 1798, that is, several years after the *cartón* paintings for the royal tapestries I discussed in the introduction to this book. The raw quality of the *Caprichos* is a veritable underside of the tapestries showing proper representations of everyday life for royal consumption. The group of eighty prints was published as an album in 1799. Of the eighty etchings and aquatints, sixteen (20 percent) are related in one way or another to the multileveled topic of prostitution. There are more plates on the topic of prostitution than on the other main topics of the series: witchery (fifteen plates) and criticism of the clergy (eleven plates). These statistics are sufficient reason to read more carefully the role the artist gave to the consequences of prostitution. In his advertisement promoting the sale of the prints (320 *reales* for the set) in the *Diario de Madrid* of February 6, 1799, Goya explained that his work aspired to offer the same kind of edifying criticism usually connected to essays and poetry, and that in his condemnation of vices and errors he had used instances of the whimsicality and the misguided character of human beings: "The author, persuaded that the censure of human errors and vices (although apparently particular to eloquence and poetry) can also be the object of painting: he has selected as subjects proportioned to his work, among the multitude of extravagances and errors that are common in any civil society, and among the everyday preoccupations and fabrications, authorized by custom, ignorance or interest, those which he has believed to be the most apt for the provision of material for ridicule, and to exercise at the same time the fantasy of the creator."[25]

Like Cabarrús and other enlightened authors discussed in this volume, Goya wanted to shed light on dark subjects that were usually confined to the private realm. He is aware that many moments of misguided character stem from lack of knowledge and the lack of reason that accompanies the "heated passions": "He has needed to expose to the eyes those forms and attitudes that have, until now, only existed in the human mind, obscured and confused due to the lack of illustration or overheated with the abandon of the passions."[26] *Desenfreno* and *pasión*, the axiomatic keywords of the time, appear once again, indicating that the problem is lack of restraint, which turns actions that are otherwise natural into faults. This balanced view of human desire is the reason Goya's portrayal of prostitution is more nuanced than one may think at first sight. Some of the plates condemn prostitutes and procuresses as abusers who take advantage of gullible men, but in other plates the young women are instead the victims of a legal system that overpowers and abuses them. The force behind these imbalances of injustice and the lack of ethical frame is, of course, the constant search for money, power, and satisfaction of desire that moves human social activity. Goya's representation of prostitution's dynamics in his *Caprichos* shows that he wanted to indict its practice, but at the same time it also reveals that he was closely acquainted with what sexual commerce entailed at several levels. Even though his aim was to present what really happened on the streets and in the bedrooms of Madrid from a universal perspective, his art relies on his knowledge of many particular instances, or, as he puts it in his ad in the *Diario de Madrid,* "Painting (like poetry) chooses in the universal that which it judges to be most relevant for its ends: it gathers up, in just one fantastic character, circumstances and characteristics which nature presents spread in many, and in this blending, ingeniously laid out, that happy imitation comes about."[27] His repeat visits to the topic of prostitution signal his familiarity with it, his interest in it, his fear of its consequences, and his use of etchings reveals a way to examine his ambivalent feelings.

Men like Goya felt both attraction and fear in relation to sexual exchanges, and the main source of this lies in the difficulty of distinguishing between a *petimetra* (smart lady) of high society and a well-dressed prostitute. Goya hints at this problem in *Ni asi la distingue* (Not even like this can he see her for what she is), the seventh etching in his *Caprichos,* in which a man, monocle in hand, observes a young woman whose dress and demeanor conceal her provenance (see fig. 11). He is mystified about whether she is a prostitute or an affluent lady. A manuscript in the collection of the Museo Nacional broaches the idea directly in its interpretation of the image: "Lecherous men are so blind that even using a lens they cannot tell that the woman they are pleasing is a prostitute" (Carrete Parrondo 355).[28] That there are two kinds of women who look alike doubles the odds of acquiring *gálico.* As I discussed before, Moratín's solution to this predicament is for his pupil to avoid women in luxurious clothes altogether, and instead to find young, humble women from the countryside who will be modestly dressed but untainted by the disease. For Cabarrús, the solution is for these women to wear a distinguishing yellow feather.

In *Ni asi la distingue,* the male subject's optical device does not help him discern whether the young woman is a prostitute or a lady. Its use indicates that science is able to offer knowledge only of the material world; it is not adequate to distinguishing moral character. In *La musa refractada* (The refracted muse), Enrique García Santo-Tomás offers insights on how the images and meanings of optical devices are richly linked to literature in Spain's Baroque period. For example, he studies how Francisco de Quevedo uses the image of the spyglass, an instrument that reveals truth and prevents deception, to comment on the difficulty of acquiring knowledge, which helps us interpret the attempt of Goya's *petimetre* (fop) to separate appearance from fact: "Quevedo himself had already reflected on the powers of sight in texts like *Spain Defended* and in passages of 'The World Inside,' . . . in which one could see the mediocrity and worldly craziness 'under the table,' that is to say, beyond appearances" (241).[29] Goya is hinting that the man would be able to see if this woman was a prostitute—and thus a carrier of *gálico,* as was the understanding at the time—only if, instead of a monocle, he had a powerful microscope, like the one mentioned by Feijoo or Moratín, which would allow him to see the

Figure 11. *Capricho 7: Ni asi la distingue,* Francisco de Goya, ca. 1797–98. Etching and aquatint.
(© Photographic Archive Museo Nacional del Prado)

animalcules that produced the disease. The latent qualities of the disease, acknowledged in Goya's etching, would be among the most important elements in representations of syphilis during the nineteenth century, and the driving force of prevention discourses in the early twentieth century.

Two of the characters in *Ni asi la distingue* already have their roles clearly defined. The man is a suitor or a client, and the young woman is either a bachelor girl or a prostitute. If behind the façade of her stylish dress she is a prostitute, how did she end up in this public role? Is the woman in the background the *celestina* or procuress who connected the young woman to the man? In the world of sexual commerce, a procuress convinced one or both parties to go ahead with their transaction; she arranged meetings and maintained channels of communication, all under the guise of her age, her feigned religious zeal, and her apparently innocuous attitude. In the *Caprichos,* Goya portrays the character of the go-between on several occasions, typically as an old, short, hunched woman who wears a cloak, a veil, or other covering.[30] All these features stress her double moral standard—that is, her ability to move between the spaces of the private home and the public church or street while arranging exchanges outside of socially accepted standards. Almost all of Goya's procuresses have apelike, wrinkled, toothless, and somewhat bloated faces that are framed by their clothing and contrast sharply with the pleasant faces of the young women, who walk or sit upright. Goya's images of young women with procuresses stress the idea of complementary opposites, whereby the old woman represents the future of the young prostitute, as well as her noxious inner self.

This juxtaposition is clearly present in plate 15 of the series, with the open fan held by the young woman and the closed fan clutched by the procuress (see fig. 12). The open fan and the direct gaze—shaded by her mantle—state the young woman's sexual availability, while the seemingly demure attitude of the procuress emphasizes her clandestine strategies. The meaning of the image becomes more nuanced with the sarcastic title that accompanies it: *Bellos consejos* (Lovely advice). The advice is of course not related to moral correctness; instead, the title stresses the role of the old woman as the experienced voice of illicit sexual exchanges and her aptitude for finding the best advantage for her and her pupil. But this is not only about monetary gain, it is also about survival in a more literal sense, given that *gálico* was a constant presence in the equation of sexual encounters. Beyond abstinence, there were not many ways to prevent sexually transmitted diseases during the eighteenth century. The skin sheaths or condoms mentioned by Moratín in his *Arte* were neither common nor completely reliable, and this meant that a prostitute had only two avenues for avoiding contagion: she could reject clients who might have *gálico* by recognizing clues to its presence—an awareness possible only through the advice of a knowledgeable person such as the *celestina*—or she could pray that nothing would go wrong. This appeal to the divine is cynically portrayed by Goya in plate 31, titled *Ruega por ella* (Praying for her) (see fig. 13). The description of this engraving in the manuscript of the Biblioteca Nacional in Madrid is not subtle: "While the whores deck themselves out and dress, the *alcahuetas* pray that God should give them great fortune, and teach them certain lessons" (Carrete Parrondo 357).[31] This situation, in which a person prays to succeed in a morally wrong activity, could be viewed as an irrational practice to be condemned, but economic and medical realities did not

Figure 12. *Capricho 15: Bellos consejos,* Francisco de Goya, ca. 1797–98. Etching and aquatint. (© Photographic Archive Museo Nacional del Prado)

leave much room for theological consistency.[32] Goya's title in fact underlines the sincerity of the *alcahueta* (procuress), because her prayer is a true plea for her pupil to be delivered from evil, including the evil of the feared *gálico.* In this sense, the fortune and lessons mentioned in the manuscript are not simply references to taking advantage of a prospective client, but also a reaction to a trade in which money and health were at stake. The young woman's enticing leg, dressed in a fancy stocking, intersects with the rosary in the hand of the old procuress, mirroring the crossroads faced by women in the lower strata of society, who did not have many economic options.

Figure 13. *Capricho 31: Ruega por ella,* Francisco de Goya, ca. 1797–98. Etching and aquatint. (© Photographic Archive Museo Nacional del Prado)

Goya describes this lack of possibilities in plate 73, *Mejor es holgar* (It is better to remain idle) (see fig.14). The young peasant woman has stopped her work of helping the older woman spin wool. The fact that she is holding a ball of yarn at the level of her genitals, and that her legs are open, points to the sexual connotation of her posture. The sexual tension is amplified by her coquettish look, which is directed at the viewer. Goya's title plays with the double meaning of the word *holgar* in Spanish: it means to remain at leisure or without work, but it is also a euphemism for having sexual relations.[33] It is unclear whether the old man is a family member or a client, but the etching suggests that the old woman is spinning the loose end of the thread that connects the young peasant to the old man. The image shows that tedious work and scarce economic opportunity in the countryside made peasant women

Figure 14. *Capricho 73: Mejor es holgar,* Francisco de Goya, ca. 1797–98. Etching and aquatint. (© Photographic Archive Museo Nacional del Prado)

envision sexual commerce, with its promise of profit and leisure, as a way out. The availability of countrywomen as prospective prostitutes is also clear in Moratín's *Arte,* where he recommends young peasants as a safe source of sexual pleasure.

The dyad of an old woman and a young woman in the rural environment corresponds to the urban setting's *alcahueta* and prostitute in other *Caprichos.* The first is plate 16, *Dios la perdone: Y era su madre* (May God forgive her: And she was her mother) (see fig. 15). The hunched old woman clutching a rosary in her hands follows the young woman with the open fan, who locks her gaze on the viewer. Although some describe the scene as that of a young

Figure 15. *Capricho 16: Dios la perdone: Y era su madre,* Francisco de Goya, ca. 1797–98. Etching and aquatint. (© Photographic Archive Museo Nacional del Prado)

woman pretending not to recognize her mother, the ambiguity of the image and the title allow for another plausible interpretation—that the mother is acting as the manager of the sexual encounters of her daughter. In this reading, the ethical criticism would be directed not at the young prostitute for disowning her mother, but to the old woman for prostituting her own daughter. Both scenarios are conceivable because both situations were equally real. In the first, a young woman of limited means finds upward mobility through severing family ties and pursuing the dynamic trade of prostitution—although the momentary improvement will likely fade when she ages or acquires a venereal disease.[34] In the other, the etching evinces the common situation of sexual

Figure 16. *Capricho 17: Bien tirada está,* Francisco de Goya, ca. 1797–98. Etching and aquatint. (© Photographic Archive Museo Nacional del Prado)

trade as a source of income that offered sustenance to entire families of lower extraction—a reality that persists to our day.

The ambiguity of the relationship between these two characters is absent in one of the best-known images of the series, plate 17, titled *Bien tirada está* (It has been properly stretched) (see fig. 16). The prostitute is preparing herself for the encounter with a client or a lover, and as a final touch she ensures that her stocking is stretched to show the beauty of her leg. The title plays with the meaning of the vulgar word *tirar* (to pull, or to shoot), which is used colloquially to denote a sexual encounter. In contrast to the young woman, her companion is portrayed as wrinkled and undesirable. The title singles out the young woman as a prostitute who has had many sexual encounters and will continue, like the stocking, to be stretched, while the *alcahueta* represents the opposite—a life of unrestrained sexual commerce that is ending in a state of indolence.

Goya's encompassing depictions of social reality in Spain do not rely on abstract ideas. Quite the contrary: the power of his etchings lies in his clear knowledge of details—the stretched stockings, the adorned fan, the feminine shoe, and the wrinkled face of the procuress do not come from his imagination but from his synthesis of what he has seen many times. Our understanding of his capacity to portray prostitutes in their rooms and on the streets is made more complex by his rendering of situations that required going deeper in the world of prostitution. This firsthand knowledge is visible in plate 36, *Mala noche* (Bad night) (see fig. 17) and plate 26, *Ya tienen asiento* (They are well-seated now) (see fig. 18). *Mala noche* shows the harsh life of prostitutes waiting for clients; the icy wind is so strong that it has lifted one woman's skirt over her head, almost turning her into a mock ghost. The lower part of her body is barely covered by her petticoat and her thin stockings. This is a bad night not only because the inclement weather affects her clothes but also because the cold conditions mean fewer clients and thus less income.

The image in plate 26 shifts from the public to the private realm. The two young women are turning convention on its head: their petticoats have become coats, and chairs are propped on their heads. The title goes beyond the common meaning of *asiento* as "chair" and its connection to the idea of having good judgment, and the scene is one of Goya's clearer depictions of the intimate reality of prostitution, but the general spirit of this image seems more innocent and simple than many other plates in the *Caprichos*. This is the only plate in the album where we can see the bare feet of women; in contrast, the feet Goya typically draws are tamed and constricted by shoes that make them look smaller than they really are. All the other barefoot women in the *Caprichos* are witches and their apprentices. The light, relaxed atmosphere produced by the silly attitude of the young women in *Ya tienen asiento* is reinforced by the sincere laughter of the two men with them. Although one of the men is pointing and laughing in a ridiculing manner, the mischievous face of the girl and the way she is looking at the spectator gives her agency and puts her in charge of the joke. The most striking aspect of this plate is that these are adults playing and laughing like children—a contradictory image in this age of reason. It is clear that the bracketed space of the prostitutes' room is one in which the button-down attitude of reasonable men out in public and in *tertulias* is literally and figuratively rejected. The great number of brothels and prostitutes in Madrid—reaching more than seven hundred at some point,

Figure 17. *Capricho 36: Mala noche,* Francisco de Goya, ca. 1797–98. Etching and aquatint. (© Photographic Archive Museo Nacional del Prado)

as I have mentioned before—is a symptom of the need for spaces where social constraints were temporarily lifted. This suspension of social restrictions may also be one of the reasons men continued frequenting these places, even though they were aware of the presence of the deadly venereal disease.

Another scene that shows Goya's intimate knowledge of the relationship between prostitutes and clients is titled *Le descañona* (Fleecing him), where the act of barbering the beard against the grain, a technique used to get a better shave, becomes synonymous with taking economic advantage of someone (see fig. 19). Goya depicts the man with his legs covered by a petticoat, making him look like a woman and hinting at his loss of virility—that is, his loss of control

Figure 18. *Capricho 26: Ya tienen asiento,* Francisco de Goya, ca. 1797–98. Etching and aquatint. (© Photographic Archive Museo Nacional del Prado)

over his feminine counterpart. In this sense, *descañonar* could also mean that the prostitute is stripping this man of his manhood, a possibility corroborated by his feminine features.[35] The title of this plate brings to mind other instances in the series where the metaphor of plucking or shaving clean is applied to men being swindled by prostitutes, or prostitutes being abused by officials of the law; I will show that is also related to the feared transmission of *gálico* in the environment of the brothel.

There are three consecutive plates in the *Caprichos* that illustrate multiple meanings of *desplumar* (to pluck): plate 19, *Todos caerán* (All of them will fall) (fig. 20); plate 20, *Ya van desplumados* (They have been plucked) (fig. 21); and plate 21, *¡Qual la descañonan!* (That's how they pluck her!) (fig. 22). In *Todos*

Figure 19. *Capricho 35: Le descañona,* Francisco de Goya, ca. 1797–98. Etching and aquatint. (© Photographic Archive Museo Nacional del Prado)

caerán two prostitutes and a procuress are in the last stage of yanking tail feathers from a man-bird. The creature is in pain, his head is shaven, and saliva drips from his mouth while the three women nonchalantly continue with their task. In the background of the image, a third prostitute, with birdlike features, is surrounded by a flock of winged men that include a military man with his saber, a monk cloaked in his religious garments, and an elegant *petimetre.* The descriptions accompanying this plate, which coincide with the idea of men being attracted to prostitutes and inevitably being swindled by them, stress the preoccupation of public policy officials and thinkers with devising regulations to help contain and keep watch on sexual exchanges. Another contemporary

Figure 20. *Capricho 19: Todos caerán,* Francisco de Goya, ca. 1797–98. Etching and aquatint. (© Photographic Archive Museo Nacional del Prado)

manuscript, the Ayala manuscript, states that "every kind of *avechucho,* soldiers, countrymen, and monks swarm around a lady who is half hen: they fall, the lasses hold them by their wings, make them vomit and pull out their guts" (Carrete Parrondo 356).[36] The manuscript in the Biblioteca Nacional explains that "a whore puts herself in the window as a lure, and soldiers, countrymen, and even monks and every kind of *avechuchos* swirl around; the madam asks God for them to fall, and the other whores pluck them, make them vomit, and pull out their guts, like hunters do with partridges" (Carrete Parrondo 356).[37] Nevertheless, there is more to this image. Several words in the annotations clue us into an interpretation related to the venereal disease. The image of the

Figure 21. *Capricho 20: Ya van desplumados,* Francisco de Goya, ca. 1797–98. Etching and aquatint. (© Photographic Archive Museo Nacional del Prado)

men and the prostitute as birds, and their designation as "avechuchos," connect us to double meanings and the slang of the underworld. The *Diccionario de autoridades* explains that *avechucho* is a metaphorical and familiar word to denote "the subject who is contemptible because of his figure or habits" (RAE 1770, s.v. "avechucho").[38] More tellingly, *avechucha* is slang for *mujer de vida libre* (woman of free life), as well as a generally disparaging word for presumptuous women who are interested only in luxury (Chamorro, s.v. "avechucha"). *Búho* (owl), another slang term for a prostitute, very likely refers both to the nocturnal habits of birds of prey and to the practice of the trade of prostitu-

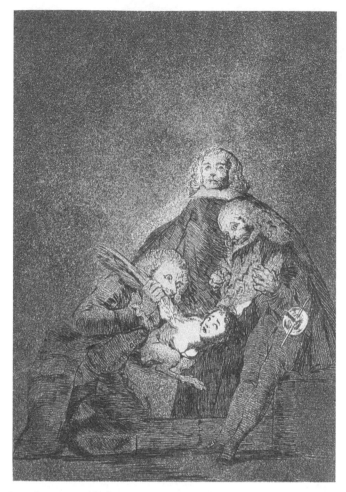

Figure 22. *Capricho 21: ¡Qual la descañonan!* Francisco de Goya, ca. 1797–98. Etching and aquatint. (© Photographic Archive Museo Nacional del Prado)

tion at night (Chamorro, s.v. "búho"). Goya organized the image in order to tell a chronological story: in the background scenery, the woman-bird with big breasts, perched on a sphere, entices all types of men. One of the men has fallen, and is currently being plucked. In the lower right, his bald head and his mouth, in the act of spitting or vomiting, foretell his future. The title for the plate indicates that everyone in the image is doomed, including the women. The third plate in this group of images reinforces that the woman-bird will meet an ominous end; there she is being attacked and plucked by three officers of the law.

In discussions of *Todos caerán,* critics have commented in passing on the presence of fake *lunares* (beauty marks) on the faces of the women, which can be seen in plates 15, 16, and 27 as well. The focus tends to be on the fashion of beauty marks promoted by ladies of high society, such as the queen consort Maria Luisa and the Duchess of Alba (Martín Gaite 225; Stoichita and Coderch 261). Stoichita and Coderch explain that the "black patch (usually referred to as a *lunar* in Spain and as a *mouche* in France, which also means 'a fly') is the descendant of the 'beauty spot' or 'mole' that decorated the faces of beautiful ladies in the eighteenth century. The 'cosmetic' function of the '*lunar*' was to bring out whiteness (and thereby the beauty) of the face on which it was placed" (260). Yes, the large beauty mark on the temple is usually a sign of sublime royal elegance or a "talisman of supremacy" (261), but there is another highly probable reason that large, fake beauty marks can be seen on several prostitutes in the *Caprichos: gálico.*

The English graphic satirist William Hogarth (1697–1764) was an important influence on Goya's work in the *Caprichos.* Javier Docampo Capilla, who offers an excellent overview of the aesthetic and thematic linkages between the two artists in relation to the topic of prostitution, summarizes the critical literature that has established Goya's probable knowledge of *A Harlot's Progress* (1732), a group of six prints by Hogarth that narrate the life and death of the character Moll Hackabout (Docampo Capilla 127–28). The first of these prints, "Moll Hackabout arrives in London at the Bell Inn, Cheapside," shows a London brothel keeper inspecting the naive protagonist, who has just arrived from the countryside in search of a job (fig. 23). The procuress, who has been identified as a real woman, Elizabeth Needham, has several fake beauty marks on her face that cover scars left by syphilitic wounds. The biggest mark is on her temple, the same place where Goya usually places it on his characters. In the third plate, "Moll has gone from kept woman to common prostitute" (fig. 24), and in the fourth plate, "Moll beats hemp in Bridewell Prison" (fig. 25), beauty marks appear on the temple of Moll's servant and on the cheekbone and forehead of Moll herself, and are clearly visible as she processes hemp for textiles, supposedly as a part of her reformation. Plates 5 and 6 present the consequences of *gálico,* which brings about the death of the protagonist. The scenes show repeatedly, and in different characters, the presence of the disease as a mark on the face (see figs. 26 and 27). The beauty marks in Hogarth's prints go beyond fashion; they are the physical representation of moral and physical decay, which are connected to unregulated sexuality and prostitution. Correspondingly, the beauty marks on the temples of Goya's female characters should be interpreted as double-layered sources of meaning. One layer is related to the fashion among upper-class women in the court of Madrid, and

Figure 23. *A Harlot's Progress* 1: "Moll Hackabout arrives in London at the Bell Inn, Cheapside," William Hogarth, 1732. (© The Trustees of the British Museum)

Figure 24. *A Harlot's Progress* 3: "Moll has gone from kept woman to common prostitute," William Hogarth, 1732. (© The Trustees of the British Museum)

Figure 25. *A Harlot's Progress* 4: "Moll beats hemp in Bridewell Prison," William Hogarth, 1732. (© The Trustees of the British Museum)

Figure 26. *A Harlot's Progress* 5: "Moll dying of syphilis," William Hogarth, 1732. (© The Trustees of the British Museum)

Figure 27. *A Harlot's Progress* 6: "Moll's wake," William Hogarth, 1732. (© The Trustees of the British Museum)

the other is a clear reference to the reality of *gálico.* The connection between the two strata of meaning suggests that, in works where the fake beauty mark appears, Goya was presenting to the viewer a hidden criticism of nobility, their beauty marks the result of both the French disease and a pervasive moral disease among those who ruled the country.

Fake beauty marks had their own semiotic system in the high circles of Madrid. Martín Gaite has commented on the disproportionate effort required for a lady's toilette, which included protracted discussions about where to place *lunares* to signify jealousy, disdain, or attraction (188–89). Martín Gaite's discussion is based in part on a very popular publication—which appeared in at least six editions between 1763 and 1764—titled *Colección de diferentes escritos relativos al Cortejo, con notas de varios, por Liberio Veranio, recogidos por D. Luis de Valdeflores* (Collection of writings related to Courtship, with notes from many, written by Liberio Veranio, collected by don Luis de Valdeflores). Luis José Velázquez de Velasco, marqués de Valdeflores (1722–72), wrote several books on the history of Spain and on numismatic themes. His *Colección* is a humorous manual on the tactics, secrets, fashions, and incidents of the *cortejo,* a practice that he defines as "the art of showing off, with noisy and brilliant pompousness, the love that one does not have" (8).[39] The relevance of this

seemingly conceited system of signification for my purposes justifies the following lengthy citation from Valdeflores's work:

> *Topography of Moles,* divided in two parts: the first addresses the moles that are
> placed on the temples; and the second with those placed on other parts of the
> face. The author, who is an arbiter in courtship, suggests that the moles which, to
> date, have been only used on the faces of ladies to produce a good appearance, can
> have a more sublime and more serviceable use in courtship. He says that the large
> moles, when placed on the left temple can denote that the place is taken; placed
> on the right that she is willing to break with her current suitor and take a new
> wooer; their lack on both temples can indicate that the place is vacant. Further,
> that the dexterous distribution of small moles across the face can denote the cur-
> rent, even momentary state of their caprices; for example, near the right eye will
> mean that the order is given for the suitor to not look at such or such a person
> with any attention; placed together near the left eye they will mean that the suitor
> can look where he pleases; placed together near the mouth on the right side, they
> will mean that the suitor ought not speak to this person or that; placed together
> on the left side they will denote that the suitor can look wherever he wants; put
> to the right side of the mouth they will mean that he should not speak on that day
> with whatshisname or other; put to the left side they will denote that the suitor
> has been very sweet, and that they have said things, etc.; and finally, placed below
> the nose they will be able to denote, that she has smelled some misstep by the at-
> tached person. (22–23)[40]

Although it was schematic and impoverished, this system of connotation,
based on fashion and appearance, was one of the few tools that women had for
exercising some type of control over their relationships with men. In addition
to the work of Goya that we are tracing, several of Lorenzo Baldissera Tiepolo's (1736–76) paintings of Spanish *tipos populares* (popular characters), finished around 1770, show women donning these fake oversized beauty marks.
In *Framing Majismo,* Zanardi explains convincingly that the central figure of
Tiepolo's *La vendedora de acerolas (The Cherry Vendor)* is not really a peasant
stared at by soldiers and a *majo,* but a handsomely adorned aristocratic lady
dressed as a *maja* (114) (see fig. 28). Nevertheless, the art critic's explanation of
the silk patch as simply a popular gypsy fashion fails to reveal the complex origin and meaning of the accessory. The implicit sexual availability of the young
woman selling cherries is made obvious by the spot on her right temple, which
states, for the knowledgeable courtly spectator, that she is ready to entertain a
new liaison. The use of fake beauty marks was common throughout Europe,
and it was used in the Spanish colonies as well.

Indeed, the peninsular custom of beauty patches as courtly communication

Figure 28. *La vendedora de acerolas* (*The Cherry Vendor*), Lorenzo Tiepolo, ca. 1770. (Palacio Real, Madrid; © Patrimonio Nacional)

and as signifiers of high status traveled to colonial Spanish America and is noticeable in the portraits of nobility in New Spain. The aesthetic reverberation of fake *lunares* from the Spanish metropole appears in many examples, including the Brooklyn Museum's portrait of doña María de la Luz Padilla y Gómez de Cervantes (1734–76), painted by the important colonial artist Miguel Cabrera (1695–1768) (fig. 29), who is known for his iconic portrait of Sor Juana Inés de la Cruz; the likeness of doña Ana María de la Campa y Cos (1734–1804), countess of San Mateo de Valparaíso, painted by the prolific Andrés de Islas (fig. 30); and *Young Woman with Harpsichord,* painted in Mexico in the early 1700s and held today at the Denver Art Museum (fig. 31). These fake beauty marks were known in Mexico as *chiquiadores* or *chiqueadores*. A century later, masculine fear and condemnation of *chiquiadores* as signs of flirtatious behavior can still be seen, for example in a stanza by the Mexican poet Guillermo Prieto. The title of the poem, "Un retrato (estilo moderno)" (A portrait [modern style]), reveals the connection between a woman's control

Figure 29. *Doña María de la Luz Padilla y Gómez de Cervantes,* Miguel Cabrera, ca. 1760. Oil on canvas, 43 x 33 in. (109.2 x 83.8 cm.). (Brooklyn Museum, Museum Collection Fund and Dick S. Ramsay Fund, 52.166.4)

Figure 30. *Doña Ana María de la Campa y Cos, Condesa de San Mateo de Valparaíso,* Andrés de Islas, 1776. (Rodrigo Rivero-Lake, Mexico City, Mexico; Artstor, library.artstor.org/asset /UNC_VRL_9719645516)

of her body (via adornment) and changing times, here dubbed as "modern": "I do not want, dear readers / that the beauties move backward, / Nor to see our maidens / in big bows and fake *chiquiadores*" (70).[41]

The signification of the patches becomes more complex as a result of the imbrication of European and American knowledges. *Chiquiadores,* which were made out of tortoiseshell (Batres Jáuregui 222), were not only seen as aesthetic additions but also known as a treatment for headaches or toothaches,

Figure 31. *Young Woman with a Harpsichord,* unknown artist, ca. 1735–50. (Denver Art Museum Collection; gift of the Collection of Frederick and Jan Mayer, 2014.209; photograph courtesy of the Denver Art Museum)

in the form of poultices that very likely came from the indigenous medical tradition. In his *Florilegio medicinal* (1712), the Jesuit doctor Juan de Esteyneffer explained that placing this "parchecito redondo" (little round patch) on the temple of the same side where the person had the pain or toothache helped to stop the noxious accumulation of liquids, known in Spanish as *fluxión* (64). Esteyneffer's method was to melt incense or mastic powder onto a piece of chamois cloth of the size of a "real de à dos" coin (64). In 1936 the American anthropologist Elsie Clews Parsons reported that in Mexico in general, and specifically among the Zapotec population in Mitla, "circular patches, black, white, or brown, may be seen on women's temples, *chiquiadores,* for headache. . . . They are mostly black—black paper, the wrapping of needles, stuck on with a gum, *tecomaca*" (125–26). In other places they were made with snakeskin, tobacco, or even a coin. The plasters used different medicinal plants and were glued to the skin with wax, resin, turpentine, or animal fats, such as lard. The medical logic of the *chiquiadores* was related to both the European theory of humors and the indigenous belief of hot or cold elements inside the body that were "brought out" with the help of the medicine in the little poultice. In their double quality as adornments and as medicinal technique, *chiquiadores* served both for healing and for hiding in eighteenth-century Mexico.

In addition to the references to María Luisa, the duchess of Alba, and the noblewomen in colonial Mexico, we also know about the use of beauty marks thanks to the depiction of María Ladvenant y Quirante (1741–67), a popular actress and singer who reached great heights in the theatrical circles of the time, and who provided plenty of material for gossip because of her torrid relationships with several prominent men in Madrid. Her standing, her performance style, and her beauty gained her the favors of several noblemen—favors that she returned. She was known by derivative names such as "Lavenant," "La Venant," "Lavenal," and "Lavenala," and more commonly by the stage names of "La Divina" and "Lavenana." Ladvenant's dramatic force and beauty were admired by many *ilustrados* and mentioned in poetic works by Gaspar Melchor de Jovellanos, Leandro Fernández de Moratín, and José Cadalso. Ladvenant did not belong to the Spanish aristocracy; she was the daughter of actors and rose in fame, becoming a lead actress and director of a theater company. Ladvenant was the kind of woman that Cabarrús saw as problematic—in the same way as high-end prostitutes—because her popularity, the quality of her dress, and the interest she produced in men from the higher stratum of society made her equal to aristocratic women, thereby attacking the logic of difference that sustained the system of power in the Spanish court. Martín Gaite claims that theater actresses like Ladvenant, who she believes are the same as *majas,* were the most successful vehicles of transferring popular customs, fashion, and attitudes to the aesthetic inclinations of the nobility (86).

In addition to her theatrical and physical qualities, Ladvenant was known for leading an ardent amorous life. She maintained affairs with several well-off figures and had three children with two of these noblemen outside of her marriage. She also had various minor affairs with other admirers, and her moral conduct was criticized, to the point that in 1765 there were rumors that blocked her ability to act or to lead a theater company. Bypassing the Junta de

Comedias, the official theater organization, Ladvenant sent a request to the king to reinstate her. It is clear that Ladvenant had the protection of people in high places, but this time it was not enough; she had overstepped in going directly to the king, and with her dissolute behavior it landed her in jail for a brief period of time. The scandal produced by her overindulgence, the protection she received from those she intimately engaged with, and the imminent possibility of her ending up in a reformatory house were noticed and turned into piquant satirical rhymes that were passed from one person to the next in the streets. Ladvenant's biographer, Emilio Cotarelo y Mori, quotes one such criticism, in which a poet wishes for Ladvenant to be sent to the *galera,* even if she had a protector from the nobility on her side, such as the theater enthusiast Countess-Duchess of Benavente:

> But, in the end, while it is not much,
> I am left with a great satisfaction,
> that you shall not learn your lesson
> even if you were reprimanded,
> because since your dwelling
> was founded during the time
> when you were given to vice, and deception,
> stealer of jewels and earrings,
> although there may be a thousand Benaventes,
> you'll end up in the *galera.* (123–24)[12]

The best-known depiction of Ladvenant is an engraving by an artist by the name of Rodríguez that appeared at the time of her death; copies are preserved in the Museo Nacional del Teatro de Almagro and the Museo de Historia in Madrid (see fig. 32). Its most striking feature are the many beauty marks on Ladvenant's face, especially one on her right temple, a placement very similar to those in Goya's images. It is difficult to know whether these beauty marks were natural, fake, or a combination of both. It is also difficult to prove that if the *lunares* were fake, they were used to cover syphilitic scars, such as those on Hogarth's character of Moll Hackabout and some of the characters in Goya's paintings. Nevertheless, some clues hint that the *lunares* were covering wounds from *gálico.* Cotarelo y Mori does not give much information about the cause of Ladvenant's death at the very early age of twenty-five but instead leaves a murkiness that insinuates that the cause of her death was shameful: "Perhaps she came to believe herself cured, but the 26th of March, a violent and unknown illness came over her, which by the end of six days snatched away her triumphs and pleasures. // She died the first of April of 1767, in a fit of continued vomiting that impeded her from receiving last rites" (133–34).[43]

Figure 32. *María Ladvenant,* Rodríguez, ca. 1770. (Museo Nacional del Teatro, Almagro)

Her passing is further complicated by cryptic verse written by Gaspar Melchor de Jovellanos fourteen years after her death:

> He will recall for you of Guerrero and Catuja
> long-lasting memories, and of the ill-fated one
> of the divine Lavenant, who now
> *walks through fields of light, grazing stars,*
> her flair, the poise, her airs, her jokes,
> the fame and her illustrious mishaps
> he will remember with tears . . . (34, vv. 78–84; my emphasis)[44]

Critics have frequently used these seven lines to show how much the actress was admired. In some cases, these lines have been quoted as a hint that Jovellanos himself was giving homage to Ladvenant.[45] Yet this is not the case. The lines are part of the "Sátira segunda a Arnesto," a text in which Jovellanos harshly criticizes the lack of effort, focus, education, and entrepreneurship of the young Spanish elite. The poetic voice describes a young nobleman, a far-removed descendant of a king, who spends all his time on unproductive activities such as watching bullfights, debating the merits of bulls and bull-fighters, learning about fashionable trinkets, smoking cigars, and showing his great knowledge of what happened in the theater. The poetic voice explains that this unsuitable member of society can lecture about the feats of actors like Guerrero and la Catuja, or about the fight between the theater factions of "chorizos" and "polacos," but these are things that do not help the progress of the country. It is in this context that the reference to Ladvenant appears. The indolent young man laments and even cries over the death of the actress, who was famous for her coquettishness, her showiness, and her "ilustres contratiempos" (illustrious mishaps), a euphemism for her scandalous affairs with members of the aristocracy. The line that appears to be the most poetic, the one often quoted as an encomium, is the one in which the young man is thinking of the dead actress, who "walks through fields of light, grazing stars" ("anda en campos de luz paciendo estrellas").[46] The line seems to praise Ladvenant, placing her among the heavenly stars, but it is important to realize that Jovellanos's main goal is to present a negative example to those members of society who he thought had to become productive leaders for the good of the country. The multileveled denotation of *gálico* comes into play in this example. The word *pacer* in the poem does not merely describe a flock of grazing animals; Jovellanos is employing the second meaning of the word, which is still used today (although not commonly) and still recorded in the dictionary of the Real Academia as "to eat up, to gnaw, or to wear out" ("comer, roer o gastar algo," RAE 2001, s.v. "pacer"). The *Diccionario de autoridades* of 1737, which perhaps Jovellanos had read, sheds further light on the interpretation of the line. One of its examples for the word *pacer* comes from a medical treatise translated and commented on by Andrés de Laguna titled *Pedacio Dioscorides Anazarbeo: Acerca de la materia medicinal y de los venenos mortíferos* (Pedacio Dioscorides Anazarbeo: About the medicinal matter and lethal poisons), in which papyrus ash "stops the *gnawing* sores, and not only those in the mouth, but also those of the whole body" (RAE 1737, s.v. "pacer").[47] This use of *pacer,* which also appears in phrases such as "llagas que van paciendo la carne" (sores that are eating up the skin), is repeated at least twenty-five times in Laguna's work. In every occurrence, the word is related to sores, which indicates that the meaning was well known to those who dealt in one way or another with sickness, including the intended audience of Jovellanos's satirical poem. Another example in the *Diccionario de autoridades* comes from Francisco de Quevedo's *Caballero de la Tenaza,* in which the protagonist writes to a lady he is courting and tells her that he will not keep paying for the food that she and her entourage eat: "It has been two months, three days and six hours since your excellency and two old hags, three girlfriends, a page and your sister began eating me up night and day."[48]

Jovellanos is using the word *pacer* in this negative sense of being gnawed at or eaten up by something or someone, and the medical reference from Laguna is clear about the word's relation to sores that gnaw at the human body. The meaning of *pacer* in this section of the poem becomes yet more revealing when one takes into account the mention of stars, which does not mean those in the sky but is a euphemism for syphilitic wounds on the face of "la Divina" Ladvenant. Two centuries before, in Francisco Delicado's celebrated novel *La Lozana andaluza* (trans. as *Portrait of Lozana: The Lusty Andalusian Woman*) (1528), the character of Lozana complains to the character of Sevillana about an old prostitute who had told her that she had "greñimón" because of a wound on her forehead. The words *greñimón, griñimón,* and *grillimón* denote a disease that produces buboes, and more specifically the disease of *gálico.* Hiding the wound under a headdress in the "Genovese style," Lozana claims that the sore actually came from beating her head in rage. Sevillana advises that a doctor be summoned, because it seems that what Lozana has is an "estrellica" (little star) on her forehead, which means that she does indeed have a syphilitic bubo:[49]

> Loz.: My lady, that youth told the mother [madam] that she should give me a good place, and the bearded old whore, astromancer, said: Can't you see that she has *greñimón?*... She thought that, because I wear my headdress low, and tied in the Genovese fashion, and me having beaten myself in the head so many times in a spell of rage that I had, that I wonder at the fact that I'm alive, that, seeing as how on the ship I had neither doctor nor any goods, it has touched me between the eyes, and I think I will be left with a mark.
> Sev.: It won't be anything, by my life. We will call here a doctor to see it, because it looks to be a little star. (192–93)[50]

Thus, Jovellanos's "anda en campos de luz paciendo estrellas" suggests that Ladvenant had died of the disease that produces starry facial wounds that eat up the skin: *gálico.* That the disease affected the life of this important figure in Spanish theater is further confirmed in Moratín's *Arte de las putas,* the work we studied earlier as an unorthodox manual for preventing the spread of the

French disease. It also names people involved in unsanctioned sexual relations in Madrid at the time. Given the secretive and supposedly limited nature of the poem's readership, one can assume that the poetic voice is that of Nicolás Fernández de Moratín. In the fourth canto, he reveals that he had a sexual relationship with María Ladvenant when she was very young. Unlike Jovellanos, Moratín is overt about the highly contagious nature of Ladvenant's disease:

> In that way the inimitable Lavenana
> gave herself to a servant of yours for two pesetas
> being a child, still almost a maiden and healthy.
> But after the courtly lust
> ran unchecked, eagerly and stubbornly,
> each one took himself for lucky
> if he could call himself the father of her children,
> after those long-winded encounters
> which my genius provokes me to count,
> yet the muse puts her finger on my mouth.
> After this, he considered himself a hero
> the one who managed to catch in his crotch
> five months of green blennorrheas,
> at the cost of a fine dress and a hundred doubloons. (4:120–33)[51]

Moratín uses "Lavenana," the popular stage name used by the public, to address the actress. In a new instance of tension between high forms of expression and displeasing language, the text recognizes Ladvenant's artistic qualities—describing her as "inimitable"—but then goes into scatological detail a few lines later, describing the infection as "verdes purgaciones" (green blennorrhea), a depiction that borders on debasement. The author also harshly criticizes the many aristocrats who had sexual relations with Ladvenant, and clearly suggests that her downfall was the result of Madrid high society's two-faced dynamic, which he condemns as unbridled courtly lust. Ironically, this tension is reproduced in Moratín's own text because only the secretive nature of the poem allows him to make explicit his profound criticism. He himself is not able to evade the double standard, given his need to boast of his early sexual possession of the coveted woman, even as he reviles her and her memory.

It is important to clarify that the name "Lavenana" in this passage of the *Arte* refers to the infamous actress María Ladvenant y Quirante and not to her sister Francisca Ladvenant (1750–72).[52] Francisca is also named once, as "Isidora," in the will of her popular sister (qtd. in Cotarelo y Mori 175).[53] In an early work dealing with Moratín's *Arte,* the American critic David Thatcher

Gies asserted that Francisca was the real person behind the name of "Dorisa," Moratín's subject of inspiration: "Her real name was Francisca Ladvenant, a singer, and sister of the famous actress known as the 'Divine' María" ("El cantor" 320).[54] In another work, Gies clarifies that the identification of Francisca Ladvenant as Dorisa had first been suggested by Cotarelo y Mori (*Moratín* 71). Although Gies offers relevant clues about the name—for example, the anagrammatic nature of "Isidora" and "Dorisa"—the likelihood of this connection is still unclear, given that Cotarelo does not back his claim with any proof: "It is plausible that this Isidora or Francisca Ladvenant is the *Dorisa* praised by don Nicolás de Moratín in so many and so exquisite verses" (Cotarelo y Mori 43).[55] More information and further research are needed to confirm the name of Moratín's muse, as well as the real cause of Francisca's death. In any case, if Francisca is Dorisa, it is highly improbable that Moratín would refer in such a censorious way to the woman he had chosen to be his muse. "Lavenana" here is the sister, the woman with the stars on her face. The beauty marks on her temple testify both to her majestic status as an artist and to the disease that may have ended her days.

Let us get back to Goya's *Caprichos*. The story of *Todos caerán* begins with the woman-bird—who has a venereal beauty mark—being surrounded by "avechuchos" who will soon have a sexual exchange with her. It continues with the man-bird having his tail plucked by the prostitutes—of whom at least one has the same mark. The final outcome is that the man-bird is not only swindled for money but also infected with *gálico*. As we know, baldness, vomiting, and profuse salivation are consequences of *gálico*'s evolution and treatment. The reader may remember the account of a *gálico* patient offered by Torres Villarroel in his *Los desauciados del mundo,* which could almost be used to describe the bird characters in Goya's plates: "Inundated by sticky and fetid sweat, unsettled by distress, and swallowed by agonies and suffocations.... The head hulled of its hair, and plagued in swaths by scabs, warts, pustules, tubercules and other promontories and bumps. The mouth covered in blisters, pooling with saliva" (57).[56]

The title of plate 19 also acquires new meaning with this interpretation: all the characters in the images will in fact fall, because they *all* have the mark of *gálico*. Men from all walks of life frequented prostitutes because they wanted to satisfy their sexual desire and, from a patriarchal perspective, were plucked of both money and health. At the same time, prostitutes offered sex because doing so was one of the few options available to them for obtaining sustenance. As a result, they were not exempt from the physical suffering produced by the disease, even if this experience never made it to the anacreontic poetry of the *ilustrados*.

It is obvious that in this mercantile cycle service and profit function only with high numbers: for a prostitute to make ends meet, more clients have to be serviced. For this reason, the scene of plucked man-birds in the plate titled *Ya van desplumados* makes sense: they appear as crestfallen clients being pushed away to make room for new clients, such as the one being serviced in the upper right corner—he still has his feathers intact and is mounting the woman-bird. The market's lack of regulation, lamented by Cabarrús, allowed for price and demand to fluctuate, an unstable situation made even more dangerous by the incurable and highly contagious venereal disease that could destroy earning power entirely. Plate number 21, titled *¡Qual la descañonan!,* shows a group of three well-dressed man-cats plucking the feathers from a prostitute's wings. Goya chooses feline features for these characters to mirror the common image of cats preying on and toying with birds. In the language of *germanía* (slang used by criminals), the term *gato* was also used to denote the apparently contradictory meanings of both "thief" and "bailiff" or "court clerk" (Chamorro, s.v. "gato").[57] The cats in this image represent the officers in charge of processing women accused of prostitution who have been captured in street raids. As in any system where venality is present, the accused women had few tools for freeing themselves from punishment: they could either bribe the officers, thereby picking their own pockets, or accept the officers' advances, a possibility suggested by the man-cat on the left, who is biting the young woman's wing from behind. This abuse of power is commented on in the Biblioteca Nacional manuscript, which states that "the Superior judges regularly cover up for the scribes and clerks, that they may rob and pluck the poor whores" (Carrete Parrondo 356),[58] a criticism that is also present in Moratín's *Arte,* where he signals that bailiffs and clerks do not fulfill their duty of reforming prostitutes: "And though they know that swindling them is not / a means to correct them, when remaining / poor, they will continue forever whoring, / they rob them with the pretext of reforming them" (4:109–12).[59]

That said, he advises his pupil to feign friendship with these officials because, thanks to their position, they know where the newer, healthy prostitutes live. This theme of venal, corrupt law enforcement is also present in the "Sátira primera a Arnesto" by Gaspar Melchor de Jovellanos, which Goya may have used as a point of departure for other engravings in the series. The use of the image of plucking as a metaphor for swindling and for transmitting *gálico* reflects Goya's balanced view of the dynamic of prostitution. At the same time, its mix of irony, humor, and grotesqueness brings to viewers a sobering understanding of Goya's society—one in which the plucker is plucked, the "law" is unlawful, and pleasure equals death.

The next plate in the series shows two young women being escorted by a pair of law officers (fig. 33). The sequence of images on plates 19–21 indicates that they had been hauled into court after a raid, and that they are now on

Figure 33. *Capricho 22: Pobrecitas!* Francisco de Goya, ca. 1797–98. Etching and aquatint. (© Photographic Archive Museo Nacional del Prado)

their way to a *galera* or another institution for rehabilitation. It is dark, and it is indeed a bad night, but it has gone wrong in a different way than in the plate where the wind made the trade of prostitution difficult. The women's faces are completely covered, but this time it is their shawls that make them look half like monks and half like ghosts. Specters or friars, women or prostitutes, healthy or diseased, they are en route to confinement and punishment. Goya's title for the plate, *Pobrecitas!* (Poor things!), reveals a trace of sympathy: like many other enlightened individuals of his time, Goya knows that the women have ended up on this path because of the unbalanced dynamic of money, social relations, and desire. Contemporaneous with this etching is a drawing that was never developed as a plate for the *Caprichos.* Titled *San Fernando ¡Cómo hilan!* (San Fernando. Good spinners!), it shows three women in the act of spinning yarn. According to the visual narrative we have been tracing, the bailiffs ushered the women to the reformatory institution of San Fernando. According to Victoria López Barahona, San Fernando comprised "some facilities with the capacity to take in many more inmates—and workshops—than the *Galera,* with a very similar disciplinary regimen, but whose administration falls under the Assembly of Hospices. From its foundation, the inmates of this establishment were set to looms, spinning wheels, and other means of textile manufacture, because their objective was that poor women should learn the 'labors proper to their sex' and to 'serve honorably'" (46).[60]

While Rebecca Haidt comments that prostitutes and women without a known trade caught wandering on the street were locked up in San Fernando, where they were put to work producing textiles (120–21), Beatriz Sánchez Hita and Bárbara Salas García explain that this type of institution was part of efforts to teach prostitutes lawful skills with the aim of reinserting them into society. The difference here is between Haidt's consideration of these institutions as places of punishment and Sánchez Hita and Salas García's view of them as places of reformation (86).[61] This, of course, is one of the cruxes in interpreting the public policy goals of enlightened officials in their time and to this day. Some examples of their social institutions are the reformatory in Goya's drawing, the hospitals, and the *casas de arrepentidas.* In addition to providing the medical treatment women might need, such places trained their inhabitants in traditionally feminine trades such as needlework.

The hair of the three women in Goya's drawing has been shaved off, perhaps as a measure to prevent the spread of lice and other infestations. The uniformity of the women's shaven heads and their identical dresses is indicative of the new level of organization and homogenization of individuals that was taking place in the country's punitive and reformatory system. It is possible to see here the erasure of the prisoners' individuality as they are transformed into a system of able bodies that can be trained to perform a productive task. The absence of hair reminds us of the man-birds' shaven heads in earlier plates, reinforcing the idea that both men and women suffer negative outcomes within the dynamic of prostitution, but loss of hair was also a consequence of *gálico* and its treatment, which prompts an alternate interpretation of the women's appearance—that the three women have been touched by the disease. Goya's critique of this type of reform institution can be seen in the title's double meaning. Women may have been sent to these institutions to learn an "appropriate" trade, like spinning yarn, but the truth was that they would very likely go back to the streets to resume practicing the "inappropriate" trade of sex. The word *hilar* (to spin) means "to have sex" in the slang language of *germanía* (Chamorro, s.v. "hilar"), and in the drawing's exclamatory title Goya uses irony to indicate that before and after their correctional stay in San Fernando, these women will continue in prostitution. But *hilar* as a synonym for having intercourse—the eye of the needle as the vagina, the thread as the penis—may also allude to the filaments of saliva that result from the use of mercury to treat *gálico*.[62] The sexual reference is further developed by the mischievous looks between two of the women, and the phallic shapes of the spindle and the distaff. The thread held by the woman in the center of the image appears to come out from her mouth, and can be viewed as allusion to saliva or seminal fluid. Perhaps Goya did not publish *¡Cómo hilan!* as a plate in the *Caprichos* because its multileveled meaning was too obvious. A great deal of the power of the series rests in its allusive capacity, and it was too easy to connect the drawing's composition, together with its title, to obscenity or to criticism of the system of the government that had organized reformation institutions like San Fernando. The fact is that the narrative in the *Caprichos* jumps from the scene of street prostitutes being led to the reformatory facility to depictions of women in cells and other spaces of punitive isolation, as is the case in plate 32, *Por que fue sensible* (Because she had too much feeling), which shows a languid young woman confined to a cell (see fig. 34). In this precarious situation of dark seclusion there is not even the hope of natural light, only the stifled reflection of a dying lamp. As with the image of the tapestry with the blind singer I used at the beginning of this book, Goya uses the emblem of this woman to represent, perhaps, the inescapable situation of Spain's reality. Pondering, in barefoot indolence, with no visible way out of the social tensions and economic problems, including those stemming from the widespread nature of *gálico,* Spain awaits with folded hands, while the shadow of a rat approaches her body.

Such an ethos of darkness and doom had been hovering in the collective mind for many years before Goya prepared his engravings. Francisco de Quevedo had already contemplated it more than a century before in his glum sonnet "Miré los muros de la patria mía." However, it became a topic of heated discussion after the publication of an entry on Spain, written by French encyclopedist Nicolas Masson de Morvilliers (1740–89), for the *Encyclopédie méthodique* in 1782, approximately ten years before Goya produced his engraving. Masson insistently represents Spain as a lethargic nation. He characterizes such indolence with the qualities of a disease, and the country as a patient who rejects the treatment that may lead to health: "Today she resembles those weak and unfortunate colonies that always need the protective embrace of the metropolis. It is thus necessary to aid her with our arts and our discoveries. What is more, she resembles those sick, desperate people who, unaware of their disease, reject the arm that brings them life!" (77).[63] The encyclopedic geogra-

Figure 34. *Capricho 32: Por que fue sensible,* Francisco de Goya, ca. 1797–98. Etching and aquatint. (© Photographic Archive Museo Nacional del Prado)

pher describes Spain as passive and sick. The situation is so dire, he points out, that the arts and the sciences in the country are dependent on the work of their French neighbors to survive. This, the entry seems to suggest, puts Spain in the same situation as that of the colonies, rendering the country an object of pity and derision. From Masson's perspective, this lethargy and lack of initiative are aggravated by the depopulation of the country—the worse in Europe, he claims, together with that of Italy (47)—one of the most feared problems in the eye of political theorists of the time. We have seen this concern and need for solution in Cabarrus's ideas to halt the spread of smallpox, or in the

Peruvian Pablo de Olavide's unsuccessful population of the Sierra Morena—a region considered as no-man's-land—with laborers brought from the Flemish region, Germany, and Switzerland. Masson blames the reduction of population in Spain on multiple factors, including the expulsion of the Moors that deprived the country of industrious hands; the unnecessary abundance of monks, religious orders, and celibates that consumed human resources that could be better employed in agriculture and manufacturing; the Inquisition as an "odious tribunal" that restrained thought, knowledge, and progress (49); the heavy taxation of raw materials that reduced the supply of laborers and in consequence depopulated urban centers; the diet of Spaniards (heavy wine, too much pepper, too much chocolate) that causes "the fluids and the nerves to dry up" (49); the hot climate that produces "strong evaporation" (51); and the great exodus of Spanish people to Asia, Africa, and the New World. The author also sees the great riches that Spain extracts from its colonies as detrimental to the cause of increasing population because these assets foment indolence by "making them [Spaniards] prefer to obtain from abroad what they might find at home in abundance. This gold circulates throughout the rest of Europe and enriches it while Spain sacrifices more than a tenth of her inhabitants to obtain it" (51). Among these factors, smallpox and *gálico* clearly represent a direct menace to the number of denizens of the country. But he deems that *gálico* is "even more deadly" because it "attacks the human race's very ability to reproduce" (49): "though more neglected in Spain, and more contemptible in appearance, is nevertheless making silent advances that are gradually undermining the nation as it spreads throughout the entire population. It is mainly to this cause that doctors attribute the current low fertility among Spanish women" (49). Masson's reproof in relation to the disease does not take into account that there was already great preoccupation with the pervasive nature of *gálico* as a factor in depopulation, clearly traceable at all levels of the vast administrative machinery of the Spanish Empire. The general concern with *gálico* in the last part of the eighteenth century would produce focused works on containment like those of Foronda, Cibat, or Cabarrús. Nevertheless, the ideas for halting and managing its negative influence can also be observed as apparently fleeting, yet symptomatically repetitive marks in public policy treatises, as well as in the bureaucratic reports of employees of the state at all levels on the peninsula and the colonies. Parallel to this preoccupation was the concern for the Spanish Empire's viable future amid the political, Napoleonic *mal gálico* and its venereal counterpart. The final years of the 1700s and the first years of the 1800s would see drastic changes that transformed the political map of the world and the future of Spain and its former colonies.

16

The Future in Jeopardy

In his *Instituciones del derecho público general de España* (1800) Ramon Lázaro de Dou y de Bassóls (1742–1832), a Catalonian moderate reformer who would become the first president of the Cortes de Cádiz in 1810, explained the menace of *gálico* as an obstacle in fostering future generations for the country: "The French disease is another cruel enemy of the people, which not only ravages and debilitates the one who suffers it, but also his very sons and descendants, and they are born with this second sort of original sin, and they grow up weak, sickly, and disqualified for work and tiring things" (40).[1] The unchecked presence of *gálico* that Masson had criticized as a main factor of depopulation in Spain is further attacked by Dou as a destructive factor akin to original sin, whereby the fault of the parents ends up being atoned for by their descendants. Such condemnation of future generations based on actions of the past would become the main interpretation of *gálico* by the second half of the nineteenth century, leading authorities to stress containment and prevention as the main tools to secure the survival of the nation.[2] In line with the idea of prevention, Dou agrees with Cabarrús on the need to make the institution of matrimony more flexible, with Moratín in avoiding contagion, with Jovellanos in his *Sátira a Arnesto* in fighting against idleness, and with Meléndez Valdés in the implementation of a more effective system of hospitals to treat *gálico*. The difference with previous viewpoints is that Dou is thinking not only about the present but also about the jeopardized future, which he intends to protect through his ideas on policing Spanish society: "The care for the growth of the population is without a doubt one of the things that are generally useful to all parts of the state: for it is that population that will provide men for all of the occupations and ministries of religion, justice, strength, wisdom, economy, and police" (23).[3]

A year after the publication of Dou's treatise, José Celestino Mutis (1732–1808) sent to King Charles IV his "Informe sobre el estado de la medicina, la cirugía y la farmacia en el Nuevo Reino de Granada y forma de remediarlo" (Report on the state of medicine, surgery, and pharmacy in the New Kingdom of Granada and means of remedying it), a report on the colony's state of health. A doctor, mathematician, and botanist, Mutis was the proposer and leader of the Royal Botanical Expedition in that region, and a key figure in the dissemination of enlightened ideas that would influence the uprising of the Viceroyalty of Nueva Granada, today Colombia, in 1810. Mutis agrees with Masson that climate directly influences the health and vitality of the population. He also concurs with the French author on the dangerous impact of depopulation on the future wealth of a region. Mutis underlines the natural riches of Nueva Granada, which he qualifies as opulent, but laments that many of the villages were established in places conducive to diseases that prevent them from becoming truly prosperous: "A realm of middling opulence, which by dint of its native resources could be most opulent, walks by slow steps in her population because of the endemic diseases which are the result of the casual and arbitrary choice of the sites in which her residents have congregated" (34).[4] According to Mutis, the unsuitable location of villages and towns promoted scrofula and *gálico,* two of the most harmful "endemic plagues" afflicting the populace: "The scrofulas, called goiters or buboes by the common folk, sores, and other vices that accompany the primitive *gálico,* certainly original to that climate, have gone on propagating themselves to the point that some towns seem veritable hospitals" (35).[5] The doctor and botanist adheres to the theory of *gálico* as a disease from the New Continent, and as a malady that radically hinders the economy of the colony, especially when some towns are becoming almost hospitals as a result of the widespread contagion bolstered by adverse climate. According to Mutis, the difficult situation of a colony like Nueva Granada derives not only from confronting these two radically insidious diseases, already a major obstacle, but also from dealing with other common afflictions derived from a bad diet, ordinary contagious diseases, incompetent doctors, and inadequate treatment centers. The result, according to Mutis, is that of a population sick and unfit for productivity: "with so many calamities gathered together, as daily displayed to view, they form the dreadful image of a generally ailing population, which maintains a full half of its individual members unutilized for society and public happiness, some for much of the year and others for the rest of their lives" (35).[6] In other words, Mutis thinks that the Nueva Granada has the same problems of any other place in the world, of any other province in Spain, but only worse. In between the lines, the scientific and enlightened man from Cádiz in Spain, who had become a man from Nueva Granada after forty years of residence there, implies that the situation is worse in the colony because the original conquerors, colonizers, and settlers chose to found their villages in the inadequate places; worse because the crown appointed incompetent administrators to manage riches and provide health and organization; worse because the metropolis that seemed so far away was interested in extracting resources but neglected to give voice and determination to this colony.

Mutis did not overtly call for a movement for autonomy, but the work of the botanical expedition did galvanize many learned men who were born in the colony. We have seen some of them before, like Antonio Nariño, translator of the Declaration of the Rights of Man, or Francisco José de Caldas, the inventor of the hypsometer; but other key thinkers affiliated with the expedition that set in motion the push for autonomy include Francisco Antonio Zea (1766–1822), who later accompanied Simón Bolívar (1783–1830) in the campaign for the liberation of Venezuela; Jorge Tadeo Lozano (1771–1816), a zoologist who became the first president of the independent state of Cundinamarca and was later executed by Pablo Morillo (1775–1837), the envoy sent by the Spanish crown to put out the flames of the revolution; or José Manuel Restrepo (1781–1863), who served in several offices after the definitive independence of the colony of Nueva Granada.

In several instances, the Spanish authorities, seeking to break off the revolutionary movement, went after the French books that these scientists-turned-politicians had in their bookshelves. The parallel of French egalitarian discourses and the venereal disease was used once again to condemn the ideas of autonomy and self-determination that inspired the revolutionary movements at the very beginning of the nineteenth century. A case in point of this linkage between revolutionary convictions in the New Continent, French ideas, and the venereal disease is the depiction of Miguel Hidalgo y Costilla (1753–1811) by José Mariano Beristáin y Souza (1756–1817). Hidalgo is a key figure of the beginning of the War of Independence in Mexico. Being a priest, and using the image of Our Lady of Guadalupe as a banner, Hidalgo led, together with Ignacio Allende (1769–1811), Juan Aldama González (1774–1811), Mariano Abasolo (1783–1816), and José Mariano Jiménez (1781–1811), a successful uprising in New Spain (today Mexico) in 1810. Hidalgo was imprisoned in 1811, before the success of the independence movement in 1821, and was executed, his body decapitated. The heads of Hidalgo, Jiménez, Allende, and Aldama were displayed on the corners of a public building in Guanajuato known as Alhóndiga de Granaditas, and remained there for ten years as a warning to future insurgents.

On the other side, Mariano Beristáin y Souza was a Mexican priest, archdeacon of the Metropolitan Cathedral of Mexico, and author of a *Biblioteca hispano-americana septentrional* (1816–19). A strong critic of Hidalgo's uprising, Beristáin defended Spanish rule while advocating for a new system based on deliberations in the Cortes de Cádiz—which he saw as a way to preserve the colonies' connection with Spain. In his *Diálogos patrióticos* (1811), Beristáin published a series of conversations between the fictional characters of Filopatro (the name means "devoted to the motherland"), Aceraio (Sincere), and Morós (Foolish) to attack any remaining ideas supporting the uprising after the execution of the rebel priest. The character of Filopatro qualifies the liberation ideas defended by Hidalgo as "pus gálico-napoleónico" (*gálico-Napoleonic pus*), that is, diseased beliefs from France and the Napoleonic expansion that infected places such as Mexico or Nueva Granada: "The *gálico-Napoleonic* purulence that for some time had come on paper, but as it came with its essence lost, had little and weak effect. Some infected emissaries came too, who prepared imperceptibly and cautiously the contagion, indisposing with their miasmas the diverse humors of this body; but seeing as they did not dare to inoculate *from arm to arm,* they did not achieve a complete eruption. There arrived at last from the north to the inland towns the Frenchman Delmivar, and very much knowingly he inoculated the priest Hidalgo. This one propagated the infernal pox in Allende, Aldama, Abasolo, and others; and from these the plague was communicated to a multitude of the incautious and unhappy" (123).[7]

The dialogue between Filopatro and his interlocutors is a lengthy play of signification, coupling the ideas of contagion and disease—sometimes described as something similar to *gálico,* but other times also connected to smallpox—with the incidents of Hidalgo's uprising and its consequent radical suppression. In this sense, the ideas of revolution and independence are presented as an infection that first arrived through writings without much incidence.[8] Then the "miasmas," or sickening vapors, carried by blighted messengers upset the body, that is, infected the country (123).[9] Filopatro indicates that these messengers were not able to completely infect the body because they could not inoculate their ideas "arm to arm." This image uses the idea of variolation, whereby a wound in the arm of a person with smallpox is applied to a wound opened in the arm of a healthy person to expose that individual to the disease in order to develop immunity. But in the end, the French ideas infected Hidalgo, who in turn passed the "infernal pox" to the other leaders of the uprising, expanding the disease's influence among the unsuspecting and naive—very much like the credulous and gullible man that acquired the venereal disease. Filopatro continues the allegorical ramifications, indicating that the infection was unstoppable until a good doctor, sent by Divine Providence to take care of the colony's health, arrived in Veracruz: "The practitioners [*practicantes*] brought by the physician were dexterous, and with the excellent *antipyretics* that existed here, they marvelously impeded that it be occupied by confluent pox (those with a great density of marks), and in little time they were banished to less noble parts. Straightaway they have been attacked wherever they have appeared, evicting them from the places that they had occupied with most fervor and tenacity. At the end, the evil is only in the legs; the head always firm and clear, the chest free, the breathing natural, the stomach strong" (123–24).[10]

Morós decodes the indirect representation, revealing that the good doctor is the recently arrived viceroy Francisco Javier Venegas (1754–1838), who
defended the capital city of Mexico from the disease—the head that had not
been infected by the "viruelas de insurreccion gàlica" (124). The "practicantes," or physician assistants, are the able commanders who lead what he calls a
"curación" (healing process) in conjunction with soldiers of the colony, whom
he compares with "febrífugos" (antipyretics), a medical term used to name an
agent—such as *quina*—that helps to reduce fever. The chest and stomach of
this veritable colonial body represent minor and more important cities near
the capital, and the legs, far away but still diseased, are cities and villages like
Guadalajara where the pox of insurrection has retreated (124). Filopatro is
confident that the disease will be eradicated because the name of the disease,
"[mal] gálico-napoleonico," is now known. Following medical precepts of the
time, naming the disease was the first step to finding a treatment to cure it,
a knowledge that convinces Filopatro that within a year "the beautiful body
of New Spain shall be left free and clean of all leprosy" (125).[11] Nevertheless,
Morós worries about the possible scars left by the pox. Filopatro is quick to explain that to take care of the blemishes left by the disease there are "good soaps
and elixirs in our pharmacy,"[12] such as the "soap of repentance" that erases the
flaw of those who contracted the disease of mild revolutionary ideas. In more
difficult cases of contagion, the soap needs to be stronger in order to tear off
the infected loose skin and stimulate new and beautiful integument. But for
the more persistent renegades—presented here as scabs and warts—the harsh
metaphors used by Filopatro are indeed not so subtle: the ugly scabs are to be
washed with "jabon de piedra infernal" (hellstone soap) (125), a highly toxic
preparation made out of silver nitrate—a poison if ingested, but a beneficial
caustic treatment when applied on ulcers and wounds (*Suplemento*, s.v. "piedra
infernal"). But the image and the name of this soap, as related to hellish punitive measures against those who persisted in their defiance of the establishment, leave no room for any misunderstanding. Finally, the political physician
warns that for "llagas pùtridas y tenaces" (putrid and tenacious pustules), the
remedy will not be soap, but cauterizing iron and fire (125).

Although using allegorical language, Father Beristáin does not mince
words to condemn those he sees as enemies and a disease to the Spanish rule
of the colony. After advising on the course of action against the "French putrefaction," which he connects to the revolutionary ideas of Miguel Hidalgo,
Beristáin has the three companions discuss the possible consequences of the
recently suffocated uprising after the political situation stabilizes in Spain.
Morós explains that he has heard people fearing that if the Spanish royal family prevails in power, the memory of the turmoil will make the king act with
harshness against the colony. Filopatro retorts, calling any person making

such comments a conspirator working for Napoleon who seeks to divide the country by making people afraid of royal retaliation and preferring to support French rule instead. Beristáin's mouthpiece, the righteous character of Filopatro, forecasts that the French political disease will be eradicated from New Spain by the end of 1811. Nevertheless, like its allegorical venereal counterpart, the contagion of ideas of autonomy that had started with the likes of Clavijero and Teresa de Mier, that had shown its first clear symptoms in the festering turmoil led by Hidalgo, that had been radically treated with a regimen of executions, beheaded corpses, and "enhanced interrogations," remained relatively dormant for ten years until Agustín de Iturbide (1783–1824) became president of the Regency in 1821, and later emperor of Mexico in 1822. There was no cure for what Filopatro dubbed the "pus *gálico.*"

The high metonymic quality of *gálico* blurred the meaning of the disease every time it was used to qualify the enemy. Given its hazy quality, the two sides of the same conflict used the trope to insult their opponent with the same accusation of being an embodiment of the venereal disease. For Beristáin, the supporter of Spanish rule in Mexico, *gálico* represents the contagion with putrid ideas coming from Napoleon in particular—the invader of the Spanish peninsula who sought to control the colony of New Spain—and from France in general. Conversely, for Servando Teresa de Mier, the steadfast defender of Mexican autonomy who wrote about the origin of the disease, *gálico* was a representation of Spain as one of the many evils brought by the Spaniards to the New Continent. In one of the documents collected by the historian Juan E. Hernández y Dávalos in his *Colección de documentos para la historia de la guerra de independencia de México* (Collection of documents for the history of the war for Mexican independence) (1882), there are details of the case against Teresa de Mier in the Holy Inquisition as apostate and traitor to the king and the country. After several years in exile in Europe, Teresa de Mier returned to New Spain in April 1817 beside the Spanish revolutionary Francisco Xavier Mina (1789–1817) with the goal of taking part in the struggle for independence of the country. But he was taken prisoner only three months after his arrival and sent to the jail of the Inquisition in Mexico City, where he remained until 1820. Xavier Nicolas de Lecuona, one of the witnesses brought to testify against Teresa de Mier in the Inquisition's legal action, recalls a conversation he heard between Teresa de Mier and two officers while in the town of Atotonilco: "In his own home he heard indistinctly two persons, who were Captain don Antonio Castro and, of equal class, don Felix Ceballos: then that father Mier had said: What is it that the dirty Spaniards have brought to America? *Gálico,* mange, the pox, cockroaches, and other such corruptions" (Hernández y Dávalos 694).[13] Lecuona's testimony is believable because we know that Teresa de Mier was convinced of, and had written about, the European origin of *gálico*. The statement is also credible because the rebellious priest names the Spaniards with the pejorative term of "gachupín," meant to offend the parvenus coming from the peninsula with the intention of taking the established criollos' place in society. While for Teresa de Mier the tangible disease of *gálico* was the upshot of the "gachupines," for Beristáin the "pus gálico" was the result of the ideological infection brought by the "gabachos," another derogatory term used in Mexico to name the French. In the end, ambiguously, no matter what point of view, "gabacho" or "gachupín," *gálico* was the idea or the reality that embodied the evil brought by the other. The only thing that could pinpoint *gálico* with some clarity was its obscurity, that is, the fact that once it touched the physical body or the immaterial social body, its contagion, with no cure in prospect, would bring the symptoms that announced gloomy demise.

By the end of the eighteenth century, a time we have come to know under the rubric "Age of Enlightenment," there was not much clear about *gálico*, its origin, the mechanics of its contagion and development once acquired, its treatment, or its cure. By 1810, with the Napoleonic *mal francés* on the Spanish peninsula or the insurgency in Mexico seen by Beristáin as "pus *gálico*," not much more was known about the disease than at the outset of the century and the mysterious ailment of "the Bewitched" last king of the Hapsburg family. In this sense, the only real understanding of *gálico* was its extraneous quality: anything and everything different was either appealing or had to be rejected, even if it looked like an enemy within. Ambiguously, the reality of *gálico* and its connection with sexuality also meant that, in order to preserve life, what was appealing also had to be rejected.

But the Enlightenment is not about well-defined facts or overconfident knowledge; its light is made of inquiry, observation, formulation of questions, the challenging of previous judgments, and the debunking of inveterate convictions. By this measure, the understanding of *gálico* during this time was far-reaching and highly consequential; it conformed an organic social experience that touched many realms at the same time. The multifarious unfolding of the meanings of the disease studied in this volume show that *gálico* was indeed not only enlightened but also luminous.

Notes

Introduction

1. The Scottish doctor and bacteriologist Alexander Fleming (1881–1955) discovered the antibiotic properties of the *Penicillium chrysogenum* fungus. The pure culture of the fungus became what is known today as penicillin. The antibiotic is still used effectively in the treatment of syphilis and other contagious diseases.

2. For a comprehensive study of the crafting and reception of medical treatises between the beginning of the fourteenth century and 1650 on the Spanish peninsula, see Solomon's *Fictions of Well-Being.* Solomon aptly follows the way in which writers developed strategic discourses of healing and improvement to boost sales of their work. He also shows how ailing patients sought in these texts ways of recovering their health.

3. There is a wealth of active discussion on the perceptions of the French disease from a historical perspective. For scholarship on syphilis in early modern Europe, see the pivotal work by Arrizabalaga, French, and Henderson, *The Great Pox;* in addition to Arrizabalaga's ongoing efforts in this area, also see the work by Kevin Siena. Other relevant works include, chronologically, Rosebury's *Microbes and Morals;* Temkin's "On the History of 'Morality and Syphilis'"; Quétel's *History of Syphilis;* Foa's "The New and the Old"; Schleiner's "Moral Attitudes toward Syphilis"; and Oriel's *The Scars of Venus.*

4. For an initial discussion on the relation between the venereal disease and feminine gender roles, see Schleiner's "Infection and Cure through Women." Merians's edited volume, *The Secret Malady,* includes two studies in the eighteenth-century European context: Norberg's "From Courtesan to Prostitute," and Stewart's "'And blights with plagues the Marriage hearse.'" On the nineteenth century, see Spongberg, *Feminizing Venereal Disease.* For studies on representations of venereal disease in connection with gender, see Rollerston, "Venereal Disease in Literature"; Conway, "Syphilis and Bronzino's London Allegory"; and Gilman, *Disease and Representation.* In connection with pictorial representations, see Morton, "Syphilis in Art."

5. For the French context, a general overview of syphilis can be found in Martineaud's *L'amour au temps de la vérole.* For France during the eighteenth century, see Merians's *The Secret Malady.* For the Spanish context, see López Terrada's "El tratamiento de la sífilis en un hospital renacentista." For the German context, see Stein's *Negotiating the French Pox in Early Modern Germany,* and Jütte's "Syphilis and Confinement." For the English context, in addition to Siena's work, see Bentley's *Shakespeare and the New Disease,* as well as Fabricius's *Syphilis in Shakespeare's England,* and Hentschell's "Luxury and Lechery." For the Italian context, refer to McGough's *Gender, Sexuality and Syphilis in Early Modern Venice* and her essay

"Quarantining Beauty"; see also Gentilcore's "Charlatans, the Regulated Market-place and the Treatment of Venereal Disease in Italy," Zanrè's "French Diseases and Italian Responses," and Hewlett's "The French Connection," all of these in Siena's *Sins of the Flesh*. For the North American context from an archaeological perspective, a thorough argument on the implications of nonvenereal treponematosis in the dispute about the American origin of syphilis, see Cook and Powell's *The Myth of Syphilis*. Other current scientific discussions on the origin of syphilis include Zimmer's "Can Genes Solve the Syphilis Mystery?" and Mitchell's "Pre-Columbian Treponemal Disease." For the United States during the nineteenth century, see Brandt's *No Magic Bullet*.

6. José María López Piñero's work is the most salient of the initial studies of Spanish medicine and science in this period. Luis S. Granjel developed early extensive work of synopsis and compilation in his *Historia general de la medicina española*. Relevant works in this period include Goodman, *Power and Penury;* Cañizares-Esguerra, *Nature, Empire, and Nation;* the edited volume *Science in the Spanish and Portuguese Empires, 1500–1800,* by Bleichmar et al.; Clouse, *Medicine, Government and Public Health in Philip II's Spain;* and the compelling analysis by Enrique Fernández, *Anxieties of Interiority,* which shows the incidence of anatomical studies in the thinking about the individual's being and the fear of exposing the intimate self in the Spanish early modern period. For the case of the Spanish colonies, see Risse's "Medicine in New Spain," and Barrera-Osorio's *Experiencing Nature*.

7. After the *Reconquista* and the expulsion of Muslim and Jewish populations in Portugal and Spain, the *limpieza de sangre* was the substantiation of not having ancestors accused of practicing a heretical religion or belonging to a race considered shameful. The demand to demonstrate being "cristiano viejo" (Old Christian) aimed at excluding this part of the population from jobs, positions, associations, and professions of influence.

8. For an understanding of the process of acculturation, whereby the incorporation of Moorish and Islamic cultural and scientific nodes into the now-dominant culture meant the obliteration of these practices and knowledges, see the chapter "La minoría musulmana y morisca" in García Ballester's *Historia social de la medicina en la España,* and his book *Los moriscos y la medicina*. For a corresponding study of the influence and vicissitudes of the Jewish population on the peninsula, see Kottek and García Ballester, eds., *Medicine and Medical Ethics in Medieval and Early Modern Spain*.

9. For a study on nontraditional healers, the role of superstition, and the practice of the so-called *saludadores*—those who healed through prayers and incantations, as well as with their spit or other healing powers—see Camagne's "Entre el milagro y el pacto diabólico," and Tausiet's "Healing Virtue."

10. For a more developed discussion on the Galenic doctrine of humors, see the sidebar "Humoral Equilibrium" and figure 3 (pp. 34 and 35).

11. For revealing research on Philip II's interest in alchemy and his influence in con-

temporary discussions, see Rey Bueno's *"La Mayson pour Distiller des Eaües* at El Escorial," "Juntas de herbolarios y tertulias espagíricas," "El informe Valles," and *Los señores del fuego.*

12. For more developed research on the Protomedicato in Peninsular Spain, see the dossier "El Tribunal del Real Protomedicato en la Monarquía hispánica (1593– 1808)," edited by Martínez Vidal and López Terrada. From that dossier, the overarching nature of Campos Díez's "El Protomedicato en la administración central de la Monarquía hispánica" and Gardeta Sabater's "El nuevo modelo del Real Tribunal del Protomedicato en la América española" have been especially useful for my purposes, and I have used them as my guide here. An early study for the Peninsular case is Iborra, Granda-Juesas, and Riera's *Historia del Protomedicato en España (1477–1822).* The most extensive study on the history and role of the Protomedicato in the Spanish colonies in America is Lanning's posthumous volume *The Royal Protomedicato.*

13. For more developed information on Feijoo, see the sidebar on p. 63. For my discussion of his observations about changes in medical perspective, see pp. 62–66.

14. The complete title of Harvey's revolutionary publication is *Exercitatio Anatomica de Motu Cordis et Sanguinis in Animalibus* (An anatomical exercise on the motion of the heart and blood in living beings). The slow pace of the incorporation of Harvey's ideas in Spanish medical discussion is revealed by the fact that the first complete edition of his *De Motu Cordis* in Spanish did not appear until 1936, translated by the Mexican doctor and professor José Joaquín Izquierdo in *Harvey, iniciador del método experimental.* Nevertheless, it is also true that during the second half of the sixteenth century Harvey's ideas were known in Spain in the original, Latin version.

15. López Piñero emphasizes in several of his publications the watershed quality of Cabriada's book. For a focused discussion on this topic, see his *"La Carta filosófica, medico-chymica* (1687) de Juan de Cabriada."

16. José Colmenero, a professor at Salamanca, published in 1697 his *Reprobación del pernicioso abuso de los polvos de la corteza de Quarango o China-China* against the use of quinine. Colmenero's claims were refuted the following year by Tomás Fernández in his *Defensa de la china-china y verdadera respuesta a las falsas razones,* published in Madrid. Also in 1697, Salvador Leonardo de Flores published in Seville his *Desempeño al método racional en la curación de las calenturas tercianas.* Both Flores and Fernández develop a clear defense of the new ideas heralded by Cabriada ten years before.

17. For more information on the cinchona bark, see the sidebar on p. 168.

18. Attempting to offer even a cursory list of authors who have produced meaningful research in this area would be both inadequate and inequitable. Refer to the works in the critical apparatus of this volume to locate the main sources that have informed my approach.

1. This Book Is (the Back of) a Tapestry

1. For portrayals of important world personages and their relation to or experience with syphilis from the fifteenth to the twentieth centuries, see Hayden's *Pox*.

2. "si no nos desdeñáramos de aprender de estas gentes sencillas, y procuráramos tratarlos con intimidad, descubriríamos específicos mas importantes que las Disertaciones mas eloqüentes, y que losa descubrimientos mas curiosos de la Anatomía."

2. A Mysterious Disease Changes the Political Map of the World

1. For example, in the article "Sífilis congénita en el siglo XXI" (Congenital syphilis in the twenty-first century), Rodríguez-Cerdeira and Silami-Lopes explain the prevalence of syphilis among the Habsburgs, including the hereditary syphilis of Charles II: "Philip II and his third wife, Elisabeth of Valois, were syphilitics, just like his son Carlos, who had symptoms of hereditary syphilis. King Philip IV of Spain contracted syphilis and infected Mariana of Austria, who in her turn transmitted it to their son Charles II." (680; Fueron sifilíticos Felipe II y su tercera esposa, Isabel de Valois, así como su hijo Carlos, que tenía síntomas de sífilis hereditaria. El rey Felipe IV de España contrajo sífilis e infectó a Mariana de Austria, que a su vez la transmitió al hijo de ambos Carlos II.)

2. "Morbus itaque Gallicus, est dispositio mala epatis ad frigiditatem, & aliqualem siccitatem declinans cú qualitate occulta per venas, & porositates toti corpori communicate, & est contagiosa, cum qua fiunt sæpissime pustula malæ per totum corpus, vel in aliquibus membris, & quampluribus apparent in primis in capite, & fronte circa originem capillorum, & in virga, & vulva in illis qui per coitum inficiuntur."

   All translations are mine, unless stated otherwise.

3. "Otros, como Geronimo Fracastoreo, la llaman sifila, que quiere dezir, enfermedad nacida de mucho amor, y Concordia que ay entre la muger, y el hombre, la qual pluguiesse à Dios no la huviesse tanta en esta parte."

4. For a study of Calvo's treatise in the 1500s and the purposeful concealment of same-sex relations as possible causes of the French disease, see Berco's "Syphilis and the Silencing of Sodomy." Berco notes that Calvo's was "the medical treatise on the French disease most widely read in the Spanish Golden Age" (93).

5. For a discussion on the clash between unlicensed practitioners and surgeons and university-trained physicians in Europe two centuries before, see French and Arrizabalaga's "Coping with the French Disease." This essay also gives a good overview of the tension between Galen's and Avicenna's defenders.

6. "se enseña su origen, causas, y curación, el modo de hazer el vino santo, dar las unciones, y corregir sus accidentes."

7. "de humores acres corrosivos, y malignos, ò de la massa sanguinaria corrompida, la qual unas veces declina biliosa, otras à melancolica, y aun otras à atrabile."

8. "señal es que el tal tiene, yà las bubas confirmadas."

9. "el humor se ha buelto de las partes de afuera à las de adentro."

10. "buelto al coraçon, y sufocarà el calor natural dèl, y sin duda el enfermo se morirà."

11. "à los quales llama el vulgo incordios, y con razon, porque los que los tienen, libremente no pueden andar, sino coxos, y con grande pena."

12. "Tiene esta enfermedad tres especies; en la primera, y los que la padecen, no ay dolores, y es dificil de conocerle. Rastrease de ver que ay destemplanças de higado, y opilaciones en èl, y flaqueza de estomago. En las galicos de la segunda especie suele aver gonorreas, y dolores universales, como arteticos. En los de tercera especie ay gomas, y sobrehuessos; y en todas, finalmente, se halla lo que en la primera."

13. "la nariz, entre Roma y Francia, porque se le había comido de unas búas de resfriado, que aún no fueron de vicio, porque cuestan dinero."

14. "los que carecen dellos se tienen por personas afeminadas, y porque el morbo galico muchas vezes es causa que se caygan."

15. "porque el humor vicioso que tiene su assiento en el higado, acude no solamente à la boca, pero à todo el cuerpo."

16. "Notan aqui algunos Doctores que esta enfermedad suele librar de otras mas graves, saliendo por el cuero el humor vicioso, y maligno del cuerpo."

17. For more on baldness and syphilis in early modern Spain, see Berco's "The Great Pox," especially the section "Hairlessness as Symptom and Shame" (232–36).

18. "ayre infecto, y podrecido" ... "sino de contacto de personas bubosas."

19. "el superfluo coyto destruye, y desvarata universalmente toda la maquina de el cuerpo humano" ... "se bambonea, desmorona, y tiembla" ... "Los actos venereos destruyen, marchitan, desflorecen, y afean toda la hermosura, gentileza, y brio de el hombre, dexandole seco, y marchito."

20. "Crudezas de estomago, resolucion de los miembros, debilidad de fuerzas, torpeza en los sentidos, perdida de memoria, perlesia, gota, mal de reiñones, y de orina, colica, mal olor de boca, dolor de muelas, esquinancia, thysis, hydropesia, [...] dolores de cabeza, de las cervices, de espaldas, brazos, ancas, rodillas, pies, y de todo el cuerpo. Resultan gomas de la cabeza, brazos, y piernas, ulceras corrosivas en todo el cuerpo, garganta, campanilla, y paladar; morseas, pustulas, empeynes, berrugas, ulceras en las partes verendas, gonorreas galicas, bubones, alopecias, lamparones, topos, talparias, corrupciones de huesos."

21. "Quanto mas se detienen, mas se abren las porosidades, se escalientan los humores, y se buelven mas aptos, y aparejados para recibir la dicha enfermedad. De aquí colegimos, que las que sienten mas delectación en el acto venéreo se inficionaràn mas presto; y de aquí es, que las personas jobenes se inficionaràn mas presto que las viejas; y los sanguineos, que los melancolicos; y las mugeres que los hombres, porque ellas doblada delectación sienten que los hombres."

22. For a discussion on the history of the condom and its use in Spain, see the section dealing with Moratín's *El arte de las putas* and the sidebar "The Craft of Condom Making" (p. 212).

23. "Como se podrà defender cada uno despues del coito desta enfermedad" ... "haze mas el que detiene y preserva à otro para que no cayga, que el que le levanta despues de caydo."

24. "porque no se debiliten de tal manera, que estorven la cura: y tambié porque con aquella agitacion se encienden los humores, y se pueden seguir muchos accidentes."

25. "Ayudàranles otras diligencias, que son, hazer exercicio corporal, mas que el acostumbrado; andar bien abrigados; dormir moderadamete, guardarse de los serenos; lavarse las manos, y la cara à menudo; cortarse las uñas de manos, y pies; no cohabitar con mugeres, aunque seã casados, sino lo menos q puedan; no enojarse, no entristecerse, ò melancolizarse, sino procurar divertirse contra qualquier pesar."

26. "Lo q ha de bever es agua cozida con el palo santo, ò zarçaparrilla, que sea muy simple: como se aya de hazer, luego lo dirèmos." In the section about products used to cure the disease, I will show important implications of the qualities and the origin of these medicines.

27. "estas quatro cosas con toda su sustancia, y con propiedad oculta à nosotros, curan admirablemente todo genero de bubas."

28. "los medicamentos que curan à esta enfermedad fueron por experiencia hallados. Esta experiencia nos vino à nosotros de los Indios, los quales beviendo el agua en que era cozida esta fusta, ò palo santo, y sudando con ella, y guardando buen regimiento, curan perfectamente de las bubas [...] este es el palo santo que nos traen de las Indias: cierto es gran providencia de Dios ver que venga la medicina de donde vino la enfermedad."

29. "Dio noticia del un Indio a su amo, enesta manera. Como un Español padeciesse grandes dolores de Bubas que una India se las avia pegado, el Indio que era delos Medicos de aquella tierra, le dio el agua del Guayacan, con que no solo se le quitarõ los Dolores que padescia, pero sano muy bien del mal: con lo qual otros muchos Españoles, que estavan inficionados del mismo mal, fueron sanos: lo qual se comunico luego por los que de alli vinieron aqui a Sevilla, y de aqui se divulge por toda España, y della por todo el mundo."

30. "que con toda su sustancia, y no con calidad manifiesta cura el morbo galico, ò bubas." . . . "la qual la traxo de primera vez de la Nueva España, y despues de Honduras, y esta es la mejor, y la que haze mejores efectos."

31. "Dicen efectivamente, que si un enfermo del mal Venereo, no toma otro alimento, le salen al principio muchos granos por todo el cuerpo, los que elevandose en punta, supuran mucho, y de este modo creen que en un mes se arroja todo el virus oculto en el cuerpo [...] los Pyratas llamados comúnmente Hibustiers, que infestan los Mares de America, no se curan de otro modo."

32. "Porque los ricos, y nobles, que se han de curar con este remedio, quieren las unturas mas delicadas, y olorosas: los pobres se contentan con las que bastan para sanarlos[,] los muchachos, y hombres delicados, y otros que fácilmente sudan, y resuelven, se han de tratar con mas delicadeza, y blandura."

33. "Los pobres, ò mendigos, ò siervos, que ni tienen lugar para curarse, ni con que, despues de haberse sangrado, y purgado, se pueden untar blandamente con sus propias manos todas las coyunturas, ò las que mas pareciere que hacen al caso, usando de algun unguento liviano de los dichos, y despues se vestiràn, y acudiràn a sus negocios, y en viendo alguna de las señales que diximos, cessarà el untar."

34. "El Mercurio de Voticas, / Aun no alcanza à los bubosos, / Y assi puse al Dios Mercurio, / Porque en fin: Dios sobre todo."

35. "A diez maridos, sin lloverse en oro, / Convirtió en Aries, Capricornio y Toro."

36. "en lo mejor destos engaños / Gálico Cáncer le royó los años."

37. "Otros la pica al hombro, / Sobre murallas puestos, / Hambrientos y desnudos / Pero de gloria llenos."

38. "Que hay de Vénus á Marte, / Que hay de Mercurio á Vénus."

39. "Si le dices, que sin despreciar el mérito de aquellos dos grandes hombres, los modernos han adelantado en esta facultad por el mayor conocimiento de la anatomía y botánica que no tuviéron los antiguos; á mas de muchos medicamentos, como la quina y mercurio, que no se usáron hasta ahora poco, también hará burla de ti."

40. "ciencias positivas, para que no nos llamen barbaros los estrangeros: haga nuestra juventud los progresos que pueda: procure dar obras al público sobre materias útiles. [. . .] Dentro de dos años se ha de haber mudado el sistema científico de España insensiblemente y sin estrépito."

41. "Cuéntese, pues, por nada lo pasado, y pongamos la fecha desde hoy, suponiendo que la península se hundió á mediados del siglo XVII, y ha vuelto á salir de la mar á últimos del XVIII."

42. "A la literatura actual: Soneto improvisado en broma y de pies forzados."

43. "El delirio, el furor se llaman *genio;* / ya Diana no es más que un *plenilunio;* / sólo se usa en el gálico *Cilenio.*"

44. "Ay muchas que lo sacan del vientre de su madre, quales son las que se han engendrado de padres que tienen la misma enfermedad; que como el semen, que es causa eficiente de la generacion [. . .] quando marido, y muger estàn infectos, cierto es, que assi la sangre mentrua, como el semen (de los quales se ha de formar la criatura, y sus partes) seran viciosos, y corrompidos; y que aunque se ajunten en el utero, por ser malos, ò dellos no se seguirà generación, ó será cosa enfermiza: porque de malos principios en las cosas naturales, nunca se sigue buen fin, si ya Dios no lo remedia."

45. A few examples show how open and prevalent was the discussion on *gálico* in the sixteenth century. *La pícara Justina* (1605), a novel full of satire and mordant wit published under the authorship of Francisco López de Úbeda, presents the protagonist Justina discussing with her bristly quill about her own lack of hair as a result of *gálico,* and pondering how to negotiate between a public life where she must appear as desirable and healthy and a private reality of covert disease and deterioration (8). In Cervantes's *El casamiento engañoso* (1613), Lieutenant Campuzano has no qualms about telling Licenciado Peralta that he just finished treatment for *bubas* in the Hospital of the Resurrection in Valladolid (177). For a complete list of hospitals that treated *gálico* in the Hispanic context, see the sidebar "The Geography of Hospitals" (p. 97). As I will show later in my discussions of Torres Villarroel and Valle y Caviedes, Francisco de Quevedo's poems such as "Tomando estaba sudores" and "A Marica la chupona" were unambiguous about the physical consequences of *gálico* and its treatment.

46. "(como perro al vomito) buelven à tener exceso con mugeres infectas, las quales les volverán una, y muchas vezes à inficionar."

47. "One must understand the same of women, so that when we see them we flee from them as from the plague. *For if a bull has hay in his horns, flee far away.*" (Calvo, 545; Lo mismo se ha de entender de las mugeres, pues quando las viéremos nos apartaremos dellas como de peste. *Quia fænum habent id fronte, longe fuge.*) The Latin phrase is Calvo's adaptation of Horace's "faenum habet in cornu, longe fuge."

48. "de menos de cien años à esta parte conocida, aldemenos en nuestras partes, porque en las Indias mas antigua es."

49. "una question mas curiosa que provechosa."

50. "conversaban con las Indias que venian tocadas del mal."

51. "El titulo solo pone grima, y espanto; y es tan odioso, que ninguna de aquellas Naciones, de quien se tiene sospecha alguna que primero la contraxo, le quiere dàr su nombre, teniendose por afrentada, que tan pestilente mal tenga origen, y nombre de su Patria, y assi lo atribuyen à otra."

52. "En nuestras partes tuvo origen esta enfermedad de los dichos Indios, y ellos fueron los que la pegaron, assi à los Franceses, Italianos, Españoles, y otras Naciones, que en el dicho tiempo se hallaron alli en Napoles porque en las Indias es muy común, y familiar, por ser, como eran ellos, muy luxuriosos, mundanos, y vorazes, que no solo comían carnes de animales, mas aun de hombres."

3. Judging Books by Their Covers

1. "A Maria santissima, madre del verbo Humanado; madre del hermoso Amor, Temor, y Sabiduria; mar benefico, estrella celestial, y patrona segura de todos los mortals."

2. "no contiene cosa contra nuestra Santa Fè Catholica, ni Christianas costumbres."

3. "A quien no desmayarà el animo la empressa de escribir, viendo unos Heroes ta grandes como nuestros aplaudidos (aun mas de los Estrangeros, que de nuestros Españoles) los doctissimos Feyjoò, Rodriguez, Martinez, y otros, que debiendo esculpirse en letras de oro cada rasgo de sus plumas, aun no bien estas descubren sus preciosos caracteres, quando yà la emulacion, ossadamente atrevida, quiere assaltarles; pero no es lo peor, que debe repararse, las impertinentes impugnaciones, con que obstinadamente solicitan combatirles, sino que pisando las lindes del decoro, suelen salpicar tambien los respetables, tal vez con desordenados satyricos vituperios."

4. "Siendo Medico Titular de la Villa de Gargantalaolla, me llamaron desde Aldea Nueva para que visitasse à cierta joven, que padecia un fluxo menstrual inmoderado, y periodico. [. . .] Entonces procurè con animo generoso echar mano de mis rotulas anti-emorragicas. [. . .] Tratè de destruir al fermento galico, cuerpo de dicha sombra, hechando mano del hydragiro, por confiar de experiencia, que es el fuego que consume à los accidos venereos, la carcel que los aprisiona, y el monarcha que los doma, por ser el mas noble precipitante, absorvente, y correctivo, que hasta el siglo presente se ha descubierto."

5. "A todos siete Planetas / En tu primer Tomo pones, / Y es, que en esto te antepo-

nes / A todas las influencias; / Pues Minerva de las sciencias, / Hazes, que yà los
metales, / En tan dulces minerales, / Cobre, plomo, azogue, estaño, / Se opongan
à tanto daño / Marte, Sol, Luna, en raudales."

4. The Awakening of Reason Produces Befuddlement

1. "Usado regularmente en plural. Enfermedad bien conocida y contagiosa, llamada
   tambien mal Francés, y Gálico, porque (segun algunos) la contraxeron los Fran-
   céses, quando entraron en Italia con el Rey Carlos Octavo, por medio del comercio ilicito que tuvieron con las mugéres de aquel Pais; pero otros dicen haverla padecido los españoles en el descubrimiento de las Indias, tambien con el motivo del
   trato inhonesto, que freqüentaron con las mugéres de aquellas nuevas Regiones.
   Ló cierto es ser enfermedad sumamente Antigua, cuyo conocimiento llegó à unas
   Provincias mas tarde que à otras, y que por indecente, ninguna quiere confessar
   haver sido la priméra à sentirla, y comunicarla" (REA 1726, s.v. "buba").
2. "Costando unas bubas menos, / que una libra de pepinos."
3. "En los hombres de negocios (como los papelistas, y los que son dados à la tarea
   literaria) haze el fermento galico su mayor assiento en la cabeza, y en el estomago.
   [...] Se debilita grandemente la cabeza con el continuo estudio [...] y por este
   motivo relucen tantos accidentes capitales, como emicranias, sorderas, &c."
4. "y no menos à los actos venereos con desproporcion."
5. "Dialogo entre un enfermo, y sus tripas en occasion de ir à tomar un caldo, por haver mandado el Medico no tomasse otro alimento hasta que bolviesse, y no haver
   buelto."
6. "**Enf.** Agua và, tripas mias, Agua và. / **Trip.** No por amor de Dios, tengase ustèd, /
   Salir nos dexe, y haganos mercèd. / **Enf.** Què se entiende salir? Tenganse allà. //
   Trip. Pues buelva el assesino. **Enf.** Bolverà. / **Trip.** Mirad que perecèmos. **Enf.**
   Tienen sed? / **Trip.** Necessidad tenèmos. **Enf.** Pues tenèd / Esse caldo en substancia. **Trip.** Bueno està. // **Enf.** Cien caldos llevan yà. Gran resistir. **Trip.** Mirad,
   que nuestro riesgo es el mayor. / **Enf.** Pues naden, sin que tiren á salìr. // **Trip.** San
   Blàs! San Blàs! **Enf.** Aguarden al Dotor, / Suspendan el clamor; que ha de venir, /
   Y no es razon sin èl, que aya clamor."
7. "La Sanguijuela primera / me embistió con gran enojo, / y Yo viendola tan fiera, /
   porque mas colera hiciera, / todo fue guiñarla el ojo."
8. "Pues tanto ardid / de este Pueblo me revelas: / Hà, Pobrecito Madrid, / cargado
   de Sanguijuelas!"
9. "Aquì està un Cavallero, /que es muy galante: / 2. En la Calle de Francos /debe
   hospedarse. / 1. Donde irà este que tiene / males de Francia? / 2. A la Calle, que dicen, / que es de la Zarza." The numbers at the beginning of the stanzas correspond
   to each one of the characters involved in the dialogue about the names of streets
   and urban geography.
10. "Dando las gracias al Señor Don Gaspar de Mendoza, hijo de los Excelentísimos
    Señores Marqueses de Mondejar, por haverle remitido las Obras de Pantaleon."
11. "Muriò el Gran Pantaleon; / pero no muriò su fama, / que el cuerpo de tales

obras, / no serà cuerpo sin alma. / Muriò pobre! Fue Poeta; / y de bubas: Què desgracia! /Dàr à entender, que tenia / poca lana, y essa en zarzas. / Influyò Apolo en su Numen, / Venus, Señor, le guiaba, / y Mercurio hizo à su vena, / que aùn sin discurrir, sudàra. / Su flaqueza le llevò / à ser triumpho de la Parca; / pero no llevò à su Musa, / siendo mas lo que adelgaza. / No muriò, no, sin la Uncion, / porque viendo que tardaba / el Cura, le diò el Barbero, / de Unciones, mas de una carga. / Era de ingenio tan vivo, / que aùn muerto (fue cosa rara!) / le vieron, que hasta los huessos / como azogados estaban. / Siendo en extremo discreto / lo dissimulò con gracia, / pues cada instante, y por todo, / se le caìa la baba. / El que muriesse me admira, / y no me admira sin causa: / pues quando muriò de veras /quien siempre viviò de chanza? / Aunque muriendo, su aplauso / para siempre le afianza, / que està segura la Gloria / siempre que no falte gracia. / A ser cierta la opinion / de que se heredan las almas, / dixera que era la tuya, / muy Apantaleonada." (Benegasi 38; The Great Pantaleon Died; / but his fame didn't die, / because the body of such works, / will not be a body without soul. / He died poor! He was a poet; / and because of buboes: What a disgrace! / It leads one to believe, that he had / little wool, and that (wool was) tangled in brambles. / Apollo influenced his numen, / Venus, Sir, guided him, / and Mercury influenced in his [poetic] vein, / such that even without running, he would sweat. / His weakness led him to become the triumph of Fate (Atropos); / but it didn't take his muse, / being [the muse], rather, the one who thins. / He didn't die, no, without the anointment, / because seeing that the priest / was running late, the barber gave him, / of anointments, more than one dose. / He was of such a lively wit, / that even when he was dead (it was a strange thing!) / they saw, that even the bones / were covered in quicksilver. / Being most discreet /he hid gracefully, / the fact that continually, and all over / he drooled. / It amazes me that he died, / and it doesn't amaze me without reason: / because when did anyone truly die / who always lived by wit? / Although he dies, his applause / guarantees him forever, / for glory is certain / as long as grace is not lacking. / If the opinion were true / that souls are inherited, / I would say that yours, / was very Pantaleon-like.)

12. "Entre los Modernos, unos culpan en las fiebres los Acidos, y quieren que se curen con Alkalis; otros culpan los Alkalis, y quieren que se curen con Acidos; y otros entre tanto se burlan de quanto se dice de Acidos, y Alkalis. ¿Infundió tres dictámenes tan opuestos Dios à Adán y Salomón? Pero en tantas partes de mis Obras tengo mostrado, que no hay cosa alguna bien assentada entre los Medicos, à excepción de curar las fiebres intermitentes con la Quina, el galico con el Mercurio, la disenteria con la Hipecuana, y la sarna con el Azufre, (y aun en estos remedios, en orden al quándo, al quánto, y al cómo hay batallas a cada passo), que es escusado detenerme mas ahora en cosa tan notoria."

For more information on the history of medical use of the bark of the cinchona tree (*Cinchona officinalis*), see the sidebar on p. 168.

13. "consiste unicamente en unos gusanillos, ó menudos insectos, cuya figura es muy parecida á la de la Tortuga. Estos gusanos viven dos, ó tres días separados de el

cuerpo, por lo que es facil contraher la sarna con el contacto de la ropa, ó guantes de el que padece esta infección."

14. "Es verdad que esta opinion no se funda en inspeccion ocular, sino en mera conjetura, tomada de que el mercurio, que es el grande antídoto de los gusanos, es el remedio específico de esta dolencia."

15. For a discussion on a particular literary ramification of germ theory, see the sidebar "From Humoral Theory to Germ Theory" (p. 107) and the analysis of Nicolás Fernández de Moratín's *Arte de las putas.*

16. "Algunos Phýsicos, con el señor Paulini, citado en el Diario de los Sabios de París año de 1704, estienden esto mucho mas, aseverando que todas, ò casi todas las enfermedades epidémicas consisten en unos insectos, que passan de unos cuerpos à otros, en los quales, por medio de la propagacion, aumentan su número; por lo qual no hay que admirar, que de un cuerpo solo tocado de enfermedad contagiosa se vaya estendiendo el daño à todo un Reyno."

17. "Es probable, que todas las enfermedades contagiosas provienen de varias especies de insectos que se engendran en el cuerpo humano."

18. "los Principes, que poseen las piedras preciosas de mejor calidad, y en mayor cantidad, adornandose continuamente de ellas en los anillos, y otros ajuares, no solo no viven mas que los demás hombres, pero, á proporcion, mucho mas que los de la inferior condicion, padecen la alevosía de los venenos."

19. "los celebres medicos y medicas, que haviendo muerto santamente, son venerados por nuestra Santa Madre Iglesia Catholica Romana."

20. "Desengañado, Santos mios, de las grandezas del Mundo, os sacrifico este Tomo primero de mi Obra."

21. "Y pues los ojos del cuerpo no pueden por sì discernir lo dicho, se conseguirà, aplicandoles algun microscopio; entonces sì, que registuràn al Mercurio dissuelto en la orina, formando diferentes aculeos, ò puntas Salinas, como unos agudos cuchillos; porque dicho acido salino venereo le hizo perder al Mercurio su figura globulosa, la mas blanda, y suave de todas las figuras."

22. "De las Sales Hydraulicas previene el expertissimo Physico Conde de la Garaye: dice este insigne Varon, en comprobacion de las famosas virtudes, y eficacia de estas Sales" . . . "El cèlebre Academico Chymista Monsiur Geofroy, de la Real de las Ciencias de Parìs, presentò una memoria en aquel sabio Congresso, la que se extractò despues el Jornal de los Sabios."

23. "Salen à luz en un tiempo tan abundante de Escritos, que son, sin exageracion, muchos mas los Autores, que los que han de leerlos. He dicho Autores, no siendo en realidad assi, pues apenas he visto tiempo tan escaso de esta especie de hombres. Ha ya diez años, que no se hace en España otra cosa, que traducir à nuestro Idioma muchos escritos de otras Naciones, de modo que como si se huviera acabado en ella el ingenio, se buscan los Escritores Estrangeros, para tributarles aquel honor, que debiera con mucha razón adjudicarsele à los nuestros."

24. "llave maestra, para abrir las puertas al verdadero conocimiento del mercurio, remedio, que en forma de unciones, vence las fatigas, hijas del morbo gálico."

25. "una melancholia tan honda, y tan desesperada, que no se me puso en aquel tiempo figura à los ojos, ni idèa en el alma."

26. "la furia de sus recipes, y sus desaciertos [...] y sin saber el nombre, el apellido, la casta, ni el genio de las dolencias las curaban, y perseguian à costa de mi pellejo con todos los disparates, y frioleras, que se venden en las Boticas."

27. "Muchas veces la oì llamar Hypocondrìa, otras Coagulo en la sangre, Bubas, Hictericia, Passion de alma, Melancolìa morbo, Obstrucciones, Brujas, Echizos, Amores, y Demonios."

28. "todos los males, que se resisten, que hacen porra en los cuerpos, y que se burlan de otras medicinas, se deben conocer por Bubas, y curar con unciones."

29. "ahunque yo ignoraba como ellos la casta de mi passion, yo bien sabìa, que no eran Bubas, porque estaba cierto, que ni en herencia, ni en hurto, ni en cambio, ni en emprestito habìa recibido semejantes muebles; ni en mi vida sentì en mis humores tales inquilinos."

30. "ò à lo menos haberme libertado de la multitud de las congojas, y dolores, que lleva detràs de sì este utilissimo medicamento."

31. "una habitacion hermosa, capaz, y distinguida con algunos escudos, y tarjetas."

32. "anegado en pegajoso, y fetido sudor, rebuelto en congojas, y tragado de agonias, y sofocaciones. [...] La cabeza monda de cabello, y plagada à trechos de costras, berrugas, postillas, tuberculos, y otros promontorios, y chichones. La boca cubierta de vexigas, encharcada en babas. [...] Los labios negros, duros, y arremangados, como el borde de un barreño; la nariz llena de mordiscones, y tan arañada, y comida, que enseñaba por sus roturas los huessos de los lacrimales, y las orbitas de los ojos: ladraba en vez de articular vozes."

33. "hozicar en otros sucios, y descorteses vicios."

34. "diòle segundo aviso con demonstraciones mas vivas, y sensibles, rociandole toda la pièl de manchas menudas à manera de lentejuelas versicolores, y tan inquietas, que no las pudo acallar con las uñas, las sangrias, las unturas, las orchatas, las aguas de malvas, y otros absorventes, y dulcificantes."

35. "postillas, tuberculos, y costras en la frente, orejas, boca, cabeza, y otras partes vergonzosas de su cuerpo."

36. "las pildoras de el leño Guiaco, el de sasafras, la zarzaparrilla, la raiz de china, la soponaria, y los mas exquisitos alexifarmacos, como el antidoto, el agua cardiaca, y los polvos de palmario, el agua theriacàl de Rondeleto."

37. "Aquella parte de el cuerpo, que recibe el veneno, es la que primeramente se daña, luego se comunica, y corre por las venas, y de estas al higado, en donde adquiere una depravada disposicion, con la que destruye la bondad de la sangre, y de todos los demàs liquidos."

38. "Es regularmente el morbo galico enfermedad perezosa y diuturna, y los que la padecen andan arrastrando con la vida muchos años."

39. "brutalidades de su costumbre [...] le corrompiò las partes sòlidas de sus huessos, tendones, membranas, y nervios, desgarrando, y royendo toda su textura, y conformidad. Plagòle de llagas, fistulas, cavernas, cancros, y topos: arrancòle todo el cabello de la barba, y la cabeza: comiòle las narizes, tragòle las gorjas, tapiòle los

oìdos, y finalmente lo introduxo la calentura ectica, que es la que rapidissimamente le està sorbiendo el humido vital."

40. "No quiero hablarte mas en las causas de la condenacion de este ajusticiado; que aunque soy Demonio, me averguenzo de que salga por mis negros labios la relacion de sus feos delitos."

41. "les borra de su conocimiento los peligros, los Dolores, y aun todo el horror de el Infierno."

42. "sumergido en mas abundante, y hediondo sudor, descompuesta toda la harmonia de el semblante, furioso de miraduras, y lidiando con tan rigurosos accidentes, y congojas, que sospechè, que aquellas eran las que daban el ultimo termino à su vida."

43. "fortaleza de el argento vivo, y la rebeldia de el pegajoso humor producen essa batalla tan furiosa."

44. "las que los hombres solicitan, por no descontentar a su gula, y por agassajar à su lascivia, no merecen la compassion, ni el disimulo."

45. "sin duda el antiveneno de todas sus ansias, y no permitiria, que llegassen à inficionar sus pensamientos, ni los mas penetrantes, y agudos espinos de la lascivia."

46. "Aunque no tuviesse este voluntario, y asqueroso insulto otros enemigos, ni aflicciones, que el enojo, el asco, el desprecio, y olvido con que es tratado el que le sufre, havian de huir los hombres cien leguas de su contagio."

47. "todos los que se ven libres de su impression, se rien, y mofan de el que la padece."

48. "bien empleado le está, con esto verèmos si escarmienta: si se estuviera recogido en casa, ò empleado con las gentes de honra, no le sucederia esto: no hay que tener lastima de el que se busca, y se toma por su mano los males; y si se lo quiso menga, que se lo tenga."

49. "apenas puse recta mi figura, vì anublado el retrete de el reboltoso nubarron de los demonios que nos seguian, que con rabiosa algazara se llevaron el espiritu de aquella asquerosa carne á padecer eternamente mayores castigos."

50. "ya porque era el simple cubierto mas vecino y mas desocupado ó ya porque aquel lugar es el mas oportuno para sacudirse de las humedades que se pegan á los que andan ociosos por la Corte."

51. "Entre el seo Piscator, que este es el sitio propio de los Estrelleros. Venga acá, que aquí tiene el Mercurio que ha menester, y déxese de perseguir al del Cielo, que ese no le ha de chupar los malos humores. Pase adelante, que aquí vomitará las Catalinas que se le han pegado con el comercio de las Pepas y las Antonias."

52. For further discussion on the double meaning of "stars" as wounds produced by syphilitic buboes, see the section below on María Ladvenant y Quirante, and the link to Francisco Delicado's *La lozana andaluza* (1528).

53. "Callen en hora mala los báberas [. . .] que las bubas solamente las arrebañan los bobos, los miserables, los desocupados y aborrecidos de las conversaciones honradas."

54. In "Torres Villarroel, Quevedo y El Bosco," Russell P. Sebold comments on elements of connection and differentiation between the two authors. In his introduction to Torres Villarroel's *Visiones y visitas de Torres,* he also points to the consonance between Torres's *Vida* and Quevedo's *La cuna y la sepultura* (xxx).

Henry Ettinghausen's "Torres Villarroel's Self-Portrait" traces their correlation with more detail, especially showing the influence of Quevedo in the writing of Torres's *Vida*. The section "Los procedimientos expresivos" in Martínez Mata's *Los "Sueños" de Diego Torres Villarroel* offers an organized approach to Torres's craft and shows the connections with Quevedo's writing. Also dealing with their proximity in technique, in particular for the satirical representation of characters, is Paul Ilie's "Grotesque Portraits in Torres Villarroel."

55. "un hedor mas intolerable que regüeldo de estómago avinagrado, mas pegajoso que gargajo de vieja comilona, y tan espeso y tupido que se podia serrar."

56. "estaban purgando sus escandalosos gustos, y sus culpables majaderías, hasta dos docenas de delinqüentes tontos, Galanes morciélagos, lascivos de boca de noche, que andan con la luxuria de rebozo, en acecho de los portales obscuros y los meaderos escondidos, enamorados bozales, que compran los delitos y la condenacion á costa de su pellejo, y finalmente pecadores roñosos, y chalanes mentecatos, que piensan que por poco dinero se puede encontrar buena muger y sabrosa salud."

57. "los tumbados sensuales, empezaron á descargar sobre mí otro turbion de satirillas arrolladas entre madejones de espuma y mazorcas de flema, porque arrojaban las palabras de los muladares de sus podridas bocas, embadurnadas de mugre, rellenas de podre, y tan rebutidas en el seboso estiercol de sus babas, que ni se podían distinguir lo que eran, ni conocer á dos tirones su significado."

58. "Raspóse los labios con el mangón de la camisa, y revolviéndose con pereza lastimosa sobre los codos, nos presentó la cara; pero, ¡Jesus mil veces! tan disforme, y tan abominable, que no puede tener el Infierno semejante monstruosidad. Tenia acinado en la frente y en la mollera un pedregal de gomas, y talparias garrafales; en la gorja un hormiguero de berrugas de á folio; y en los brazos un enxambre de sobrehuesos, porcinos, garrapatas, y otros burujones hinchados y rabiosos. Estaba con la boca de par en par, arremangados los labios sobre las narices y la barba; y las honduras de las carrilleras tan emborradas de porquería, que me pareció un barreñon en tiempo de mondongo, relleno de sebo, sangraza y cebollones. Andaban sus dientes esparramados por los arrabales de la caverna de su boca, y quando queria revolver la lengua (la que tenia mas torpe que el porro de un Vaquero) para pronunciar alguna voz, le sonaba la dentadura como costal de nueces en poder de muchachos."

59. The proximity of Torres Villarroel's work to Quevedo's is evident: "Saturdays he tended to send some eggs, with as much stubble, by virtue of his own hairs and grey hairs, that they could could aspire to become a mayor or to practice law. Well, using the fire shovel in place of the ladle and sending out a bowl of stony soup, was very normal, A thousand times I came upon bugs, and sticks, and burlap of the sort that was spun, in the pot; and he put it all in so that it would establish some presence in the intestines." (Quevedo, *El buscón* 44; Los viernes solía enviar unos huevos, con tantas barbas, a fuerza de pelos y canas suyas, que pudieran pretender corregimiento o abogacía. Pues meter el badil por cucharón y enviar una escudilla de caldo empedrada, era muy ordinario. Mil veces topé yo sabandijas, y palos, y

estopa de la que hilaba, en la olla; y todo lo metía para que hiciese presencia en las tripas.)

60. "tomando estaba sudores / Marica en el Hospital; / que el tomar era costumbre, / y el remedio es el sudar" (4:497). "A Marica la chupona / las goteras de su cama / la metieron la salud / en la venta de la zarza" (4:414).

61. The article "la" was used to characterize the name of a public woman.

62. "por boca de un moribundo: / con desengaño profundo / acusaré tus errores, [...] uno que en Martin Anton/ *tomando estaba sudores.*"

63. "Disfrazados de Galenos / andan Perico y Marica, / y el uno y el otro aplica / por triacas los venenos."

64. "anda el Anti-Medicato / vertiendo sus aforismos: / soltando está solecismos / que no podrá reparar, / y la cura se ha de errar, / porque en esta hipocondría / se receta la sangría, / *y era remedio el sudar.*"

65. "En venerables bestias se montaba / toda la Escuela, que Mercurio aprueba, / y cada qual en la cabeza lleva, / señales de la ciencia, que estudiaba: // Viva, y beba, en confuso se escuchaba, / de pintados chillones en voz nueva, / y en todo Licenciado se renueva / al escuchar el viva, tanta baba: // Toda la gente, y la Ciudad se emboba, / azia la Plaza el Esquadròn arriba, / corrense Toros, sorbese una cuba; // Cenan, y se resfrian de la soba, / y acaba la funcion, que dixe arriba, / en baba, beba, viva, boba, y buba."

66. For more on the environment and organization of the hospital wards treating *gálico,* in particular the Hospital de Santiago in Toledo during the 1600s, see chap. 5, "Between Body and Soul: Treatment at the Hospital de Santiago," in Berco's *From Body to Community.*

5. Inhospitable Hospitals

1. "Si Castro fue à Anton Martin / con su Romance Jocoso, / que yo le embie el Mercurio, / no debe estrañar el Docto."

2. "Erase un borrachon Tunante, con sus amenazas de Petardista, rubio, tuerto, tiñoso, malas barbas, rodeado de paperas, engullido en sarna, atiborrado de bubas, y esclavo perdurable de la universal laceria con que paga la señora luxuria las malas inclinaciones de los apetitos prontos, rateros y baratos. Era su merced el dicho Señor Don Desdicha, un vivo y asqueroso retrato de la podre, una copia andante de la desvergüenza, un mapa de la embriaguez, y un Anton Martin en abreviatura."

3. There was a constant influx of patients in Spanish hospitals. For example, Elisa Torres Santana describes the statistical variation of *gálico* patients in the Hospital de las Bubas during Philip V's reign: "The increase is perceived in the hike in contagion of venereal diseases observed in the Hospital de las Bubas, which during the War of the Spanish Succession went from attending the usual monthly average of 40–50 men and 20–25 women to registering 130–150 men and 30–40 women." (333–34; El aumento se percibe por el incremento del contagio de enfermedades venéreas, apreciado en el Hospital de las Bubas, que durante la Guerra de Sucesión

pasó de atender una media habitual de 40–50 hombres y 20–25 mujeres al mes, a registrar a 130–150 hombres y 30–40 mujeres.)

4. "Al joven, que sin saber / Qué cosa lujuria fuera, / Por sola la vez primera / Que visitó á una mujer, / Vé el pobre que ha menester / Entrar en Santa María, // Le cayó la Lotería."

5. "Por la misericordia de Dios, todavia dura fuera de los muros de Salamanca un Casaròn Viejo, y pobre, que es la sola acogida, y el remedio de todos los pobres heridos de la lepra, la sarna, las bubas, y otros achaques contagiosos, y el unico amparo, y hospedaje de los Peregrinos, Passageros, Vagos, y otros infelices, à quienes la fortuna, y la desdicha tiene en el mundo sin la triste cobertera de una choza. [. . .] rechazados de su piedad, para que las hediondas malicias de sus dolencias no añadan más perniciosas infecciones à los calenturientos, y à los postrados de otros achaques menos pegajosos, que se curan en sus Salas."

6. "sobre la necesidad de prohibir la impresión y venta de las jácaras y romances vulgares, por dañosos a las costumbres públicas, y de susutituirles con otras canciones verdaderamente nacionales, que unan la enseñanza y el recreo."

7. For context on the unification of hospitals and the work of Meléndez Valdés in this regard, see Astorgano Abajo's "El regalismo borbónico y la unificación de hospitales."

8. "No he podido hacer este cotejo con los libros y diarios del Hospital de San Joaquín, porque ni en él he hallado tales libros de entradas ni ninguna formalidad en este ramo, ni más que unos cuadernetes sucios y sin forro, cuales no se tendrían en la más miserable taberna. [. . .] Tampoco remito a Vuestra Alteza estados comparados del Hospital de Dios Padre, porque curándose en él sólo el mal *gálico* y en una escasa temporada de cuarenta días de primavera, y entrando y saliendo todos los enfermos en un mismo día señalado para ello por su Patrono, no puede haber lugar a estas diferencias como en los demás. Pero [. . .] sus enfermos toman las raciones exorbitantes de cinco y aun de diez libras de pan, una y dos de carnero, y media azumbre y una de vino; que las panaderas, el pastor, el aguador, y parece que cuantos iban a él, iban sólo a comer y beber, y que pudieran con sobra reducirse sus raciones a la mitad de lo que son" (Meléndez, *Teatro y poesía* 495).

9. "mando que al Hospital General de la ciudad de Ávila, para cuyo establecimiento estuvo por Real Orden comisionado mi marido cuando se hallaba de Oidor en la Chancillería de Valladolid, y al cual miró siempre con particular cariño e interés, tanto por el amor que tenía a los pobres, como por los afanes, y aún la enfermedad que le costó dicho establecimiento y reunión [. . .] se le den hasta en cantidad de veinte mil reales de vellón."

10. "Tiene *Piura* un Hospital al cuidado de la Religion *Bethleemitica;* y aunque se curan en èl toda suerte de enfermedades, es famoso por la del *Morbo Galico;* pues contribuyendo sensiblemente para su mejor curacion la qualidad del Clima, acuden à èl de todas partes los que se hallan infestados de este mal; y en muchos se experimenta, que con menos cantidad del especifico, que se suela aplicar en otros Paìses, y sin tanta molestia del paciente, se logra el fin de restablecerse à la primera salud."

11. "sabes con evidencia que eres un reo sentenciado a muerte, aunque ignores quando ú como se ha de executar la sentencia."

12. "Animate Christiano y pasa á aceptar la muerte con todas las condiciones que el Señor, te la tiene preparada, sea de una suave enfermedad, sea con crueles dolores."

6. The Transformation of the Medical Understanding of *Gálico*

1. "Presbytero, Medico-Socio de la Real Sociedad Medica de Madrid, y de la Villa de San Vicente" (Brunet, front page).

2. "mas que olvidados de los propios, tanto, que, sin exageracion, puedo decirte, que estos grandes hombres estàn entre nosotros dos veces muertos."

3. "El galico es incurable, y ciertamente mata à el enfermo en llegando su causa à corromper alguna parte interna. [. . .] Si llega à hacer concreción de materias en alguna de las internas vísceras, que es lo que se llama apostema, es irremediable."

4. "Esto lo acreditarà de docto, y disculparà el ruìn exito de la curativa."

5. "mas estos alivios, despues de padecer algunas contingencias, no son de mucha duracion."

6. "un traydor enemigo, [que] dà la herida, y esconde la mano, y la cara."

7. "la gota arthetica, la hipocondria, la piedra, el cancro, la lepra, la flegma salada, las ulceras malignas, las rheumas impertinentes."

8. See the sidebar "*¡Eres un incordio!*" (p. 223) for a more developed discussion on the medical understanding of the word and its popular meaning.

9. "Tomad de harina de linaza una libra, de queso añejo rallado sutilmente media libra, cuezase todo en caldo de pies de puerco, y hagase emplastro, y ponedlo sobre el encordio; y sabed que es un grande remedio."

10. "Esta es el agua con que grandes Autores curaron el morbo galico desesperado. Curbo assegura ser testigo de vista, de tres dolientes tan tullidos que no se podian rebolver en la cama, y solo con esta agua cobraron perfectissima salud."

11. "Quien tomara cinco, ò seis dias por la mañana en ayunas dos onzas de zumo de limon agrio, mixturado con dos cucharadas de azucar, quedarà libre de la gonorrhea, como consta por infinidad de experiencias."

12. "Què maravillas nos refieren de ellos sus Autores! Què Milagros nos dicen haver conseguido con su aplicacion! El Medico visoño al leer esto ya le parece, que le han conferido despotico dominio sobre la muerte. Toma aquellas armas, y quando se discurria ser vencedor, se halla vencido, porque es una rueca lo que le parecia espada."

13. "las funestas consequencias que ha ocasionado muchas veces el Mercurio por su mala elaboracion, por administrarse en excesiva cantidad, ò por no hallarse preparados los enfermos hasta aquel grado que es menester [. . .] se conocerá quanto importa à la humanidad desterrar en quanto sea posible el uso si interno como externo del Mercurio en la curación del galico."

14. "arriesgadas, y que obrando alguna vez sobre los intestinos pueden causar colicas muy peligrosas, y que si llegan à comunicarse a la masa de la sangre explicando su

accion sobre las fibras de la viscera mas delicada, causarán terribles irritaciones, que se corrigen dificultosamente."

15. "el licor anti galico de *Visseman* celebre Cirujano Inglés, el licor anitivenero de *Ricardo Hautesureq;* el del Varon de *Wanswieten;* las pildoras de *Pablo Hartmanc;* los anises de *Mr. Keyser,* mi gragéa anti-galica, y otras composiciones de la misma estofa."

16. "lo cura todo, como se maneje con acierto."

17. There is also a noticeable formal change. The typographic setting of the Spanish version, which avoids using the letter "c" with cedilla (ç) and the "long s" (ſ), and spells out the word "que," which had been previously written as a contraction (a letter "q" with a tilde on top). All these typographical features, which were present in Calvo's work back in 1703, were abolished in the publication of 1772.

18. "por el *Padre,* porque las particulas del semen comunican el embrion, e virus Venereo de que están inficionadas: y por la *Madre,* porque proveyendo esta de alimento al fetus todos los nueve meses de su preñado, al mismo tiempo le hace participar del mal que ella padece [. . .] un padre, que padece esta enfermedad, engendra algunas veces hijos verdaderamente inficionados de ella, y cubiertos de ulceras, aunque la madre esté sana."

19. "acaso tambien todas estas Historias, no son mas que invenciones de los enfermos, que con mentiras procuran ocultar sus desordenes."

20. "Debe tambien entenderse del uso abominable, y contra la naturaleza, entre personas de un mismo sexo; pues de este ultimo modo, el que está sano, adquiere de la misma manera el mal del que está inficionado y aun un mal mucho mas peligroso."

21. "pues no es creíble que jamás pueda engendrarse en el cuerpo humano un veneno tan pernicioso, y activo, sino que es una comparacion que sirve mas para dar alguna idea del virus Venereo, que para explicar exactamente su naturaleza."

22. "el mal Venereo se produce por los animales pequeños que nadan en la sangre."

23. "Pero no me detendré en refutar las ideas de los que creen, que el virus Venereo no es otra cosa mas que un numeroso enjambre de animales muy pequeños, ágiles, vivos, y muy fecundos, que recibidos una vez se multiplican prontamente, se mudan con frequencia à diferentes partes del cuerpo, que pican, agujerean, y muerden las partes à donde se pegan, y de este modo las inflaman, corroen, y ulceran; y finalmente, sin alteración alguna de los humores, producen todos los simptomas del mal Venereo."

24. "y en una palabra, de todas las enfermedades, trastornando toda la theorica de la Medicina."

25. "del mismo modo que los Perros de caza destruyen las Liebres, ò los Alcones à las Palomas."

26. "Estos son los artificios que este astuto, y desvergonzado Charlatan tuvo la osadía de exponer al publico en un Siglo tan ilustrado, y instruído en materias de Physica, como el nuestro, y en una Ciudad como Paris, llena de sugetos tan hábiles."

27. "Despues de haver inficionado las partes por donde se introdujo, penetra insensiblemente à la sangre, lo que segun mi dictamen, sucede de dos modos, ò por la

circulacion de la sangre, que regando las partes dañadas, recoge de paso algo del virus, ò por la circulacion de limpha, que bolviendo de estas mismas partes, lleva consigo à la sangre á donde vá à parar, por vasos particulares, muchas gotas de este virus."

28. "suelen carecer de libros por falta de medios, y abundar en el pueblo el Mal Venéreo por sobra de vicios" (Astruc and Galisteo v).

29. "En la segunda mitad del siglo se va a producir en la España ilustrada la puesta al día de la Cirugía y a Medicina; las traducciones de la bibliografía extranjera serán las que hagan posible esta realidad. [. . .] La intensa actividad desarrollada en torno a la traducción por los hermanos Juan y Félix Galisteo Xiorro, cirujano y medico respectivamente, hace que podamos considerarlos como verdaderos traductores de textos médicos gracias a las numerosas versiones de tratados de medicina y cirugía que publican incansablemente entre los años 1761 y 1807, con las que introducen en nuestro país los últimos avances de la medicina europea ilustrada."

30. "Son excusados los elogios ni la recomendación para una obra que está ya tan acreditada, cuyo método es hoy seguido por todos los Facultativos juiciosos, y que ha merecido que el Soberano apruebe la elección que de ella han hecho los Maestros á cuyo cargo está la enseñanza de este ramo de Cirugía en el nuevo Colegio erigido en esta Corte baxo su Real protección" (Astruc and Galisteo vi).

7. Naming the Disease: The French Malady

1. "Pues que tanta parte del oro destas Indias ha pasado á Italia é Francia, y aun á poder assi mesmo de los moros y enemigos de España, y por todas las otras partes del mundo, bien es que como han goçado de nuestros sudores, les alcançe parte de nuestros dolores é fatigas, porque de todo, á lo menos por la una ó por la otra manera, del oro ó del trabajo, se acuerden de dar muchas graçias a Dios."

2. "Muchas veces, en Italia me reia, oyendo á los italianos deçir el *mal francés,* y á los franceses llamarle el *mal de Nápoles;* y en la verdad, los unos y los otros le açertaran el nombre si le dixeran el mal de las Indias."

3. "hay peste de traductores, porque casi todas las traducciones son una peste."

4. "Lo que digo es que, con efecto, los malos, los perversos, los ridículos, los extravagantes o los idiotas traductores son los que principalísimamente nos han echado a perder la lengua, corrompiéndonos las voces tanto como el alma. Ellos son los que han pegado a nuestro pobre idioma el mal francés, para cuya curación no basta ni aun todo el mercurio preparado por la discreta pluma del gracioso Fracastorio *unicum illum Ulcera qui jussit castas tractare camenas.*

   "Ellos son los que han hecho que ni en las conversaciones, ni en las cartas familiares, ni en los escritos públicos nos veamos de polvo *gálico,* quiero decir, que parece no gastan otros polvos en la salvadera que arena de la Loira, del Ródano o del Sena, según espolvorean todo cuanto escriben de galicismos o de francesadas."

5. "La cual, sin embargo de ser problema entre los sabios si es más perjudicial que provechosa, ha logrado, no obstante, un séquito prodigioso. No hay librería pú-

blica ni particular, no hay celda, no hay gabinete, no hay antesala, ni aun apenas hay estrado donde no se encuentre, tanto, que hasta los perrillos de falda andan jugueteando con ella sobre los sitiales."

6. "Escríbenle sin regla ni cuidado; / Háblanle por costumbre; / Sus delicados fueros no veneran; / Nadie lo estudia; todos le adulteran."

7. "Ellos son, o Dalmiro, los perversos / Traidores al lenguage de su tierra, / Y que haciéndole están continua guerra. / Oh! quiera el justo Apolo, / (Pues se lo pido así en mis pobres versos) / Que quanto aquéllos en su vida escriban, / Quede, como archivado en protocolo, / Del mas necio Librero en la trastienda; / Que ni los Confiteros la reciban, / Ni aun merezca servir para cohetes, / O para alfombra en lóbregos retretes! / Sí, legos Traductores: / Caiga sobre vosotros mi anatema, / Viciosos Corruptores, / Los que á la pura lengua Castellana / Pegasteis una Gálica apostema, / Que en su cuerpo no dexa parte sana."

8. "Que solo de ello los gusanos vivan / Y eterno polvo empuerque tal hacienda."

9. "Dos siglos ha Maestra de las Ciencias, / Y en el nuestro Aprendiz de las del Norte!"

10. "*Dr. Murillo.* Diré o cognominaré el morbo, si Vm. tiene probabilidad para darme esta licencia; pero no daré el antidotal específico, porque entonces haría que Vm. desde sus cavernosos meatus eche la última baba. // *Dr. Mera.* Siendo Vm. médico no necesitaba mi licencia para advertirme del mal y avisarme del remedio. Mas éste ya se entiende mi Doctor, cuál sea. Quiere Vm. decir el uso del mercurio. // *Dr. Murillo.* Sí, Señor, unas unciones metálico-mercuriales."

11. "*Dr. Mera.* Mas ¿dónde padezco yo mal francés? // *Dr. Murillo.* En todos sus óseos intercostales, en todas sus miológicas vísceras, en toda su rubra quilífera substancia, en todo su maquinal cuerpo y en todo su inteligencial espíritu. Todo Vm. está amiasmado de morbo gálico, y afrancesado en todo el pútido aliento que respire."

12. "Pero vamos, que es Vm. hijo legítimo de los más altísonos poetas, y que para decir una cosa usa de más metáforas y alegorías que todos ellos. Como al presente, para decirme que soy adicto a los franceses."

13. "quieren que sigamos su piocha poética, dejando nuestro rizado copete y nuestra encastillada cofia; su frigorosa naturalidad, abandonando nuestra meteórica altísona sublimidad. Así ha dado Vm. en ser galiquiento. Digo otra vez que necesita babeo."

14. "*Dr. Murillo.* Alto allí, Señor mío. No quiera el Trino Omnipotente, que yo vea ni lea a los tales Monsiures. Eso sería dar en ateísta, por eso no quiero doctrinarme en ese maldito idioma, que vuelve a todos heresiarcas. No los he de leer. Pero he oído que ellos, y muy en capite Voltaire, herejete más hereje que el mismo Arrio dicen con herética pravedad que esos poetas ignoraban lo que se poetizaban. // *Dr. Mera.* Le han dicho a Vm. muy mal. Lo primero que ha de advertir Vm., es (óigalo bien, no sea que me ande con que también éste es centón francés) que en todas las naciones ha habido literatos de buen gusto, que han hablado o contra la corrupción de la poesía, o contra el abuso de ella."

15. "Apolo ha decretado ahora este castigo a los asesinos de nuestra lengua y de ellos ha elegido con especialidad a los semigalos, por incorregibles y porque han ocasio-

nado la muerte a la respetable matrona con la enfermedad más sucia y hedionda. Hicieron ímpetu en ella con furiosa desesperación. Y, viéndose debilitada, ya con la horrible persecución que la suscitaron casi en mi tiempo los culteranos, ya con innumerables martirios que recibió de los equivoquistas y conceptistas posteriores, ya con la inmensa y extravagante carga de adornos con que, creyendo hermosearla, la abrumaron (y faltó poco para que la ahogasen) los predicadores y novelistas de este vuestro siglo, sin defensores, sin padrinos que le valiesen, resistió vanamente los insultos de la caterva engalicada y se dejó violar a más no poder. Púsose hidrópica, contrajo la enfermedad que la comunicaron y abortó, en fin, del infame y forzado ayuntamiento una muchedumbre de molas, frutos espurios de la ceguedad y de una furia desesperada."

16. "mui bien, me dixo; pues si un sisthema por el modo de la francia se intentase introducir en el Pais, aseguro á U. (me replicó con viveza) que mas bien querríamos que los americanos españoles continuasen por un siglo súbditos obedientes baxo del opresivo goviero del Rey de España, que verles submergidos en las calamidades del abominable sisthema de los franceses!"

17. "Mui bien, dixe, y es precisamente para evitar un contagio semejante, y precavernos con tiempo del influxo galico, que hemos pensado en emancipamos inmediatamente; y formar alianza con los E.U. de America y con la Ynglaterra á fin de combater unanimente (si fuese necesario) los monstruosos y abominables principios de la pretendida Libertad francesa!"

18. These five issues had been lost but were rediscovered by scholar Elisabel Larriba at the University of Connecticut's Dodd Research Center. Larriba reproduced the text of these issues in her article "La última salida al ruedo del *Memorial Literario*."

19. "Los franceses fueron el objeto primitivo de las críticas que se empezaron a publicar en el *Memorial literario* en los primeros números; los franceses son y serán el blanco de nuestros tiros […] y así nuestro periódico será como siempre anti-francés."

20. "Sermón del R. P. Fr. Josef *Malaparte* (alias Botellas) predicado en Gentil, y traducido en Sibarita por el Padre compañero el Ex-español, Patriarca de la legua. Puesto en castellano arbitrario por un curioso oyente que entiende algo de telégrafos."

21. "Españoles, ¡mal empecé! Vasallos, ¡mal dije! Demonios, que ningún otro título merecen los *rebeldes,* ¿cómo tenéis valor de hacer armas contra vuestro tan legítimo como bien admitido rey?"

22. "Mi familia edificará el sólido trono premeditado de la redención de la Europa. Hará que cada cual atienda a su juego, y ¡ay de vosotros, si os metéis en hacer una pepitoria tan siquiera! Si lo intentáis, ¿qué es intentar?, si lo imagináis solamente, dejadme tomar por lo menos un alón para probarla, que yo os aseguro por Baco, mi dios tutelar, que el mal gálico hará en vuestros hogares lo que acostumbra, y no os libertaréis de la tal plaga sin embargo blasonáis de haber descubierto el específico contra su influjo venenoso."

23. "anotado honrosamente en la lista sanguinaria de Bonaparte."

24. "el monstruo mayor que el infierno ha vomitado."

25. "jactanciosamente, à la *francesa,* [han hecho] profesión de regicídas, atéos, vandídos y en una palabra, jacobinos."

26. "todo el mundo leyó los libros franceses, ó el diluvio de traducciones afrancesadas, que alteraron y afrancesaron nuestra armoniosa lengua y lo peor nuestras costumbres y nuestras ideas [...] y por este vil conocimiento toda la nacion se vistió, comió, anduvo, visitó, tosió y estornudó *á la francesa.*"

27. "Contagiados con el mismo espíritu de inconstancia y de vértigo, hemos aplaudido y execrado con el mismo entusiasmo francés las sucesivas constituciones, partidos y gefes que rápidamente se sucedieron y precipitaron unos sobre otros, envueltos en sangre y carnicería, nunca vista en las proscripciones mas espantosas que conoce la historia."

28. "¡Feliz goticismo, barbarie y fanatismo español! ¡felices con nuestros frayles y con nuestra Inquisicion, que en el concepto de la ilustracion francesa nos lleva tras de las otras naciones un siglo por lo menos de atraso! Oh! ¡y si pudiéramos recular aun otros dos! Esto seria alejarnos trescientas leguas morales de la Francia, ya que no podemos separarnos físicamente de unos vecinos tan contagiosos."

29. "Lejos pues de conciliar la benevolencia francesa tomemos todas las medidas posibles para separarnos eternamente de esta contagiosa y pérfida nacion, de esta tierra maldita en donde se viola la santa hospitalidad tan agradable á Dios."

30. "vecindad pestífera, es preciso construir un alto y grueso muro que separe al pueblo escogido de estos tártaros excomulgados."

31. "la filosofía francesa exige precauciones muy mas superiores á quantas se toman contra la fiebre amarilla y todas las pestes."

32. "no faltaron algunos pocos, P. Isla, P. Feijóo, P. Interian de Ayala, que, llevados de la pestífera corriente, dieron cabida en sus escritos á formas galicanas."

33. "Así se daba á conocer el gran secreto del lenguaje español, conviene á saber, que las causas que habían concurrido á formarle, esas concurrían á mantenerle en su ser; quiero decir, la religión en conformidad con el amor patrio; causas ambas, que dábanse las manos amigablemente en los varones religiosos antedichos, por más que en algunos el trato frecuente con los heridos del mal gálico derramase la maldita ponzoña que ponía en peligro la sanidad de la lengua."

34. "¡Bendito Dios! Sigan gabacheando, barbarizando, modernizando, que al fin esto es hecho; el romance castizo se murió de gálico mal; lo que peor es, murióse á necias, sin esperanza de pasar á mejor vida."

8. Naming the Disease: *Mal americano*

1. "los unos y los otros le açertaran el nombre si le dixeran el mal de las Indias."

2. "como más inmediato, proveyese de treinta hombres con su cabo, con armas, municiones y víveres, así para nuestro resguardo como para que con el temor de las bocas de fuego (que le tienen grande) consigamos reducirlos á pueblos, á que vivan conforme á la ley de Dios, con buenas costumbres y policía Cristiana."

3. "No se espantará V.S. de que le tiemble la barba á los seis que dicen están señalados para la Talamanca de esta santa provincia, aunque sean de mucho espíritu, valor

y robusta naturaleza, pues tienen experiencia que yo, de dos años que estuve, salí con humor gálico que hasta hoy padezco aún mejorado, y mi compañero salió á los cuatro con cuartanas, cuajado de granos y diviesos y muy mal humorado; pero con la gente se podrán abrir los caminos que entren bestias y ganado para el sustento y otras conveniencias razonables para conservar la vida."

4. According to Holliday, "The tragic, precipitous decline in California's Indian population began in the Spanish-Mexican eras, from an estimated 300,000 in 1769 to under 150,000 in 1848. Epidemic diseases remained the primary cause of death among the native people as syphilis, cholera, malaria, measles, smallpox, and other contagious diseases further reduced the Indian population to an estimated 30,000 in 1870" (164).

5. "Todos padecen un mal gálico y así están siempre llagados, y no solamente omiten avisar al Padre sus enfermedades, sino que, positivamente, resisten su curación, aunque se solicite por aquel. Vi y oí de uno que llego a engusanarse de manera, que, con un palo como a una bestia, se le sacaban los gusanos. Y fue tal el descuido de su propia vida que, si por accidente no se advierte su lastimoso estado, se lo comen los gusanos" (*Espinosa de los Monteros*).

6. "La enfermedad dominante es el Gálico, pero muy reconcentrado, de donde se origina una infinidad de enfermedades, unos se llenan de llagas, éstos viven más tiempo aunque no tiran mucho; a otros se les internan y mueren antes, otros se van resolviendo por Pujos. El temperamento para esta enfermedad puede ser algo contrario porque es húmedo y fresco. Alguna diarrea de sangre que siendo executiva acaba con el individuo" (*Apóstol y civilizador*, no. 180, 377).

7. "No se ha descubierto hasta ahora, que los Californianos tengan remedio alguno para curar sus dolencias. Siendo acometidos de algún accidente, mueren sin remedio, si provida no los socorre la naturaleza. Pero és la muerte aun para los bautizados poco, ó nada temida, y assi la dejan acercar con mucha indiferencia, y dejan de existir con suma tranquilidad. En Sta. Cruz carecemos de aguas termales; pero en donde las hay, como en la Mision el Sñor. Sn. Jph. usan de ellas los Indios para baños en cualquiera de sus dolencias, y enfermedades. También és mui comun entre ellos el Temascal, que es un Subterraneo, en que hacen mucho fuego, y sudan con estremo. Sus males dominantes son el dolor de costado, la insolacion, y disenteria, y les acometen en la Primavera y Otoño. Pero el más comun, y de todos tiempos, és el Gálico" (*Apóstol y civilizador*, no. 209, 117).

8. This kind of outbreak is what epidemiologists call "virgin soil epidemics"—that is, "those in which the populations at risk have had no previous contact with the diseases that strike them and are therefore immunologically almost defenseless" (Crosby 289).

9. For more on the Escuela Literaria Salmantina, see the sidebar on p. 92.

10. "Esta epidemia empezó por Octubre del año de 1788, y en dicho mes se sublevaron ellos, apostataron de la Fe, se rebelaron contra España y mataron á los Misioneros. Y con el mismo órden que ellos se manifestaban enemigos de la religion, con el mismo les acometia la epidemia. [. . .] Todas estas circunstancias hacen ver que esta epidemia fue castigo del cielo; pero sea lo que fuere, para nuestro asunto, de

los granos que afligian á los Indios se iban formando unas llagas pútridas que salian en los genitales, y esta enfermedad es la que ha cundido por toda esta provincia: y aunque, como dixe, á los Gentiles no les aflige, pero vemos que lo mismo es hacerse Christianos, que de alli á poco ya están imposibilitados: este es el origen de este mal que por aquí llaman gálico."

11. "será para siempre señalada en los fastos de la historia humana, no tanto por los sucesos de su fortuna, sino por haberse manifestado entonces la enfermedad horrible y dolorosa que empezó á declarar la violencia de su ponzoña al tiempo que este Príncipe tenia sitiados los castillos de Nápoles. Llamósela mal frances, porque los de esta nacion fueron los primeros que se conocieron estragados con ella. La América nos la inoculó como en represalia de nuestras violencias; y las generaciones siguientes, atacadas en los órganos de la propagacion y los placeres, han maldecido y maldecirán muchas veces la imprudencia y la temeridad de sus abuelos."

12. "Con sangre están escritos / En el eterno libro de la vida / Esos dolientes gritos / Que tu labio afligido al cielo envía. / Claman allí contra la patria mía, [...] // ¿No cesarán jamás? No son bastantes / Tres siglos infelices / De amarga expiación? Ya en estos días / No somos, no, los que á la faz del mundo / Las alas de la audacia se vistieron / Y por el ponto Atlántico volaron; / Aquellos que al silencio en que yacías, / Sangrienta, encadenada, te arrancaron."

13. "Yo volaré; que un numen me lo manda; / Yo volaré; del férvido Océano / Arrostraré la furia embravecida, / Y en medio de la América infestada / Sabré plantar el árbol de la vida."

14. "No crece ya en Europa / El sagrado laurel con que te adornes. / Quédate allá, donde sagrado asilo / Tendrán la paz, la independencia Hermosa; / Quédate allá, donde por fin recibas / El premio augusto de tu accion gloriosa."

9. The Rejection of the Origin of *Gálico* as a Nucleus of Self-Identity in the Spanish Colonies

1. "Bulle carmín viviente en tus nopales, / que afrenta afuera al múrice de Tiro."

2. "esa abundancia de imágenes, ese ímpetu entusiasta de la descripción, ese orgullo en el fruto americano y en su nombre indígena."

3. I am quoting from the Spanish translation by José Joaquín de Mora that appeared under the title *Historia antigua de México:* "No tengo que disputar tan sólo con Mr. de Paw, sino con casi todos los europeos, entre los cuales está muy propagada la opinión de que el mal venéreo debe su origen al Nuevo Mundo, recurso que tomaron las naciones de Europa, como de común acuerdo, después de haberse estado echando en cara, unas a otras, por espacio de treinta años, el origen de tan vergonzosa enfermedad."

4. Francisco Guerra offers insight on the arguments around the origin of the disease in his "The Dispute over Syphilis." For the larger context of the controversy of the New World as decaying and degenerated in comparison to Europe, see Gerbi and Alatorre, *La disputa del Nuevo Mundo.*

5. "provincias interiores del África situadas a una y otra orillas del Senegal."

6. I have already discussed Jean Astruc, who was regarded as the main expert on *gálico* at the time, in relation to the changes in medical discourse.

7. "He aquí todo el argumento de Mr. Astruc en apoyo de su sistema sobre el mal venéreo, lleno todo, desde el principio hasta el fin, de falsedades, como pienso demostrar; pero suponiendo que todo ello sea cierto, sostengo lo que he dicho antes, es decir, que lo mismo que él refiere de la isla de Haití pudo suceder en Europa."

8. This claim will reverberate over two hundred years later in misconceptions about the AIDS virus, when some scientists will assert that the syndrome originates from humans having sexual intercourse with monkeys.

9. "Antes de terminar este artículo no puedo menos de mencionar la ridícula y absurda opinión del Dr. Juan Linder, escritor inglés, acerca del origen del mal venéreo, para que se vea hasta dónde puede llegar el empeño de desacreditar en este punto a los americanos. Asegura, pues, aquel extravagante naturalista que este contagio tuvo por principio la unión de los americanos con las hembras de los sátiros o grandes cercopitecos. Por fortuna de los habitantes de la isla de Haití, no había en ella cercopitecos grandes ni pequeños."

10. A similar logic was used in 2012 by Tennessee senator Stacey Campfield in an interview with *Huffington Post* journalist Michelangelo Signorile when he erroneously linked homosexuality and bestialism to the origin of AIDS: "Most people realize that AIDS came from the homosexual community—it was one guy screwing a monkey, if I recall correctly, and then having sex with men. It was an airline pilot, if I recall" (Signorile).

11. Referring to Father José de Acosta (1540–1600), who had observed that, when they applied themselves, the crafts of Peruvian indigenous people were superior to those of Europeans, Clavijero affirms that "this naive confession from a European with such healthy criticism and who is so impartial in his opinions, is worth something more than all the invectives from a Prussian philosopher and from a Scottish historian who are poorly instructed on the things of the New World, and strangely predisposed against the people who inhabit it" (esta ingenua confesión de un europeo de tan sana crítica y tan imparcial en sus opiniones, vale algo más que todas las invectivas de un filósofo prusiano y de un historiador escocés, mal instruidos uno y otro en las cosas del Nuevo Mundo, y extrañamente prevenidos contra los pueblos que lo habitan) (406).

12. "una preocupacion generalísima, que puede retraer del Comercio, y habitacion de la Española à los Europeos," . . . "necesario desvanecer por principios y razones sólidas, è intergiversables una Fábula tan perjudicial para el fomento de aquella Isla."

13. "el primer difamador de la Isla de Hayti."

14. "No podemos pasar tan por alto al Filósofo Prusiano Paw, que consumió diez años haciendo inquisiciones filosóficas sobre los Americanos: trabajo que hubiera ahorrado, empleando siquiera un año en dar vuelta por aquellas tierras. Este Sábio, como los otros de la opinión común, gastan mucho papel, y tiempo en indagar las causas de qué se originó el Gálico en las Indias Occidentales, delirando, ó mintiendo."

15. "Mr. de Paw, aquel enemigo capital de todo el Nuevo Mundo, aquel gran investigador de las inmundicias americanas" (Clavijero 474).

16. "¿Qué quieren decir estas contradiciones, sino que estos AA. sistematicos pintan á los Americanos con aquellos colores, que les viene á qüento? Quando quieren ponderar la apatia ó insensibilidad de aquellos hombres, dicen, que son friísimos; pero quando tratan de desacreditar sus costumbres, ó recargarles con el gálico, entonces afirman, que son por extremo libidinosos."

17. "Yo prescindo ahora de los errores del Español, del Francés, y de este Sabio de Berlin [...] en que se encuentra, no solo diferencia notable, sino contradiccion manifiesta entre los tres, como que los dos ultimos jamás vieron Iguanas; y el primero, si vió alguna, no pudo observar la especie, y escribió de ella por qüentos." Sánchez Valverde is referring to a type of treatment with lizards that I will address in more detail when I discuss Joseph Flores's treatise on the topic.

18. "Cosa bien particular, que la misma especie de Iguanas, que comida en Indias es principio venereo, segun Pavv, sea antivenereo en el Asia meridional, donde produce los propios efectos, y no pueda ser lo mismo en las Indias, como lo afirman los que han estado en ellas."

19. "Yo no puedo creer ignorante á Mr. de Pavv: pero me persuade á que en su celebro habia ciertamente una semilla Anti-Americana, que le trastornaba, y viciaba, quanto escribia sobre aquellos países, y sus naturales, ó que queria á toda costa consolar á la Prusia de su defecto de establecimientos en la America."

20. "Parece ésta una Hermosa, y robusta Doncella, y la Europa, una Vieja consumida y estéril. La América ofrece por todas partes à la vista los hermosos atractivos de verdes, y frondosisimos bosques, que en Enero, como en Mayo, y todo el año, están vestidos, y cargados de sus frutos. [...] La favorecida Europa, para mostrar tres meses alguna gallardia, pasa los nueve en trabajosísimo embarazo, árida, erizada, y seca, como un esqueleto. Aquella produce, y cria sin mas fatiga, que la de echarla las semillas: esta, como vieja, necesita que se la fomente con mil diligencias."

21. "del Gremio y Claustro de la Real Universidad de dicha Goatemala su Patria." For an extensive discussion of Flores's work, its dissemination in European medical discourse, and the rich dispute about the effectiveness of the treatment with lizards, see Miruna Achim, *Lagartijas medicinales.*

22. According to Jesús Kumate Rodríguez, Dr. Flores would later advocate at the Spanish court for the implementation of Francisco Javier Balmis's expedition to the New Continent to inoculate against smallpox: "En 1804, a iniciativa de Joseph Flores, médico de San Cristóbal de las Casas, por entonces en la capitanía de Guatemala, a la sazón médico de la Corte en Madrid, se organizó la expedición de la vacuna para llevarla a las colonias de España" (8).

23. "En los fecundos Paises de esta América no solo encuentran los Indios su alimento, vestido, muebles, y quanto necesitan para conservar la robusta salud que gozan, sino que entre las producciones naturales hallan remedios tan simples como eficaces, para curar enfermedades que hasta aquí se habían burlado del Arte, y sus mas sabios Profesores. De suerte, que si no nos desdeñáramos de aprender de estas gentes sencillas, y procuráramos tratarlos con intimidad, descubririamos específicos

mas importantes que las Disertaciones mas eloqüentes, y que los descubrimientos mas curiosos de la Anatomía."

24. "D. Nicolas Verdugo, Profesor de Cirugía, que le habia asistido, y quantos vieron corrompida no pequeña parte del rostro de Ferrer, no cesaban de admirar la pronta restitucion á su natural figura."

25. "hacer menos desagradable el remedio, é imitar el método de los Indios," . . . "con la brevedad posible, para tomar la carne lo mas viva que se pueda, segun el método de los Amatitanecos."

26. "El calor, sudor, y babeo hacen ver que las Lagartijas son un ventajoso equivalente del mercurio. No es necesario guardar las escrupulosas precauciones con que se toma este mineral; ni hay temor alguno de sus resultas."

27. "Se puede encontrar en estos animales un excelente vermifugo, un antihidrofóbico, y el específico antivariólico, que el célebre Boerhave pensaba se podia hallar en cierta composicion preparada con el antimonio, y mercurio."

28. "Este conocimiento nos puede abrir camino á muchas experiencias, que se pueden aventurar, con otros animales comidos en la misma forma."

29. "para examinar su vida, sus sexos, su generacion, y conservacion, con el fin de enviarlas vivas al Real Gabinete de Historia Natural, y que la Europa participe de tan precioso hallazgo."

30. "muger India, última de su familia, que lo había usado desde tiempo inmemorial en Acapuacáro."

31. For concise information on the state of medicine in the colony of New Spain in the sixteenth and seventeenth centuries, see Rissc's "Medicine in New Spain."

32. "Quarenta hombres y veinte mugeres, afectos de casi todos los grados de la lüe venérea."

33. "variar y aun desterrar, si fuese posible, el uso del Mercurio, establecido en todas las Naciones."

34. "á pesar del *empirismo* con que se habia administrado hasta entónces, y sin embargo de haberse dado determinados dias en iguales dósis á todos los enfermos, sin distinction de edad, sexô, ni temperamento."

35. "maduro exâmen, modificar, simplificar y poner en buen método la nueva medicina."

36. "No es mi ánimo criticar ni censurar la práctica empírica de Viana: se dexa conocer fácilmente, que su falta de método y las desproporcionadas formulas de que usaba, son conseqüencias precisas de su ningun conocimiento de la Medicina: pero lo que hay digno de admiración es, cómo logró este hombre con su método tan felices curaciones."

37. "Profesores del Reyno para la curación del mal Gálico, por el interés de la Humanidad, por su poco costo, simplicidad, seguro uso, y poco tiempo que se emplea en la curación."

38. "El amor que yo profeso á los hombres; la distinguida confianza que mecí á S. E.; el deseo que me animaba (como á este sabio Prelado) de ser útil á mi Nacion, dando principio á un nuevo ramo de comercio activo por el consumo de estas raices, que solamente se vegetan en aquel Reyno, y muchas otras ventajas importantes

á la Humanidad; me precisáron, sin arbitrio, á admitir gustosamente la Comision de transportar á la Europa el conocimiento medicinal de estas plantas, á costa de muchísimos peligros y disgustos, y mil otras incomodidades."

39. From another perspective, Flores's proposal prefigures the present dynamic of research, use, and abuse of native plants by multinational pharmaceutical companies that do not care about overharvesting, the reduction of availability of plants for traditional medicine, or the loss of land that leads to the extinction of plants that have not been properly studied. Flores's small treatise mirrors the complexity of the search for differentiation through engagement, and the problematic consequences of emulation, self-determination, and dependency.

40. "hubo particularmente un punto de la historia de la medicina que llamó la atencion de Bello, I sobre el cual ejecutó muchas investigaciones durante su permanencia en Inglaterra, aunque, por desgracia, no tuvo tiempo de coordinarlas, I mucho ménos de darlas a luz. Ese punto fué el del orijen de la sífilis." The introduction to vol. 6 (xxxvi–lxxxvi) contains Bello's annotations on the discussion of the origin of *gálico,* which occupy all of section 3.

41. "la interesante i erudita disertacion sobre el *Orijen del mal venéreo,* compuesta en 1780 por el ex-jesuita mejicano don Francisco Saverio Clavijero."

42. "manifestar las contradicciones que se echan de ver en los autores que han tratado esta materia."

43. "No puedo prescindir de mencionar aquí un ejemplo de la lijereza con que han procedido los que sostienen que la sífilis fué llevada de América a Europa."

44. "Cornelio de Pauw, escritor azas lijero, i aficionado a sostener tesis paradojales, compuso su obra para demostrar que la raza indíjena de América era mui inferior a las del antiguo mundo."

45. "Al comunicarla a sus conquistadores, vengaron superabundantemente las injurias que éstos les hicieron."

46. The complete title given by Teresa de Mier to his manuscript explains his political objectives: *Idea de la Constitución dada a las Américas por los reyes de España antes de la invasión del antiguo despotismo. Dábala a conocer desde el castillo de S. Juan de Ulúa, donde le tiene el nuevo despotismo, el Dor. Don Servando Teresa, José de Mier, Noriega y Guerra. Para corregir los errores prejudicialísimos, que por ignorar esa Constitución se han estado cometiendo en España y América desde 1808, e impedir otros nuevos. Impresa en Veracruz y reimpresa en la Habana con doble extensión y notas del autor* (Thoughts on the Constitution given to the Americas by the kings of Spain before the invasion of the old despotism. He made it known from S. Juan de Ulúa's castle, where he is held by the new despotism, by Dr. Don Servando Teresa, José de Mier, Noriega y Guerra. To correct the most injurious errors, that by ignoring that Constitution they have been committing in Spain and America since 1808, and stop other new ones. Printed in Veracruz and reprinted in Habana with double the size and notes by the author).

47. For more information on the Cortes de Cádiz, see the sidebar on p. 256.

48. José María Blanco Crespo (1775–1841), better known as Joseph Blanco White— an important figure I will examine in more detail when I discuss his long poem

"El incordio"—introduced the two American scholars and politicians while they were in London.

49. "Hubo un incrédulo llamado Paw que nació en Prusia; pero que no debió de escribir sus *Investigaciones sobre los americanos* sino más allá de los círculos polares; pues de otra suerte era imposible escribir con tan supina y absoluta ignorancia de la América y todas sus cosas: aunque dice que estuvo trabajando nueve años en acopiar su material."

50. "Cartas de Tulitas Cácalo-xochitl le cogí 500 mentiras en lo que escribió sobre México, amén de los innumerables dislates y contradicciones."

51. "De ella extrajo las muchísimas mentiras y desatinos que por pique contra mí, que lo había impugnado y a sugestión de don Luis Trespalacios, montañez mentecato, vomitó en contra los mexicanos don Pedro Estala, *viajero universal,* sin haber salido más que del claustro de las Escuelas Pías."

52. "Pero lejos de convenir los europeos en que también les debemos el mal venéreo, dan por supuesto, con sus elegantes habladores Paw y Raynal, que de la América les ha ido este funesto regalo, llevado por las naves de Colón. Mas esta voz no tiene otro origen que la autoridad de Oviedo, enemigo y tirano de los indios, en su falsa y nefanda *Historia de las Indias.*"

53. "Bernal Díaz os dirá mucho más que Solís y que Robertson. Interrogad a cada civilización en sus obras; pedid a cada historiador sus garantías. Esa es la primera filosofía que debemos aprender de la Europa. Nuestra civilización será también juzgada por sus obras; y si se la ve copiar servilmente a la europea aun en lo que ésta no tiene de aplicable, ¿cuál será el juicio que formará de nosotros, un Michelet, un Guizot? Dirán: la América no ha sacudido aún sus cadenas; se arrastra sobre nuestras huellas con los ojos vendados; no respira en sus obras un pensamiento propio, nada original, nada característico; remeda las formas de nuestra filosofía, y no se apropia su espíritu. Su civilización es una planta exótica que no ha chupado todavía sus jugos a la tierra que la sostiene."

54. "Pero nuestro Sánchez Valverde, natural de Santo Domingo, hizo contra Paw en su eruditísima disertación sobre el origen del gálico, una demostración sin replica con los monumentos de la historia."

55. "Yo no niego que en alguna parte de nuestra inmensa América pudiese haber mal venéreo, aunque los indios son los menos susceptibles; pues como sienta Fracastor ésta parece ser una de las enfermedades que suelen rodear el globo, y es como la pensión anexa a todo exceso en cada género. Tal vez lo habría en México como había moscas, que a las islas trajeron los buques de España; pero es evidentemente falso que de América se llevase a Europa. Precisamente, cuenta Pedro Mártir de Angleria, que los indios de las islas dieron guerra a los españoles por haberles inficionado sus mujeres."

56. "Gracias a Dios que así como nos ha venido el conocimiento de la vacuna de la Europa, de donde nos trajeron las viruelas, nos va a venir el remedio o a lo menos el preservativo del gálico."

57. "Historia natural, civil, y geographica, de este gran rio, y de sus caudalosas vertientes: govierno, usos, y costumbres de los indios sus habitadores, con nuevas, y utiles

noticias de Animales, Arboles, Frutos, Aceytes, Resinas, Yervas, y Raìces medicinales: Y sobre todo, se hallaràn conversiones muy singulares à nuestra Santa Fè, y
casos de mucha edificacion."

58. "En los ríos de *Chire, Tate, Punapuna,* y otros muchos de aquellos llanos, se halla
la *zarza* tan celebrada, y aprobada contra el mal gálico."

59. "El *amor venereo,* se difine asi: un deseo de unirse con la cosa amada. El Poeta lo
pinta como un suave incendio de los huesos, ó una oculta herida en el Corazon:
est mollis flamma medullas. Interea, & tacitum vivit sub pectore vulnus. La causa es
el deseo de poseer un bien deleitable. Los que caen en sus redes padecen enagena-
mientos, inedias, desvelos, y fiebres; creen las sospechas, no los aterran los impo-
sibles, ni las dificultades los contienen, el consejo no los persuade, ni la mente los
sujeta. Son unos ciegos á la razon: *quid deceat non videt ullus amans.* Ovid."

60. "Me esfuerzo en esta obrita á que el Publico tenga en un pequeño tomo, no solo lo
mas util que se halla esparcido en muchos libros, sino tambien lo que tengo observado en nuestra America, declarando con franqueza todo lo que he experimentado
ser más provechoso á los enfermos."

61. "Por brillante, y grande que parezca el numero de libros filosoficos, quimistas, y
botanicos que adornan las librerias; y por exquisitos, y de buen gusto que sean los
discursos de los doctos Médicos, á pesar de el aparato de voces pomposas en las juntas, y de disertaciones eruditas, una infeliz vieja, un pobre paisano, ó un estupido
Indio, se burlan muchas veces de ellos con el uso feliz de una droga despreciada."

62. "Si á los mas consumados Botanicos les presentamos una planta extraña, jamás nos
darán con los *Sistemas* la menor luz para la seguridad de los usos á que debamos
aplicarla."

63. "La América es la bolsa de la Omnipotencia, y el Paraiso terrenal que enriquece
á la Europa, no solo con sus preciosos metales, sino tambien con muchos de sus
nobilisismos vegetales, en palos, raices, plantas, frutos, gomas, balsamos &c. [...]
Exemplo sean la *Quina,* y la *Xalapa.* Estas indigenas drogas, cuya preferencia es
innegable en muchos casos á los mas preciosos remedios, no explican tan generalmente sus virtudes en su propio suelo Americano, como lo experimentan las
Regiones Septentrionales, y Paises frios de la Europa."

64. "pencas del nopal de tuna tapona, suasadas, y abiertas por el medio."

65. "Y asi, no habiendome propuesto escribir la Historia Natural de estos Reynos.
[...] me contento con proponer las mas eficaces medicinas, que he experimentado
ser provechosas en *esta nuestra América.*"

10. José Joaquín Fernández de Lizardi's Diseased Characters

1. Some of the most relevant recent scholarship on Fernández de Lizardi's *Periquillo*
is by Beatriz de Alba-Koch, Juan Pablo Dabove, Mariela Insúa Cereceda, Danuta
Teresa Mozejko, and several works by Nancy J. Vogeley.

2. "Vd. y otros escribanos ó receptores tan pelotas y maliciosos como vd. tienen la
culpa de que el vulgo poco recto en sus juicios, mire con desafecto, y aun diré con
odio, una profesion tan noble. [...] ¿No es pues una lástima que cuatro zaragates

desluzcan con sus embrollos, necedades y raterias, una profesion tan recomendable en la sociedad?" (Fernández de Lizardi, *Obras* 1:173).

3. "Hablaba gangoso y rociaba de babas al que lo atendia, á causa de que el galico y el mercurio lo habian dejado sin campanilla ni dientes: no era nada liberal y sobre tantas prendas tenia la recomendable de ser celosísimo en extremo" (*Obras* 1:179).

4. "Hablo en comun y solo contra los malos médicos, empíricos, y charlatanes que abusan de un arte tan precioso y necesario de que nos proveyó el Autor de la naturaleza para el socorro de nuestras dolencias" (*Obras* 2:43).

5. "Pues, no señor, le interrumpí: yo no soy de esos: yo sé mi obligacion y estoy examinado y aprobado *nemine discrepante,* 'con todos los votos,' por el real Protomedicato de México: no ignoro que las partes de la medicina son: Fisiología, Pathología, Semeiótica y Terapéutica: . . . sé cuántos y cuáles son los humores del hombre, como la sangre, la bilis, la flema, el chîlo y el gástrico . . . conozco las enfermedades con sus propios y legítimos nombres griegos, como la ascitis, la anasarca, la hidrophobia, el saratán, la pleuresia, el mal venéreo, la clorosis, la caquexia, la podagra, el parafrenitis, el priapismo, el paroxismo, y otras mil enfermedades que el necio vulgo llama hidropesía, rabia, gálico, dolor de costado, gota y demás simplezas que acostumbra" (*Obras* 2:43–44).

6. For a more developed discussion on the role and history of the Protomedicato, as well as on the particularities of this institution on the peninsula vis-à-vis the American colonies, see the introduction.

7. "Que me echen apopléticos á miles á ver si no los levanto 'en el momento,' *ipso facto,* y no digo apopléticos, sino lazarinos, tiñosos, gálicos, gotosos, parturientas, tabardillentos, rabiosos y cuantos enfermos hay en el mundo. Tú tambien lo haces con primor; pero es menester que no corras tanto los dedos ni profundices la lanceta, no sea que vayas á trasvenar á alguno, y por lo demás no tengas cuidado que tú saldrás á mi lado no digo barbero, sino médico, cirujano, químico, botánico, alquimista, y si me das gusto y sirves bien, saldrás hasta astrólogo y nigromántico" (*Obras* 2:22).

8. "Se pondrá el enfermo desnudo al sol, hasta que el cuerpo se haya calentado mucho. Entonces se meterá en la cama, tomará el chocolate bien caliente, y se abrigará quanto pudiere, conservandose en la mayor quietud por algunas horas, en cuyo tiempo prorrumpirán las babas, y el sudor copiosamente."

9. "En otras partes tienen la santa devocion de enviar al hospital de san Lázaro, la ropa y colchon del que murió de tisis, de gálico, ó de otra enfermedad maligna y contagiosa, y dicen que les envian aquella pestilencia á los miserables enfermos, *de caridad.* ¡Desgraciados! harto tienen que sufrir y padecer con sus malos humores, ¿aun es fuerza envenenarles mas la sangre *por caridad?*"

10. "Esta no es limosna, ni puede llamarse caridad, sino mezquindad, ruindad, hipocresía. Esto es querer engañar á Dios, y comprar sus misericordias con basura."

11. "Porque la crianza acaba a las mujeres, y por fin no es moda ni se quedan estas cosas para las personas de nuestra clase, sino para las pobretas y gente ordinaria."

12. "Pero yo conseguí salirme con la mía y que la criara una negra retobada como el diablo y creo que gálica, por señas que el niño se murió a pocos días medio po-

drido, y desde entonces ya mi marido tiene buen cuidado de buscar chichis robustas a sus hijos."

13. "Sobre un gálico irremediable, como lo decían bien claro las úlceras de boca y nariz y las llagas de las piernas, tenía una fiebre voraz de que no podía escapar."

14. "En medio de los más vehementes dolores y agitación, auxiliada por los padres camilos, que se habían llamado, entregó su alma al Criador, dejando un patético y sensible ejemplo y escarmiento a las mujeres sin juicio que siguen las mismas ideas y conducta de la infeliz Pomposa."

11. Sick Humor

1. I am not interested here in reviewing the existing literature on Valle's work, namely, the influence and affinities of his style with Francisco de Quevedo, or his acrid criticism of doctors, a theme that has been revisited several times after Daniel R. Reedy started that vein in the mid-1960s, or his critical portrayal of the city of Lima as explored by Pedro Lasarte. In addition to Lasarte's work, see Lorente Medina's *Realidad histórica y creación literaria.* For the situation of medicine in the viceroyalty of Lima and the racial implications of the profession of medicine, see Rivasplata Varillas's "Los médicos y los cirujanos mulatos."

2. In *Realidad histórica y creación literaria,* Lorente Medina uses the mentions of real doctors in the poems to establish the sequence and possible dates of their composition: "El Dr. Bermejo, citado en 'A una dama que paró en el Hospital de la Caridad,' dejó de ser el médico de dicho hospital en 1687, y el Dr. Revilla, que aparece en 'A una dama que por serlo paró en la Caridad' no empezó su labor profesional en él hasta 1691. Luego entre ambos poemas distan, al menos, cuatro años" (181n30).

3. "Tanto despreciar amantes, / tanto deshacer maridos, / tanto hacer de los oídos / arracadas de diamantes, / claro está, que habían de dar / ocasion al Amor / para vengar tu rigor."

4. "Purgando estaba sus culpas / Anarda en el hospital, / que estos pecados en vida / y en muerte se han de purgar."

5. "Tomando está las unciones / En la Caridad Belisa, / Que la caridad le vale / A quien es caritativa."

6. See Rossi Rubí's "Historia de la Hermandad y Hospital de la Caridad."

7. "la limosna y socorro que se dá à uno: y con especialidad la llaman assi los que la piden, ò reciben."

8. The play with the multilayered meanings of charity is similarly developed in "Que paró," where the author further emphasizes the idea of giving alms—in this case sexual favors—to anyone who solicits them: "In the Caridad is / because of her great charity, / since to any beggar love / she never denied alms" (En la Caridad se halla / por su mucha caridad, / si a ningún amor mendigo / negó limosna jamás) ("Que paró" vv. 49–52).

9. "Como gusanos de seda / babas por la boca hila, / que el andar con dos capullos / no ha olvidado todavía."

10. Valle y Caviedes's poems show a preference for the use of double meanings to refer to the penis. In one case they are called "pífanos" (fifes) (v. 59), later "caños" (pipes) (v. 62). In other instance, the author incorporates an obscene reference to the quality of the erection of Belisa's lovers and of her ability to satisfy each one of them: "She was always triumphant over all / who had them the stiffest / because in love laxness / is the greatest bravery" (Siempre triunfaba de cuantos / más tiesos se las tenían / que en amor la flojedad / es la mayor valentía) ("Que por serlo" vv. 101–4).

11. "que quien con pífanos anda / a los parches se dedica."

12. "de tantos caños corría / que le salía agua al rostro / por rebosar la vasija."

13. "Los billetes se le han vuelto / papelillos de botica, / y sus continuas ayudas / en costa de otras jeringas."

14. "La costumbre del pedir / su propio dolor la imita / porque en un continuo 'ay' / está de noche y de día." In "Que paró" Valle uses the euphemism of *clavar* (to nail or hammer a pin-shaped object) to allude to sexual intercourse. In addition to the meaning of *clavo* as a nail or metal pin, this word is also used to name the type of callus known in English as a corn. The author indicates that it is surprising that after being penetrated or nailed so many times there is only one syphilitic wound or callus in her heel: "She has a bubo nail / riveting her heel / and it is lucky indeed that in only one / so much hammering ended up" (Un clavo tiene de bubas / remachado el carcañal, / y es mucha dicha que en uno / parase tanto clavar) ("Que paró" vv. 77–80).

15. "El amor cobra en dolores / lo que le prestó en cosquillas, / conque á pagar viene en llanto / deuda que contrajo en risa."

16. "No extrañará sudadero / quien tanto se ha hecho ensillar, / copla que en la matadura / de medio a medio le da."

17. "Dicen que la campanilla / sin remedio se le cae, / o se le raja, a los golpes / de tanto badajear."

18. "Parece se solicita / por gusto la enfermedad, / si le han venido a medida / las llagas del paladar."

19. "No hay hueso que bien la quiera, / que esta enfermedad maldita / que por la carne se adquiere / siempre a los huesos se libra."

20. "De su estrella se lamenta / porque en luceros peligra."

21. "Sudando está y trasudando / por delante y por detrás, / sin que extrañe en sus bureos / que se le pegue el pañal."

22. "Un mal francés le da guerra, / gabacho tan militar / que cercó a Fuenterrabía / y entró por el arrabal."

23. *Arrabal* was defined at the time as a "settlement adjoining and adjacent to populated cities and towns outside the ramparts or fences" ("Población contígua y adyacente à las Ciudades y Villas populosas fuera de las murallas ò cercas"), and in its second meaning, "understood in jest as the rear part, or the buttocks" ("Se toma jocosamente, por la parte posterior, ò las assentadéras," RAE A 1726, s.v. "arrabal").

24. "Ella tiene un mal francés, / tan hijo de estas provincias, / que es nacido en la ciudad / que llaman de Picardía." The same trope appears in the earlier poem:

"For the ones that catch a cold from love / the effective remedy is / to sweat out a French [illness] who is / of picardy a native" (Las que de amor se resfrían / es el remedio eficaz / sudar un francés que es de / picardía natural).

25. "Como a plata con azogue / beneficiándola está / un mal médico a repasos / de sobar y más sobar."

26. "A puro azogue presume / la tiene de volver piña, / la cual tiene más estacas / que todas las de las Indias." Reedy's edition reads "la tiene de volver pina" (v. 82), but our discussion of the use of mining terminology makes clear that the wordplay is related to the silver *piña,* and therefore I've corrected it here.

27. "Venganza es de las estafas, / si a sus amantes decía / el alma den, cuyo azogue / lo venga Huancavelica."

28. "piensa que él solo entiende lo que el otro dice."

29. "Supo Inés que un Oficial, / De gálico muy lisiado, / En su casa habia mandado / Que en nada le echasen sal. / Y dixo en risa: no entiendo / Cómo la sal cause enfado / A este, que por mas de un lado / Aprisa se va pudriendo."

30. For a fuller discussion of this poem, see chap. 4.

31. "carta jocoseria escrita por el autor a su cuñado Don Gerónimo Mendiola, describiendo a Guayaquil y Quito."

32. "ciudad hermosa, / de la América guirnalda, / de la tierra bella Esmeralda / y del mar perla preciosa."

33. "Hermano, en aqueste Quito / muchos mueren de apostemas / de bubas, llagas y flemas, / mas nadie muere de ahíto . . ."

34. "viendo los asientos rotos / y quebradas las tablillas, / dije: bien pueden ser sillas, / mas yo las tengo por potros."

35. "Que, despues de mis males me ha brotado / en la espina medula del trasero / una potra mas grande que un harnero."

36. "siempre de chiste, o por lo retumbante, o por lo cómico, o por lo facultativo, o por algún retruecanillo . . . *Parentación dolorosa, oración fúnebre, epicedio triste.*"

37. "Guárdate bien de decir nunca la *vara de Aarón,* porque juzgaría que es la vara de algún alcalde de aldea; en diciendo la *aaronítica vara,* se concibe una vara de las Indias, y se eleva la imaginación." The friar is referring to Aaron's rod in the Old Testament. Moses and his brother Aaron owned walking sticks with miraculous power. For example, Moses was commanded by God to raise his staff over the Red Sea to part its waters (Exodus 14:16), and Moses's rod was used to produce water from a stone (Numbers 20:11). God also commanded Aaron to cast his staff in front of Pharaoh to produce the miracle of turning it into a serpent (Exodus 7:8–11), and later makes it blossom to show that Moses's brother was the chosen one with authority to lead the Israelites (Numbers 17:1–11).

12. Moratín's *Arte de las putas*

1. For more on clandestine literature and associations to erotic topics for the Spanish case, see the breadth of the corpus in José Antonio Cerezo's *Literatura erótica en España: repertorio de obras, 1519–1936;* Gies's compiled work in *Eros y amistad,* es-

pecially chaps. 1–5; and the work by Philip Deacon, in particular "El libro erótico en la España dieciochesca," "El espacio clandestino del erotismo literario en la España dieciochesca," and "Las fronteras del erotismo poético español a finales del siglo XVIII." For the French milieu, given its connections to literary production in Spain, see Robert Darnton's *The Corpus of Clandestine Literature in France, 1769–1789,* and *The Forbidden Best-Sellers of Pre-Revolutionary France.*

2. "por estar lleno de proposiciones falsas, escandalosas, provocativas a cosas torpes, injuriosas a todos los estados del Christianismo, blasfemas, hereticas, y con sabor de Ateismo, y Politeismo"; quoted in Fernández Nieto, Introducción, 14n1.

3. Scholarly work has focused on establishing the text (Colón Calderón and Garrote Bernal, Fernández Nieto, Velázquez); the relations between the text, the life of the author, and the production of his contemporaries (Colón Calderón and Garrote Bernal, Franco Rubio, Gies, Goldman, Juárez Nissenberg); the geographies of prostitution (Goldman); the dynamic of scandal and festive mood (Gies, Ribao Pereira); its didacticism (Colón Calderón and Garrote Bernal, Fernández Nieto); the state of prostitution in Madrid and Spain (Goldman); misogyny, eroticism, and sexuality (Franco Rubio, Schlünder); and the traces of scientific discourse (Colón Calderón and Garrote Bernal, Gies).

4. "Si fuera la dulzura de mi canto / capaz de impresionar el horroroso / gálico inmundo y su extinction lograse, / ésta sí fuera de mi canto hazaña."

5. "¡Oh putañero, a quien la musa mía / condujo a tal altura peregrina / por nuevos rumbos que otros no surcaron, / no mis buenos propósitos cesaron!"

6. "mas si Apolo a los míseros mortales / quiso enseñar algo útil por mi labio."

7. "En esto has de estudiar de noche y día, / que es malo porque quieren que lo sea."

8. "el derramar la orina, el mismo oficio / viene a ser casi y con la propia cosa, / y a nadie afrenta acción que es tan forzosa."

9. "De solo a solo, ni romper deseo / la coyunda que enlaza el himeneo: / sufra el cuello magnánimo y robusto / su yugo tan pesado como justo, / y evitará el horror de mis lecciones."

10. "¡De cuántos infortunios libertada / fuera la humanidad si este contrato / le anularan violadas condiciones!"

11. According to Max Rheinstein, "The first country in which these new tendencies were to reshape marriage legislation was Prussia, whose King, Frederick II (the Great), constituted the very prototype of the "enlightened" eighteenth century monarch. His decree of 1752 was the first legislative act in modern Europe by which marriage was declared to be a private affair" (12).

12. "Y no siendo posible que se impida / lo que naturaleza a veces clama, / justa o injustamente, inevitable / es de amor apagar la ardiente llama."

13. "Si moderan los gastos excesivos / que pierden a los jóvenes lascivos, / y el contagio venéreo se destierra / de las ardientes ingles y, seguros / los tálamos nupciales, los futuros / frutos de bendición esperan ciertos . . . / el daño menor debe / sufrirse por obviar mayores daños."

14. "se alzarán para ti todas las faldas / de cualquier hembra."

15. "quien por pobre dice que pleitea / y pretende comer bueno y barato."

16. "Más fácil fuera al estrellado globo / contarle los luceros, las arenas / al mar que baña desde al Indo al Moro, / primero que yo cuente las muchachas / que hay en Madrid."

17. "un buen chocho y un buen culo, / tetas y carnes duras, pero sanas."

18. "con boca de carmín bañada en risa."

19. "y según yo los iba recitando / la incontinente y disoluta hembra / se iba en pura lujuria electrizando."

20. Gies suggests that Moratín died as a result of syphilis, a disease that would have been covered in his death certificate under the vague description of "mysterious sickness": "His death certificate reveals that he had suffered from mysterious illnesses. That mystery followed him to the grave: they buried him in secret, and to this day we remain ignorant of the reason why. But it is not illogical to suggest that the supposedly correct and rational neoclassical author don Nicolás Fernández de Moratín should have died from that selfsame 'horrific and vile *gálico*,' that fearful shadow that informs the entirety of *The Art of Whoring.*" ("Cantor" 322; Su certificado de muerte revela que había padecido de enfermedades misteriosas. El misterio le sigue a la tumba: lo enterraron "a secretas," la razón de la cual desconocemos hoy. Pero no es ilógico sugerir que el supuesto correcto y racional autor neoclásico don Nicolás Fernández de Moratín muriera de aquel mismo "horroroso gálico inmundo," aquella temida sombra negra que informa la totalidad de *El arte de las putas.*)

21. In *The Age of Wonder,* Richard Holmes develops an encompassing introductory study of scientific advances in the context of English Enlightenment, including Cook's expedition and the resonance of the work of Joseph Banks (1743–1820) in fostering scientific exploration.

22. "¡Qué chusca estabas antes / de haber virotes ablandado / que te encajaron de asquerosas bubas, / y en un portal baldada te han dejado!"

23. "la Chiquita, a quien el Padre Angulo / le pegó purgaciones en el culo."

24. "y a cualquiera que ven, el miembro agarran / y están muy diestras en ponerlo tieso, / y a quien se lo metió luego le plagan."

25. "cual vieja o fea, puñetera; / y así saliste, a fuerza de ejercicio, / la más diestra de todos los humanos."

26. "y en vez de una belleza soberana / se encontró un miembro femenil podrido, / lleno de incordios, unos reventados, / otros por madurar, otros maduros, / sobresaliendo el clítoris llagado / sin un labio y pelado a repelones; / colirios de las séptimas unciones / con cicatrices, churre y talpapismos; / de hediondo aliento y corrompido podre; / sucio de parches, gomas y verrugas, / cuantiosas y abundantes purgaciones, / que inundaban de peste la entrepierna, / pringando de materia las arrugas / de la muy puerca tripa renegrida."

27. "Muchas ponderan la excelencia rara / del encabronamiento, que preserva / de la infección venérea; son errores / del vulgo; estar tal pueden tus humores / que aunque estés con mujer no galicada / se corrompa tu linfa de escaldada, / pues la disposición está en nosotros."

28. "que a las gorronas van de las tabernas / —llenas de lancetazos y botanas, / con todo Antón Martín entre las piernas— / y lo sacan más limpio que una espada."

29. "La sarna así, la peste y las viruelas / no se pegan a muchos asistentes, y ningún otro lo pegó al primero."

30. "Mas si acaso pequeñas purgaciones / destila por desgracia tu ciruelo, / dura abstinencia observa y ten consuelo / de que arraigarse el mal es imposible."

31. "del trato inhonesto, que freqüentaron con las mugéres de aquellas nuevas Regiones."

32. "Enciéndese la sangre recaliente . . . / en un joven robusto y muy ardiente, / en un viejo, en un clérigo o en un fraile, / y exprimiendo la pringue a los riñones, / baja por sutilísimas canales / a esponjar los pendientes compañones, / los músculos flexibles extendiendo, / y el instrumento humano entumeciendo, / hasta el ombligo se levanta hinchado, / del semen abundante retestado, / que, reventando por salir, comprueba / ser venenoso estando detenido, / según el docto Hipócrates de Cos."

33. "si son las bubas multitud viviente / de insectos minutísimos y tiernos, / como sienten los físicos modernos, / porque el mercurio a todo bicho mata, / la comunicación evitar quiero, / haciendo escudo de la ropa santa."

34. "Feliz principio a esta artimaña puso / de un fraile la inventiva, que de un fraile / sólo u del diablo ser invención pudo."

35. "Tú así del Soto a casa ve a atacarte; / más yo quiero del todo asegurarte, / facilitando del gondón el uso."

36. "Supongo que continuo armado sales / del gondón, tu perenne compañero, / y así no ensuciarás los hospitales."

37. The most up-to-date and reliable publication on the history of the condom is Amy and Thiery's "The Condom." The authors clarify many misunderstandings and myths about the name of the object and its history as a contraceptive. Perhaps one of their most important elucidations is a discussion of the long-held belief that condoms were used to protect against syphilis. According to the authors, it has been repeatedly claimed that in his *De morbo gallico* (1563) Gabriel Fallopius discussed a trial on the use of an initial type of condom made out of linen as a prophylactic against *gálico*. Amy and Thiery explain that there has been a misinterpretation of the Latin word *coiverit* in the future perfect tense in the original Latin text, which means that the linen cloth mentioned by Fallopius's was to be placed on the glans *after* having sex and not as a preventative. This explanation also means that the first mentions of the prophylactic use of condoms are from the late seventeenth century, but they are only clearly discussed in the eighteenth century.

38. "después los sutilísimos ingleses, / filósofos del siglo, le han pulido, / y a membrana sutil le han reducido."

39. In the "Ventas" (sales) section of the *Diario de Madrid* on Sunday, September 23, 1810, an announcement appears of the sale of five pine shelves and a large red armoire with drawers and a lock. Those interested in the furniture could inquire at

Geniani's: "Will give information in the store of Don Simon Geniani, Montera Street, no. 13" ("Darán razón en la tienda de Don Simon Geniani, calle de la Montera, núm. 13").

40. "Los miércoles y sábados durante el Carnaval enfrente de la Real Biblioteca, y todos los días del año en la Puerta del Sol, Calle Mayor, casas de Geniani, Perez, Lumbreras, Tarsi, Larus, Vallejo, Gallinas, y otros de la misma clase y orden."

41. "un relox de oro de repetición esmaltado y guarnecido de brillantes, que se compró en casa de Geniani en precio de 18.000 reales."

42. "Mercanti di Bijouterìes e Chincaglierìe . . . [sono] Geniani e Perez" (Metrà 379).

43. For a thorough study of Paret's painting and insights on performativity, gender, literature, dressing, costumes, and masked balls during Charles III's reign, see Gómez Castellano's "Misterios en la trastienda"

44. "si los pagares bien y con secreto."

45. "y por los secretarios de embajada, / que a la nuestra remiten las naciones."

46. "Pero si acaso tu salud estragan / las puercas que lo tienen con gusanos / y les huele a chotuno en los veranos, / Urbina, Juan de Dios y Talavera, / (muy experimentados cirujanos / en ingles de mancebos disolutos) / te sajarán con delicadas manos, / y los humazos del vermellón rojo / las tenaces ladillas desagarran."

47. "y las putas de Londres son multadas / si no ofrecen bandejas de gondones, / que les hacen venir desde la China."

48. "Es fama que un proyecto han ofrecido / al Ministerio, por el cual se obligan / a abastecer la Corte de pescados / y carne fresca y sana."

49. "que servirán al público barato, / y con tanto cariño y abundancia, / que no hará falta ni podrá quejarse / la insaciable lujuria cortesana."

50. "y con tal pacto a tributar se obligan / mayor farda que un tiempo los judíos."

51. "También alrededor de los cuarteles / rondan los putañeros más noveles / las putas mal pagadas de soldados, / pues en Madrid hay más de cien burdeles / por no haber uno sólo permitido / como en otras ciudades, que no pierden / por eso: y tú, Madrid, nada perdieras / antes menos escándalo así dieras."

52. "verás que estas ajadas / en vil plomo son perlas engastadas."

53. "muchas veces / bajo un vestido rústico y villano / te encontrarás la Venus del Tiziano, / como buen bebedor en mala capa."

54. "[trocar] las hermosas por las sanas."

55. "Llévala al cuarto, y si la ropa ofende / la vista, ropa afuera, y en pelota / como la borra, métela en la cama."

56. "Y en fin, todo Madrid al ser de noche / le da a un hombre de bien mil portaleras / y, aunque pobres, no gálicos infieras / que albergan sus ingles."

57. "pues valen sus noticias un tesoro. / Ahorrarás tiempo, males, plata y oro / si buscar sabes las recién venidas, / pues no piden ni baldan, que aún no tienen / ni salud ni costumbres corrompidas."

58. "Arriba de dos veces no permite / nuestra arte a una gozar—aunque ella fuera / la salerosa y chusca Saturnina—, / a no ser que lo dé por solo gana, / que entonces no hay peligro si no hay gasto."

59. "El Parador del Sol, de Zaragoza, / y Barcelona, y Parador de Ocaña, / todo lo

anduve; que es donde se goza / del género a Madrid recién venido, / porque lo antiguo todo está podrido."

13. An Epic Chant to the Syphilitic Bubo

1. "Shortly after my arrival in Madrid, a grave illness overcame me by my own fault, which left me confined to my room for two months. However, such was the intoxicated happiness—as I am unable to find another, more appropriate name for what I felt—produced in me by the pleasure of seeing myself free from the controls of my family and my city, that my spirits were always high. My only recourses in those days were to read the worst books of the French philosophers. [...] As soon as I had fully recuperated, I returned with new vigor to seeking out the more turbulent and tumultuous pleasures." (Blanco, *Escritos* 65; Poco después de mi llegada a Madrid me sobrevino por mi culpa una grave enfermedad que me tuvo confinado en mi cuarto durante dos meses. Sin embargo tal era la borrachera de felicidad—porque no soy capaz de encontrar otro nombre más apropiado para lo que sentía—que me producía el disfrute de verme libre de los controles de mi familia y mi ciudad, que siempre tuve el espíritu alegre. Mis únicos recursos en aquellos días eran leer los peores libros de los filósofos franceses. [...] En cuanto me hube recuperado del todo volví con nuevos ímpetus a buscar los placeres más turbulentos y borrascosos.)

2. Ríos Santos's doctoral dissertation, although repetitive, develops a careful examination of Blanco's correspondence. His method reveals very useful information that would greatly inform a solid biography of the Sevillian writer.

3. There are hints that Godoy liked to read salacious compositions: "The poem, according to Antonio de Campmany (*Manifesto by D. Antonio de Campmany in Response to the Answer by D. Manuel Quintana*, Cádiz, Imprenta Real, 1811) served Blanco in 'gaining the protection of the tyrant [Godoy],' and circulated through Quintana's salón" (El poema, según Antonio de Campmany [*Manifiesto de D. Antonio de Campmany en respuesta a la contextación de D. Manuel Quintana*, Cádiz, Imprenta Real, 1811] le sirvió a Blanco para "ganarse la protección del tirano [Godoy]," y circuló por la tertulia de Quintana) (Blanco, *Obra* 235n2).

4. "The fact that I had obtained liberation from my duty to live in Seville by means of a royal order, itself obtained through the Prince of the Peace [...] made it so that I should not join the scandalous joy of my friends after the mutiny of Aranjuez. I could not help but observe in many of them certain cold expressions and even something close to suspicion, because I had taken advantage of Godoy's influence, an action which they well knew had no other objective than avoiding the odious obligation of having to live in Seville." (Blanco, *Escritos* 66; El hecho de que había obtenido la liberación de mi deber de vivir en Sevilla por una real orden conseguida por medio del Príncipe de la Paz [...] hicieron que no me uniera a la escandalosa alegría de mis amigos tras el motín de Aranjuez. No pude menos de observar en muchos de ellos ciertas expresiones de frialdad e incluso algo parecido a la sospecha por haberme valido de la influencia de Godoy, que ellos sabían bien

que no había tenido otro objetivo más que el de evitar la odiosa obligación de tener que vivir en Sevilla.)

5. "Quedaos en vuestro monte recatadas / Cuidándole el pegazo a vuestro hermano."

6. "Para qué quiero yo Musas ni Apolo: / A cantar un incordio basto solo."

7. "Y si es que por fuerza ha de haber Musas, / Venid, venid, oh Ninfas del Barquillo, / Que no os paráis en dengues ni en excusas."

8. "La gran casa también es bien que trates / a quien Jácome Roque dio su nombre, / y entrando en ella no saldrás para hambre. / Los barrios del Barquillo y Leganitos, / Lavapiés bajo y altas Maravillas / remiten a millares las chiquillas, / con achaque de limas y avellanas; / salado pasto a lujuriosas ganas."

9. "le hande poner en el Arpa, que es lo mismo, que un trato de Cuerda, con que ellas castigan á lo polytico."

10. For an instructive review of the philosophical debates on the use of judicial torture in Europe and Spain in the eighteenth century, see Pereiro Otero's introduction to *La abolición del tormento*.

11. "y las Mulatas le tienen ya puesto sobre las cuerdas de las Harpas al lado de D. Pantaleon, y de Juan Puerco" (Lavandera [19]).

12. "La parte inferior del vientre entre las ingles."

13. "El es bolsón del infierno, / del Diablo faltriquerilla / pues de los que lo frecuentan / cuenta lo que no tenía / él es un cilindro en donde / se refina y rectifica / el mal francés y las bubas / corren como agua por pila; / todo en él es pajas y en ellas / nadie duerme ni aun dormita / y de noche más petites / hay que petates de día. / Y aunque juzgen vocableros / lo que con verdad se avisa, / para ferias del infierno / hay más que tiendas tendidas. / Allí es donde a todas horas / a Venus se sacrifica, / por medio de sus infames / inmundas sacerdotisas."

14. "tocados del veneno / que mata con tiranía."

15. "De estos callejones nace / en muchos la alferecía / y es herir, porque sus madres / están del gálico heridas / y casi todas las amas / de leche tienen la misma / enfermedad, por el pecho / que han pagado a la lascivia."

16. "Más a decir su nombre no me atrevo, / Que esto es ir contra Horacio, quien encarga / Que nunca se comience por el huevo."

17. "No vas a ver aquel rapaz alado / A quien Amor llamaron los poetas, / Aquel niño travieso, aquel taimado / Con venda y una carga de saetas."

18. "Con un *carajo* dicho en voz tan fiera / Que no pude dudar que de un dios era."

19. "Sin duda descendía de guiferos: / Traje de jerezano lo adornaba, / Con aire jaque y respirando fieros."

20. In Manuel Silvestre Martínez's *Librería de jueces* (1791), a series of books with a history of laws in Spain, there is a section on the arbitration of weapons that comments that a law of 1761 "prohibited absolutely the use of short firearms and edged weapons . . . daggers, bodkins, almaradas (narrow-bladed knives that are only sharp on the point), spring-loaded knives with a notch or ferrule . . ." (prohibió absolutamente el uso de las Armas cortas de fuego y blancas . . . Puñales, Guiferos, Almaradas, Navajas de muelle con golpe ó virola . . .) and states that the punishment

was "For nobles, six years in prison; for peasants the same period in the mines" (A los nobles la de seis años de Presidio; y á los Plebeyos los mismo de Minas) (351).

21. "Pues aquí aunque no limpio se ama claro."

22. "Vencer esa canalla que ahí delante / Ves de berrugas, llagas, purgaciones, / Es cosa tan pequeña, tan sencilla, / Que es vencer partidas de guerrillas."

23. "Tenía el grueso rostro abigarrado / De morado y carmín, y a costurones / Tan caprichosamente variado / Que apenas descubría las facciones. / De mitras el vestido era bordado, / De bandas, cruces, llaves y cordones; / Luego vistosamente terminaba / En un crespo cerquillo que lo orlaba."

24. "Y gracias a sus buenas condiciones / Me vi muy pronto echando bendiciones."

25. "Pronto me hallé de púrpura vestido. / ¡Oh tiempo en que me vi leyes dictando! / Vi el orbe a mi obediencia tan rendido, / Tan confiado en mi saber profundo / Que con un pergamino partí el mundo."

26. "En la Secretaría de Estado se conserva una carta del enviado de España que dice que el Papa tenía una llaga en el *carajo.* En aquel tiempo se hablaba claro."

27. In 1545, Pope Paul III nominated Girolamo Fracastoro (1478–1553) as medical adviser to the Council of Trent. Fracastoro is the author of the poem *Syphilis sive de morbo gallico,* which gave the name to the venereal disease.

28. " "incordio primitivo / Que el insigne Colón condujo a España."

29. "Los Sitios frecuenté, secretarías, / Antesalas, tertulias y paseos, / La guardia hice en Palacio muchos días / Mas no lograba el fin de mis deseos."

30. "El bestia por salir de tal ladilla / Me llevó a que habitase una guardilla."

31. "En esta situación desesperado / Aguardé al que llegase allí primero / Para escapar con él. De este malvado / Me fie bajo fe de caballero / Y en vez de libertarme ha batallado / Hasta entregarme a un enemigo fiero, / Enemigo tan fuerte y poderoso / Que de terror nombrarle apenas oso."

32. "Mas luego apeteciendo los honores / De las ciencias, cursé universidades, / Confundí sublimísimos doctores / y les hice decir mil necedades."

33. "Di trabajos a muchos escritores, / que ellos no han transmitido a estas edades. / Picado así en mi honor, las obras mías / Impresas doy ya a luz todos los días."

34. The legend of the balm of Fierabrás has its origin in a French *chanson de geste* of the twelfth century. The magic potion was supposed to be made out of the special unction used to embalm the body of Christ and had the quality of curing the ailments of those who consumed it. According to the story, Fierabrás and his father, King Balan of Spain, took over Rome and looted some barrels that contained the balm. In chap. 10 of the first part of Cervantes's *Don Quixote,* after having been beaten and gotten his ear split in an encounter with a man from Biscay, who was in truth a lady's attendant, the knight claims to know a formula to prepare the balm. He tells Sancho Panza that the balm is so effective that even if his body is split in two, the squire only has to put the two parts back together and give him the potion to drink.

35. "Un auxilio dulcísimo y seguro / En él tendrán mis fieles seguidores; / No aquel dios de Almadén, terrible y duro, / Perseguidor cruel de los amores. / Tal vez ten-

drán algún pequeño apuro / Más sufrirán alegres sus Dolores / Y en Fierabrás de confianza llenos / Firmes dirán: Incordio más o menos."

36. "tiene efectos maravillosos en varias enfermedades, especialmente en las venéreas, que cura con suavidad admirable."

37. "que con tanto beneficio comun han merecido la poderosa acogida de V. Em.ª"

38. "disenterias pertinaces, en la angina maligna y otras enfermedades."

39. "La gran diputación que se acercaba / De médicos compuesta, hospitalarios, / Frailes, enterradores, boticarios."

40. "yo no se latín ni jansenismo, / Pero sabré caparte aquí ahora mismo."

41. "A Fierabrás colocaré a mi lado / Y en él tendrá mi reino mil ventajas. / Una gran pipa de licor sagrado / Mandaré conservar con mis alhajas / Y en vez de insulso néctar y ambrosía / Beberé una botella cada día."

42. "sirve para Dolores venéreos, úlceras exóstosis, tumores endurecidos y escrófulas. No falta en Madrid quien vende esta tisana por un secreto en botellas y á buen precio."

14. Samaniego's Sticky Fable

1. The understanding of Samaniego's canonical work started to change with the publication of his erotic and obscene poems, which had only circulated in clandestine versions, very much like those of Blanco and Moratín we just studied. The French Hispanist Raymond Foulché-Delbosc included several of these poems in his *Cuentos y poesías más que picantes* (More than spicy stories and poems) (1899), and a more complete edition appeared in 1921 under the title *Jardín de Venus* (Garden of Venus), edited by Joaquín López Barbadillo. López Barbadillo's work has been expanded and refined by Emilio Palacios Fernández in later editions of 1977, 1991, and 2004.

2. "Se trata pues, de una moral no definida, naturalista, telúrica, carente de religión. Es una moral utilitaria, y con frecuencia instintiva. Se coloca al hombre al nivel del animal, en lucha con la vida por la supervivencia ... El instinto de conservación domina sobre muchos sentimientos de la moral cristiana" (Palacios Fernández, "Caracterización" 189).

3. "Samaniego retoma la tradición de las fábulas de una manera crítica y personal. Si los temas pasaron por el tamiz de su ingenio, mayores razones le asistían para controlar las moralejas."

4. "si es que queremos entender como es debido qué era la literatura de las *Fábulas* y qué papel jugaba en el conjunto de la producción literaria dieciochesca."

5. "Que en estos versos trato / de daros un asunto / que instruya deleitando."

6. "A un panal de rica miel / dos mil moscas acudieron, / que por golosas murieron / presas de patas en él. / Otra dentro de un pastel / enterró su golosina. / *Así, si bien se examina, / los humanos corazones / perecen en las prisiones / del vicio que los domina.*"

7. "Metaphoricamente se toma por qualquier cosa que deleita el gusto, ò incluye en si especial suavidad y delectación."

8. "Inclinado à comer sin nesessidad, y que busca manjáres exquisitos y regalados, atendiendo mas al gusto, que à dár buen mantenimiento al estómago. Formase del nombre Gula."

15. *Gálico,* Prostitution, and Public Policy

1. "Es una harpía inhumana, / veneno de licenciosos, / *escarmiento de golosos* / y ruina de gente sana; / monstruo que come sin ganas, / anillo de todas manos, / azote de hombres livianos, / género común de dos, / censo de San Juan de Dios / y hacienda de cirujanos."

2. "En esta gran capital, donde abundan por comun desgracias á cada paso y donde quiera los objetos de la mas vergonzosa prostitucion; donde la corrupción imprudente camina sin freno tan libre y descocada, insultando á la virtud y la decencia pública; donde malgrado la severa vigilancia de V. A., la liviandad, el ocio, la miseria, la infame seduccion ofrecen sin cesar al vicio nuevas y nuevas víctimas; donde mil infelices van dia y noche por esas calles brindando á todos con sus sucios y venales favores; donde, en fin, es tan fácil, ¡ojalá no lo fuese!, sacrificar el vicioso á su sensualidad y lascivo desenfreno."

3. "¡Y que veneno, amigo mio, aquel que se encubre igualmente entre las rosas de la hermosura, y los indicios ménos equívocos del recato y de la virtud, que inficionando generaciones enteras, suele dormir y reconcentrarse en la inocente que sin saberlo lo abriga, y le ha de propagar, hasta que prevaleciendo con mas furor, imprima en los semblantes y en los miembros exteriores las vergonzosas señales de una espantosa degradación!"

4. "Es menester hacer a las enfermedades venéreas la misma guerra que a las viruelas, y voy a arriesgar mis ideas sobre este asunto."

5. "de la mayor providad, y con dotaciones que los hiciesen inaccesibles á toda seducción [. . .] y baxo la misma pena de deportacion habian de avisar sin perder un instante de cualquiera que se hallase contagiada [. . .] hasta que se conduxese la enferma al hospital destinado a este objeto."

6. "La Prostitution n'a pas, à la vérité, produit la honteuse contagion qui desole l'univers: mais elle la propage; elle en est le réservoir, la fource impure, & toujours renaissante."

7. "Propre á prévenir les Malheurs qu'occasionne le *Publicisme* des Femmes."

8. I will later refer to the actress María Ladvenant, an important figure who can be placed in this realm and who supposedly had contracted *gálico.* Cabarrús's system for controlling *gálico* includes the management of actresses who combine their histrionic profession with that of prostitution. At the same time, he advises that women actors should be encouraged and protected in their careers so that they will not see self-degradation as a necessity: "Actresses should be subject to the brothel system, and live there if they prostitute themselves, it not being just to defame them solely for their profession, which should be promoted and preserved from the almost inevitable necessity that leads them to this point of degradation" (Las actoras debian ser sujetas á la mancebía, y vivir en ella si se prostituyesen,

no siendo justo infamarlas solo por su profesion, que se habia de fomentar y preservar de la quasi inevitable necesidad que las conduce á este punto de degradacion) (780).

9. For a more in-depth explanation of the aesthetic attraction that *petimetras* (high society's fashionable women) felt toward *majas,* the mimicking of their demeanor, and the idea of "majismo," see chap. 2 of Martín Gaite's study. In *Framing Majismo,* the art historian Tara Zanardi offers a comprehensive study of the power of dress and the public attitudes of *majas* and *majos,* analyzing pictorial representations of these popular characters that were crafted for consumption by Spanish society's higher echelons. Zanardi further instantiates Martín Gaite's insights on the use of these iconic figures to establish common identity for Spanish society.

10. "para que en los paseos y teatros estas mugeres fuesen conocidas."

11. Moratín is using macaronic Latin, French, Italian, and English to mask real places, people, and situations. Here he must be referring to the somewhat quiet Jesús del Valle Street, less than a kilometer away from the popular Puerta del Sol.

12. "Por el solo hecho de exercer este infame oficio sin la autorizacion de la policía, estaria expuesta á una graduacion de penas, desde la condenacion á la mancebía, que seria la primera, hasta la deportacion á las colonias, que seria la mas grave."

13. "En fin, las mugeres que despues de curadas y declaradas sanas del contagio por dos veces diesen lugar á una tercera curacion, serian irremisiblemente conducidas del lazareto ú hospital á las colonias, baxo las condiciones que exige la poblacion de estas, y de que hablaré separadamente."

14. "la pena de muerte, ó á lo menos de destierro perpetuo á las colonias [. . . debería] determinarse irremisiblemente."

15. "Los Regimientos habian de hacer registrar exáctamente la ropa de sus soldados, y al menor indicio de contagio, consignar los contagiados, sin dexarlos salir hasta su curacion."

16. "Permitid pues que se procuren disminuir los riesgos que acompañan á este desórden inevitable, y tal vez os convencereis de que las precauciones que exige la sanidad pública, redundarán en beneficio de las costumbres mismas."

17. For a more developed study of Cibat's work, see Jean-Louis Guereña's *Médicos y prostitución,* on which my own discussion is based.

18. "Billete de sanidad impreso y firmado del profesor encargado de visitarlas, fijado en la cabecera de la cama, el que las servirá de patente o testimonio de seguridad para sí y los contratantes."

19. "para no entregarse a ellos si los hallasen enfermos."

20. Institutions of this sort were also created outside the peninsula during the sixteenth and seventeenth centuries and were aimed not only at prostitutes but also at women going against the rules of appropriate behavior. According to Josefina Muriel, there were houses in Buenos Aires, Cuzco, Lima, Manila, Mexico, Santiago de Chile, and Santo Domingo.

21. For a study of the changes in administration and the irregular effectiveness of the *galeras* in the city of Madrid, see Domínguez Ortíz's "La galera o cárcel de mujeres de Madrid."

22. "Y la Hermosa Gertrudis, carpintera / muy diestra en toda su arte de meneo, / de cuyo bien nos priva hoy la galera."

23. For more in-depth discussions on the topic of prostitution in Goya's *Caprichos,* see Alcalá Flecha's *Matrimonio y prostitución en el arte de Goya..*

24. Although it is not an unlikely phenomenon, I have not found information on women forced into prostitution. There are of course the economic factors that, yesterday and today, can prod women into this practice.

25. "Persuadido el autor de que la censura de los errores y vicios humanos (aunque parece peculiar de la eloqüencia y la poesia) puede tambien ser objeto de la pintura: ha escogido como asuntos proporcionados para su obra, entre la multitud de extravagancias y desaciertos que son comunes en toda sociedad civil, y entre las preocupaciones y embustes vulgares, autorizados por la costumbre, la ignorancia ó el interés, aquellos que ha creido mas aptos á subministrar materia para el ridículo, y exercitar al mismo tiempo la fantasia del artifice."

26. "Ha tenido que exponer a los ojos formas y actitudes que solo han existido hasta ahora en la mente humana, obscurecida y confusa por la falta de ilustración o acalorada con el desenfreno de las pasiones."

27. "La pintura (como la poesia) escoge en lo universal lo que juzga más a propósito para sus fines: reúne en un solo personage fantastico, circunstancias y caracteres que la naturaleza presenta repartidos en muchos, y de esta convinacion, ingeniosamente dispuesta, resulta aquella feliz imitacion."

28. "Se ciegan tanto los hombres lujuriosos, que ni con lente distinguen que la Señora que obsequian, es una ramera."

29. "El propio Quevedo había reflexionado ya sobre los poderes de la vista en textos como *España defendida* y en pasajes de 'El mundo de por dentro,' . . . en el cual se observaba la mediocridad y locura mundana por 'debajo de la cuerda,' es decir, más allá de las apariencias."

30. Goya also depicts *celestinas* as messengers for and confidantes of women in high society. In plate 28, *Chiton* (Hush), a young woman dressed in black shares a secret with an old woman, who listens to her with rosary in hand.

31. "Mientras se aderezan y visten las putas, rezan las alcahuetas para que Dios las de mucha fortuna, y las enseñan ciertas lecciones."

32. For a discussion of the harmonization of morally reproachable actions and principled religious attitudes and poses, see Martín Gaite, chap. 6, esp. pp. 163–64 and 169–72.

33. In the *Diccionario panhispánico de dudas,* "holgar(se)" is defined as "sometimes it is used, euphemistically, with the meaning of 'maintaining sexual relations with someone': 'It was she who confirmed to me that Mario was trying to induce Celia to liberate herself . . . and that Celia . . . feared that it was only a request, on Mario's part, to *holgar* with other women'" (a veces se usa, eufemísticamente, con el sentido de 'mantener relaciones sexuales con alguien': 'Fue ella quien me confirmó que Mario trataba de inducir a Celia a liberarse . . . y que Celia . . . temía que fuera solamente . . . una petición de permiso, por parte de Mario, para holgar con otras mujeres') (RAE 2005, s.v. "holgar[se]").

34. The manuscript in the Biblioteca Nacional refers to this scenario: "Una hija viciosa que se echa a puta, luego no conoce ni aun a su madre que anda tal vez pidiendo limosna" (A dissolute daughter who turns into a whore, later on doesn't even recognize her mother who may be begging for money) (Carrete Parrondo 356)

35. Stoichita and Coderch connect this image to the idea of men under the rule of women who are "on top," a theme they link to the representation of Hercules being forced by Queen Omphale to wear feminine clothes (42). The positioning of the woman's left hand, holding the man's hair and head, and her right hand, holding the sharp razor close to his face, runs parallel to images of Judith and Holofernes, a well-developed pictorial theme known to Goya and other masters. The fear of loss of manhood and its expression in stories about male decapitation would be profusely revisited during the nineteenth century, after the re-creation of Salome's story and the decapitation of John the Baptist in Oscar Wilde's play *Salomé* (1891).

36. "toda especie de avechuchos, militares, paisanos y frailes revolotean alrededor de una dama medio gallina: caen, las mozas los sujetan por los alones, los hacen vomitar y les sacan las tripas."

37. "una puta se pone de señuelo en la ventana, y acuden militares, paisanos y hasta frailes y toda especie de avechuchos revolotean alrededor; la alcahueta pide a dios que caigan, y las otras putas los despluman, y hacen vomitar, y les arrancan hasta las tripas como cazadores a las perdices."

38. "el sugeto despreciable por su figura ó costumbres."

39. "el arte de ostentar con ruidosas, y brillantes exterioridades el amor que no se tiene."

40. "*Topografía de los Lunares,* dividida en dos partes: la primera trata de los Lunares que se colocan en las cienes; y la segunda de los que se colocan en las demàs partes del rostro. El Autor, que es arbitrista, en punto de Cortejo pretende que los Lunares que hasta oy no han tenido otro uso en los rostros de las Damas que hacer buen viso pueden tener uso mas sublime, y mas util en el Cortejo. Dice, que los Lunares grandes puestos en la sien izquierda pueden denotar, que la plaza está ocupada; puestos en la sien derecha, que està dispuesta à romper, y tomar otro Cortejo; y su falta en ambas sienes puede ser señal de estàr la plaza vacante: Que los Lunares pequeños distribuidos diestramente por el rostro pueden denotar el actual, y momentaneo estado de los caprichos; por exemplo, puestos junto al ojo derecho querràn decir, que està dada la orden para que el Cortejo no mire con atención à tal, ò tal persona: puestos junto al ojo izquierdo querràn decir, que el Cortejo puede mirar adonde quiera: puestos junto à la boca al lado derecho querràn decir, que no hable con fulano, ú zutano: puestos junto al lado izquierdo denotarán, que aquel dia el Cortejo ha estado muy mono, y que ha dicho cosas, &c. y en fin, puestos debaxo de la narìz podràn denotar, que el Cortejo ha olìdo algun mal passo de la adjunta persona."

41. "No quiero, amados lectores, / Que retrograden las bellas, / Ni ver á nuestras doncellas / De zorongo y chiquiadores."

42. "Pero, al fin, aunque no es nada, / me queda grande contento / que no tendrás

escarmiento / aunque has sido amonestada; / porque como tu morada / se funda sólo en la era / de disoluta, embustera, / quita joyas y pendientes, / aunque haya mil Benaventes / pararás en la Galera."

43. "Quizá llegó a creerse curada; pero el día 26 de Marzo le acometió una enfermedad violenta y desconocida, que al cabo de seis días, escasos la arrebató á sus triunfos y placeres. // Falleció á las once y cuarto de la mañana del 1.o de Abril de 1767, en medio de continuos vómitos que le impidieron recibir el Viático."

44. "Haráte de Guerrero y la Catuja / Larga memoria, y de la malograda / de la divina Lavenant, que ahora / anda en campos de luz paciendo estrellas, / la sal, el garabato, el aire, el chiste, / la fama y los ilustres contratiempos / recordará con lágrimas . . ."

45. In the *Historia de la música española,* Antonio Martín Moreno writes that "Leandro Fernández de Moratín la llamó 'incomparable y grande'; José Cadalso la declaró 'reina de los teatros'; y Gaspar Melchor de Jovellanos aludía a ella en una poesía diciendo que 'anda en campos de luz paciendo estrellas'" (411). This is the same reading of the passage by Cruz Peterson in her accomplished *Women's Somatic Training in Early Modern Spanish Theater,* where she understands the poem as showing that Ladvenant "was so loved by her audience for her extraordinary acting skills that after her death poets mourned her loss with poems and prose" (3–4).

46. Jovellanos's text renders warped homage to Luis de Góngora by paraphrasing a verse from his *Soledad* primera: "en campos de zafiro pace estrellas" (grazes stars amid fields of sapphire) (*Soledades* I, v. 6), part of the dense beginning of the poem (vv. 1–6). Góngora explains that he started writing in the spring, when the sun is in the constellation of Taurus, thus the image of a bull grazing stars. Jovellanos, outwardly praising Ladvenant but implicitly asserting that she was tainted by a not very poetic malady, inverts Góngora's cryptic imagery. I want to thank one of the readers of the manuscript for calling my attention to this link.

47. "ataja las llagas, que van *paciendo,* y no solamente las de la boca, empero las del cuerpo universo."

48. "Dos meses, tres dias y seis horas há que V.m. y dos Viejas, tres amigas, un Page y su Hermana me *pacen* de día y de noche."

49. For a more in-depth discussion of *La Lozana andaluza* in relation to the discourse of syphilis, see Herrero Ingelmo and Montero Cartelle, "El *Morbus gallicus.*"

50. *Loz.:* Señora mía, aquel mozo mandó a la madre que me acogiese y me diese buen lugar, y la puta vieja barbuda, estrellera, dijo: ¿No véis que tiene greñimón? . . . pensó que, porque yo traigo la toca baja y ligada a la ginovesa, y son tantas las cabezadas que me he dado yo misma, de un enojo que he habido, que me maravillo cómo so viva; que como en la nao no tenía médico ni bien ninguno, me ha tocado entre ceja y ceja, y creo que me quedará señal. // *Sev.:* No será nada, por mi vida. Llamaremos aquí un médico que la vea, que parece una estrellica.

51. "Así la inimitable Lavenana / se dio a un servidor vuestro en dos pesetas / siendo niña, aún casi doncella y sana. / Mas ya que la lujuria cortesana / se desenfrenó ansiosa y a porfía, / cada cual por dichoso se tenia / con llamarse algo padre de

sus hijos, / después de aquellos lances tan prolijos / que a contarlos el genio me provoca, / mas la Musa me pone dedo en boca. / Después de esto se tuvo por un héroe / el que logró coger en su entrepierna / cinco meses de verdes purgaciones, / a costa de un gran traje y cien doblones."

52. In his travel diary, the French diplomat Jean-François de Bourgoing transcribes the epitaph of Francisca Ladvenant while in the cemetery of the Valencian church of Sant Miquel de Burjassot. In his comments he confuses Francisca with her sister María, but the transcription allows us to place the birthdate of Francisca in 1750: "Here lies / Francisca / l'Advenant / twenty two years and eight days / of age, immortal / for her very sharp / talent and admi- / ration, unique in / her profession, she di- / ed the eleventh of April 1772, / giving special / signs of her fer- / vent contri- / tion; pray to God / for her" (A qui jace /Francisca /l'Advenant /de edad de veinte y dos annos /y ocho dias, immortal /por su agudissimo /talento, y admi- / racion unica en / su profession, mu- / rio en onze de abril 1772, / dando especiales / muestras de fer- / vorosa contri- / cion; ruegen a Dios / por ella) (Bourgoing 119).

53. For biographical information on both María and Francisca Ladvenant, see Juliá Martínez's "Documentos sobre María y Francisca Ladvenant."

54. "En realidad se llamaba Francisca Ladvenant, cantante y hermana de la conocida actriz, la 'divina' María."

55. "Es probable que esta Isidora ó Francisca Ladvenant sea la *Dorisa,* cantada por D. Nicolás de Moratín en tantos y tan delicados versos."

56. "Anegado en pegajoso, y fetido sudor, rebuelto en congojas, y tragado de agonias, y sofocaciones. . . . La cabeza monda de cabello, y plagada à trechos de costras, berrugas, postillas, tuberculos, y otros promontorios, y chichones. La boca cubierta de vexigas, encharcada en babas."

57. In the section titled "On Goya's Bestiary," Stoichita and Coderch develop a nuanced interpretation of the artist's use of animal physiognomy as an overarching metaphor in his work (59–73). The bailiff-cat and the prostitute-bird were not Goya's only animalized people; his engravings also show a student as a frog; an aristocratic woman, dressed as a maja, as a snake on a scythe; and a *petimetre* who looks like a monkey.

58. "los Jueces superiores hacen capa regularmente a los jueces superiores y alguaciles para que roben y desplumen a las putas pobres."

59. "Y aunque saben que no es el estafarlas / medio de corregirlas, pues quedando / pobres, prosiguen siempre puteando, / las roban con achaque de enmendarlas."

60. "unas instalaciones con capacidad para acoger a muchas más internas—y talleres—que la Galera, con un regimen disciplinario muy similar, pero cuya administración recae en la Junta de Hospicios. Desde su fundación, las reclusas de este establecimiento fueron aplicadas a los telares, los tornos de hilar y otras manufacturas textiles, porque su objetivo era que las pobres aprendieran las 'labores propias de su sexo' y a 'servir honradamente.'"

61. Although Salas García and Sánchez Hita do not develop an interpretation of Goya's "San Fernando" drawing, I am indebted to their article for my discussion.

62. I have already discussed a similar image in the Peruvian author Valle y Caviedes's poem "A una dama que por serlo paró en La Caridad." The character of Belisa is presented as drooling either because of the treatment with mercury or because of her performing oral sex: "like silkworms / she threads spittle from her mouth, / because going around with two cocoons / is something she has not yet forgotten" (Como gusanos de seda / babas por la boca hila, / que el andar con dos capullos / no ha olvidado todavía) (vv. 37–40).

63. I use the translation from French by Clorinda Donato and Ricardo López in their *Enlightenment Spain and the* Encyclopédie méthodique. Donato and Lopez's volume contains the original "Espagne" entry by Masson de Morvilliers with a parallel translation into English. It also includes the Spanish entry and parallel translation of "España" written by the translator-adaptor Julián de Velasco that appeared as a riposte to Masson in the *Encyclopedia metódica* in 1792.

16. The Future in Jeopardy

1. "El mal *gálico* es otro cruel enemigo de la poblacion, que no solo estraga y debilita al que le padece, sino también á los mismos hijos y descendientes, que con esta especie de segundo pecado original nacen, y se crian débiles, enfermizos é inhábiles para el trabajo y la fatiga."

2. In fact, this preoccupation with inherited disease would be the characteristic mantra of Henrik Ibsen's great play *Ghosts* (1881), which deals with the concealment of syphilis.

3. "El cuidado del aumento de la población es sin duda una de las cosas generalmente útiles á todas las partes del estado: pues ella es la que subministra hombres para todas las ocupaciones y ministerios de religion, justicia, fortaleza, sabiduría, economía y policía."

4. "Un reino medianamente opulento, que por sus nativas riquezas pudiera ya ser opulentísimo, camina a pasos lentos en su población a causas de las enfermedades endémicas que resultan de la casual y arbitraria elección de los sitios en que se han congregado sus pobladores."

5. " "Las escrófulas, llamadas vulgarmente cotos y las bubas, llagas y demás vicios, que acompañan al primitivo mal-gálico, ciertamente original del propio clima, se han ido propagando hasta el punto de representar algunos pueblos un verdadero hospital."

6. "reunidas tantas calamidades que diariamente se presentan a la vista, forman la espantosa imagen de una población generalmente achacosa, que mantiene inutilizada para la sociedad y felicidad pública la mitad de sus individuos, a los unos por mucha parte del año y a otros por todo el resto de la vida."

7. "El *Pus* gálico-napoleonico ha tiempo que habia venido en papeles; pero como llegó desvirtuado, hizo poco y débil efecto. También vinieron algunos Emisarios apestados, que preparaban insensible y cautelosamente el contagio, indisponiendo con sus miasmas los humores diversos de este Cuerpo; mas como no se atrevian á inocular *de brazo á brazo,* no lograron la erupción completa. Llegó por fin por

la parte del Norte á los Pueblos de Tierradentro el Francés Dalmivar; y muy á su sabor inoculo al Cura Hidalgo. Este propago la infernal viruela en Allende, Aldama, Abasolo y otros; y de estos se comunicó la peste á una multitud de incautos e infelices."

8. These authors would include the French Denis Diderot (1713–84), François-Marie Arouet (Voltaire) (1694–78), Jean-Baptiste Rousseau (1671–1741), Jacques-Hyacinthe Serry (1659–1738), and Antoine Augustin Calmet (1672–1757), but this list could also include other names that awakened ideas of autonomy or autonomous thought, such as the aforementioned Feijoo or Clavijero.

9. For more on miasma, see the sidebar on p. 120.

10. "los Practicantes que trahia el Facultativo eran diestros, y con los *febrífugos* excelentes, que aqui habia, se impidio maravillosamente que la ocupasen las viruelas confluentes, y en poco tiempo fueron rechazadas acia partes menos nobles. En seguida se les ha ido atacando dó quiera que han aparecido, y desalojandolas de los lugares que habian ocupado con mas furor y tenacidad. Al fin el mal está sólo en las piernas; la Cabeza siempre firme y despejada, el pecho libre, la respiración natural, el estómago fuerte."

11. "quedara el hermoso Cuerpo de la Nueva España libre y limpio de toda lepra."

12. "buenos jabones y elixíris en nuestra Botica."

13. "Que en su misma casa oyó indistintamente á dos personas que fueron el Capitan D. Antonio Castro y el de igual clase D. Felix Ceballos: que el Padre Mier había dicho: ¿Qué es lo que han traido los gachupines á la america? El galico, la sarna, las viruelas, las cucarachas, y otras inmundicias como estas."

Bibliography

Primary Sources

Aguirre, Juan Bautista. "Breve diseño de las ciudades de Guayaquil y Quito (carta jocoseria escrita por el autor a su cuñado Don Gerónimo Mendiola, describiendo a Guayaquil y Quito)." In *Los dos primeros poetas coloniales ecuatorianos*. Quito: Biblioteca Ecuatoriana Mínima, 1960.

Apóstol y Civilizador. Boletín de Divulgación del Beato Fray Junípero Serra 180 (March 1991). Mallorca: Fraternidad de Franciscanos Petra.

Apóstol y civilizador. Boletín de divulgación del beato fray Junípero Serra 209 (September–October 1995). Mallorca: Fraternidad de Franciscanos Petra.

Arjona, Manuel María de. *Exercicios de preparacion para la hora de la muerte que se practica en una de las distribuciones del santo retiro espiritual, en la Iglesia del Hospital de las Bubas de esta ciudad.* Seville: Por la viuda de Hidalgo y Sobrino, 1805.

Astruc, Jean. *De morbis venereis libri novem: in quibus disseritur tum de origine, propagatione & contagione horumce affectuum in genere: tum de singulorum natura, aetiologia & therapeia, cum brevi analysi & epicrisi operum plerorumque, quae de eodem argumento scripta sunt.* Lutetiae Parisiorum [Paris]: Apud Guillelmum Cavelier, 1740.

———. *Traité des maladies vénériennes; où, après avoir explique l'origine, la propagation, & la communication de ces maladies en général, on décrit la nature, les causes, & la curation de chacune en particulier.* Paris: Guillaume Cavelier, 1740.

Astruc, Jean, and Félix Galisteo y Xiorro. *Tratado de las enfermedades venéreas, en que despues de haber explicado el orígen, la propagacion, y la comunicacion de estas enfermedades en general, se trata de la naturaleza, de las causas, y curacion de cada una en particular.* Madrid: En la imprenta de don Benito Cano, 1791.

Astruc, Jean, Félix Galisteo y Xiorro, Pedro Marín, Francisco Fernández, and Miguel Copín. *Tratado de las enfermedades venereas: en que despues de haver explicado el Origen, la Propagacion, y la Comunicacion de estas Enfermedades en general, se trata de la Naturaleza, de las Causas y Curacion de cada una en particular.* Madrid: En la imprenta de Pedro Marin, 1772.

Baglivi, Giorgio, and Giovanni Domenico Santorini. *Opera omnia medico-practica, et anatomica.* Antwerp: Apud Joh. Fridericum Rüdigerum, 1715.

Balmis, Francisco Javier. *Demostración de las eficaces virtudes nuevamente descubiertas en las raices de dos plantas de Nueva-España, especies de ágave y de begónia, para la curacion del vicio venéreo y escrofuloso, Y de otras graves enfermedades que resisten al uso del Mercurio, y demás remedios conocidos.* Madrid: En la imprenta de la viuda de D. Joaquin Ibarra, 1794.

Beccaria, Cesare. *Dei delitti e delle pene.* Trans. as *On Crimes and Punishments*, by David Young. Indianapolis: Bobbs-Merrill, 1963.

Bello, Andrés. *Obras completas de don Andrés Bello.* Santiago de Chile: Pedro G. Ramírez, 1881–90.

Benegasi y Luján, Francisco, and Joseph Joachín Benegassi y Luxán. *Obras lyricas joco-serias, que dexó escritas el Sr. D. Francisco Benegasi y Luxan . . . Van añadidas algunas poesias de su Hijo don Joseph Benegasi y Luxán, posteriores á su primer Tomo Lyrico.* Madrid: Juan de San Martin, 1746.

Beristáin y Souza, José Mariano. *Diálogos patrióticos.* [Mexico]: María Fernández de Jáuregui, 1810.

Blanco White, Joseph. *Autobiografía de Blanco-White.* Ed. Antonio Garnica. Seville: Servicio de Publicaciones de la Universidad de Sevilla, 1988.

———. *Escritos autobiográficos menores.* Ed. Antonio Garnica. Huelva: Universidad de Huelva, 1999.

———. "El incordio: Poema épico-gálico en un canto." *Rara Avis* 2–3 (1987): 65–73.

———. *Obra poética completa.* Ed. Antonio Garnica and Jesús Díaz García. Madrid: Visor, 1994.

Bourgoing, Jean-François. *Travels in Spain: Containing a New, Accurate, and Comprehensive View of the Present State of that Country.* London: G. G. J. and J. Robinson, 1789.

Bretonne, Restif de La. *Le pornographe, ou idées d'un honnête-homme sur un projet de réglement pour les prostituées.* London: Chez Jean Nourse; A La Haie [The Hague]: Chez Gosse junior, & Pinet, libraires de S.A.S, 1770.

Brunet de la Selva, Ramón. *Dissertaciones physico-medicas, sobre varios curiosos assumptos de Medicina. Tomo Segundo. Que contiene tres disertaciones. I. Dissertacion Apologetica contra una Carta anónima. II. Sobre las señales, prognostico, y curativa del Morbo galico, y su verdadero remedio. . . .* Madrid: En la Oficina de Domingo Fernandez de Arrojo, 1758.

Cabarrús, Francisco de. *Cartas sobre los obstáculos que la naturaleza, la opinion y las leyes oponen a la felicidad pública.* Vitoria: Imprenta de don Pedro Real, 1808.

Cabriada, Juan de. *Carta filosófica, médico-chymica. En que se demuestra, que de los tiempos, y experiencias se han aprendido los mejores remedios contra las enfermedades. Por la nova-antigua medicina.* Madrid: L.A. de Bedmar y Baldivia, 1687.

Cadalso, José. *Cartas marruecas.* Paris: Bobée é Hingray, Libreros, 1827.

———. *Obras inéditas.* Ed. Raymond Foulché-Delbosc. Madrid: M. Murillo, 1894.

———. *Poesías del Coronel D. José de Cadalso.* Madrid: En la imprenta de Sancha, 1821.

Calvo, Juan, and Andrés de Tamayo. *Primera y Segunda Parte de la Cirugía Universal, y Particular del Cuerpo Humano, que Trata de las Cosas Naturales, no Naturales, y Preternaturales . . . Añadidos Tres Tratados, Uno de Anatomía, y Otro de Morbo Gálico.* Valencia: Vincente Cabrera, 1703.

Capitulos de reformacion, que su magestad se sirve de mandar guardar por esta ley, para govierno del Reyno. Madrid: Por Tomas Junti, 1623.

Carrió de Lavandera, Alonso. *El lazarillo de ciegos caminantes desde Buenos-Ayres, hasta Lima con sus Itinerarios segun la mas puntual observacion, con algunas noticias utiles á los Nuevos Comerciantes que tratan en Mulas, y otras Historicas. Sacado de las memorias que hizo Don Alonso Carrió de la Vandera en este dilatado Viage, y Comision que tubo por la Corte para el arreglo de Correos y Estafetas, Situacion, y ajuste de Postas, desde Montevideo. Por Don Calixto Bustamante Carlos Inca, alias Concolorcorvo Natural del Cuzco, que acompañoò al referido Comisionado en dicho Viage, y escribió sus Extractos.* Gijón [Lima]: En la Imprenta de la Rovada, 1773 [1775].

Castro, Adolfo de. *Poetas líricos de los siglos XVI y XVII.* Madrid: M. Rivadeneyra, 1854.

Cibat, Antonio. "Medidas propuestas por D. Antonio Cibat para contener los progresos de la sífilis." *El Siglo Médico* 8.379 (1861): 221–22.

Cervantes Saavedra, Miguel de. *Don Quijote de la Mancha.* Preliminary study by Fernando Lázaro Carreter, critical text and direction by Francisco Rico. Barcelona: Crítica, 1998.

———. "El casamiento engañoso." In *Novelas ejemplares* II, edited by Francisco Rodríguez Marín. Madrid: Espasa Calpe, S. A., 1965, 175–207.

Clavijero, Fransisco Saverio. *Historia antigua de México: sacada de de los mejores historiadores españoles, y de los manuscritos y de las pinturas antiguas de los indios: dividida en diez libros . . . e ilustrada con disertaciones sobre la tierra, los animales y los habitantes de México.* Trans. José Joaquín de Mora. Mexico: Departamento Editorial de la Dirección General de las Bellas Artes, 1917.

———. *Storia antica del Messico: cavata da' migliore storici spagnuoli, e da' manoscritti, e dalle pitture antiche degl' indiani . . . e corredata di carte geografiche, e di varie figure e dissertazioni sulla terra, sugli animali, e fugli abitatori del Messico.* Cesena [Italy]: Per Gregorio Biasini all' Insegna di Pallade, 1780.

Colmenero, José. *Reprobación del pernicioso abuso de los polvos de la corteza de Quarango o China-China.* Salamanca: Eugenio Antonio García, 1697.

Covarrubias Orozco, Sebastián de. *Tesoro de la lengua castellana, o española.* Madrid: Por Luis Sanchez, 1611.

Curvo Semmedo, João. *Secretos medicos y chirurgicos del doctor don Juan Curbo Semmedo: traducidos de lengua vulgar portuguesa en castellana, por el Doct. Thomas Cortijo Herraiz . . . ; con un breve diccionario Lusitanico Castellano, para los que tienen las obras de dicho Autor.* Madrid: En la Imprenta de Bernardo Peralta, 1735.

Delicado, Francisco. *Retrato de la Lozana andaluza.* Ed. Claude Allaigre. Madrid: Cátedra, 1985.

Dioscorides Pedanius, of Anazarbeo. *Pedacio Dioscorides anazarbeo, Acerca de la materia medicinal y de los venenos mortíferos.* Trans. and ed. Andrés de Laguna. Antwerp: En casa de Iuan Latio, 1555.

Dou y de Bassóls, Ramon Lázaro de. *Instituciones del derecho público general de España con noticia del particular de Cataluña, y de las principales reglas de gobierno en qualquier estado.* Vol. 3. Madrid: Oficina de don Benito García y Compañía, 1800.

"Edicto manuscrito de la Inquisición de corte." 22 de Junio, 1777. Archivo Histórico Nacional, Inquisición, Legajo 4.428, expediente núm 30, folio 3v. Y 4r.

Espinosa de los Monteros, Manuel. Archivo General de la Nación (AGN). Sección "Misiones" (141, fol. 30v.). Sección: Capitanía General. Año 1786. Caracas, Venezuela.

Estala, Pedro, and Joseph de Laporte. *El viagero universal; ó, Noticia del mundo antiguo y moderno.* Vol. 26. Madrid: Imprenta de Villalpando, 1799.

Esteyneffer, Juan de. *Florilegio medicinal, de todas las enfermedades, sacado de varios, y clasicos autores, para bien de los pobres, y de los que tienen falta de Medicos, en parti-cular para las Provincias remotas, en donde administran los RR. PP. missioneros de la Compañia de Jesus. Reducido a tres libros, el primero de medicina; el segundo de Ciru-gia, con un Apendix, que pertenece al modo de sangrar, abrir, y curar fuentes, aplicar ventosas, y sanguijuelas; el tercero contiene un Catalogo de los Medicamentos usuales, que se hacen en la Botica, con el modo de componerlos.* Mexico: Por los Herederos de Juan Joseph Guillena Carrascoso; Madrid: Por Alonso Balvas, 1729.

Feijoo, Benito Jerónimo. *Cartas eruditas, y curiosas: en que por la mayor parte se continúa el designio de el Theatro critico universal, impugnando, o reduciendo a dudosas varias opiniones communes.* Madrid: Por Blas Roman, impressor de la Real Academia de Derecho Español y Público, 1781.

———. *Obras escogidas del padre fray Benito Jerónimo Feijoo y Montenegro.* Introduc-tion by Vicente de la Fuente. Madrid: M Rivadeneyra, 1863.

———. *Teatro critico universal, ó Discursos varios en todo genero de materias, para desen-gaño de errores comunes. Tomo Septimo [vol. 7].* Madrid: En la imprenta de Antonio Marin . . . a costa de la Real Compañia de Impresores, y Libreros del Reyno, 1765.

———. *Theatro critico universal, ú Discursos varios en todo género de materias, para desengaño de errores comunes: escrito por el muy ilustre señor D. Fr. Benito Geronymo Feyjoó y Montenegro, Maestro General del Orden de San Benito, del Consejo de S.M. &c.. Tomo octavo [vol. 8]. Nueva Impresion. En la qual van puestas las Adiciones del Suplemento en sus lugares.* Madrid: Por Pedro Marín, 1779.

Fernández, Antonio. *Reflexiones sobre las calenturas remitentes é intermitentes.* Madrid: En la imprenta de la Administracion del Real Arbitrio de Beneficencia, 1805.

Fernández, León. *Coleccion de documentos para la historia de Costa Rica, publicados por el Lic. D. Léon Fernández. Documentos especiales sobre los límites entre Costa Rica y Colombia.* Vol. 5. Paris: Imprenta Pablo Dupont, 1886.

Fernández, Tomás. *Defensa de la china-china y verdadera respuesta a las falsas razones, que para su reprobación trae el Doct. Don Joseph Colmenero, Cathedratico de Prima de la Vniversidad de Salamanca.* Madrid: Diego Martínez Abad, 1698.

Fernández de Lizardi, José Joaquín. *The Mangy Parrot: The Life and Times of Periquillo Sarniento, Writen by Himself for His Children.* Trans. David Frye, with an introduc-tion by Nancy Vogeley. Indianapolis: Hackett, 2004.

———. *Noches tristes y Día alegre.* Mexico: Oficina de la calle del Espíritu Santo, á cargo del C. José Uribe y Alcalde, 1831.

———. *Obras.* Ed. Jacobo Chencinsky Veksler, Luis Mario Schneider, and María Rosa Palazón Mayoral. Vol. 7. Mexico: Centro de Estudios Literarios, Universidad Nacio-nal Autónoma de México, 1963.

———. *El Periquillo sarniento.* Mexico: En la librería de Galván, 1842.

Fernández de Moratín, Nicolás. *Álbum de Venus seguido del Arte de putear de Moratín.* Madrid: Visor Libros, 2014.

———. *Arte de las putas.* Ed. Manuel Fernández Nieto. Madrid: Ediciones Siro, 1977.

———. *Arte de las putas.* Ed. Enrique Velázquez. Madrid: A-Z, 1990.

———. *Arte de las putas.* Ed. Pilar Pedraza. Valencia: Editorial La Máscara, 1999.

———. *Arte de las putas: Poema.* Madrid, 1898.

————. *Arte de putear.* Ed., with intro. and notes, Isabel Colón Calderón and Gaspar Garrote Bernal. Archidona, Málaga: Aljibe, 1995.

————. *Diario (Mayo 1780–Marzo 1808).* Ed. René Andioc and Mireille Andioc. Madrid: Castalia, 1967.

Fernández de Oviedo y Valdés, Gonzalo. *Historia general y natural de las indias.* Asunción: Editorial Guaranía, 1944.

Ferrer Gorraiz y Beaumont, Vicente. *Cartilla de cirujanos y manual para todos. Deducida de las observaciones de Mr. Goulard, cirujano de la academia de Montpeller. Con varias prevenciones y notas que ha demostrado la experiencia, para curar todo mal exterior con brevedad, seguridad, y à placer con el uso de una sola medicinia diferentemente modificada.* Barcelona: En la imprenta de los herederos de María Angela Martí, 1780.

Flores, José. *Específico nuevamente descubierto en el reyno de Goatemala para la curacion radical del horrible mal del cancro, y otros mas frecuentes.* Madrid: Por Doña Maria Razola, calle de la Cruz, 1782.

Flores, Salvador Leonardo de. *Desempeño al método racional en la curación de las calenturas tercianas, que llaman notas; fundado en las sólidas vasas de la Razón, y adornado con la autoridad de los Antiguos Principes de la Medicina; y corroborado de la de los mas doctos Medicos Modernos de la Europa.* Seville: Juan Francisco de Blas, 1697.

Forner, Juan Pablo. *Exequias de la lengua castellana: sátira menipea por el Licdo. Don Pablo Hipnocausto.* Ed. José Jurado. Madrid: Consejo Superior de Investigaciones Científicas, 2000.

Foronda, Valentín de. *Cartas sobre la policía.* Madrid: Imprenta de Cano, 1801.

Freyre de Castrillón, Manuel. *Remedio y preservativo contra el mal francés de que adolece parte de la nación española.* Valencia: Por la viuda de Martin Peris, 1809.

Gallego, Juan Nicasio. *Obras completas. Obra poética,* ed. Ana María Freire López. Zamora: Inst. de Estudios Zamoranos "Florián de Ocampo," 1994.

Gerard, John. *The herball, or, Generall historie of plantes.* London: By Iohn Norton, 1597.

Góngora y Argote, Luis de. *Letrillas.* Ed. Robert Jammes. Madrid: Castalia, 2001.

————. *Soledades.* Ed. Robert Jammes. Madrid: Editorial Castalia, 1994.

Goya, Francisco de. *Diario de Madrid.* Vol. 37 (1799), 149–50.

Gumilla, Joseph. *El Orinoco ilustrado; historia natural, civil y geográfica de este gran río.* Bogotá: Editorial ABC, 1944.

Hernández y Dávalos, Juan Evaristo. *Colección de documentos para la historia de la guerra de independencia de México de 1808 a 1821.* Vol. 6. Mexico: José María Sandoval, impresor, 1882.

Hutten, Ulrich von. *Of the vvood called guaiacum: that healeth the Frenche pockes, and also healeth the goute in the feete, the stoone, the palsey, lepree, dropsy, fallynge euyll, and other dyseases.* Trans. Thomas Paynell. London: In aedibus Tho. Bertheleti, 1536.

Iglesias de la Casa, José. *Poesías póstumas.* Salamanca: F. de Toxar, 1793.

Iriarte, Tomás de. *Coleccion de obras en verso y prosa.* Vol. 2. Madrid: En la Imprenta de Benito Cano, 1787.

————. *Fábulas literarias* Ed. Ángel L. Prieto de Paula. Madrid: Ediciones Cátedra, 1992.

Isla, José Francisco de. *Historia del famoso predicador fray Gerundio de Campazas, alias Zotes.* Ed. Joaquín Alvarez Barrientos. Barcelona: Planeta, 1991.

Jovellanos, Gaspar de. *Obras publicadas é inéditas.* Ed. Cándido Nocedal and Miguel Artola. Madrid: M. Rivadeneyra, 1858.

Juan, Jorge, and Antonio de Ulloa. *Noticias secretas de América.* 1826. Ed. Luis Javier Ramos Gómez. Madrid: Historia 16, 1991.

———. *Relación histórica del viage a la América Meridional hecho de orden de S. Mag. para medir algunos grados de meridiano Terrestre, y venir por ellos en conocimiento de la verdadera Figura, y Magnitud de la Tierra, con otras varias Observaciones Astronomicas, y Phisicas.* Second Part, Vol. 3. Madrid: Antonio Marin, 1748.

La Porte, Joseph de. *Le voyageur françois ou la connoissance de l'Ancien et du Nouveau Monde.* Paris: Chez L. Cellot, 1772.

López de Araujo y Ascárraga, Bernardo, Matheo Giorro y Portillo, and Antonio Marín. *Impugnacion de los Triunfos Partidos Entre el Cancro Obstinado, y el Cirujano Advertido, y Discurso Sobre la Naturaleza del Cancro.* Madrid: Por Antonio Marin: se hallarà en la libreria de Juan de Moya, 1738.

López de Úbeda, Francisco. *La pícara Justina.* Paris: Baudry, Librería Europea, 1847.

López Pinna, Pedro. *Tratado de morbo gallico, en el qual se declara su origen, causas señales, pronosticos, y curacion. Ponese la virtud de la Raiz de la China, Palo santo, y Zarzaparilla; el Methodo que se tendrà en prepararlos para curar el Morbo Gallico: Methodo de dar las unciones, y corregir sus accidentes, y el Methodo de dar los humos del Cinabrio, y aplicar los Parches del Emplastro Viperino. Unas pildoras mercuriales de precipitado blanco, de intencion del autor, medicina noble para curar este mal, y el methodo de consigir* [sic] *este polvo, con variedad de recetas para curarle, y todos sus efecto.* Seville: J. de la Puerta, 1719.

Martínez, Manuel Silvestre, and J. León Helguera. *Librería de jueces, utilísima y universal: para todos los que desean imponerse en la Jurisprudencia Práctica, Derecho Real de españa, y Reales Resoluciones mas modernas de rigurosa observancia; y en especial para Abogados, Alcaldes, Corregidores, Intendentes, Prelados Regulares, y Jueces Eclesiásticos, Párroco, Regidores, Escribanos, Diputados, Síndicos, y Personeros.* Vol. 7. Madrid: En la Imprenta de don Benito Cano, 1791.

Massa, Niccolò. *Liber de morbo gallico.* Venice: Ex officina Jordani Zileti, 1563.

Masson de Morvilliers, Nicolas. "Spain." In *Enlightenment Spain and the* Encyclopédie méthodique, trans. and ed. Clorinda Donato and Ricardo López. Oxford: Voltaire Foundation, 2015.

Meléndez Valdés, Juan. *Discursos forenses.* Madrid: Imprenta Nacional, 1821.

———. *Poesía y prosa.* Barcelona: Planeta, 1990.

———. *Obras completas,* Vol. 3: *Teatro, Poesía,* ed. Emilio Palacios Fernández. Madrid: Fundación José Antonio de Castro, 1996.

Metrà, Andrea. *Il mentore perfetto de' negozianti, ovvero guida sicura de medesimi, ed istruzione, per rendere ad essi più agevoli, e meno incerte le loro speculazioni, trattato utilissimo: diviso in cinque tomi, e compitato da Andrea Metrà.* Trieste: Wage, Fleis e Comp., 1794.

Mir y Noguera, Juan. *Prontuario de hispanismo y barbarismo.* Madrid: Sáenz de Jubera hermanos, 1908.

Miranda, Francisco de. *América espera.* Ed. J. L. Salcedo-Bastardo. Caracas: Biblioteca Ayacucho, 1982.

Monardes, Nicolás. *Primera y segunda y tercera partes dela Historia Medicinal: delas cosas que se traen de nuestras Indias Occidentales, que sirven en Medicina. Tratado de la Piedra Bezaar, y dela yerua Escuerçonera. Dialogo delas grandezas del Hierro, y de sus virtudes Medicinales. Tratado de la nieve, y del bever Frio.* Seville: En Casa de Fernando Diaz, 1580.

Mutis, José Celestino "Informe sobre el estado de la medicina, la cirugía y la farmacia en el Nuevo Reino de Granada y forma de remediarlo. Santafé, 3 de junio de 1801." In *Escritos científicos de don José Celestino Mutis.* Vol. 1, ed. Guillermo Hernández de Alba. Bogota: Instituto Colombiano de Cultura Hispánica, 1983, 33–62.

Ochoa, Eugenio de, ed. *Epistolario español. Coleccion de cartas de españoles ilustres antiguos y modernos, recogida y ordenada con notas y aclaraciones históricas, críticas y biográficas.* Vol. 2. Madrid: Impr. de la Publicidad, á cargo de M. Rivadeneyra, 1870.

Pauw, Cornelius de. *Selections from Les Recherches Philosophiques Sur Les Américains of M. Pauw.* Bath: Printed by R. Crutwell, 1789.

Peralta Barnuevo, Pedro de. *Dialogo de los muertos: la causa academica.* Cumas [Lima]: En la oficina de la Sybila, con otras Obrillas mas que despues saldran, [1725].

Pérez Bravo, Diego, and José Navarro y Armijo. *Dissertacion botanico-pharmaceutica sobre la calaguala, su analysis chymico, y medicinales virtudes dicha en la Real Sociedad de Sevilla el dia 21 de marzo de 1754.* Seville: En la Imprenta del Colegio Mayor, y Universidad, 1755.

Plenck, Joseph Jakob von. *Farmacología quirúrgica ó ciencia de medicamentos externos e internos para curar las enfermedades de cirugía; con un tratado de Farmacia relativo á la preparacion y composicion de los medicamentos.* Madrid: Imprenta de D. Fermín Villalpando, 1819.

Prieto, Guillermo. *Versos inéditos.* Mexico: Imprenta del comercio, de Dubuan y Comp., 1879.

Quevedo y Villegas, Francisco Gómez de. *El buscón.* Ed. Américo Castro. Madrid: Ediciones de "La Lectura," 1927.

———. *Obras de D. Francisco Quevedo Villegas.* Ed. Pablo Antonio de Tarsia. Vol. 4. Madrid: Joachin Ibarra, 1772.

Quintana, Manuel José. *Obras completas.* Madrid: Imprenta y Estereotipía de M. Rivadeneyra, 1852.

———. *Vidas de españoles celebres.* Madrid: En la Imprenta Real, 1807.

Real Academia Española (RAE). *Diccionario de la lengua castellana: en que se explica el verdadero sentido de las voces, su naturaleza y calidad, con las phrases o modos de hablar, los proverbios o refranes, y otras cosas convenientes al uso de la lengua.* Madrid: En la Imprenta de la Real Academia Española, 1726.

Real Academia Española. *Diccionario de la lengua castellana: en que se explica el verdadero sentido de las voces . . . con las phrases o modos de hablar, los proverbios o re-*

franes y otras cosas convenientes al uso de la lengua. Tomo Quarto que contiene las letras G. H. I. J. K. L. M. N. Madrid: En la imprenta de la Real Academia Española: Por los herederos de Francisco de Hierro, 1734.

Real Academia Española. *Diccionario de la lengua castellana: en que se explica el verdadero sentido de las voces . . . con las phrases o modos de hablar, los proverbios o refranes y otras cosas convenientes al uso de la lengua. Tomo Quinto que contiene las letras O. P. Q. R.* Madrid: en la imprenta de la Real Academia Española: Por los herederos de Francisco de Hierro, 1737.

Real Academia Española. *Diccionario de la lengua castellana.* Madrid: Joachim Ibarra, Impresor de Cámara de S.M., 1770.

Real Academia Española. *Diccionario de la lengua castellana compuesto por la Real Academia Española, reducido á un tomo para su mas fácil uso.* Madrid: por D. Joaquin Ibarra, 1780.

Real Academia Española. *Diccionario de la lengua española. Madrid: Editorial Espasa Calpe, 2001.*

Real Academia Española, and Asociación de Academias de la Lengua Española. *Diccionario panhispánico de dudas.* Madrid: Real Academia Española, 2005.

Restif de La Bretonne. *Le pornographe: ou idées d'un honnête-homme sur un projet de règlement pour les prostituées.* London: Chez Jean Nourse; A La Haie [The Hague]: Chez Gosse junior, & Pinet, libraires, 1770.

Ribera, Anastasio Pantaleón de. *Obras.* Madrid: A. Garcia de la Iglesia, 1670.

——— . *Vejámenes literarios.* Ed. Gerónimo Cáncer. Madrid: Biblioteca "Ateneo," 1909.

Rossi Rubí, José. "Historia de la Hermandad y Hospital de la Caridad." *Mercurio Peruano* [Lima], January 6, 1791, 9–11.

Ruiz López, Hipólito. *Memoria sobre la legitima calaguala y otras dos raices que con el mismo nombre nos vienen de la America meridional.* Madrid: En la imprenta de D. José del Collado, 1805.

——— . *Quinologia, ó tratado del árbol de la quina ó cascarilla, con su descripcion y la de otras especies de quinos nuevamente descubiertas en el Perú.* Madrid: En la oficina de la viuda é hijo de Marin, 1792.

Salas, Francisco Gregorio de. "Una mujer de mala vida." In *Poetas líricos del siglo XVIII.* Biblioteca de Autores Españoles, compiled by Leopoldo Augusto de Cueto. Vol. 67. Madrid: Imprenta de los Sucesores de Hernando, 1911.

Samaniego, Félix María. *Cuentos y poesías más que picantes.* Ed. Raymond Foulché-Delbosc. Barcelona, 1899.

——— . *Fábulas en verso castellano para el uso del Real Seminario Bascongado, por Don Felix Maria Samaniego, del número de la Real Sociedad Bascongada de los Amigos del Pais.* Vols. 1 and 2. Madrid: En la Imprenta de Josef Lopez, 1797.

——— . *Jardín de Venus: Colección absolutamente íntegra de los graciosísimos cuentos libertinos.* Ed. Joaquín López Barbadillo. Madrid: Biblioteca de López Barbadillo y sus amigos, 1921.

——— . *El jardín de Venus: cuentos eróticos y burlescos con una coda de poesías verdes.* Ed. Emilio Palacios Fernández. Madrid: Biblioteca Nueva, 2004.

Sánchez Valverde, Antonio. *La America vindicada de la calumnia de haber sido madre del mal venereo. Por el autor de La idea del Valor de la Isla Española.* Madrid: En la Imprenta de Don Pedro Marin, 1785.

Santa Cruz y Espejo, Francisco Xavier Eugenio de. *Obra educativa.* Ed. Philip L. Astuto. Caracas: Biblioteca Ayacucho, 1981.

Sarmiento, Martín. *Antiguedad de las bubas. Extracto de un discurso del R.P.M.F. Martín Sarmiento* (n.p.: Por don Blas Roman, 1787).

Septalius, Manfredus. "Some Observations Communicated by Signior Manfredus Septalius from Milan, Concerning Quicksilver Found at the Roots of Plants, and Shels Found upon In-Land Mountains." *Philosophical Transactions (1665–1678)* 2 (1666): 493.

Suárez de Ribera, Francisco. *Arcanismo anti-galico, o Margarita mercurial.* Zaragoza: En la imprenta de Pedro Ximenez, a costa de Juan Oliveras, 1731.

———. *Ilustracion, y publicacion de los diez y siete secretos del doctor Juan Curvo Semmedo, confirmadas sus virtudes con maravillosas observaciones.* Madrid: En la imprenta de Domingo Fernandez de Arrojo, 1732.

———. *Manifiestas demonstraciones de las mas seguras, y suaves curaciones del morbo galico.* Madrid: En la imprenta de Manuel de Moya, se hallarà en la Librerìa de Luis Correa, 1745.

———. *Pedacio Dioscorides Anazarbeo.* Based on the edition of Andrés de Laguna. Madrid: En la Imprenta de Alonso Balbas; se hallarà en la Libreria de Luis Correa, enfrente de las gradas de San Phelipe el Real, 1733.

Suplemento al diccionario de medicina y cirugía del profesor D. Antonio Ballano. Vol. 3, Second Part, by Manuel Hurtado de Mendoza and Antonio Ballano. Madrid: Imprenta de Brugada, 1823.

Timonius, Emanuel, and John Woodward. "An Account, or History, of the Procuring the Small Pox by Incision, or Inoculation; as it has for some time been practised at Constantinople." *Philosophical Transactions* 29 (1714): 72–82.

Torre y Valcarcel, Juan de la. *Espejo de la philosophia, y compendio de toda la medicina, theorica, y practica.* Madrid: Por Juan Garcia Infançon, 1705.

Torres Villarroel, Diego de. *Los desauciados del mundo, y de la gloria: sueno mystico, moral, y phisico, util para quantos desean morir bien, y conocer las debilidades de la naturaleza.* Madrid: En la Imprenta de Joachin Sanchez, 1736.

———. *Entremés famoso: El médico sordo y el vecino gangoso.* Valencia: Imprenta de Agustín Laborda, 1765.

———. *Extracto de los pronosticos del gran piscator de Salamanca, desde el año de 1725 hasta el de 1753: Compone este Libro todas las Dedicatorias, Prólogos, invenciones en verso, y prosa de dichos Pronosticos.* Madrid: En la Imprenta de la Viuda de Ibarra, 1795.

———. *Juguetes de Thalia, Entretenimientos de el numen.* Salamanca: En la Imprenta de la Santa Cruz, por Antonio Villarroèl, quien las saca à la luz, 1738.

———. *Quinto trozo de la vida, ascendencia, nacimiento, crianza, y aventuras de el Doct. D. Diego de Torres.* Salamanca: Por Pedro Ortiz Gomez, 1750.

———. *Sexto trozo de la vida, y aventuras de el Doctor D. Diego de Torres Villarroel.* Salamanca: Por Antonio Villargordo, 1758.

————. *Viaje fantastico del Gran Piscator de Salamanca. Jornadas por uno, y otro mundo. Descubrimiento de sus substancias, generaciones, y producciones. Ciencia, juizio, y congetura de el eclypse de el dia. 22. de Mayo de este presente año de 1724 (de el qual han escrito los Astrologos del Norte) y reglas generales para judiciar de todos los eclypses, que puedan suceder hasta la fin de el mundo*. [Salamanca], 1724.

————. *Visiones y visitas de Torres, con D. Francisco de Quevedo, por la Corte*. Madrid: Por Antonio Marin, Vendese en su casa . . . y en la Libreria de Juan de Moya, 1727.

————. *Visiones y visitas de Torres, con D. Francisco de Quevedo, por la Corte*. Ed. Russell P. Sebold. Madrid: Espasa-Calpe, 1966.

Vega, Lope de. *Arte nuevo de hacer comedias: edición crítica, fuentes y ecos latinos*. Cuenca: Universidad de Castilla-La Mancha, 2016.

————. *Las bizarrias de Belisa: comedia famosa*. [Madrid]: Se hallará en la Librería de Castillo . . . y en el Puesto de Sanchez, 1804.

Velazquez de Velasco, Luis José. *Coleccion de diferentes escritos relativos al cortejo con notas de varios por Liberio Veranio; recogidos por D. Luis de Valdeflores*. Madrid: Imprenta de Manuel Martín, Calle de la Cruz, 1764.

Venegas, Juan Manuel. *Compendio de la medicina: ó, Medicina practica, en que se declara laconicamente lo mas util de ella, que el Autor tiene observado en estas Regiones de Nueva España, para casi todas las Enfermedades que acometen al cuerpo humano, dispuesto en forma alfabetica*. Mexico: Por D. Felipe de Zúñiga y Ontiveros, 1788.

Secondary Sources

Achim, Miruna. "From Rustics to Savants: Indigenous Materia Medica in Eighteenth-Century Mexico." *Studies in History and Philosophy of Science, Part C: Studies in History and Philosophy of Biological and Biomedical Sciences* 42.3 (2011): 275–84.

————. *Lagartijas medicinales: remedios americanos y debates científicos en la ilustración*. Mexico: Consejo Nacional para la Cultura y las Artes, 2008.

————. "Making Lizards into Drugs: The Debates on the Medical Uses of Reptiles in Late Eighteenth-Century Mexico." *Journal of Spanish Cultural Studies* 8.2 (2007): 169–91.

Alba-Koch, Beatriz de. "'Enlightened Absolutism' and Utopian Thought: Fernández de Lizardi and Reform in New Spain." *Revista Canadiense de Estudios Hispánicos* 24.2 (2002): 295–306.

————. *Ilustrando la Nueva España. Texto e imagen en* El periquillo Sarniento *de Fernández de Lizardi*. Cáceres: Universidad de Extremadura, 1999.

Alcalá Flecha, Roberto. *Matrimonio y prostitución en el arte de Goya*. [Cáceres]: Servicio de Publicaciones de la Universidad de Extremadura, 1984.

Anderson Imbert, Enrique, and Eugenio Florit. *Literatura hispanoamericana: antología e introducción histórica*. Vol. 1. Hoboken, NJ: John Wiley, 2003.

Amy, Jean-Jacques, and Michel Thiery. "The Condom: A Turbulent History." *European Journal of Contraception and Reproductive Health Care* 20 (2015): 1–16.

Arnáiz, José Manuel. *Francisco de Goya, cartones y tapices*. Madrid: Espasa Calpe, 1987.

Arrizabalaga, Jon. "The Changing Identity of the French Pox in Early Renaissance Castille." In *Between Text and Patient: The Medical Enterprise in Medieval & Early Modern Europe,* ed. Florence Eliza Glanze and Brian K. Nance. Florence: SISMEL-Ed. del Galluzo, 2011, 397–17.

———. "Medical Responses to the 'French Disease' in Europe at the Turn of the Sixteenth Century." In *Sins of the Flesh: Responding to Sexual Disease in Early Modern Europe,* ed. Kevin Siena. Toronto: Centre for Reformation and Renaissance Studies, 2005, 33–55.

———. "Medicina universitaria y morbus gallicus en la Italia de finales del siglo XV: El arquiatra pontificio G. Torrella." *Asclepio* 40 (1988): 3–38.

———. "Los médicos valencianos Pere Pintor y Gaspar Torrella, y el tratamiento del mal francés en la corte papal de Alejandro VI Borja." In *El hogar de los Borja,* ed. Jon Arrizabalaga. Valencia: Consorci de Museus de la Generalitat Valenciana, 2000, 141–58.

———. "Práctica y teoría en la medicina universitaria del siglo XVI: el tratamiento del mal francés en la corte papal de Alejandro VI Borgia." *Arbor* 153 (1996): 136–51.

———. "Syphilis." In *The Cambridge World History of Human Disease,* ed. Kenneth F. Kiple. Cambridge: Cambridge University Press, 1993, 1025–33.

Arrizabalaga, Jon, Harold John Cook, and Teresa Huguet-Termes. *Health and Medicine in Hapsburg Spain: Agents, Practices, Representations.* London: Wellcome Trust Centre for the History of Medicine at UCL, 2009.

Arrizabalaga, Jon, Roger French, and John Henderson. *The Great Pox: The French Disease in Renaissance Europe.* New Haven: Yale University Press, 1997.

Astorgano Abajo, Antonio. "El regalismo borbónico y la unificación de Hospitales: La lucha de Meléndez Valdés en Ávila." In *Felipe V y su tiempo,* coord. Eliseo Serrano Martín. Zaragoza: Institución 'Fernando el Católico' (CSIC), 2004, 37–66.

———. "Los testamentos del matrimonio Meléndez Valdés." *Boletín de la Real Academia de Extremadura* 16 (2008): 247–404.

Bakhtin, Mikhail. *The Dialogic Imagination. Four Essays.* Trans. Michael Holquist. Austin: University of Texas Press, 1981.

Barrera-Osorio, Antonio. *Experiencing Nature: The Spanish American Empire and the Early Scientific Revolution.* Austin: University of Texas Press, 2006.

Batres Jáuregui, Antonio. *Vicios del lenguaje y provincialismos de Guatemala; estudio filológico.* Guatemala: Encuadernación y tipografía nacional, 1892.

Bellón Cazabán, Juan Alfredo. "La ética del siglo XVIII: las fábulas y los cuentos. El caso de Samaniego." In *Cadalso* 1 (1983): 7–28.

Bentley, Greg W. *Shakespeare and the New Disease: The Dramatic Function of Syphilis in Troilus and Cressida,* Measure for Measure, *and* Timon of Athens. New York: Peter Lang, 1989.

Berco, Cristian. *From Body to Community: Venereal Disease and Society in Baroque Spain.* Toronto and Buffalo: University of Toronto Press, 2016.

———. "The Great Pox, Symptoms, and Social Bodies in Early Modern Spain." *Social History of Medicine* 28.2 (2014): 225–44.

————. "Syphilis and the Silencing of Sodomy in Juan Calvo's *Tratado del morbo gálico.*" In *The Sciences of Homosexuality in Early Modern Europe,* ed. Kenneth Borris and George S. Rousseau. London: Routledge, 2008, 92–115.

————. "Syphilis, Sex and Marriage in Early Modern Spain." *Journal of Early Modern History* 15.3 (2011): 223–53.

————. "Textiles as Social Texts: Syphilis, Material Culture and Gender in Golden Age Spain." *Journal of Social History* 44.3 (Spring 2011): 785–810.

Bleichmar, Daniela, et al. *Science in the Spanish and Portuguese Empires, 1500–1800.* Stanford: Stanford University Press, 2009.

Brandt, Allan M. *No Magic Bullet: A Social History of Venereal Disease in the United States since 1880.* New York: Oxford University Press, 1987.

Camagne, Fabián Alejandro. "Entre el milagro y el pacto diabólico: saludadores y reyes taumaturgos en la España moderna." In *Ciencia, poder e ideología: el saber y el hacer en la evolución de la medicina española (siglos XIV-XVIII),* ed. María Estela González de Fauve. Buenos Aires: Instituto de Historia de España "Claudio Sánchez-Albornoz," Facultad de Filosofía y Letras, Universidad de Buenos Aires, 2001, 247–90.

Campero Carrasco, Hebbe Isabel. "*Elementos para la historia de la farmacia boliviana en la Real Audiencia de Charcas.*" Thesis, Universidad Complutense de Madrid, Facultad de Farmacia, Departamento de Farmacia y Tecnología Farmacéutica, 2006.

Campos Díez, María Soledad. "El Protomedicato en la administración central de la Monarquía hispánica." *Dynamis: Acta Hispanica ad Medicinae Scientiarumque Historiam Illustrandam* 16 (1996): 43–58.

Cañizares-Esguerra, Jorge. *Nature, Empire, and Nation: Explorations of the History of Science in the Iberian World.* Stanford: Stanford University Press, 2006.

Cantera Ortiz de Urbina, Jesús. "Refranes y locuciones del español y el francés en torno al bazo, el hígado, el corazón y los riñones." *Cuadernos de Investigación Filológica* 9 (1983): 47–62.

Carnero, Guillermo. *La cara oscura del Siglo de las Luces.* Madrid: Fundación Juan March, Cátedra, 1983.

Carrete Parrondo, Juan. *Goya: estampas, grabado y litografía.* Barcelona: Electa, 2007.

Cerezo, José Antonio. *Literatura erótica en España: repertorio de obras, 1519–1936.* Madrid: Ollero y Ramos, 2001.

Chamorro Fernández, María Inés. *Tesoro de villanos: lengua de jacarandina: rufos, mandiles, galloferos, viltrotonas, zurrapas, carcaveras, murcios, floraineros y otras gentes de la carda* (Barcelona: Herder, 2002).

Clouse, Michele L. *Medicine, Government and Public Health in Philip II's Spain: Shared Interests, Competing Authorities.* Farnham: Ashgate, 2011.

Colón Calderón, Isabel, and Gaspar Garrote Bernal, eds. *Arte de putear,* by Nicolás Fernández de Moratín. Archidona, Málaga: Aljibe, 1995.

Conway, J. F. "Syphilis and Bronzino's London Allegory." *Journal of the Warburg and Courtauld Institutes* 49 (1986): 250–55.

Cook, Della Collins, and Mary Lucas Powell. *The Myth of Syphilis: The Natural History of Treponematosis in North America.* Gainesville: University Press of Florida, 2005.

Cotarelo y Mori, Emilio. *María Ladvenant y Quirante, primera dama de los teatros de la corte.* Madrid: Est. tipog. "Sucesores de Rivadeneyra," 1896.

Crosby, Alfred W. "Virgin Soil Epidemics as a Factor in the Aboriginal Depopulation in America." *William and Mary Quarterly,* 3rd ser., 33.2 (April 1976): 289–99.

Cruz Peterson, Elizabeth Marie. *Women's Somatic Training in Early Modern Spanish Theater.* London and New York: Routledge, Taylor & Francis Group, 2017.

Dabove, Juan Pablo. *Nightmares of the Lettered City: Banditry and Literature in Latin America, 1816–1929.* Pittsburgh: University of Pittsburgh Press, 2007.

Dante Alighieri. *The Divine Comedy.* Ed. John Ciardi. New York: Norton, 1977.

Darnton, Robert. *The Corpus of Clandestine Literature in France, 1769–1789.* New York: W. W. Norton, 1995.

———. *The Forbidden Best-Sellers of Pre-Revolutionary France.* New York: W. W. Norton, 1995.

Deacon, Philip. "El espacio clandestino del erotismo literario en la España dieciochesca." In *Redes y espacios de opinión pública. De la Ilustración al Romanticismo. Cádiz, América y Europa ante la Modernidad, 1750–1850,* ed. Marieta Cantos Casenave. Cádiz: Universidad de Cádiz, 2006, 219–30.

———. "Fábulas frutosóficas, o la filosofía de Venus en fábulas." In *Encyclopedia of Erotic Literature,* ed. Gaëtan Brulotte and John Phillips. New York: Routledge, 2006, 1:448–50.

———. "Filosofía y sensualismo: la estética del placer en *Los besos de amor* de Juan Meléndez Valdés." In *Juan Meléndez Valdés y su tiempo,* ed. Jesús Cañas Murillo et al. Cáceres: Junta de Extramadura, Consejería de Cultura y Editora Regional de Extremadura, 2005, 163–81.

———. "Las fronteras del erotismo poético español a finales del siglo XVIII." In *Para Emilio Palacios Fernández. 26 estudios sobre el siglo XVIII español,* ed. Joaquín Álvarez Barrientos and Jerónimo Herrera Navarro. Madrid: Fundación Universitaria Española, 2011, 281–96.

———. "Imágenes de la mujer en la poesía erótica española del siglo XVIII." In *Ecos silenciados: la mujer en la literatura española. Siglos XII al XVIII,* ed. Susana Gil-Albarellos Pérez-Pedrero and Mercedes Rodríguez-Pequeño. Valladolid: Junta de Castilla y León, 2006, 419–31.

———. "El libro erótico en la España dieciochesca." In *La memoria de los libros: estudios sobre la historia del escrito y de la lectura en Europa y América.* Vol. 1. Salamanca: Instituto de Historia del Libro y de la Lectura, 2004, 825–37.

Docampo Capilla, Javier. "*Love for Sale*: prostitutas, alcahuetas y clientes en la obra de Hogarth." *Cuadernos de Ilustración y Romanticismo* 15 (2007): 99–144.

Domínguez Ortíz, Antonio. "La galera o cárcel de mujeres de Madrid a comienzos del siglo XVIII." *Anales del Instituto de Estudios Madrileños* 9 (1973): 277–85.

Donato, Clorinda, and Ricardo López, trans. and ed. *Enlightenment Spain and the Encyclopédie méthodique.* Oxford: Voltaire Foundation, 2015.

Edelstein, Dan. *The Enlightenment: A Genealogy.* Chicago: University of Chicago Press, 2010.

Ettinghausen, Henry. "Torres Villarroel's Self-Portrait: The Mask behind the Mask." *Bulletin of Hispanic Studies* 55.4 (October 1978): 321–28.

Fabricius, Johannes. *Syphilis in Shakespeare's England.* London: Jessica Kingsley, 1994.

Fernández, Enrique. *Anxieties of Interiority and Dissection in Early Modern Spain.* Toronto: University of Toronto Press, 2015.

Fernández del Castillo, Francisco. *Los viajes de don Francisco Xavier de Balmis. Notas para la historia de la expedición vacunal de España a América y Filipinas (1803–1806.* Mexico: Galas de México, 1960.

Fernández Nieto, Manuel. "Entre popularismo y erudición: la poesía erotica de Moratín." *Revista de Literatura* 42.84 (1980): 37–52.

———. Introducción to *Arte de las putas, by Nicolás Fernández de Moratín.* Madrid: Ediciones Siro, 1977.

Fleming, John V. *The Dark Side of the Enlightenment: Wizards, Alchemists, and Spiritual Seekers in the Age of Reason.* New York: W. W. Norton, 2013.

Fletcher, John Edward. *A Study of the Life and Works of Athanasius Kircher, "Germanus Incredibilis."* Leiden and Boston: Brill, 2011.

Foa, Anna. "The New and the Old: The Spread of Syphilis (1494–1530)." In *Sex and Gender in Historical Perspective,* ed. Edward Muir and Guido Ruggiero. Baltimore: Johns Hopkins University Press, 1990, 26–45.

Franco Rubio, Gloria Ángeles. "Nicolás Fernández de Moratín y *El Arte de las putas.*" In *Feminismo y misoginia en la literatura española: fuentes literarias para la historia de las mujeres,* ed. Cristina Segura Graiño. Madrid: Narcea, 2001, 97–122.

French, Roger, and Jon Arrizabalaga. "Coping with the French Disease: University Practitioners' Strategies and Tactics in the Transition from the Fifteenth to the Sixteenth Century." In *Medicine from the Black Death,* ed. French et al., 248–87.

French, Roger, et al., eds. *Medicine from the Black Death to the French Disease.* Aldershot, Hants; Brookfield, VT: Ashgate, 1998.

García Ballester, Luis. *Historia social de la medicina en la España de los siglos XIII al XVI. Vol. 1: La minoría musulmana y morisca.* Madrid: Akal Editor, 1976.

———. *Los moriscos y la medicina: un capítulo de la medicina y la ciencia marginadas en la España del siglo XVI.* Barcelona: Labor Universitaria, 1984.

García-Escudero López, Ángel, A. Arruza Echevarría, J. Padilla Nieva, and R. Puig Giró. "Charles II: From Spell to Genitourinary Pathology." *Archivos Españoles de Urología* 62.3 (2009): 179–85.

García Regueiro, Ovidio. *Francisco de Cabarrús: un personaje y su época.* Madrid: Centro de Estudios Políticos y Constitucionales, 2003.

García Santo-Tomás, Enrique. *La musa refractada: literatura y óptica en la España del Barroco.* Madrid: Iberoamericana; Frankfurt am Main: Vervuert, 2015.

Gardeta Sabater, Pilar. "El nuevo modelo del Real Tribunal del Protomedicato en la América española: transformaciones sufridas ante las Leyes de Indias y el cuerpo legislativo posterior." *Dynamis: Acta Hispanica ad Medicinae Scientiarumque Historiam Illustrandam* 16 (1996): 237–59.

Garnica Silva, Antonio. "Notas a El Incordio: poema inédito de José María Blanco White." *Rara Avis* 2–3 (1987): 63–64.

Geiger, Maynard J., and Clement W. Meighan. *As the Padres Saw Them: California Indian Life and Customs as Reported by the Franciscan Missionaries, 1813–1815.* Santa Barbara: Santa Barbara Mission Archive Library, 1976.

Gentilcore, David. "Charlatans, the Regulated Marketplace and the Treatment of Venereal Disease in Italy." In *Sins of the Flesh: Responding to Sexual Disease in Early Modern Europe,* ed. Kevin Siena. Toronto: Centre for Reformation and Renaissance Studies, 2005, 57–80.

Gerbi, Antonello, and Antonio Alatorre. *La disputa del Nuevo Mundo: historia de una polémica, 1750–1900.* Mexico: Fondo de Cultura Económica, 1960.

Gies, David Thatcher. "'El cantor de las doncellas' y las rameras madrileñas: Nicolás Fernández de Moratín en *El arte de las putas.*" In *Actas del Sexto Congreso Internacional de Hispanistas.* Toronto: University of Toronto, 1980, 320–23.

———. *Eros y amistad: sobre literatura y cultura en España (siglos XVIII y XIX).* Barcelona: Calambur, 2016.

———. *Nicolás Fernández de Moratín.* Boston: Twayne Publishers, 1979.

Gilman, Sander. *Disease and Representation: Images of Illness from Madness to AIDS.* Ithaca, NY: Cornell University Press, 1988.

Goldman, Peter B. "*El arte de las putas* and the Death of the Elder Moratín: Charting the Borderland between Literature and Life." *Kentucky Romance Quarterly* 32.3 (1985): 279–90.

Gómez Castellano, Irene. *La cultura de las máscaras: disfraces y escapismo en la poesía española de la Ilustración.* Madrid: Iberoamericana, 2012.

———. "Misterios en la trastienda: Luis Paret, *La tienda del anticuario* y el debate en torno a los bailes de máscaras durante el reinado de Carlos III." *Revista de Arte Goya* 352 (July–September 2015): 228–43.

Gómez de Enterría Sánchez, Josefa. "Notas sobre la traducción científica y técnica en el siglo XVIII." *Quaderns de Filologia: Estudis Lingüístics* 8 (2003): 35–67.

Gómiz León, Juan José. "Goya y su sintomatología miccional de Burdeos, 1825." *Historia de la Urología Española* 60.8 (2007): 917–30.

González de Fauve, María Estela, ed. *Ciencia, poder e ideología: el saber y el hacer en la evolución de la medicina española (siglos XIV–XVIII).* Buenos Aires: Instituto de Historia de España "Claudio Sánchez-Albornoz," Facultad de Filosofía y Letras, Universidad de Buenos Aires, 2001.

Goodman, David C. *Power and Penury: Government, Technology, and Science in Philip II's Spain.* Cambridge and New York: Cambridge University Press, 1988.

Gordon, Anthony G. "Goya Had Syphilis, Not Susac's Syndrome." *Practical Neurology* 9 (2009): 240.

Granjel, Luis S. *Historia general de la medicina española.* Vols. 3–4. Salamanca: Ediciones Universidad de Salamanca, 1978.

Guereña, Jean-Louis. "Médicos y prostitución. Un proyecto de reglamentación de la prostitución en 1809: la 'Exposición' de Antonio Cibat (1771–1811)." *Medicina & Historia* 71 (1998): 3–28.

Guerra, Francisco. "The Dispute over Syphilis: Europe versus America." *Clio Medica* 13 (1978): 39–61.

Gutiérrez Girardot, Rafael. "Cultura de viñeta." In *Manual de historia de Colombia,* coord. Jaime Jaramillo Uribe. Bogotá: Instituto Colombiano de Cultura, 1979, 3:447–53.

Haidt, Rebecca. *Women, Work and Clothing in Eighteenth-Century Spain.* Oxford: Voltaire Foundation, 2011.

Hayden, Deborah. *Pox: Genius, Madness, and the Mysteries of Syphilis.* New York: Basic Books, 2004.

Hentschell, Roze. "Luxury and Lechery: Hunting the Great Pox in Early Modern England." In *Sins of the Flesh: Responding to Sexual Disease in Early Modern Europe,* ed. Kevin Siena. Toronto: Centre for Reformation and Renaissance Studies, 2005, 133–57.

Hernández Franco, Juan. "El precio del trigo y la carne en Lorca: su relación con el mercado nacional durante la segunda mitad del siglo XVIII." *Revista Murgetana* 61 (1981): 81–97.

Herrero Ingelmo, María Cruz, and Enrique Montero Cartelle. "El *Morbus gallicus* o *Mal francés* en *La Lozana andaluza* de Francisco Delicado." *Asclepio* 65.2 (2013): 021, doi: http://dx.doi.org/10.3989/asclepio.2013.21.

Hewlett, Mary. "The French Connection: Syphilis and Sodomy in Late-Renaissance Lucca." In *Sins of the Flesh: Responding to Sexual Disease in Early Modern Europe,* ed. Kevin Siena. Toronto: Centre for Reformation and Renaissance Studies, 2005, 239–60.

Hill, Ruth. *Hierarchy, Commerce and Fraud in Bourbon Spanish America: A Postal Inspector's Exposé.* Nashville: Vanderbilt University Press, 2005.

———. "The Roots of Revolt in Late Viceregal Quito; Eugenio de Espejo between Adam Smith and St. Rose." *Bulletin of Spanish Studies* 86.7–8 (2009): 143–55.

———. *Sceptres and Sciences in the Spains: Four Humanists and the New Philosophy (ca. 1680–1740).* Liverpool: Liverpool University Press, 2000.

Holliday, J. S. *Rush for Riches: Gold Fever and the Making of California.* [Oakland]: Oakland Museum of California, 1999.

Holmes, Richard. *The Age of Wonder: How the Romantic Generation Discovered the Beauty and Terror of Science.* London: HarperPress, 2008.

Homer. *The Odyssey: Rendered into English Prose for the Use of Those Who Cannot Read the Original.* London: Fifield, 1900.

Horace. *Quinti Horatii Flacci Opera omnia: The Works of Horace with a Commentary by E. C. Wickham. . . .* Vol. 2: *The Satires, Epistles, and De arte poetica.* Oxford: At the Clarendon Press, 1891.

Huguet-Termes, Teresa, Jon Arrizabalaga, and Harold J. Cook, eds. *Health and Medicine in Hapsburg Spain: Agents, Practices, Representations.* London: The Wellcome Trust Centre for the History of Medicine at UCL, 2009.

Huxley, Anthony. *New RHS Dictionary of Gardening.* London: Macmillan, 1992.

Iborra, Pascual, Juan Granda-Juesas, and Juan Riera. *Historia del Protomedicato en España (1477–1822).* Valladolid: Universidad de Valladolid, Secretariado de Publicaciones, 1987.

Ilie, Paul. "Grotesque Portraits in Torres Villarroel." *Bulletin of Hispanic Studies* 45 (1968): 16–37.

Insúa Cereceda, Mariela. "La falsa erudición en la Ilustración española y novohispana: Lizardi." *Estudios Filológicos* 48 (2011): 61–79.

———. "Figuraciones modelicas y antimodélicas del military en la obra de Fernández de Lizardi." *Revista Chilena de Literatura* 85 (2013): 229–43.

———. "Hacia la constitución del maestro ejemplar en el México ilustrado: el caso de Fernández de Lizardi." *Hispanófila* 171 (2014): 59–75.

Iparraguirre, Enrique, and Carlos Dávila. *Real Fábrica de Tapices, 1721–1971.* Madrid: Gráficas Reunidas, 1971.

Izquierdo, José Joaquín. *Harvey, iniciador del método experimental. Estudio crítico de su obra* De motu cordis, *y de los factores que la mantuvieron ignorada en los países de habla española, con una reproducción facsimilar [sic] de la edición original y su primera versión castellana.* Mexico: Ediciones Ciencia, 1936.

Jarcho, Saúl. *Quinine's Predecessor: Francesco Torti and the Early History of Cinchona.* Baltimore: Johns Hopkins University Press, 1993.

Jiménez Salcedo, Juan. "Las *Cartas* de Cabarrús (1808) y la tradición reglamentarista europea en materia de prostitución." *Anales de Filología Francesa* 16 (2008): 129–40.

Juárez Nissenberg, Gilda. "Nicolás Fernández de Moratín: la teoría neoclásica y su aplicación práctica." Ann Arbor: University Microfilms International, 1979.

Juliá Martínez, Eduardo. "Documentos sobre María y Francisca Ladvenant." *Boletín de la Real Academia Española* 1 (1914): 468–69.

Jütte, Robert. "Syphilis and Confinement: Hospitals in Early Modern Germany." In *Institutions of Confinement: Hospitals, Asylums, and Prisons in Western Europe and North America, 1500–1950,* ed. Norbert Finzsch and Robert Jütte. Cambridge and New York: Cambridge University Press, 1996, 97–115.

Kent, Molly E., and Frank Romanelli. "Reexamining Syphilis: An Update on Epidemiology, Clinical Manifestations, and Management." *Annals of Pharmacotherapy* 42 (2008): 226–36.

Kottek, Samuel S., and Luis Garcia Ballester. *Medicine and Medical Ethics in Medieval and Early Modern Spain: An Intercultural Approach.* Jerusalem: Magnes Press, Hebrew University, 1996.

Kumate Rodríguez, Jesús. "Vacunas, cultura de la prevención." *Confluencia XXI: Revista de Pensamiento Político* 10 (2010): 7–11.

Lanning, John Tate. *The Royal Protomedicato: The Regulation of the Medical Professions in the Spanish Empire. Edited by* John Jay TePaske. Durham: Duke University Press, 1985.

Larriba, Elisabel. "La última salida al ruedo del *Memorial Literario* (10 de octubre– 20 de noviembre de 1808)." *Cuadernos de Ilustración y Romanticismo* 16 (2010): 1–88.

Lasarte, Pedro. *Lima satirizada (1598–1698): Mateo Rosas de Oquendo y Juan del Valle y Caviedes.* Lima: Pontificia Universidad Católica del Perú, Fondo Editorial, 2006.

Lloyd, Genevieve. *Enlightenment Shadows.* Oxford: Oxford University Press, 2013.

Loewen, James W. *Lies My Teacher Told Me: Everything Your American History Textbook Got Wrong.* New York: New Press, 1995.

Lohmann Villena, Guillermo. "Un poeta virreinal del Perú: Juan del Valle y Caviedes." *Revista de Indias* 33–34 (1948): 771–94.

López Barahona, Victoria. "La caza de vagabundas: trabajo y reclusión en Madrid durante la edad moderna." In *La prisión y las instituciones punitivas en la investigación histórica,* coord. Pedro Oliver Olmo and Jesús Carlos Urda Lozano. Cuenca: Ediciones de la Universidad de Castilla-La Mancha, 2014, 31–48.

López Piñero, José María. "La *Carta filosófica, medico-chymica* (1687) de Juan de Cabriada, manifiesto renovador de la medicina española." In Lopez Piñero, *Medicina moderna y sociedad española,* 175–89.

———. *Ciencia y técnica en la sociedad española de los siglos XVI y XVII.* Barcelona: Labor Universitaria, 1979.

———. "Eighteenth-Century Medical Vitalism: The Paracelsian Connection." In *Revolutions in Science: Their Meaning and Relevance,* ed. William R. Shea. Canton, MA: Science History Publications/U.S.A., 1988, 117–32.

———. *La introducción de la ciencia moderna en España.* Barcelona: Ediciones Ariel, 1969.

———. "The Medical Profession in Sixteenth-Century Spain." In *The Town and State Physician in Europe from the Middle Ages to the Enlightenment,* ed. Andrew W. Russell. Wolfenbüttel: Herzog August Bibliothek, 1981, 85–98.

———. *Medicina moderna y sociedad española: Siglos XVI-XIX.* Valencia: Cátedra e Instituto de Historia de la Medicina, 1976.

López Terrada, María Luz. "El tratamiento de la sífilis en un hospital renacentista: la sala del *mal de siment* del Hospital General de Valencia." *Asclepio: Archivo Iberoamericano de Historia de la Medicina y Antropología Médica* 41.2 (1989): 19–51.

Lorente Medina, Antonio. *Realidad histórica y creación literaria en las sátiras de Juan del Valle y Caviedes.* Madrid: Universidad Nacional de Educación a Distancia, 2011.

Macgregor, Arthur. "Medicinal *Terra Sigillata:* A Historical, Geographical and Typological Review." In *A History of Geology and Medicine,* ed. C. J. Duffin, R. T. J. Moody, and C. Gardner-Thorpe. Bath: Geological Society of London, 2013, 113–36.

Manetti, Daniela. "Galen and Hippocratic Medicine: Language and Practice." In *Galen and the World of Knowledge,* ed. Christopher Gill, Tim Whitmarsh, and John Wilkins. Cambridge: Cambridge University Press, 2009, 157–74.

Martineaud Jean-Paul. *L'amour au temps de la vérole: Histoire de la syphilis.* Paris: Glyphe, 2010.

Martínez Lois, Andrés. *El Padre Feijoo: naturaleza, hombre y conocimiento.* A Coruña: Diputación Provincial de A Coruña, 1989.

Martínez Mata, Emilio. "La predicción de la muerte del rey Luis I en un almanaque de Diego de Torres Villarroel." *Bulletin Hispanique* 92.2 (1990): 837–45.

———. "Pronósticos y predicciones de Diego Torres Villarroel." In *Revisión de Torres Villarroel,* ed. Manuel María Pérez López and Emilio Martínez Mata. Salamanca: Ediciones Universidad de Salamanca, 1998, 93–102.

———. *Los "Sueños" de Diego de Torres Villarroel.* Salamanca: Universidad de Salamanca, 1990.

Martínez Vidal, Àlvar, and María Luz López Terrada, eds. "El Tribunal del Real Protomedicato en la Monarquía hispánica (1593–1808)." *Dynamis: Acta Hispanica ad Medicinae Scientiarumque Historiam Illustrandam* 16 (1996): 17–259.

Martín Gaite, Carmen. *Usos amorosos del dieciocho en España.* Madrid: Siglo Veintiuno de España Editores, 1972.

Martín Moreno, Antonio. *Historia de la música española. Vol. 4: Siglo XVIII.* Madrid: Alianza Editorial, 1998.

McGough, Laura J. *Gender, Sexuality and Syphilis in Early Modern Venice: The Disease That Came to Stay.* New York: Palgrave Macmillan, 2011.

———. "Quarantining Beauty: The French Disease in Early Modern Venice." In *Sins of the Flesh: Responding to Sexual Disease in Early Modern Europe,* ed. Kevin Siena. Toronto: Centre for Reformation and Renaissance Studies, 2005, 211–37.

Merians, Linda Evi, ed. *The Secret Malady: Venereal Disease in Eighteenth-Century Britain and France.* Lexington: University Press of Kentucky, 1996.

Mitchell, Piers D. "Pre-Columbian Treponemal Disease from 14th Century AD Safed, Israel, and Implications for the Medieval Eastern Mediterranean." *American Journal of Physical Anthropology* 121 (2003): 117–24.

Monod, Paul Kléber. *Solomon's Secret Arts: The Occult in the Age of Enlightenment.* New Haven: Yale University Press, 2013.

Morel D'Arleux, Antonia. "Recogimientos y cofradías del 'pecado mortal' en los siglos XVI y XVII." In *La Prostitution en Espagne: De l'époque des Rois Catholiques à la IIe République,* ed. Raphaël Carrasco. Besançon: Annales littéraires de l'Université de Besançon, 1994, 111–35.

Morton, R. S. "Syphilis in Art: An Entertainment in Four Parts." *Genitourinary Medicine* 66 (1990): 33–40, 112–23, 208–21, 280–94.

Mozejko, Danuta Teresa. "El letrado y su lugar en el proyecto de nación: *El Periquillo sarniento* de Fernández de Lizardi." *Revista Iberoamericana* 73.218–19 (2007): 45–60.

Muriel, Josefina. *Los Recogimientos de mujeres en América.* Mexico: Universidad Nacional Autónoma, Instituto de Investigaciones Históricas, 1974.

Nicolás Martínez, María del Mar. "Galas y regalos para una novia: a propósito de la boda de María del Pilar Teresa Cayetana de Silva, duquesa de Alba." In *Congreso Internacional Imagen Apariencia. Noviembre 19, 2008—noviembre 21, 2008.* Murcia: Universidad de Murcia, Servicio de Publicaciones, 2009.

Norberg, Kathryn. "From Courtesan to Prostitute: Mercenary Sex and Venereal Disease, 1730–1802. " In *The Secret Malady: Venereal Disease in Eighteenth-Century Britain and France,* ed. Linda Evi Merians. Lexington: University Press of Kentucky, 1996, 34–50.

Olmedo Ramos, Jaime. "Repertorios biográficos colectivos antes de *L'Encyclopèdie.*" In *Las enciclopedias en España antes de l'Encyclopédie,* ed. Alfredo Álvar Ezquerra et al. Madrid: Consejo Superior de Investigaciones Científicas, 2009, 181–216.

Oriel, J. David. *The Scars of Venus: A History of Venereology.* London and New York: Springer-Verlag, 1994.

Ortiz de Urbina, Jesús Cantera. "Refranes y locuciones del español y el francés en torno al bazo, el hígado, el corazón y los riñones." *Cuadernos de Investigación Flológica* 9 (1983): 47–62.

Pagden, Anthony. *European Encounters with the New World: From Renaissance to Romanticism.* New Haven: Yale University Press, 1993.

Palacios Fernández, Emilio. "Caracterización en los personajes en las Fábulas de Samaniego." *Boletín de la Institución Sancho El Sabio* 16 (1972): 169–89.

———. "Las *Fábulas* de Félix María de Samaniego: fabulario, bestiario, fisiognomía y lección moral." *Revista de Literatura* 60.119 (1998): 79–100.

Parsons, Elsie Worthington Clews. *Mitla, Town of the Souls: And Other Zapoteco-Speaking Pueblos of Oaxaca, Mexico.* Chicago: University of Chicago Press, 1936.

Pedraza, Pilar. "Prólogo." In *Arte de las putas,* by Nicolás Fernández de Moratín. Valencia: Editorial La Máscara, 1999.

Pereiro Otero, José Manuel. Introduction to *La abolición del tormento: el inédito* Discurso sobre la injusticia del apremio judicial *(c. 1795), de Pedro García del Cañuelo,* ed. Pereiro Otero. Chapel Hill: North Carolina Studies in the Romance Languages and Literatures, 2018, 11–168.

Ponce Cárdenas, Jesús. "De burlas y enfermedades barrocas: la sífilis en la obra poética de Anastasio Pantaleón de Ribera y Miguel Colodrero de Villalobos." *Criticón* 100 (2007): 115–42.

Puerto Sarmiento, Francisco Javier. *La Triaca Magna. Discurso del Excmo. Sr. D. Francisco Javier Puerto Sarmiento, leído en la sesión del día 26 de febrero de 2009 para su ingreso como académico de número, y contestación del Excmo Sr. D. Antonio Doadrio Villarejo.* Madrid: Real Academia Nacional de Farmacia, 2009.

Quétel, Claude. *History of Syphilis.* Baltimore: Johns Hopkins University Press, 1990.

Reedy, Daniel R. *The Poetic Art of Juan del Valle Caviedes.* Chapel Hill: University of North Carolina Press, 1964.

Rey Bueno, Mar. "El informe Valles: los desdibujados límites del arte de boticarios a finales del siglo XVI (1589–1594)." *Asclepio* 56.2 (2004): 243–68.

———. "Juntas de herbolarios y tertulias espagíricas: el círculo cortesano de Diego de Cortavila (1597–1657)." *Dynamys* 24 (2004): 243–67.

———. "*La Mayson pour Distiller des Eaües* at El Escorial: Alchemy and Medicine at the Court of Philip II, 1556–1598." In *Health and Medicine in Hapsburg Spain: Agents, Practices, Representations,* ed. Teresa Huguet-Termes, Jon Arrizabalaga, and Harold J. Cook. London: The Wellcome Trust Centre for the History of Medicine at UCL, 2009, 26–39.

———. *Los señores del fuego: destiladores y espagíricos en la Corte de los Austrias.* Madrid: Corona Borealis, 2002.

Rheinstein, Max. "Trends in Marriage and Divorce Law of Western Countries." *Law and Contemporary Problems* 18.1 (1953): 3–19.

Ribao Pereira, Montserrat. "Amor y pedagogía en el *Arte de las putas,* de N. Fernández de Moratín." *Cuadernos de Estudios del Siglo XVIII* 10 (2000): 155–74.

Ríos Santos, Antonio Rafael. "Blanco White a inicios del XIX, hasta exiliarse (23 — Feb.—1810)." Ph.D. thesis, Programa Política, Sociedad y Economía en la Edad Media, Antiguo y Nuevo Régimen, Universidad de Sevilla, Facultad de Geografía e Historia, 2004.

Risse, Guenter. "Medicine in New Spain." In *Medicine in the New World: New Spain, New France, and New England,* ed. Ronald L. Numbers. Knoxville: University of Tennessee Press, 1985, 12–63.

Rivasplata Varillas, Paula Ermila. "Los médicos y los cirujanos mulatos y de otras castas en la Lima colonial/Mulatto Physicians and Surgeons from Other Castes of Colonial Lima." *Fronteras de la Historia* 19.1 (2014): 42–70.

Roberts, Justin. *Slavery and the Enlightenment in the British Atlantic, 1750–1807.* Cambridge and New York: Cambridge University Press, 2013.

Rodríguez-Cerdeira, Carmen, and V. G. Silami-Lopes. "Sífilis congénita en el siglo XXI." *Actas Dermo-Sifiliográficas* 103.8 (2012): 679–93.

Rodríguez Mateos, Maria Victoria. *Los hospitales de Extremadura, 1492–1700.* Cáceres: Junta de Extremadura, Universidad de Extremadura, 2003.

Rollerston, J. D. "Venereal Disease in Literature." *Medical History* 10 (1934): 147–60.

Romero, Ximena. *Quito en los ojos de los viajeros: el siglo de la Ilustración.* Quito: Abya-Yala, 2000.

Rosebury, Theodor. *Microbes and Morals; the Strange Story of Venereal Disease.* New York: Viking Press, 1971.

Sala-Molins, Louis. *Dark Side of the Light: Slavery and the French Enlightenment.* Minneapolis: University of Minnesota Press, 2006.

Sánchez Hita, Beatriz, and Bárbara Salas García. "La calle, la mancebía y la galera: una aproximación a la prostitución a través de la literatura dieciochesca." *Cuadernos de Ilustración y Romanticismo* 8 (2000): 71–91.

Schleiner, Winfried. "Infection and Cure through Women: Renaissance Constructions of Syphilis." *Journal of Medieval and Renaissance Studies* 24 (1994): 499–517.

———. "Moral Attitudes toward Syphilis and Its Prevention in the Renaissance." *Bulletin of the History of Medicine* 68.3 (1994): 389–410.

Schlünder, Susanne. "Erotica Hispania—Figures of Love and the Human Body in 18th-Century Spanish Literature." In *Lili-Zeitschrift für Literaturwissenchaft und Linguistik.* Göttingen: Vandenhoeck & Ruprecht, 2004, 60–86.

———. "¿Erotismo grotesco o discursos de la sexualidad? *El arte de las putas* de Nicolás Fernández de Moratín." In *Literatura-Cultura-Media-Lengua: Nuevos planteamientos de la investigación del siglo XVIII en España e Hispanoamérica,* ed. with an introduction by Christian von Tschilschke and Andreas Gelz. Frankfurt: Peter Lang, 2005, 105–17.

Sebold, Russell P. "Torres Villarroel, Quevedo y El Bosco." *Ínsula* 159, 160 (1960): 3, 14.

Siena, Kevin Patrick. "The 'Foul Disease' and Privacy: The Effects of Venereal Disease and Patient Demand on the Medical Marketplace in Early Modern London." *Bulletin of the History of Medicine* 75.2 (2001): 199–224.

———. "Pollution, Promiscuity, and the Pox: English Venereology and the Early Modern Medical Discourse on Social and Sexual Danger." *Journal of the History of Sexuality* 8.4 (1998): 553–74.

———. "Poverty and the Pox: Venereal Disease in London Hospitals, 1600–1800." Dissertation, University of Toronto. ProQuest Dissertations Publishing, 2001.

———. *Sins of the Flesh: Responding to Sexual Disease in Early Modern Europe.* Toronto: Centre for Reformation and Renaissance Studies, 2005.

———. "The Strange Medical Silence on Same-Sex Transmission of the Pox, c. 1660–c. 1760." In *The Sciences of Honosexuality in Early Modern Europe,* ed. Kenneth Borris and George Rousseau. New York: Routledge, 2008, 115–33.

———. *Venereal Disease, Hospitals, and the Urban Poor; London's "foul wards," 1600–1800.* Rochester, NY: University of Rochester Press, 2004.

Signorile, Michelangelo. "Stacey Campfield, Tennessee Senator Behind 'Don't Say Gay' Bill, on Bullying, AIDS And Homosexual 'Glorification.'" *Huffington Post,* January 26, 2012.

Solomon, Michael. *Fictions of Well-Being: Sickly Readers and Vernacular Medical Writing in Late Medieval and Early Modern Spain.* Philadelphia: University of Pennsylvania Press, 2010.

Spongberg, Mary. *Feminizing Venereal Disease: The Body of the Prostitute in Nineteenth-Century Medical Discourse.* Washington Square: New York University Press, 1997.

Stein, Claudia. *Negotiating the French Pox in Early Modern Germany.* Farnham, England; Burlington, VT: Ashgate, 2009.

Stewart, Mary Margaret. "'And blights with plagues the Marriage hearse': Syphilis and Wives." In *The Secret Malady: Venereal Disease in Eighteenth-Century Britain and France,* ed. Linda Evi Merians. Lexington: University Press of Kentucky, 1996, 103–15.

Stoichita, Victor Ieronim, and Anna Maria Coderch. *Goya: The Last Carnival.* London: Reaktion Books, 1999.

Stolley, Karen. *Domesticating Empire: Enlightenment in Spanish America.* Nashville: Vanderbilt University Press, 2013.

Tausiet, María. "Healing Virtue: *Saludadores* versus Witches in Early Modern Spain." In *Health and Medicine in Hapsburg Spain: Agents, Practices, Representations,* ed. Teresa Huguet-Termes, Jon Arrizabalaga, and Harold J. Cook. London: The Wellcome Trust Centre for the History of Medicine at UCL, 2009, 40–63.

Temkin, Owsei, "On the History of 'Morality and Syphilis.'" In *The Double Face of Janus and Other Essays in the History of Medicine.* Baltimore: Johns Hopkins University Press, 1977, 472–84.

Tomlinson, Janis A. *Francisco Goya: The Tapestry Cartoons and Early Career at the Court of Madrid.* Cambridge: Cambridge University Press, 1989.

Torres Santana, Elisa. "Los marginados en tiempos de Felipe V." In *Felipe V y su tiempo: Congreso internacional.* Vol. 1, ed. Eliseo Serrano Martín. Zaragoza: Institución "Fernando el Católico," 2004, 323–42.

Uphof, Johannes Cornelis Theodorus. *Dictionary of Economic Plants.* Wienheim: H. R. Engelmann, 1959.

Vásquez García, Francisco, and Andrés Moreno Mengíbar. "Políticas de burdel en la

España contemporánea: de las propuestas ilustradas a la prostitución reglamentada." *Cuadernos de Ilustración y Romanticismo: Revista del Grupo de estudios del Siglo XVIII* 1 (1991): 55–78.

Velásquez, Enrique. "Estudio introductorio." In *Arte de las putas,* by Nicolás Fernández de Moratín. Madrid: A-Z ediciones y publicaciones, 1990, 11–65.

Vogeley, Nancy J. *Lizardi and the Birth of the Novel in Spanish America.* Gainesville: University Press of Florida, 2001.

Yagüe Bosch, Javier. "Aspectos de la vision de América en los ilustrados." *Cauce* 14–15 (1992): 639–68.

Zanardi, Tara. *Framing Majismo: Art and Royal Identity in Eighteenth Century Spain.* University Park: Pennsylvania State University Press, 2016.

Zanrè, Domenico. "French Diseases and Italian Responses: Representations of the *mal francese* in the Literature of Cinquecento Tuscany." In *Sins of the Flesh: Responding to Sexual Disease in Early Modern Europe,* ed. Kevin Siena. Toronto: Centre for Reformation and Renaissance Studies, 2005, 187–208.

Zimmer, Carl. "Can Genes Solve the Syphilis Mystery?" *Science* 292 (May 11, 2011): 1091.

INDEX

Abasolo, Mariano, 301, 302, 356n7
Abraham Entertaining the Angels (tapestry),
  22–23
Académie Royale des Sciences, 67
Aeneid (Virgil), 46
afrancesadas, 128–29, 328n26. *See also* language
afrancesados, 95, 123, 137, 236
agricultura de la zona tórrida, La (Bello), 143,
  168
Aguirre, Juan Bautista, 15, 196–98
"A la expedición española para propagar la
  vacuna en América bajo la dirección de don
  Francisco Balmis" (Quintana), 140–41
Alba, Padre, 92
alcaldes examinadores, 6
alchemy, 5, 41–42; in poetry, 54
Aldama González, Juan, 301, 302, 356n7
Alexander VI, Pope, 234
Allende, Ignacio, 301, 302, 356n7
almanac, 72, 78, 85
Almazán, Antonio Tavira, 92
Alphonso II, King, 3
"A Marica la chupona" (Quevedo), 83, 163,
  181, 312n60, 313n45
Amat y Junient, Manuel de, 225
*America vindicada de la calumnia de haber
  sido madre del mal venéreo, La* (Sánchez
  Valverde), 147–48
Amsterdam, 4
Amy, Jean-Jacques, 211–12, 343n37
"Anacreóntica" (Cadalso), 43
anacreónticas, 43, 93–95, 195, 292. *See also*
  poetry
anatomy, 8, 25, 44, 101, 152. *See also* medicine
Anazarbeo, Pedacio Dioscorides, 69, 289
Anderson Imbert, Enrique, 143
anthrax, 107. *See also* bacteria
"Anti-Medicato" (Torres Villarroel), 84,
  321n64. *See also Protomedicato*
Antón Martín Hospital, 13, 78–79, 82, 84,
  89–91, 97, 182–83, 205, 208, 215, 230,
  321nn1–2, 321n62, 343n28. *See also* hospitals; Madrid
apothecaries, 5, 6, 42, 71, 104, 238, 313n34,
  318n26, 339n13, 348n39, 356n12. *See also*
  medicine

Arcanismo anti-galico, o Margarita mercurial
  (Suárez de Ribera), 53, 68, 164, 208
Arcimboldo, Giuseppe, 73
Arjona, Father Manuel María de, 97–98
Arroyal, León de, 92
art, 4, 11, 17, 19, 20, 22, 26, 62, 201, 260, 262,
  281, 282, 291, 292, 297, 307n4, 332n23,
  350n9, 351n25, 354n57
arte de las putas, El (Moratín), 16, 21, 52, 193,
  200–19, 245–46, 256, 259–60, 267, 290–93
*asno erudito, fábula original, obra póstuma de
  un poeta anónimo, El* (Forner), 123
"Aspectos de la visión de América en los ilustrados" (Yagüe Bosch), 199–200
astrology, 42–44, 54, 176, 290, 319n51, 337n7,
  339n20, 353n50; predictions of, 28, 71, 78–
  79; and weather forecasts, 71
Astruc, Jean, 38, 104–9, 145–46, 149–50, 159,
  331nn6–7
"A una dama que paró en el Hospital de la
  Caridad" (Valle y Caviedes), 181–92, 338n2,
  338n8, 339n14
"A una dama que por serlo paró en La Caridad" (Valle y Caviedes), 181–92, 338n2,
  355n62
avechucho/avechucha, 274–75, 292,
  352nn36–37
Avicenna, 5, 28, 29, 48, 104, 176, 310n5
Ávila, 13; hospitals in, 94–97, 322n9. *See also*
  Spain
ayuda, 184, 185, 339n13. *See also jeringa;*
  medicine
azogue. See mercury

bacteria, 1–2, 64, 107. *See also* disease
Baglivi, Giorgio, 57
Bakhtin, Mikhail, 221
Balmis, Francisco Javier de, 15, 140–42,
  154–57, 165, 332n22
Barcelona, 85, 216, 219, 234, 344n59. *See also*
  Spain
barometer, 66. *See also* science
Bayeu y Subías, Francisco, 19
beauty, 30, 32, 61, 81, 207, 217–18, 249, 253,
  269, 277, 286, 340n32, 342n26, 352n41.
  See also women

WRITING THE EARLY AMERICAS

Sifilografía: A History of the Writerly Pox in the Eighteenth-Century Hispanic World
Juan Carlos González Espitia

Creole Drama: Theatre and Society in Antebellum New Orleans
Juliane Braun

The Alchemy of Conquest: Science, Religion, and the Secrets of the New World
Ralph Bauer

CPSIA information can be obtained
at www.ICGtesting.com
Printed in the USA
LVHW090042151019
634156LV00003B/253/P